BEYOND THE LAND OF GOLD

The Life & Times of
PERRY A. BURGESS

Burgess Family

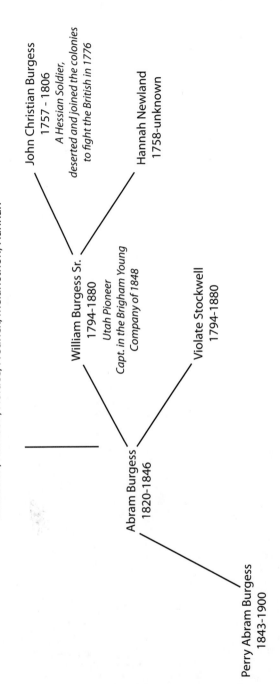

Aunts and uncles discussed in this book.
William Jr., Harrison, Horace, Fredrick, Melancthon, Hannah

John Christian Burgess
1757 - 1806
*A Hessian Soldier,
deserted and joined the colonies
to fight the British in 1776*

Hannah Newland
1758-unknown

William Burgess Sr.
1794-1880
*Utah Pioneer
Capt. in the Brigham Young
Company of 1848*

Violate Stockwell
1794-1880

Abram Burgess
1820-1846

Perry Abram Burgess
1843-1900

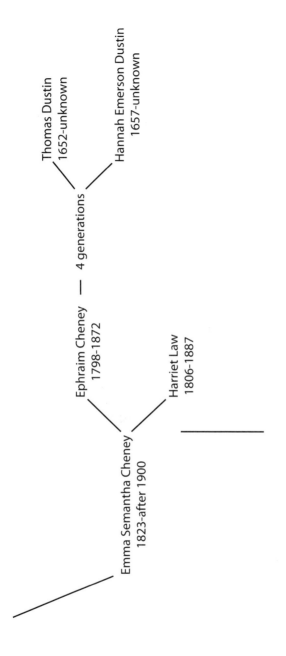

Thomas Dustin
1652-unknown

Hannah Emerson Dustin
1657-unknown

— 4 generations

Ephraim Cheney
1798-1872

Harriet Law
1806-1887

Emma Semantha Cheney
1823-after 1900

Aunts and uncles discussed in this book.
Dr. Levi, Mansel, Lewis, Lyman, Matthew, Caroline, Richard

Cheney Family

Perry A. Burgess, circa 1880
June 14,1843 - June 6, 1900
Courtesy of Tread of Pioneers Museum, Steamboat Springs, CO

Beyond the Land of Gold

The Life & Times of

Perry A. Burgess

Rebecca Valentine
Travis Thompson

October 23, 2010

To The Oak Creek Library

Rebecca Valentine

Travis Thompson

THOMPSON MEDIA

ACWORTH, GA

For more information about the Burgess story, please visit the companion website at *http://www.burgessdiary.com*

First Printing - August 2010

Library of Congress Control Number: 2010929900
ISBN: 978-0-9827089-0-3 (PB)
ISBN: 978-0-9827089-1-0 (HB)
ISBN: 978-0-9827089-2-7 (e-pub)
ISBN: 978-0-9827089-3-4 (e-pdf)

This book is dedicated to Charles Leckenby and Bruce Burgess for being the first to publish Perry's Pioneer Recollections in the *Steamboat Pilot* newspaper spanning 1896-1900. We also dedicate this book to Perry's "Cousin Charlie" and wife "Lulu" Cheney who transcribed the 1866-1868 Burgess Bozeman diaries, thus creating the only known copies that exist today. Long after the original Burgess diary was lost, Lulu donated these typed manuscripts to the Colorado State Archive, where they are housed today.

1929–$50 bill issued by the First National Bank of Boulder, with signatures of Lewis Cheney Allison and Charles Cheney Charles was referred to as 'Cousin Charlie' in the Burgess diaries

Foreword

My journey began in 2005, following a visit with my cousin Theodore Bradshaw and great uncle Joseph Cheney Thompson in Independence, Missouri. Joseph had spent his entire life in the original home of his grandfather, Dr. Levi Cheney, the uncle of diarist Perry A. Burgess. The home was purchased by Levi in the 1890s when he moved his family to Missouri to be closer to the center of the upstart RLDS Church. The home is located at 1320 West Short Street, a short walk to the original temple square that served as the cultural center of the early Mormon Church. Joseph Smith III also moved to West Short Street in 1906 and was a trusted friend and neighbor of the Thompsons. The Thompson family maintained a close relationship with the Smiths for multiple generations and remained devout followers of the RLDS, now Community of Christ Church. By 2005, the Short Street residence had been in the Cheney and Thompson family for over 100 years, and fortunately the family pictures remained undisturbed in the home (the Levi Cheney Collection).

Genealogy being a hobby of mine, I had already performed extensive family research and was able to associate the names on many of the photographs in the collection with members of Levi's extended family. These include, among others, his brother Lewis Cheney and family, as well as his nephew Perry A. Burgess. Ted and I carefully scanned the photographs, many of which have been used to illustrate sections of this book. Other images relating to the Burgess and Cheney families were obtained from various sources as noted in the list of images or directly underneath each individual photograph.

In 2007, I discovered the obituary of Perry, which credited him with writing a series of Pioneer Recollections and other essays in the *Steamboat Pilot* newspaper. These were published from 1896 to 1900, a brief period in which his son Bruce was a co-editor and partner in the paper. The essays were not credited, however I realized these were rare manuscripts relating to Perry's previously published 1866-1868 Montana Bozeman Trail diaries. In addition, there were some essays that tell of other western adventures. Unfortunately, a turn-of-the-century fire at the *Steamboat Pilot* office destroyed numerous Burgess articles. No known copies exist today.

In 2009, I began searching for a writer to craft what I knew was a great story. Aside from its historical value, Perry's story—and that of the Mormons, the Cheneys, and everyone else his life touched—is simply fascinating. I knew I needed someone with an appreciation of history and the ability to bring his story to life. I found Rebecca Valentine and after meeting her, knew her experience as a writer and researcher made her The One. That she lives in Colorado and knows the regions we needed to write about was the proverbial icing on the cake.

We have taken great care to re-create the 1866-1868 diaries as they were originally transcribed by Charles Cheney, with the exception of adding a standardized full date in front of each entry to allow for improved readability. The recollection articles were transcribed as published.

In addition to the Bozeman Trail diaries and related recollections, we have included excerpts from Perry's Steamboat Springs, Colorado, diaries. This is a collection of eight diaries dating from 1880-1900 and includes some of the earliest written daily accounts of pioneer life in Steamboat Springs. The original diaries were transcribed through a grant provided by the Tread of Pioneers Museum. Along with the Steamboat Springs diaries, we included the corresponding recollections and essays. We have inserted all of the known articles amongst the diary entries to which they relate.

In the interest of preserving the integrity and authenticity of Perry's diaries and recollections, we have chosen not to correct any errors, misspellings, or other questionable text in these primary documents. The reader will notice these quirks—and in some instances, Perry's meaning is somewhat obscured by them—but we believe they do not detract from the overall historical meaning of the writings but indeed, add to it.

There are places in this book where we felt obligated to speculate for one reason or another. Anyone who has ever conducted historical research understands that sometimes—often, actually—conclusions must be drawn. Answers are not directly provided, and to find them, one must piece together many snippets of information while taking into consideration all surrounding circumstances. In suggesting scenarios or conclusions, our goal was not to revise history, but to encourage readers to look at the big picture, to put themselves in the shoes of our story's characters, perhaps inside their minds, even. It is a liberty, we know, and we took it.

On March 29, 1866, Perry A. Burgess noted in his diary. "The long looked for day having at length arrived …bid goodbye to our friends and started on our journey toward the land of gold." This entry became an inspiration behind Susan Badger Doyle's two-volume set, *Journeys to the Land of Gold*, a compilation of all the known diaries written on the Bozeman Trail 1863-1866, including Perry's. The prospector label is the one commonly ascribed to him. But his life was so much more than that single trip. His interests were many, his abilities even more numerous. Fortunately for history's sake, one of his hobbies and skills was writing. From those accounts alone, it is clear that Perry was a Renaissance man. His multi-faceted personality and passion for discovery led him down a wide variety of paths. In order to thoroughly depict this man's influence and legacy, I wanted to present him in the most complete way possible. Hence, I chose the title *Beyond the Land of Gold: The Life & Times of Perry A. Burgess*.

This text is the only resource that combines Perry Burgess's diaries with all known recollection essays. In addition, readers will find scores of images from publications such as *Harper's*, one of the many periodicals in which Perry tried persistently to publish his work. It seemed only fitting that his writings be combined with these illustrations.

Beyond the Land of Gold: The Life & Times of Perry A. Burgess is our tribute to a remarkable man. We hope it does him justice.

~ *Travis Thompson*

Table of Contents

Acknowledgements

I would like to thank Travis for trusting me with the honor of telling your family's story. It was a journey every bit as adventurous as Perry's. Thanks to my amazing kids—Max, Tuck, Tavia, and Bella, for making do without me more often than they would have liked during the course of crafting this book. And lastly, my gratitude goes to Rick…for showing up in that moment when I most needed you and didn't even know it.

- Rebecca Valentine

First, I would like to thank my wife Becky Thompson, who has labored countless hours during this project researching, documenting, and transcribing the Burgess diaries and recollections, also for her work in publishing the story. Without Becky, this book would not have been possible. A special thanks to Rebecca Valentine for her dedication and knowledge of Colorado and Western history, and her ability to bring the Burgess and Cheney family stories to life. Love and thanks to my family Theodore Bradshaw, Nina Lewis, and Joseph Cheney Thompson (deceased) who have assisted in many ways compiling and preserving the family history. "Ted" and "J.C." saved many of the family photos of Levi Cheney and his daughter Samantha Cheney Thompson that I have used in the book. Endless gratitude goes to my grandfather, George W. Thompson (deceased) for sharing his life-long interest in the Cheney heritage. Patricia Parker Carter of Utah generously provided assistance in researching the members of the Burgess-Cheney party and shared knowledge of her home town Butler, Missouri. Many facts were uncovered through her endless hours of research and knowledge of public records. James Crawford, the great-grandson of Steamboat Springs, Colorado founders James H. and Margaret Crawford, for his input and assistance with the history of Steamboat Springs. His wealth of knowledge was invaluable in the development of these chapters. And of course, my gratitude goes to the staff of the Tread of Pioneers Museum in Steamboat Springs; the keepers of Routt County history. I bow to David Moran for salvaging many of the last known copies of the published Burgess recollections. Roger and Joyce Cusick and Charlene Stees for their knowledge and assistance in researching the Steamboat Springs information. John Rives of DiscWrite CD Promotions – www.discwritecd.com, for his graphic design production work and endless patience.

- Travis Thompson

List of Images

List of Images

List of Images

List of Images

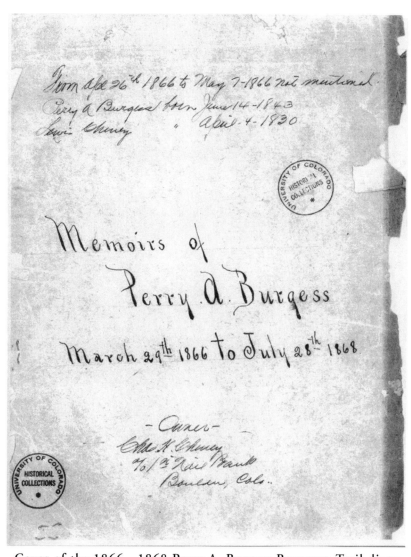

Cover of the 1866 - 1868 Perry A. Burgess Bozeman Trail diary
Colorado State Archives

Grave of Perry A. Burgess and daughter Helen.
Steamboat Springs Cemetery, overlooking the Burgess ranch

Introduction

The passages of history are replete with the names of men and women who made their mark as America became the impressive country she is today. Our tomorrows are built on the names and accomplishments of our yesterdays. Some of those names are well known. They belong to politicians and military officers, men whose attitudes and choices thrust them into the public spotlight and forever onto the printed pages of history books. Their achievements, too, are well known. They freed slaves, won battles, made or changed laws, and stood up against the majority at a time when the world believed might made right. These are the names our children are expected to memorize in school and remember throughout life.

But we shortchange our children when we teach them only about those figures whose fame elevates their status. Perry A. Burgess is one of those characters in American history whose life's achievements never cried out for attention. His explorations and adventures are not taught in our schools today, even though his life included prominent historical figures such as Brigham Young, Jim Bridger, and Sam Brannan. His story includes all the drama and adventure of a modern-day epic as he traveled—on foot and by wagon—across the plains and mountains to escape religious persecution, search for gold, and cultivate and promote the Colorado cities of Boulder and Steamboat Springs.

Perry Burgess's life is a portrait in quiet courage. Perry was a man whose determination propelled him through the American wilderness with a can-do attitude. Whether he was traveling as a refugee—as was the case throughout his Mormon childhood—as an adventurer—a role he embraced on the Bozeman Trail and into the Colorado back country—or as an entrepreneur—a hat he wore when he took up banking, assaying, and writing, Perry lived life with a dogged determination to let wonder and endless possibility be his guide.

In living this genuine life, Perry A. Burgess impacted the American West in ways far beyond what is commonly known or understood. Although gold rush history buffs know about him for his travels along the Bozeman Trail, his life prior to 1866 is virtually unknown. His personal endeavors unwittingly led him to shape much of the society and culture still being enjoyed and celebrated in Boulder, Colorado. With his uncle, Lewis Cheney, Perry established the city's banking system and became one of Boulder's most prominent citizens. His in help analyzing water content with William E. Walton—the same Walton family of Walmart fame—led him to settle 160 acres of prime wilderness in that remote part of the state, thereby becoming one of its earliest settlers in Steamboat Springs. His visionary financial investment in the Steamboat Springs Town Company made him one of the town's most influential residents.

And through it all, Perry maintained his ability to forge ahead—into the unknown—without letting fear or even life-threatening circumstances such as Native American attacks and extreme weather conditions deter him. Rather than become set in his ways in his old age, Perry continued to broaden his horizons as he explored Spiritualism right alongside the life of Jesus Christ, socialism in the face of capitalism, and environmentalism in an era of abundant natural resources. Perry was an individual, a man unencumbered by collective thought or keeping up with his peers. He lived his life according to his own compass, and that in itself is courageous.

This book is not the first ever to include the name Perry A. Burgess. His diaries have been published and written about, and his Montana diaries are one of the few existing accounts of the Bozeman Trail experience. He has been included sporadically in several texts. His name can still be found in Colorado newspaper archives. But this is the first detailed account of his life. And so it is the first—the only—treatise on the life of this pioneer whose passion for adventure led him to achieve remarkable feats both big and small. That he was able to accomplish so very much in a relatively short period of time—fewer than fifty-seven years—in an era in which technology and even the most simple of conveniences did not yet exist—is a testament to his fortitude. That he did so while maintaining a spotless reputation of integrity and kindness speaks volumes of his character.

Beyond the Land of Gold: The Life & Times of Perry A. Burgess is the first resource to combine his Montana and Colorado diaries with his Steamboat Pilot newspaper articles, thereby providing the most complete and accurate portrait of one of the lesser-known relevant pioneers of America's Wild West.

His story is presented in a way that allows each chapter to be read and understood on its own. Those readers interested only in Perry's recollection articles will find them easily accessible. Gold rush aficionados, likewise, will find the pertinent chapters without having to wade through page after page of unrelated text. And those who wish to know the whole story, from Perry's birth through his death, can read the book cover to cover and walk away knowing the man to a level of detail never before revealed.

Perry's story begs to be told. And so we tell it.

Burgess Steamboat Springs diaries
Tread of Pioneers Museum Steamboat Springs, Colorado

MoNUMENT of
HANNAH DUSTIN

PENACOOK-N.H.

Hannah Dustin statue, Dustin Island, New Hampshire
First woman to be honored with a statue in the United States

CHAPTER 1
Hannah Dustin – Perry's Infamous Ancestor

Haverhill (pronounced HAY-vrill) at the end of the seventeenth century was not the charming northeastern Massachusetts town it is today. Founded in 1640 by English Puritans and officially established by the courts in 1641, the frontier settlement of Haverhill was originally known as Pawtucket Plantation—commonly referred to as Pentucket—in honor of the Native Americans who lived there first. A friendly gesture, this honor, but friendliness between white settlers and surrounding Native American tribes was hard to come by in the late 1690s.

At the beginning of the seventeenth century, Haverhill was largely populated by the Pawtucket (Penacook) tribe and what colonists referred to as Massachusetts Indians. No one knows with any certainty just how many Native Americans lived there at the time; accounts vary, though they generally agree that the native population numbered in the low thousands. Several epidemics and the Indian Wars that swept the region in the early decades of the century decimated that population, however, and by the end of the 1600s, less than one hundred Native Americans called the Haverhill area home.

Because of King Philip's War (1675–1676) and France's subsequent funding of raids on English settlers in New England for the next fifty years, frequent Indian attacks during this time period were a fact of life for Haverhill and the residences scattered within a two-mile radius of the village. The fact that the Merrimack River helps form the east, southeast, and west borders of Haverhill made it a particularly vulnerable site for attack, as the river was a main transportation route for the region's Native Americans even before they sided with the French against North America's English.

The year 1697 was especially devastating for Haverhill residents, and for one family in particular. Thomas and Hannah Dustin (also spelled Duston, Durston, and Dunston) had lived in the same house since the early 1680s, but their ever-expanding family had outgrown its walls even before the March 9, 1697, birth of their twelfth child, Martha. At that time, Thomas was busy building a new brick home for his family, one that would serve double duty as a garrison in case of Indian attack.

Born around 1652 in either New Hampshire or Maine, Thomas had lived in the Haverhill area since 1663. Hannah Webster Emerson was born in Haverhill on December 23, 1657. No known historical accounts of their childhoods exist, but it can be assumed that the two attended the same school, with Hannah five years behind Thomas.

The two married on December 3, 1677, and their first child—Hannah—was born on August 22, 1678. By spring of 1697, the Dustins had buried four of their eleven children. Thomas supported his wife and seven remaining children through work as a bricklayer and farmer. Haverhill town records indicate that Thomas served as a constable in the early 1690s, and still he managed to find time to write his own almanacs when weather prohibited him from farming or laying bricks.

It was a hard but satisfying life, this rural existence in New England's frontier. Children were raised to be constantly aware of their surroundings, on the lookout for Indians and the signs that they were near. The men rarely left the safety of their homes without taking their flintlocks along.

And so it was on the morning of March 15, 1697, that Thomas and his seven children were working and passing the time in the fields near the family home as Hannah lay in bed, recovering from the birth of her daughter Martha just six days before. By her side was the Haverhill midwife and family friend Mary Neff, who cared for both mother and infant with the utmost devotion.

The tranquil morning was abruptly interrupted with shouts from Thomas and the children. After ordering the children to flee to the closest garrison at Pecker's Hill, Thomas burst through the front door to check on his wife and newborn daughter. Hannah directed him to flee and protect the children, and the two women and the baby were left to fend for themselves.

Thomas managed to hold back the few Abenaki warriors who had followed his children across the meadow and into the woods. Shielding himself behind his horse, he threatened to shoot his enemies any time one of them showed himself. It was fortuitous that Thomas never had to fire a shot because reloading would have taken more time than he had available to him, and doing so surely would have meant the death of him and the capture of his children. As it was, he safeguarded all seven children to the garrison.

Hannah and Mary weren't so lucky. As Mary tried to escape with Martha in her arms, both were easily overtaken, and the Abenaki looted the Dustin home while forcing Hannah to get out of bed and dress herself. In all the chaos, Hannah's shoe fell off, and she was unable to retrieve it when her captors set fire to her home. Both women and Martha were led toward the forest and were soon joined by the rest of their attackers, who had killed twenty-seven others in the vicinity and captured thirteen more. It was the beginning of what would be a long and arduous journey. As Hannah had just given birth six days earlier, it is safe to assume that she was still in a fragile physical and emotional state.

The kidnappers feared an immediate pursuit of their captives, and so they wasted no time in setting out for Canada. In all likelihood, Mary Neff was carrying Martha so as to make Hannah's efforts as painless as possible. It soon became clear that carrying the baby would impede Mary's progress, but this caused little annoyance compared to Martha's crying, which the Abenaki feared would attract unwanted attention. Without warning, one of the kidnappers ripped the days-old infant from Mary's arms and abruptly struck Martha's head against an apple tree.

We can only try to imagine what went through Hannah's mind at that moment. Under such harsh conditions—New England–cold temperatures, her fragile physical condition, deep-seated concern as to the whereabouts of her other children and Thomas, sheer terror at being led farther and farther away from the only home she'd ever known—Hannah's response to this atrocity might have been an intensification of her determination to survive. Or it might have merely numbed her. In all likelihood, Hannah went into some state of shock, and yet she had no choice but to continue forging on if she was to have any chance of reuniting with the family she didn't even know with any degree of certainty was still alive.

The Abenaki gave Hannah and Mary no time to grieve but pushed them onward at a grueling pace. The group finally reached the forest, where they joined the squaws and children who had been waiting out the raid. Here they were soon joined by the remaining Abenaki warriors and their captors. With no time to rest, the kidnapped settlers moved on, the weaker ones murdered and scalped where they stood. By her own admission, Hannah and the surviving captives marched about twelve miles that first day. The next few days would lead them through miles and miles[1] of wilderness, over rough terrain and through snow and mud. The captives were not properly clothed for such a journey, and Hannah had to keep pace wearing only one shoe. Suffering and misery surely accompanied every one of those settlers.

Add to this misery the horrifying stories told by the Abenaki, tales of the fate that awaited the captives in Canada. There they would be stripped naked and made to "run the gantlet." Bordered on both sides by Indian warriors-in-training, they would be mocked, beaten, and used as target practice for Abenaki youth just learning to wield their tomahawks. Many whites died from the torture. Others fainted and were then sold as slaves to the French. Either way, the future did not look bright for Hannah, Mary, or the others.

Upon learning of what lay in store for her, Hannah decided the risk of trying to escape was less dangerous than the certain torture and life of hardship that awaited her. Hannah began hatching a plan, but she needed the help of Mary and Samuel Lennardson, a fourteen-year-old who had been captured eighteen months earlier and was by now a trusted member of the Abenaki tribe.

At the junction of the Merrimack and Contoocook rivers, twelve Abenaki (two men, three women, and seven children) separated Hannah, Mary Neff, and Samuel from the rest of the group and headed toward what is now called Dustin Island, near present-day Penacook, New Hampshire. Dustin Island was the home of the Abenaki warrior who claimed Hannah and Mary as his own. The plan was to rest there before setting out for Canada.

This rest stop provided the perfect opportunity for Hannah to carry out her escape. She managed to discuss her plans with Samuel and Mary, and both agreed they had little to lose. Samuel was longing for the home and family he had left behind. His master, Bampico, treated Samuel as a member of his family, and when Samuel asked him how he managed to kill so many English, Bampico showed the boy how to kill with one sharp blow to the temple. Perhaps believing Samuel wanted to learn the ways of his "adopted" family, Bampico then demonstrated the method for scalping. His teaching moment would be the undoing of his family.

The group of fifteen arrived at Dustin Island some time before March 30, and conditions on the island could not have been better suited to their plans. Bampico and his family never dreamed Samuel would want to leave, and they believed neither Hannah nor Mary were physically capable of escape. They let their guard down that first night on the island and went to bed without keeping an eye on their three captives. Realizing that the flooding river waters would muffle any sound, Hannah decided the time had come to put her escape plan in action. Samuel had carefully and thoroughly shown both women how to kill and scalp, and there might never be another opportunity.

Just after midnight, Hannah woke Mary and Samuel. Using their tomahawks with remarkable dexterity, Hannah and Samuel killed their captors outright. Only Mary struggled with the task. As a result, ten of the twelve Abenaki were killed instantly. A wounded squaw and a young boy escaped into the woods, a detail corroborated by a deposition given by one Hannah Bradley in 1739.

The rogue trio quickly piled food and weapons—including the tomahawk Hannah had used to kill her master—into a canoe and set off down the Merrimack River. They soon realized that their story was too incredulous to be believed without proof, and so Hannah turned the vessel around and returned to the murder scene. There, she scalped all ten victims.

Who Did What? The World May Never Know.

Many books and accounts of Hannah Dustin's ordeal have been written and published, some more credible than others (see the Selected Bibliography section in the back of this book). And while the basic story remains the same, the details vary. For example, who was carrying baby Martha as the captured settlers marched toward Canada—Mary Neff or Hannah Dustin? What motivated Hannah to kill and scalp her captors—revenge? Desperation? Basic survival instinct? A combination of all three?

These and other questions may never be consistently and accurately answered, and emotionally charged accounts such as that written by John Greenleaf Whittier in 1831 don't help historians move any closer to the truth. His essay, titled "The Mother's Revenge," includes this passage:

> The wretched mother cast one look upon her dead infant, and another to Heaven, as she obeyed her savage conductor. She has often said, that at this moment, all was darkness and horror—that her very heart seemed to cease beating, and to lie cold and dead in her bosom, and that her limbs moved only as involuntary machinery. But when she gazed around her and saw the unfeeling savages, grinning at her and mocking her, and pointing to the mangled body of her infant with fiendish exultation, a new and terrible feeling came over her. It was the thirst for revenge; and from that moment her purpose was fixed.[2]

Now, it may well be true that Whittier's analysis is accurate, if emotional and a bit theatrical. Then again, he may have

Base of Hannah Dustin statue, Haverhill, Massachusetts

exaggerated the situation. Even Cotton Mather's account of Hannah's trials that spring, which is supposedly based on an interview with Hannah, is quite possibly exaggerated and embellished for the sake of drama and reader's interest. Mather, infamous for his influence in the Salem Witch Trials, was known for his dramatic flair.

In the end, what matters is the story itself—Hannah's kidnapping, her courage in the face of death, and her ultimate triumph. As is always true when relying on historical documents in the quest for truth, one must take into consideration the author as well as his intent.

Here is the genesis of the still-brewing controversy surrounding Hannah Dustin. While Hannah is commonly revered as a colonial heroine, she has her critics. Of the ten Abenaki killed that night on Dustin Island, six of them were children. After the deed was done and the escape in progress, Hannah turned around and collected scalps from all ten corpses. Most accounts report that she took the scalps as proof of her deed. Some say it was an act of revenge, driven by hate rather than logic. Still other critics maintain that her motive for scalping was to collect a bounty.

In hindsight, it might be prudent to address these criticisms, not for the sake of finding easy answers, but in the hope of deconstructing the logic of a traumatized mother who had just marched a hundred miles in snow and mud after watching her six-day-old daughter's brutal murder.

Were the scalps of her victims the only proof she could provide of the events of that March night? She already had the tomahawk, and she had two people who had participated in and could verify the episode. Perhaps this would have been sufficient proof of her story. Then again, she was a woman alone with "savages" in the wilderness. Women during that era were not considered capable of doing the things Hannah Dustin did. To report something like her story back in the seventeenth century would be almost akin to sharing an alien abduction story today. Most would consider the event unlikely and improbable. However, by providing the scalps of her captors, Hannah could prove beyond doubt that she was telling the truth.

And then there's the issue of Hannah's future. In all likelihood, she believed her family to be dead. What would she—a woman alone on the frontier—do to get by? Surely money for the scalps would be a start. And yet, she could not count on receiving a bounty. Although a $50 bounty had been placed on Indian scalps in 1694, that amount had decreased until the bounty was completely revoked in mid-December of 1696, three months before Hannah's fateful adventure.

There is no account of Hannah's life upon returning to her family, so there is no way of knowing how the event affected her. It does not seem to be mere speculation that she would have been haunted by the events of that dreadful March. It is, perhaps, easy to judge, from the distance of several hundred years, the choices and decisions of someone whose shoes (or in this case, shoe) we can only try to imagine walking in. There are just no easy answers to this particular scenario.

Hannah Dustin statue, Haverhill, Massachusetts

Base of Hannah Dustin statue, Haverhill, Massachusetts

The trio took turns guiding the canoe as they traveled by night and hid in the light of day. They finally reached the home of John Lovewell in what is now part of Nashua, New Hampshire. The weary travelers spent the night there and resumed their journey, eventually beaching their canoe at Bradley's Cove. The last leg of the trip was made on foot, and they managed to reach Haverhill safely. With both parties imagining the other dead, they must have celebrated with one joyous reunion.

The Dustins, Mary, and Samuel returned to the new house, which Thomas had since completed, and there rested for several days. In late April, Thomas took his wife and her companions into Boston, where they presented the scalps to the governor's office. He filed a petition asking for the now-revoked bounty to be reconsidered on the grounds that the scalps represented great courage and also because he had lost his estate in the same raid that took his wife when the Indians set fire to his home. On June 16, 1697, the General Court approved a 25-pound bounty "unto Thomas Dunston of Haverhill, on behalf of Hannah his wife" and 12 pounds, 10 shillings each to Mary and Samuel.[3]

While still in Boston, Hannah relayed her experience to the famed minister Cotton Mather, who declared her escape a miracle and did his utmost to paint it as such in his *Magnalia Christi Americana*. It is Mather's account that brought Hannah's exploits to public notice and instantly made her a heroine. Never before had a woman fought to hold her own against her Indian captors. Hannah's name was known throughout the colonies, so much so that she could be considered one of the earliest known celebrities. So impressed was Governor Francis Nicholson of Maryland that he gifted Hannah with a pewter tankard.

In addition to the Dustin house and garrison Thomas completed in 1697, other reminders of Hannah and her adventure remain. Monuments commemorating her ordeal were erected on Dustin Island (1874), in Monument Square in Haverhill (1861), and at the site of John Lovewell's home in Nashua (1902). Markers of various

Dustin Garrison House, Haverhill, Massachusetts
Built in 1697 of local Haverhill brick by Thomas Dustin

stops along the journey also serve to memorialize Hannah, Mary, and Samuel.

Samuel Lennardson made a life for himself in Preston, Connecticut, with a wife and five children. He died on May 11, 1718. As for Hannah and Mary, so little of their lives after that fateful spring of 1697 is known that it is almost as if they had fallen off the face of the earth.

Thomas and Hannah did conceive one more child—a daughter, Lydia, born October 4, 1698. And historical records indicate that Hannah died in early 1736. But for nearly 200 years, that was all anyone knew of her. Then, in March 1929, Marchus C. Jean, sexton of the Haverhill Center Congregational Church, found papers dating back more than two centuries. Among them was a letter written by Hannah to the elders of the church. In it, she is seeking membership of the congregation.

That letter is reprinted here in its entirety.

I Desire to be Thankful that I was born in a Land of Light & Baptized when I was Young : and had a Good Education by My Father, Tho I took but little Notice of it in the time of it :--I am Thankful for my Captivity, twas the Comfortablest time that ever I had; In my Affliction God made his Word Comfortable to me. I remembered 43d ps. ult-and those words came to my mind--ps. 118.17. ... I ave had a great Desire to come to the Ordinance of the Lords Supper a Great while but Unworthiness has kept me aback; reading a Book concerning +s Suffering Did much awaken me. In the 55th of Isa. Beg. We are invited to come:-- Hearing Mr. Moody preach out of ye 3rd of Mal. 3 last verses it put me upon Consideration. Ye 11th of Matthew has been Encouraging to me-- I have been resolving to offer me Self from time to time ever since the Settlement of the present Ministry: I was awakened by first Sacram'l Sermon (Luke 14.17) But Delays and fears prevailed upon me:-- But I desire to Delay no longer, being Sensible it is My Duty--. I desire the Church to receive me tho' it be at the Eleventh hour; & pray for me--that I may hon'r God and obtain the Salvation of my Soul. Hannah Duston wife of Thomas AEtat 67.[4]

It would be wrong to say that this is the end of the story. It is indeed the end of Hannah's story, but it is only one story in millions, some as yet untold. Though history tends to be studied as if it is a linear journey, the reality of it is anything but. Historical events happen simultaneously ... some unfold only eventually, and it is not until a story ends that the keen observer realizes how remarkably coincidental so much of history seems. And yet coincidence has nothing to do with it.

History is like a map, where roads and tributaries overlap, run parallel, and branch off into their own tomorrows. As history is in the making, it can be difficult, even impossible, to see where it is going, let alone where it might end. The story of Hannah Dustin is one amazing historical event. Regardless of how one perceives her actions, her ordeal was unusual and her courage makes it unforgettable. Even today, there are Hannah Dustin family reunions. A nursing home, an elementary school, and various other institutions have been named in her honor.

And yet it is just one early story in a series of events and lives comprising American history that have, until now, only been speculated upon in many ways. It is a story that leads to other stories and eventually entwines its heritage with other notable Americans, namely the Cheney and Burgess families. Those two names are recognizable for the key roles they played in the early Mormon Church, the founding of Steamboat Springs, Colorado, and the development of Boulder, Colorado.

Although their roots were in the East, the Cheney and Burgess men were pivotal players in helping tame the Wild West.

History has focused on Hannah Dustin's role in the Indian raid and subsequent kidnapping. Even Thomas Dustin is mentioned in history books for the bravery and level-headedness that allowed him to get his seven children to safety at the garrison on Pecker's Hill. No known documented account of the experience from the children's perspective exists, yet it would be absurd to think that the older children, particularly the eldest, Hannah, did nothing to help muster along their younger siblings. Hannah would have been eighteen years old at the time of the raid; the youngest child, Timothy, was two. In all likelihood, she and her sister Elizabeth helped carry and keep calm Thomas (14), Nathaniel (11), Sarah (8), Jonathan (5), and Timothy.

After her mother's safe return in April 1697, Hannah's strength probably manifested itself in how she tended to her traumatized mother and took over some of the household duties and chores. Despite this transitional period for the family, Hannah managed to find herself a husband, and in 1698 she wed Daniel Cheney II, a man nearly eight years her senior.

Born in Newbury, Massachusetts, on December 3, 1670, Daniel made his living as a farmer there. When so required, he rendered "service in the blockhouse,"[5] according to historian C. H. Pope. A blockhouse is a fortified two-story building with gunports through which defenders can ward off attackers without concern about injury. In this way, Daniel fought off untold number of Indians, and his shooting skills were put to use in "The Second Foot Company of Newbury,"[6] with which he served from 1710 to 1711.

Daniel and Hannah had seven children, and he made certain to provide generously for all of them and their children after his death in 1755. According to his will, which is reprinted in C. H. Pope's *The Cheney Genealogy*, Daniel ensured his widow a comfortable life:

> Imprimis [In the first place] I give to my Beloved Wife Hannah the Use and Improvement of all the East Half of my Dwelling House And the Cellar under said East Half. Excepting the garret. a piece of Land for a garden where she shall choose to have it well fenced. I give to my said wife the use of, also to be fenced by my Executor. During all the time she remains living my Widow.

> I do also give to my said Wife Thirty bushels of Indian Corn and Two Bushels of Wheat and Three Bushels and a Half of Rye. and Two Bushels and a half of Malt and two Barels of Cyder and Five pounds of Sheeps Wool and Eight pounds of flax from swingle [after it is separated and cleaned] and fifty pounds of Beef and as many apples as shall be needful for her. and Needful firewood brought to the Door Cut fit for the fire all which my said wife shall have yearly During the time She remains my Widow to be paid to her by my Executor. And my Executor Shall Provide and Keep a good Cow Winter and Summer for my said Wife so long as she Remains my Widow. And I Do give to my said Wife all my pork that I shall leave at my Decease and also all the money Due to me by Bonds and Notes. and all my swine that I shall leave at my Decease. and all my House Hold Goods Excepting my Andirons my Gun my Loom and my wearing apparel for her to have and Dispose of as she shall think fit. And my Executor shall provide and find a horse for my said Wife to ride as she shall have Ocation [occasion] so Long as she shall remain my widow. And my said Executor shall repair that part of the House which my Wife is to have so that it may be comfortable for my Wife so long as she shall remain my Widow.[7]

It may not seem like much according to modern standards: Half of a house and land for a garden, bushels and barrels of food and beverage, firewood cut and delivered annually, a few farm animals, some household goods, and an undisclosed amount of money. But the reality of life in the mid-eighteenth century was such that Daniel Cheney left his beloved wife everything she could possibly need to maintain the lifestyle to which she was accustomed. He left her not only money with which to buy whatever she might need, but also raw materials to turn into goods she might be able to sell to earn more income. His will directly reflects his thoughtfulness and foresight.

The Great Storm of 1635

Delve back far enough in virtually any family and some-where along the genealogy tree branches hangs a remarkable story. Hannah Cheney had only to go as far back as her childhood to find hers. Husband Daniel needed look no further than his grandfather's and great-grandfather's generations.

Daniel Cheney II was the son of Daniel Cheney and Sarah Bayley (also spelled Bailey). On May 23, 1635, Sarah's 22-year-old father John and grandfather John Sr. set sail from Bristol, England, for New England. Their passenger galleon, the *Angel Gabriel*, was originally built by Sir Charles Snell for Sir Walter Raleigh in 1617 and was accompanied on its voyage by four other ships: the *James*, the *Mary*, the *Bess* or *Elizabeth*, and the *Diligence*.

On board the *James* was the patriarch of one of America's most famous conservative colonial dynasties, the Mathers. Rev-erend Richard Mather was the father of Increase and the grand-father of Cotton, the very man who thrust Hannah Dustin into the public eye and gave her eternal life in the annals of American history. It is through Richard Mather's journals that the unfolding of the Great Storm of 1635 is understood.

From the very beginning of the voyage, the weather refused to cooperate. High winds repeatedly forced the ships back to land, where they would anchor anywhere from three to twelve days at a time. Finally on June 22, the fleet was able to leave the English coastline behind. The next day, the captain of the *James* decided to stay with the *Angel Gabriel*, as they were the only two ships sailing to New England. The remaining three headed to Newfoundland.

According to Mather's journal, the *James* reached land at Menhiggin—quite possibly Monhegan, Maine—on August 8. Six days later, they docked at the Isle of Shoales, a group of islands and tidal ledges about ten miles off the coast of New Hampshire and Maine. Some time between these dates, the *Angel Gabriel* dropped anchor at Pemaquid Point near Bristol, Maine.

On August 15, weather conditions were just right for a hurricane, and although hurricane season had not yet arrived, this particular storm carried with it a fury remarkable enough (contemporary analysis of the hurricane labels it a Category 3 at landfall) to devastate the *Angel Gabriel*. Ripped from its dock, the 240-ton ship literally fell apart, and with it sank three to five passengers and crew, cattle, and all the settlers' supplies. It was the only sailing vessel carrying immigrants from England to New England ever to sink.

The tide caused by the Great Colonial Hurricane of 1635 reached twenty-two feet in some areas, the highest ever recorded for a New England hurricane. Entire villages of Indians were drowned as 125-mile-per-hour winds destroyed wigwams and flattened everything in their path.

Both father and son survived the storm and settled in Newbury, not far from the Dustin family. John Cheney Sr. wrote to his wife Elizabeth, beckoning her to join him now that he had settled. He made the mistake of telling her about the hurricane and the terrifying experience he and their son had shared. So vivid was John Sr.'s description that Elizabeth refused to board a ship and sail to New England. John Sr. had had enough maritime adventure for a lifetime and also refused to ever sail again.

Despite a court order to reunite with his wife one way or another, John Sr. and Elizabeth never saw each other again. And so Daniel Cheney II grew up without ever knowing his maternal great-grandmother.

And the remains of the *Angel Gabriel?* Divers still search for them today.

Hannah Dustin Cheney's death date is not verifiable, but the robust spirit evident so early in the Dustin and Cheney families continued to wind its way down the family tree from one generation to the next. Eventually, the path led to Emma Semantha Cheney, mother of Perry A. Burgess. Known to most by her middle name Semantha, she was born on December 1, 1823, to Ephraim and Harriet (Law) Cheney. She was one of eleven children born to the couple and one of five to be born in Freedom, New York.

The town of Freedom in the 1820s was small but growing. According to reports given by trustees of the school districts for the school year ending March 1, 1825,[8] Freedom was home to 1,835 people, most with roots in New Hampshire and Vermont. Their values of hard work and frugality made Freedom an aesthetically appealing and successful dairy farming community.

These stoic New England transplants took their religion as seriously as their work, and until the late 1820s, most residents attended the Baptist church. In 1827, the First Methodist Episcopal Church opened its doors, as did the First Presbyterian Church. These three denominations satisfied the residents of Freedom throughout the decade.

Then came what historian Franklin Ellis refers to in his 1879 book *The History of Cattaraugus County, New York* as "the Mormon excitement."[9] And this is where one of the most fascinating chapters in American history begins: with a little girl, a Mormon, and a twist of fate.

Emma Semantha Cheney Burgess, circa 1890
Mother of pioneer diarist Perry A. Burgess
4x great-granddaughter of Hannah Dustin

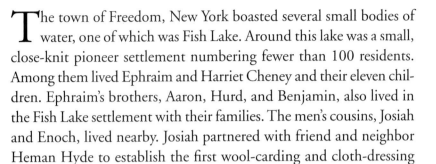

CHAPTER 2
Early Mormon Era – Birth of Perry A. Burgess

The town of Freedom, New York boasted several small bodies of water, one of which was Fish Lake. Around this lake was a small, close-knit pioneer settlement numbering fewer than 100 residents. Among them lived Ephraim and Harriet Cheney and their eleven children. Ephraim's brothers, Aaron, Hurd, and Benjamin, also lived in the Fish Lake settlement with their families. The men's cousins, Josiah and Enoch, lived nearby. Josiah partnered with friend and neighbor Heman Hyde to establish the first wool-carding and cloth-dressing works in the area in 1822. This business was erected near the home of Warren Cowdery, Fish Lake's resident physician and first postmaster, who built the first brick house in the community in 1828, four years after the first post office opened.

Fish Lake was a serene, pious farming settlement in rural Freedom. A largely self-sufficient—though not prosperous—township, Fish Lake consisted primarily of extended families that interacted and functioned as one unit. Such a dynamic was integral to the pioneer way of life in the early 1800s. Fish Lake residents led simple lives marked by poverty and relied upon one another in good times and bad.

The Hurd Cheney family was no different from its neighbors. Despite hard work and long hours, the family struggled to get by. Children were expected to help maintain the daily routines of the homestead, and attending school was secondary in importance to helping out at home. Girls especially were raised to value household contribution over schooling. Although Hurd sent his sons to school as regularly as possible, his daughters did not benefit from the same opportunity. Poverty required that they stay home not only because they provided another set of helping hands, but because they had no suitable clothing to wear. When permitted to attend school, Malinda and her sister Mariah took turns and shared the one dress they owned between them. Every night, that dress would be washed, dried in front of the fire or on the clothesline, then ironed for the next day's use. Classmates referred to the sisters as "the girls who had dresses alike," unaware of the fact that they had only the one dress. Even if their peers had known, it probably wouldn't have mattered. Poor was poor in Fish Lake, New York.

Meanwhile, in nearby Ontario County, in the town of Manchester, a young Joseph Smith spent his teenage years helping to run the family farm. A devoted reader of the Bible, Smith was raised in a family of Christian mystics, people who believed their dreams and visions were direct communications from God. Although Christian mysticism was common in the early decades of the 19th century, it was frowned upon and rejected as morally suspicious by most clergymen.

Upstate New York was considered the frontier in the early 1800s. This would change with the development of the Erie Canal, but at the time, it was on the edge of a vast wilderness leading into the unknown.

The region in which Joseph Smith and his family lived was known as the "burned over" district, so named for its abundance of evangelical zeal and fervor. There was no shortage of fire and brimstone in the revivals that led to what is now known as the Second Great Awakening.

Smith reportedly had his first vision in 1820, when he was just fourteen years old. It was a time of spiritual confusion for the boy. Living in a household in which each parent embraced a separate set of beliefs and growing up in an area known for its evangelicism, Smith was understandably torn. He was on a quest for truth, and Mormon history has it that he found it in a grove of trees.

Smith claimed to have been visited by God and Jesus Christ in this vision, and when he asked which church was true, the answer was none of them. At first, Smith shared his vision only with his family. His version of what happened that day in the grove changed over the years, and an evolved version of the vision recorded in 1838 became the official Mormon record of the event.

His first vision would not be his last. One night in September 1823, Smith was visited by the Angel Moroni in a vision. The angel directed Smith to the golden plates, a sacred book of bound

Ephraim Cheney

Harriet Cheney

Grandparents of Perry A. Burgess

Hurd Cheney

Mormon Church founder
Joseph Smith Jr.

metal plates that would eventually serve as the source for the Book of Mormon. The plates were buried in a hill called Cumorah, just outside Manchester.

Although Smith claimed to have located the plates easily and immediately, he was unable to extract them from the rock under which they were buried. Moroni purportedly told Smith that he had to have a companion—the right companion—in order to unlock the secret to retrieving the plates. It took three years, but Smith finally found himself the mate he was searching for in young Emme Hale.

On September 22, 1827, Smith took his new wife with him to Cumorah. Finally, he was able to extract the golden plates, and he locked them safely inside a chest. Moroni had instructed him not to share them with anyone, but to publish the translation of their text, which was written in ancient hieroglyphics. Smith relied on the Urim and Thummim, two divining stones[1] he found when he discovered the golden plates, as well as his wife and a few trusted friends, to complete the translation over a period of nearly two years. One of these friends was Oliver Cowdery, a teacher who, in spring of 1829, became Smith's scribe. Together they finished the translation some time around the beginning of July. When the translation was complete, Smith returned the golden plates to the Angel Moroni, as instructed. The translation was over 600 pages, and it was published in 1830 as the Book of Mormon.

Within months of the publication of the Book of Mormon, Smith and his followers founded the Church of Christ. Smith defined himself as the sole prophet of the Church and sent Cowdery, Second Elder of the Church, to lead a mission to find Zion, or the New Jerusalem. Cowdery and other Church leaders gave up ministering to Native Americans on the nearby Cattaraugus Reservation to follow Smith's orders and reached Kirtland, Ohio, in October 1830 and began to establish a dedicated Mormon community. Cowdery stayed long enough to convert and baptize, but he soon moved on toward Missouri, the Zion Joseph Smith believed was the place reserved by God for those who were pure of heart.

Back in Fish Lake, Oliver Cowdery's older brother, Warren, was busy as the community's sole physician and postmaster. While he was working with Smith to translate the golden plates in 1829, Oliver was sending proofs to Warren, who was in turn sharing the translated texts with his neighbors.

One such neighboring family was that of Heman Hyde, the business partner of the Cheney family. One of Heman's sons, William, kept a diary. In it, he wrote:

> In the year 1830 or 31 he [Heman] began to hear something concerning the Book of Mormon, and the setting up of the Kingdom of God on the earth in the last days. The little information that we gained upon this subject, until the elders came preaching, was through Warren A. Cowdery, whose farm joined with ours. Warren A. obtained from his brother Oliver, at an early date, some of the proof sheets to the Book of Mormon, some of which we had the privilege of perusing, and we did not peruse any faster than we believed.[2]

The Elders did indeed come preaching to the tiny Fish Lake community. Twice, in fact. Though less known, the first mission took place in 1831, within a year of the founding of the Church of Christ. Joseph Smith and Elder Orson Pratt reached out to the community to share with residents the gospel of the Church and the Book of Mormon. During this mission, a number of residents were baptized by the Church. Among them were several members of the Cheney family, including Ephraim (father of Semantha), Hurd, and Aaron and his wife Mehitable. Given that the Cowderys and Cheneys were friends and neighbors, it is safe to assume that the Cheney family was already familiar with Mormon gospel even before Smith and Pratt came to town. In all likelihood, at least some of the Cheneys saw the proofs of the Book of Mormon.

The "Mormon excitement," which historian Franklin Ellis refers to in his history of Cattaraugus County, took place in March and

April of 1834, though he misidentifies the year as 1835. Smith and Pratt again visited— "invaded," according to Ellis—Fish Lake, and this time they brought along a handful of men important in the Church of Christ:

> At the time mentioned, the quiet precincts of Fish Lake neighborhood were invaded by Joe Smith, Sidney Rigdon, John Gould, and Parley Pratt. They made their head-quarters at Rufus Metcalf's and Dr. Warren Cowdery's. Meetings were held, daily and nightly, in barns and dwelling-houses, and a prodigious excitement pervaded the minds of many people in that immediate vicinity... as a result, 30 men and women were induced to join the Mormons, and emigrated with them to Kirtland, Ohio. Some came back and renounced their faith in Mormonism, while others continued with them to the end of their lives.

Throughout March and into early April, Mormon officials preached and held prayer meetings in schoolhouses, where they baptized and confirmed scores of new members, including more Cheneys, Heman Hyde and his wife Polly, their sons Heman T. and William, and dozens more. The Hydes would prove to be key leaders in the early Mormon Church, and their zeal so impressed Joseph Smith that he wrote about it in his diary:

> Sunday, March 9th. Held meeting in a school house had great attention found a few desyples who were firm in faith and after meeting found many Believeing and could hardly get away from them we appointed A meeting in freedom for Monday 10th and are now at Mr. Cowderyes in the full Enjoyment of all the Blessings Both temporal and spiritual.

On April 11, 1834, the last of the Freedom baptisms were conducted. Smith and his missionaries, along with seventy-five or so followers, left the area and set out for Kirtland, Ohio, where the Mormon community was, by that time, already established and finding itself the target of persecution. Among the sojourners were Ephraim and Harriet Cheney and their children, including young Semantha and her younger brother, Levi. Ephraim and Harriet welcomed a new addition to the family that year—a boy—whom they appropriately named "Joseph" in honor of Joseph Smith.

The Mormon Threat

Persecution is a major theme in the history of the Mormon Church. Upon first consideration, public response to this renewed or revised gospel seems, perhaps, an overreaction . The early 1800s were, after all, a time of religious and spiritual questing. So what made Joseph Smith's message so undeniably controversial?

Smith had not only new messages and edicts, he had something solid to back up his claims: the Book of Mormon. And that book claimed the Mormon Church to be the One True Church. Smith preached that all Christians were guilty of corrupting Christianity in its purest form. In short, he was telling all non-Mormons that they were wrong.

Furthermore, Smith's preachings were based upon the idea that everyone had the ability to speak directly to God. Revelation could come to anyone, and the idea of worshipful distance played no part in these new teachings. God had once been embodied, as humans are. Such thought offended the majority of traditional Christians, and soon Smith and his followers were forced out of New York. Eventually, they were forced out of virtually every place they ever tried to settle.

While the residents of Fish Lake were living their quiet lives in rural Freedom, a young Harrison Burgess was busy making a life for himself in upstate New York. Burgess was born September 3, 1814, to William and Violate (Stockwell) Burgess, in Putnam, New York. The eldest of eleven children, Harrison received little formal education but instead spent his youth working to help keep the family fed and clothed.

Harrison left home at the age of fourteen but remained in the northeastern region of the state. According to his autobiography, he first heard of the gospel according to the Book of Mormon in July 1832. "I was convinced that the scriptures were true and the Book of Mormon was a divine revelation from heaven. I was baptized and spent the following winter in going to school, working for my board and in meeting with the Saints."[3] Harrison was just one of about a dozen people other than Smith to ever have reported a vision of the Angel Moroni, as published on the Latter-Day Saints (LDS) website.

In the spring of 1833, Harrison traveled to Vermont, where he was ordained a priest, and then returned to New York. Soon after, the nineteen-year-old had a life-altering experience:

> On the third Sabbath in May while speaking to a congregation I declared that I knew the Book of Mormon was true, the work of God. The next day while I was laboring something seemed to whisper to me "Do you know the Book of Mormon is true?" My mind became perplexed and darkened, and I was so tormented in spirit that I left my work and retired into the woods in misery and distress and therein cannot be described.
>
> Finally, I resolved to know whether I had proclaimed the truth or not, and commenced praying to the God of Heaven, for a testimony of these things, when all at once the vision of my mind was opened, and a glorious personage clothed in white stood before me and exhibited to my view the plates, from which the Book of Mormon was taken.[4]

Harrison's faith in the Book of Mormon was so strong that he converted his entire family to this new religion. Together they left New York for Kirtland in September 1834. While passing through Springfield, Pennsylvania, the Burgesses crossed paths with the Prophet Joseph Smith and had the opportunity to hear him preach for the first time. By the time winter had set in, the family had reached Kirtland.

And it is there that they met the Cheney family. Theirs was an ironic relationship, one that was forged on a foundation of shared faith but whose primary participants would eventually downplay that faith as they blazed trails, founded towns, and acquired an impressive magnitude of wealth.

Smith was greeted in Kirtland by Sidney Rigdon, a preacher who had brought with him his own 100-strong congregation. Another key player in Mormon history—30-year-old Brigham Young—had arrived in Kirtland before Smith and, upon meeting and listening to him, decided the prophet's preachings held the one truth. Young would learn from Smith all he needed to be a charismatic, forceful leader, and then would eventually lead the faithful into Utah after Smith's murder in 1844.

Kirtland was never meant to be anything but a stopover on the journey toward Zion for members—also known as Latter Day Saints or just Saints—of the Church of Christ. Even so, Smith claimed that God had commanded a 15,000-square-foot temple be built in Kirtland, and construction had begun in June of 1833. Paid for by Smith's followers, the temple was built from local sandstone and timber by the very people who paid for it. At the time, the temple was one of northern Ohio's largest buildings.

In the twenty-first century, the idea of building a temple even as magnificent as the one in Kirtland does not necessarily inspire awe. But consider: The trenches for the foundation were dug by hand tools and sweat equity. Timber had to be cut and hewn. The Berea sandstone was cut and hauled from a quarry at the base of Gildersleeve Mountain, two miles from the temple's site. Everything had to be built to the exact dimensions dictated by God to Joseph Smith in his revelation. As reported in a December 25, 1887, *New York Times* article:

> And yet, in those days of rapid development, the building of such a temple as that of the Mormons was the cause of wonder. Even at this day a building of such size would be a severe tax upon villages that are tenfold the size of Kirtland. But the Mormons who built it gave cheerfully each one his tenth to the labor, materials, or money for the four years from 1832 to 1836, the entire cost being estimated at $40,000.[5]

William Burgess Jr. tells of the Burgess family's arrival at Kirtland, Ohio:

> The Prophet Joseph Smith advised us to stop at Kirtland and help build the Temple. The walls of which were about four feet above the ground… I helped to build the Kirtland Temple, was at the dedication, and passed through the persecutions with the saints.[6]

The Saints, who labored not weeks or months but years on the Temple, were not affluent in most cases. But all were required to tithe one-tenth of their income to the Church. The Cheney and Burgess families toiled alongside one another, happy to be part of such a Divine undertaking. William Burgess, Harrison's father, began working on the Temple in its earliest stages and became a foreman on the construction site where he spent long days cutting roof timbers while Harrison and his brother Abram labored in whatever capacity was required of them. A carpenter's square used to set the ceiling timbers was saved and eventually handed down through the family.

After nearly three years, construction was completed and the Temple was officially dedicated on March 27, 1836. Those who participated in its genesis received their endowments, a sacred series of instructions and covenants believed to be required for salvation. It was a time of great celebration in the Mormon community of Kirtland.

The Kirtland Years: An Era of Change

Although the period of time spent in Kirtland was little more than the blink of an eye in Mormon history, it was a time of great transition and revelation. In 1834, the Church officially changed its name to The Church of the Latter Day Saints. Shortly after leaving Kirtland in 1838, Smith claimed to have a revelation that instructed him to change the name yet again, to Church of Jesus Christ of Latter Day Saints.

The Kirtland era was rife with revelation. Smith reported revelations concerning missionary work, tithing, moral conduct, the law of consecration, the Second Coming of Christ, and many other topics. Among the most significant revelations was that concerning the Word of Wisdom. This doctrine forbids the consumption of alcohol, caffeine, and the non-medicinal use of tobacco while also limiting the consumption of animal flesh.

The revelations reportedly experienced by Smith were compiled and first published in book form in 1835. Known as the *Doctrine and Covenants*, the first edition included 102 revelations and a series of lessons called the Lectures on Faith. *The Doctrine and Covenants* was accepted as one of the standard texts of the Mormon faith.

During those early months of 1836, the economy in northern Ohio was booming. Investors turned their sights to real estate, and there was an overall sense of optimism. During this time, Joseph Smith founded a bank to finance Church programs and dabbled in several other businesses. Before long, however, the national economic panic and questionable business practices on Smith's part led to the collapse of the bank. Those who had entrusted their savings to Smith lost not only their money, but their faith.

By 1837, conflict within the 2,000-strong Mormon community was tearing it apart. Add to that the fact that many of Kirtland's non-Mormon residents—of which there were about 1,000—found the Mormons smug and their religious doctrine threatening. What was brewing was akin to the Perfect Storm. The harassment experienced by the Mormons only increased in intensity until it became clear that the only option for survival was to leave Kirtland.

Smith and Rigdon escaped under cover of night in January 1838. That spring and summer, hundreds of others followed. And although not all traveled the same route, all had the same destination. In 1831, Smith had sent his missionaries to Missouri, where they had established a Mormon presence. By 1836, there were more than 5,000 Mormons living in Missouri. Those brethren from Kirtland would soon join them.

Among that first group—known as Kirtland Camp—was the Cheney family. According to Aaron Cheney, grandson of Elam Cheney,

> They intended to join the Saints at Nauvoo, but, owing to sickness, were not able to continue the journey. They stopped temporarily at Decatur, Macon Co., Illinois. While detained at this place, they were to work and fence a piece of ground, build a small house, raise a crop. It was while they were living at Decatur, that Joseph, the Prophet, started on his memorable trip to Washington for the purpose of laying the grievances of the saints before the President of the United States.[7]

Smith passed through Decatur and spent a night with the Cheney family in their home. Although no specific date is recorded, the Cheneys resumed their journey to Nauvoo, Illinois, "as soon afterward as they could."

Other Saints, like the Burgess clan, traveled in smaller groups. In the *Short Sketch of William Burgess* by Jennie Burgess Miles (William Burgess's great-granddaughter), she recounts his response to the crisis in Kirtland:

> There seemed no place was to be had for the Saints, so later, all were busy preparing to leave Kirtland... So at the noon hour of a bright July day William Burgess with his family, his married sons and wives, with friends and neighbors started on their journey. A threat was made by their enemies that they "would never leave Kirtland." But when they did leave they were the largest company of Saints that had ever traveled together...
>
> As they passed through the towns, people would stand in their doors to look at them and sometimes did worse than look—eggs, etc. were thrown with force at them. In one village they went through a cannon was placed in the street to fire on them. William Burgess with others persuaded these hateful quarrelsome men to let them pass. They did, after putting some of the brethren in prison. These were soon released and joined the company.[8]

William Burgess Jr. tells of the turmoil in Kirtland in his auto-biography:

> We found the mob spirit raging, and all the old settlers with the exception of two moved away in order to have their families safe while they were fighting us. For about three months, I did not undress only to shift my clothes. No one except those that passed through it could know the tribulations and privations that we had to endure. But it was for the Gospel's sake and we endured cheerfully. I was taken prisoner by the mob and abused while in their custody. We depended upon the Lord and He delivered us from them.

Mormon Settlements Throughout Missouri

Missouri was a state rife with Mormon settlements. One of the earliest and largest of these was Jackson County. This was the region Joseph Smith claimed had once been the Garden of Eden and would one day be the New Jerusalem. The seat, or center place, of this Zion was the city of Independence.

Mormons began moving to Jackson County as early as 1831 but were immediately met with hostility and prejudice for much the same reason they were persecuted everywhere else they went. A handful of Mormons were forced out of Jackson County in 1832 and settled in Ray County. They established the county's first town, Salem, and in late 1836, more Mormons relocated to the area. In December of that year, Missouri founded Caldwell County specifically for Mormon settlers, and by fall of 1838, its county seat—Far West—boasted a population of 5,000, most of them Kirtland transplants.

As the Mormon settlement grew, its Saints could not be contained solely within Caldwell County and began moving to Daviess, Ray, and Carroll counties. Non-Mormon settlers reacted with fear and intolerance as they felt their homes were being invaded by a threatening religion and culture. At first, the clashes between the Saints and the settlers were characterized by rudeness, prejudice, and malice. Before too long, however, culture clash morphed into violence as mob mentality became the upheld societal attitude. What ensued is referred to by historians as the Mormon War.

A Saint named Zerah Pulsipher had remained behind at Kirtland to help organize and lead the last 600 or so followers on their 1,000-mile journey to Missouri. In October 1838, his group arrived in Adam-ondi-ahman in Daviess County, Missouri. According to his journals,

> There we stayed about a month, being continually annoyed by mobs and thieves stealing everything that they could lay their hands upon that belonged to people of our church. In the time I was there I was assisted to build sixteen houses and the longest that I lived in one was four days.[9]

Pulsipher's account of his life experiences is particularly valuable because two of his family's women married into the Burgess family. Diaries and journal entries from both families provide evidence of their affection for and reliance upon one another. The Pulsiphers and Burgesses often lived together as one group from Missouri and through Ohio and, eventually, Utah.

As Mormon settlers migrated to Jackson County and particularly to Independence in droves, hostilities and violence mounted. Non-Mormon residents became alarmed that these unusual and culturally foreign newcomers were purchasing large tracts of land and exerting political influence with their tendency to vote in blocs. Rather than try to understand their new neighbors, earlier settlers reacted out of fear and resentment.

As early as 1833, non-Mormons began establishing vigilantes to drive out the unwanted. Their program was successful as Mormons were forced into outlying counties. Despite the violent persecution, they tried to achieve justice by working from within the system: They filed petitions and lawsuits, all to no avail. An effort to try to return to Jackson en masse failed as well.

Meanwhile, the exiled Mormons began establishing settlements nearby, and for a few years, the two factions of society lived peaceably. Caldwell County was designated specifically for the purpose of isolating Mormons, and that seemed to be a compromise everyone could live with. Events in Kirtland damaged that truce when the Kirtland Safety Society bank failed. As thousands of Saints began pouring into Caldwell and outlying counties, local residents became alarmed. No longer was Mormon settlement limited to Caldwell. This highly structured and self-reliant faction intimidated non-Mormons, and conflict escalated.

To make matters worse, trouble was brewing within the Mormon community itself. As the Church presidency and Missouri leaders engaged in a power struggle, the Mormon community was divided as to how to handle the situation. Several Mormon officials, including Oliver Cowdery, were excommunicated and charged as dissenters. These so-called dissenters had purchased a significant tract of land in Caldwell County, some of it for the Church. As rightful possession came into dispute, Cowdery and company threatened to sue the Church.

Sidney Rigdon delivered what became known as the "Salt Sermon," in which he urged the faithful to cast out the dissenters. He likened them to salt that had lost its savor. Simultaneously, a secret society known as the Danites was forming within the community. Its goal was to obey the Church leadership, right or wrong, and to force the dissenters into exile. The dissenters and their families left Caldwell County on June 19, 1838, and resumed life among non-Mormons. Their complaints against the Church could only have fueled the fire of anti-Mormon sentiment.

On July 4, Rigdon again gave a public address. This time, he declared zero tolerance for anti-Mormon sentiment and activity from both within and without the community. This declaration of independence from those who would threaten the faithful included a retaliation clause that promised vengeance until "the last drop of their blood is spilled."[10] The content of Rigdon's speech was published in local newspapers and is largely credited by secular and Mormon historians alike as the act that set the stage for the fateful Mormon War.

"Massacre of Mormons at Haun's Mill"

August 6 was county election day, and by that time tempers on both sides were running high. In the town of Gallatin (Daviess County), a brawl broke out as non-Mormons tried to prevent Mormons from voting. The fight—considered by many to be the first battle of the Mormon War—inspired raids throughout the region that lasted throughout the early fall, and the Mormons responded by pillaging and burning the neighboring community of Millport on October 18. Some eyewitness accounts of that day claim the Mormons also burned Gallatin, though that argument has been disputed by others. Regardless, seven days later, nearly five dozen Mormons fought a non-Mormon militia at Crooked River. The Mormons forced the militia to break ranks and retreat, but two Mormons were killed and eight more wounded.

Mormon settlements throughout Carroll, Caldwell, Daviess, and Clay counties were being attacked, their residents forced to flea. William Burgess and his family were among those driven from their homes. As word of the battle at Crooked River spread, so did the panic experienced by Missourians everywhere. Two days later, on October 27, Governor Lilburn Boggs responded to the fear by mustering a state militia numbering between 2,000 and 3,000 and issuing Executive Order 44, also known as the Extermination Order. Mormons were officially declared the enemy and were to be exterminated as a menace. Never before had a state government issued such a decree.

On October 30, about 240 militia attacked the Mormon settlement of Haun's Mill in Caldwell County. The bloody raid, which sent women and children fleeing in terror to safety in the woods, claimed the lives of seventeen (some accounts say eighteen) Mormons, including a ten-year-old boy who was executed at point-blank range. Explained his murderer, William Reynolds, "Nits will make lice, and if he had lived he would have become a Mormon."[11] Thirteen more Mormons—including women and children—were wounded. Although three militia were wounded, they suffered no fatalities.

After remaining in hiding while their attackers looted their homes and tents and chased off their horses and wagons, the survivors at Haun's Mill used an unfinished well as a makeshift grave into which they placed the corpses of their loved ones. The event would go down in Mormon history as the most vicious, vile example of persecution of the Saints. Accounts of that day use terms such as "horrid" and "wanton slaughter," and one account in particular provides grisly detail. James McBride, husband of Olive Cheney and brother-in-law to Elam, records a gruesome scene in his autobiography:

> Brother Amos... went on and passing the mill a short distance, came to Haun's house. The first object that met his eye in the human form, was the mangled body of my murdered father [Thomas McBride], lying in the door yard. He had been shot with his own gun, after having given it into the mob's possession. Was cut down and badly disfigured with a corn cutter, and left lying in the creek. Some of the women had dragged him from the creek into the door yard, and left him there. One of his ears was almost cut from his head—deep gashes were cut in his shoulders; and some of his fingers cut till they would almost drop from his hand.[12]

Joseph Young, Brigham's brother, provided an account that matched the details of McBride's.

Smith Imprisoned

Following the Haun's Mill massacre, many Mormon leaders—including Joseph Smith and Sidney Rigdon—were arrested and taken to Independence, where they were paraded through the streets and publicly humiliated. From there they went to Richmond and then to Liberty, where they were to stand trial for treason. Their crime? Defending themselves against the numerous and bloody attacks on them.

Smith and his men spent four months in the Liberty prison, where they were physically abused. Rigdon was set free in February 1839 when he became so ill that the state was afraid he would perish. In April, the remaining prisoners were set to go before a grand jury on charges of murder, treason, and arson, among others. The guards, however, had gotten to know their Mormon prisoners and knew they were not bad men. They allowed their captives to escape.

Liberty Jail - Liberty, Missouri
Joseph Smith III and RLDS Elders

Most Mormons fled to Caldwell's county seat, Far West, where they were given permission to spend the winter. Come spring, the Mormons moved on. Some headed for Lamoni, Iowa, but the majority of the faithful headed to Nauvoo, Illinois. William Burgess joined the latter, as did the Pulsipher family. Jennie Burgess Miles accounts for the crisis and subsequent pilgrimage:

> Orders were given to them to leave. Some of the homes were burned, [a] mob burned William Burgess' home to the ground and all they had in it. March 1839 William Burgess and family, his married sons and families, his dear friends and relatives, Zerah Pulsipher and family left for Illinois. They traveled two hundred miles...

Burgess and Pulsipher and their families arrived in Bear Creek, Illinois, in mid-April, 1839. John Pulsipher recorded in his diary the lifestyle the Saints enjoyed while in their new home. With a camaraderie often forged by individuals living in stressful situations, the Mormon families behaved as one highly functioning unit. "In about one month we had three good log houses built, 12 acres of land fenced and most if it planted to corn... We all enjoyed ourselves first rate. This place seemed more like home than any place I ever before saw. There were no mobs to disturb. We could lie down and sleep in peace."[13]

After years of persecution in Ohio and Missouri, the Saints must have been nearly delirious with relief at the welcome they received in Illinois. Around 15,000 Mormons left Missouri for Illinois, and though they arrived in various groups, most managed to make it there in the early months of 1839. Although their prophet was still in jail when they reached their destination, he wrote letters providing direction and guidance.

The Saints settled in Commerce, Illinois, on the bend of the Mississippi River. Although the land was swampy and prone to disease, the sojourners set down roots and immediately began to invest themselves in their new home. When Smith joined them that spring, he named the community Nauvoo.

The Mormon settlement was hard hit by a malaria epidemic the very spring in which they arrived. Smith himself left the comfort of his home and pitched a tent so that he might travel more freely among the victims, providing hope and healing. Stories of miraculous healing were documented, such as that provided by Zerah Pulsipher. Although he had come upon a house full of the near-dead that included his own daughter, he refused to give up on her. According to his journal, he asked his daughter if she wanted to raise a family and live the will of God. "She instantly opened her eyes and said she did... That hour she sat up in bed and immediately got well as did my sister."

After this initial hardship, the Mormons prospered at Nauvoo. Their internal structure and commitment to hard work allowed them to live in harmony with the land as they dug canals to drain the swampy area. And whereas most homes of the day were made of logs, the Saints built brick dwellings and structures that would last long after they left for Zion. While the nearly credit-only economy of Nauvoo prevented residents from becoming wealthy, the self-sufficient community thrived.

In 1840, Smith had another revelation directing him to build yet another temple. The cornerstone was laid on April 6, 1841, and the dimensions of the building were 60 percent greater than those of the Kirtland Temple. Like the temple before it, the Nauvoo Temple was designed to be used not only for worship, but for administrative and educational purposes as well. And as in Kirtland, so it was in Nauvoo that the faithful volunteered their labor and sold their belongings to raise money to purchase the materials needed to build their beloved temple. Several Cheney men, including the sons of Ephraim and Aaron, contributed their labor to the effort.

While in Nauvoo, the Cheney and Burgess families strengthened their bond as Semantha Cheney—the daughter of Ephraim and Harriet who had spent her early childhood years in Fish Lake—married Abraham Burgess, son of William and Violate and older brother of Harrison Burgess, on July 6, 1840. And on June 14, 1843, during the peak years of prosperity at Nauvoo—Semantha gave birth to her only son, Perry Abraham Burgess.[14]

Kirtland Temple - Kirtland, Ohio
Roof timbers set by William Burgess Sr. & sons

The Cheneys and Burgesses lived on the outskirts of Nauvoo, about 2.5 miles from the center of town, where they farmed property across the street from one another. Ephraim Cheney owned forty acres, as did his brother Aaron. Their property was adjacent while Horace Burgess, Harrison and Abraham's brother, owned land as far as the eye could see on the other side of the street. Theirs was a microcosm of the larger Mormon settlement in which families cared for and depended upon one another for survival. Harrison himself continued to be a highly respected Elder in the Church. In 1845, he baptized Mansel and Lewis Cheney, both younger brothers of Semantha.

The population of Nauvoo continued to grow, owing in large part to the successful missions overseas in England. The first boat bringing over Mormon immigrants left Liverpool on June 6, 1840, and the influx continued for several years. The voyage from England to

New York took five weeks. From there, the Saints journeyed another nineteen days to New Orleans, the primary port of arrival for overseas Mormon immigrants. From there they traveled up the Mississippi. According to records, all but nine voyages from 1840 to 1855 docked in New Orleans, bringing to America approximately 18,000 Saints.[15]

Despite the growing numbers and strength of the Mormon settlement, peace did not last long. Part of the reason for this was the economic policies of Nauvoo. With a credit-based economy, there simply wasn't much cash flow, and the Mormons brought with them debts from both Ohio and Missouri. In addition, there was a general practice of not repaying debt owed to non-Mormons. This caused problems both economic and political in nature, and outsiders held Joseph Smith responsible.

To further complicate matters, there was an assassination attempt on ex-Governor Boggs (of Missouri) in 1842, and Boggs fingered Smith as an accomplice to alleged trigger man Orrin Porter Rockwell. Both were arrested in Nauvoo. Released from custody on a legal technicality, Smith and Rockwell managed to evade re-arrest despite warrants. Missouri officials, in an effort not to be outwitted, revived Smith's years-old charge of murder and treason. Smith was eventually exonerated of the charge, but Rockwell was arrested and held prisoner. After escaping, he was captured and found guilty of jailbreak. He spent a total of five minutes in jail.

Clearly, tensions were high where Joseph Smith was concerned, from both within and outside the Church. The final event leading to Smith's murder happened in June 1844 when a handful of Smith's critics published the first and only issue of a newspaper called the *Nauvoo Expositor*. The newspaper accused Smith of trying to marry their wives. It also accused him of forcing women into plural marriage against their will and called into question his quest for power as Prophet, President of the Church, and Mayor of Nauvoo.

Smith denied the allegations, and as mayor ordered the destruction of the paper's office and printing press on June 10. This decision led to rioting in the streets, and violence was perpetrated on both sides. The printer himself was tarred and feathered, a common and excruciating form of vigilante justice that both Smith and Rigdon had experienced during the Kirtland years. In addition to being accused of violating the basic right of freedom of the press, some individuals charged Smith with destruction of property, inciting a riot, and treason. Smith and the entire community at Nauvoo were threatened with violence. The fallen prophet, his brother Hyrum, and several other Mormon friends submitted to arrest on June 25 and were held in jail in Carthage, the county seat of Hancock County.

Elam Cheney, who would have been in his early twenties at the time, witnessed Smith's arrest. Grandson Aaron L. Cheney documented Elam's recollection in his book *The History of Elam Cheney, My Grandfather.* "He was at Nauvoo, and saw the Prophet leave for Carthage and heard him make the remark, 'I am going like a lamb to the slaughter.'" Elam's cousin, Levi Cheney, was also present for Smith's arrest and would later recall seeing Joseph and Hyrum being led off to the Carthage jail. Many of the Cheneys were likely present during this event.

The trial never came to pass, as a mob of approximately 200 angry and armed men stormed the jail on June 27. They fired shots through the wood door of the jail, killing and wounding some of the prisoners. As Smith tried to escape through an open window, he was shot twice in the back and once in the chest by an enemy on the ground below.

Inez Smith Davis's book, *The Story of the Church*, reports Joseph's and Hyrum's deaths simply. "... about six o'clock in the afternoon, an armed mob invaded the jail and shot both of them to death."[16] Eyewitness William Daniels recorded in an 1845 account that Smith survived the jump/fall from the window only to be propped against a well and shot by a makeshift firing squad. He recalled that one of the mob tried to decapitate Smith but was prevented by divine intervention.[17]

The Smith brothers' bodies were carried back to Nauvoo in

wagons the following day, and the thousands of faithful back at the settlement were in shock at the death of their prophet. Harrison Burgess served as guard at the public funeral held on June 29, but the bodies were secretly buried in Joseph Smith's home so that no outsiders could find and exhume the prophet's body for a reward.

Although there was a temporary lull in the near-constant physical and emotional violence the Saints had suffered for fourteen years, the intensity of their grief took its place. Many of the highest officials of the Church, including Brigham Young, were traveling on missions and other business. Young rushed home as soon as he got word, as he was now the senior officer of the Church and knew his leadership was sorely needed. Besides, he wanted to comfort the faithful in this, their darkest hour.

Six weeks after Smith's death, two meetings were held to determine who should lead the Church. It was a time of great anxiety among the faithful, but many of those in attendance at the meetings claimed to experience a revelation that Brigham Young was to succeed Smith. Others reported that as Young addressed his audience, he looked and sounded remarkably like his predecessor. Still others, like Elam Cheney, said simply that the "mantle [cloak of authority] of Joseph" fell on Brigham Young. Whatever the case, Young was ordained as President of the Church on December 27, 1847.

As Young rose to the challenges and responsibilities of his new position, several men from the Cheney and Burgess families assisted him in caring for the faithful. At Young's request, Harrison Burgess sailed to England in search of converts. William Burgess Sr. was head of the deacons, while Ephraim and Aaron Cheney held membership in The Seventy, an elite group of men considered authorities with power equal to that of the priesthood.

If Brigham Young gave hope to his grief-stricken faithful, he could not alleviate their suffering. Conflict with non-Mormons surrounding Nauvoo soon resumed, and Young found himself at a major turning point in both the history and the future of the Mormon Church.

"Martyrdom of Prophet Joseph Smith"

Nauvoo Temple, 1840s
Nauvoo, Illinois
Courtesy of LDS Archives

CHAPTER 3
Mormon Exodus – Perry's First Trail Ride

Chaos was the order of the day after Smith's assassination. Anti-Mormon sentiment only intensified with the prophet's death, and when Illinois rescinded the charter for the city of Nauvoo in 1845, the Mormons were forced to leave. Brigham Young assured the state that they would be gone by spring of the following year. At that point, he had not yet determined a destination, but knew that westward travel was his only option.

Despite this imposed exodus, Young instructed his followers to push forward and complete construction of the half-built Temple. The faithful obeyed, and by November 30, 1845, the upper floor of the Temple was dedicated for the purpose of endowment ceremonies and sealing rituals. Endowment took on even greater meaning during these last days at Nauvoo as the Mormons were facing a life-threatening journey into a desolate land about which they knew nothing. The first of these endowments were performed in December 1845, by Harrison Burgess, William Hyde, and other leaders. Among the hundreds receiving endowment were eleven Cheneys, fourteen Burgesses, and seven Pulsiphers.[1] The endowment ceremonies brought great comfort to the Saints prior to their journey westward. The completed Temple was publicly dedicated in a three-day ceremony beginning May 1, 1846. It would be the final formal ceremony performed by Mormons in Nauvoo.

Trouble Beyond Nauvoo

Although most Mormons in Illinois lived in Nauvoo, there were some outlying settlements. Because Nauvoo city lots were small and insufficient for raising crops, several of the Cheneys and Burgesses lived in Appanoose Township, about five miles to the east. They settled a few miles from "The Big Mound," a fifty-foot-high hillock that jutted out of this prairie town. This area was used by Mormon guards as a preferred lookout as mob activity raged and outlying areas became increasingly dangerous. The Mound provided the highest point in the county from which many Mormons could view the mob fires burning throughout the countryside at night.

In his diary, John Pulsipher, a Burgess family in-law, recorded the turbulence experienced by Mormons in these settlements

> In the small settlements in the country the mobs collected, drove our brethren from their homes, burned their houses and grain and killed some who could not get out of the way... Many others died from exposure after being robbed and driven into the wood. Their sufferings were so great that they could not endure it.

These outliers included the Pulsiphers, Cheneys, and Burgesses, who were all forced to flee to Nauvoo.

By the time of the Temple dedication ceremony, the first wagon trains of Mormons had already begun the evacuation. Brigham Young had put out a call for followers to form a pioneer company that would clear the road for the later wagon trains to follow. One of the first men to answer Young's call was William Burgess Sr. With the help of his longtime friend and neighbor Zerah Pulsipher and others, they loaded provisions and seeds, said good-bye to their families and set out to blaze a trail. Zerah's son John recorded the event:

> They crossed the Mississippi River with the first of the pioneer company... When their provisions were gone, they went down to the nearest settlements in Missouri and worked for more. They made a road west thru the wilderness of what afterwards became the state of Iowa.

Brigham Young and the Twelve (men ordained as apostles of Jesus Christ and the second-highest ranking authority in the Church), along with countless Saints, left Nauvoo on February 8 and soon caught up to the Pioneer Company. Among this second group were Ephraim and Harriet Cheney and their family. Ephraim and Harriet received their endowment the very day they began their exodus.

**Capt. William Burgess Sr. - Brigham Young Company
Grandfather of Perry A. Burgess**

Those who were able to leave in February managed to do so because they sold their homes and most of their belongings. According to Governor Thomas Ford's *History of Illinois,*

> The people from all parts of the country flocked to Nauvoo to purchase houses and farms, which were sold extremely low, lower than the prices at a sheriff's sale, for money, wagons, horses, oxen, cattle, and other articles of personal property which might be needed by the Mormons in their exodus into the wilderness.[2]

John Pulsipher's diary provides a first-hand account of his experience:

> ... we were obliged to sell for just what we could get. About

$2,000 worth of property I had to sell for $300, because I could do no better. We got teams enough so as to let Horace and William Burgess, Jr—my brothers-in-law-have a yoke of oxen each... and took the family of William Burgess, senior, into one of our wagons.

John Pulsipher's company left Nauvoo on May 20 and on the fifth day of their travels met up with William Burgess Sr., Zerah Pulsipher, and Charles Pulsipher (John's brother). These men were returning to assist their fellow Saints, who they feared were being tormented or killed by their enemies.

After setting up a temporary camp along the Des Moines River, Pulsipher's company worked for two months to shore up their provisions. According to his diary, they started on their journey again on August 10 in the company of William Burgess Sr., William Burgess Jr., Horace Burgess, and "others of our neighbors."

The journey was never without its hardships. Changes in weather and lack of adequate rest were daily facts of life, but disease and death were frequent traveling companions as well. Despite the dangers of crossing the plains, pioneer children were still able to find time for recreational purposes and exploration of their new surroundings. Melancthon, a favorite uncle of Perry's, found himself facing an opportunity to prove his mettle, a virtue that seemed to run in the family and that would save various Burgesses from perilous circumstances as they journeyed west.

Melancthon's daughter, Margaret Burgess McMurtrie, recalled this piece of family lore in volume 3 of *An Enduring Legacy*, a compendium of important events, stories, and life sketches depicting Mormon history. While it's impossible to know the exact date the following event occurred, it would be reasonable to assume by Melancthon's age that this scene likely took place during the exodus heading west, perhaps between Nauvoo and Council Bluffs (also known as Kanesville), where Indian issues were often recorded.

Diarist John Pulsipher
In-law of the Burgess Family

Melancthon Burgess
Uncle of Perry A. Burgess

As a young man, Melancthon W. Burgess loved to skate, so one day when the company had camped on the banks of a river that had frozen over, to repair their wagons, wash clothes and do other jobs that had to be attended to, Melancthon thought he would skate on the river, as he had his skates where he could soon get them. He fastened the skates on securely, wrapped a red woolen scarf or muffler around his neck and was ready to start. He was told to be careful and not go so far away but what he could keep in sight of the wagons, but he was so thrilled with the skating that he kept on. He would keep looking back to keep the wagons in sight, but on he went. He didn't realize he had gone so far until he heard grunts, yells, and the barking of dogs. He looked up and saw that he was in the midst of an Indian encampment along the river bank, so he stepped quickly, as there was no escape. He thought that it was all over for him.

The Indian chief ordered him to come before him. He looked Melancthon over and by signs and grunts ordered him to sit down on the bank and take off his ice shoes, as he called the skates, and have them put on himself (the chief). He wanted to see if he could do the same. With a big grin on his face, Melancthon did as he was bid. He fastened the skates on the chief's feet the best he could. The chief stood up on the ice (or at least he tried to), and then'whack! went his head on the ice. He got up, tried it again with the same results only much worse, so, sitting flat on the ice, he ordered Melancthon to take the skates off and put them on his (Melancthon's) feet. With delight Melancthon did so and then skated around and did many tricks to the delight of the Indians. He took off his red scarf and waved it, to look more mysterious, and as he circled around and around each time he would get farther and farther from them and when he got the farthest away, instead of returning he made a bold dash and was gone like lightning. The Indians shouted and shot arrows after him, but he went like the wind, as he was an expert on skates. After a time he came in sight of the wagons and quickly told them what had happened and about the distance the Indians were from the pioneers' camp, so they prepared for the Indians in case they were attacked. Melancthon was praised instead of the scolding he expected to get, but there was no sleep for anyone that night. There was no trouble from the Indians and the company was on its way in the early morning, anxious to put more distance between themselves and the red men, but they were not molested at all and were thankful to their Heavenly Father for his care and protection of their lives.

This same quick-witted Melancthon, just years later, was directed by Brigham Young to serve as guard for the first fifty wagons of the Brigham Young Company of 1848.

While thousands of Saints were able to leave Nauvoo by the agreed-upon deadline of spring 1846, others weren't so fortunate. Unable to sell their property or belongings, they were forced to remain behind. Around the time John Pulsipher's company was leaving its temporary settlement along the Des Moines River, tensions in Nauvoo had escalated and were getting worse daily.

With the deadline to evacuate now months in the past, Nauvoo's "new citizens"[3]—as well as non-Mormons in surrounding areas and as far away as Missouri—wanted the 150 or so remaining Saints gone.

On September 12, a posse of more than 1,000 men formed and

stormed Nauvoo with a demand for surrender. Thirsty for blood, they knew their enemy was unarmed, for all weapons had been surrendered to the state per Governor Ford's dictate. When the Saints refused to surrender, the mob attacked, thus beginning the Battle of Nauvoo.

John Pulsipher's diary provides historians with one of the most emotionally charged accounts of the conflict:

> Before the Saints all got started, not being able to sell their property so they could make a fitout, the mobs continued to howl around like hungry wolves for the spoil, raised an army from Illinois and Missouri and other places to the number of 12 or 1500 men. I said MEN, but I think the right name is Devils, in human shape. Well, this host of ruffians came commanded by the notorious anti-Mormons, or in other words—savage christians, who were notorious for their zeal in seeking the destruction of Joseph and the Church that he led and laid down his life for. They supposed it would be an easy job to immortalize their name, by coming at this time when the Legion was gone and only about 100 of the poor crippled Saints left, who were mostly old and unable to run.
>
> As I said before, this mob force knowing there was no organized force in Nauvoo, and knowing also the Mormons had given up their arms to the State by order of Gov. Ford, they thought there would be no danger, so they did actually come to put an end to the Mormons that could be found there.
>
> Here the Lord showed forth his power in the deliverance of his Saints he inspired them with the Spirit of Fight, they were themselves as well as possible. Every man got something that he could knock the life out of them with. For cannon they got down old steamboat shafts and bored holes in, which, by the blessing of the Lord did well.
>
> So when the enemy came they were warmly received—a hard battle ensued but they were beat back and could not get possession of the City although they tried for 3 days and could gain no power, were loosing their men by hundreds. They had sense

enough to see that such a curse would not pay so they began to sue for peace, and thus ended the famous battle, being 3 of the Saints killed, who were not strictly obedient to counsel, and from 150 to 200 of the other party were left for Dung on the Land. By the officers of the State interfering the Saints were required to again give up their arms and then to move across the Mississippi River into the Territory of Iowa.

This move caused much suffering and many deaths; some hundreds of families mostly women and children with the sick turned out to the scorching heat of the sun and the storms in that sickly season—but the Lord was merciful to them and when they were about to suffer with hunger, countless numbers of quails were sent into the camp and so tame that the people could catch them with their hands and cook and satisfy hunger.

Almost all remaining Mormons left after the Battle of Nauvoo, although some, including Joseph Smith's widow, Emma, and her children, chose to stay behind. After her husband's death, Emma and some of the Church's leaders and faithful became estranged from Brigham Young owing primarily to their belief that a descendant of Joseph Smith should become the next president of the Church. Emma and her three children continued to live quietly as unaffiliated Latter Day Saints in Nauvoo.

The Mexican-American War was in its infant stages in the summer of 1846. President James K. Polk favored expansionism and wanted the Mexican territories of present-day California, Nevada, Utah, and Arizona for the United States.

By mid-June, weary Mormon refugees had already reached the destination of the first leg of their journey. They built hundreds of shelters and laid roads in temporary settlements on both sides of the Missouri River in Council Bluffs, Iowa, and across the border in what they called Winter Quarters, Nebraska (present-day Omaha).

The pioneers were exhausted, their provisions were dwindling and in some cases were already gone. They had been exiled from every state and town they had ever lived in, and they were focused on getting out of the United States, to a place where they hoped to be allowed to live in safety and freedom. The U.S. government had not protected the Mormons, and individual state governments aided in their persecution. Most of these Saints felt no loyalty toward the United States.

Into this atmosphere rode Captain James Allen of the U.S. Regular Army at Mount Pigsah, just outside Council Bluffs. Allen requested 500 volunteers to serve in the war against Mexico. The Saints were immediately and understandably suspicious of the request. John Pulsipher's diary entry reflects the general attitude of doubt and skepticism:

> Just before our arrival at this place the government officers had been to the camp with orders for 500 men to go across the deserts and mountains to help the United States fight the Mexicans. This was a scheme instituted at the head of government to destroy us while we were fleeing from persecution! They thought the men would not leave their wives and children to perish on the prairie and go across the entire continent to fight the battle of a nation who had sought their destruction all the day long. So thinking that we would refuse to obey such an unreasonable order, thereby they would have a pretence to come upon us and kill us for rebelling against the government. Pres. Young seeing thru the whole plan, soon raised the required number of men who left their families and friends among savages without houses and with but few days rations. Under these circumstances these men bid farewell to the camp of the saints and started, under Gentile officers, traveled on foot, lived on less than half rations, worked their way across trackless deserts and stony mountains without shoes, suffered hunger thirst and fatigue, yet they murmured not. The Lord was with them and gave them strength in time of need.
>
> Had I arrived soon enough I expect I should have been with that company but I was at work at another place and they were gone before I heard of it. This was rather a trying time to have

500 of our best men taken, leaving their helpless families as well as the widows, the sick and lame that were on our hands before. The able bodied men that were in camp were few compared with the invalids and widows that looked to those few men for their support.

Brigham Young recognized an opportunity when he saw it. As leader of thousands of weary men, women, and children, Young understood the monetary advantage that serving in the army would bring. Each volunteer would receive regular wages and allowances (which, by war's end, would total more than $71,000[4]). In addition to the money, it couldn't hurt the Mormons' relationship with the federal government if they showed a sense of loyalty, especially given that they had never been shown respect or treated with any semblance of dignity.

Within three days, Young had assembled the men and the march began. This Mormon Battalion first trekked to Fort Leavenworth, where they received their weapons and other necessary provisions. They left for Santa Fe on August 12 and reached their destination on October 9. Undernourished and fatigued, many of the men fell ill and were sent to Pueblo, where they wintered before journeying to Salt Lake. The majority of the battalion reached San Diego on January 29, 1847, where they remained for two weeks. Since there were no battles to fight, these volunteers chipped in to help develop the town by constructing houses, digging wells, and making bricks. From there they marched to Los Angeles, where they mustered out on July 16.

While some of the Battalion members were able to return immediately to Winter Quarters or on to the Great Basin, others weren't so fortunate. In 1848, the world was forever changed when a small group of this militia traveled north in search of funds for their return trip. The men found jobs constructing a mill along the South Fork of the American River for one Captain John Sutter. There along the river banks this group of immigrants would later trigger the largest human migration in American history, the California Gold Rush of

1849. This event would immediately resonate throughout the close-knit community of Mormons, and like so many others, the lives of the Burgess and Cheney families were changed forever.

As smaller groups of Saints continually poured out of Nauvoo throughout 1846, members of earlier wagon trains—such as William Burgess Sr.—backtracked time and time again to offer assistance to those who were poorly equipped to trek thousands of miles across the wilderness. The success of such a mass exodus depended heavily upon the benevolence of every able-bodied person. Cooperation and collaboration were key to reaching Zion.

Harrison Burgess
Uncle of Perry A. Burgess

In November 1846, Brigham Young ordered Harrison Burgess back to Nauvoo on business. Harrison's diary entry illustrates just how dispersed and out of touch family members were at the time.

> Upon arriving at Nauvoo I found it a lonesome, deserted camp as most of the Saints had left... I went to Warren, Henderson Co. to see my brothers. I found my brother, Abram, was dead and buried. In company with his wife and little son, Perry Burgess, I visited his new-made grave. My other brother, Frederick had gone to Galena and has not been heard from since. My brother, Abram, was buried November 9, 1846, he died of pleurisy.

Perry Burgess would have been three years old at the time of his father Abraham's death. Young Perry, Harrison, and the newly widowed Semantha Cheney Burgess stood at Abraham's grave, wearing their sorrow like a cloak to shelter them against the bitter chill of an unforgiving November. Perry would have been too young to understand the gravity of the situation, but Harrison and Semantha surely wondered what would become of her now that she was alone with a small child. The impending journey would be demanding under the best of circumstances, but how would mother and child fare now? Eventually, Semantha and young Perry would seek refuge with, and travel west with, the Cheney family.

It wasn't uncommon for members of a family to get separated from one another on the westward exodus. Harrison's diary entry mentions his older brother Frederick, who seemed to just disappear. Only Perry would cross paths with Frederick, again in 1866, as Perry's Bozeman Trail diary indicates. The rest of the Burgess family, however, never saw Frederick again, and although family lore has it that he served with Quantrill's Raiders in the American Civil War, there is no way to be certain of the accuracy of that speculation. Stories such as this are common among the histories of Mormon families, as logistics and limited means of communication made it impossible to remain in touch.

To further confuse matters, "official" records were not always accurate. Nauvoo LDS records include both Abraham and Seman-tha Cheney Burgess on the list of burials in the Nauvoo Cemetery although, in fact, neither was buried there. These records can be proved false by Perry's diary excerpts as well as by those of his Uncle Harrison.

Because Saints were journeying west in groups that had left Nauvoo at various times, they were somewhat scattered by the time winter set in. Out of necessity, they built temporary settlements wherever they found themselves. The great majority of Saints spent the cold-weather months in two specific locations: Winter Quarters, Nebraska, and Kanesville (Council Bluffs), Iowa. The two encamp-ments were directly across from each other, with the Missouri River dividing them. Church and other historic documents place the Cheneys—including young Perry and his mother, Semantha—the Pulsiphers, and the Burgesses at Winter Quarters.

In both settlements, the Mormons built sod houses and log cabins with the limited supplies and tools they were able to transport. Knowing they would be spending several months on the site, they also constructed mills in which to grind grains and corn. The settlers traded with local Native Americans, swapping household items and small amounts of cash for food and farm animals.

Despite their self-sufficiency, the Saints found life in Winter Quarters and Kanesville rife with suffering and grief caused by dis-ease and harsh conditions. Even in the midst of trade with Native Americans and the ability to fish in the earlier months of settlement life, camp residents lived on a diet consisting primarily of corn bread, bacon, and milk when it was available. They had a supply of wild berries they had gathered and preserved, but that was the extent of their fresh fruit and vegetables. A diet lacking in such basic nutrients resulted in widespread disease, including consumption (tuberculosis), a malaria-like disorder they called "summer disease," and black leg or black canker (scurvy). Hundreds of men, women, and children suffered miserable deaths at Winter Quarters.

William Burgess Sr., his sons, and the Pulsiphers helped save lives by providing a needed food source—fresh fish—a common remedy for scurvy as related by Nora Hall Lund, a Pulsipher family historian. This story would find its way into multiple Burgess family journals and biographies.

> They made a sieve net, four yards wide and forty long which served very well for bringing in the fish. They would go to a little lake about 20 miles up the Missouri River.

> They hauled in many loads of choice fish, fresh from the water, which was a great blessing to the suffering poor and the best medicine to cure the scurvy that they could get. They were very thankful to the Lord that he had made fish available.

A Permanent Temporary Settlement

The construction of Winter Quarters was an amazing feat and one that showcases the aptitude as well as the self-reliance of the Mormons.

Begun in mid-1846, construction was completed by December. In addition to 538 log cabins, 83 sod houses, and numerous dugouts in the bluffs, Winter Quarters boasted several schools, a dancing school, two commercial stores, and at least three blacksmith shops. Most of the buildings had no floors, and few included window openings. Winter Quarters was ruled by a city council and protected by its own police force, which ensured the safety of its 3,483 residents.

At its peak, the settlement was home to 5,000 Mormons, and because of the organized manner in which it was built, Winter Quarters is considered the first official city or town in the state of Nebraska. Although it was completely abandoned by May or June of 1848, one of its mills and the Mormon Pioneer Cemetery remain standing to this day.[5]

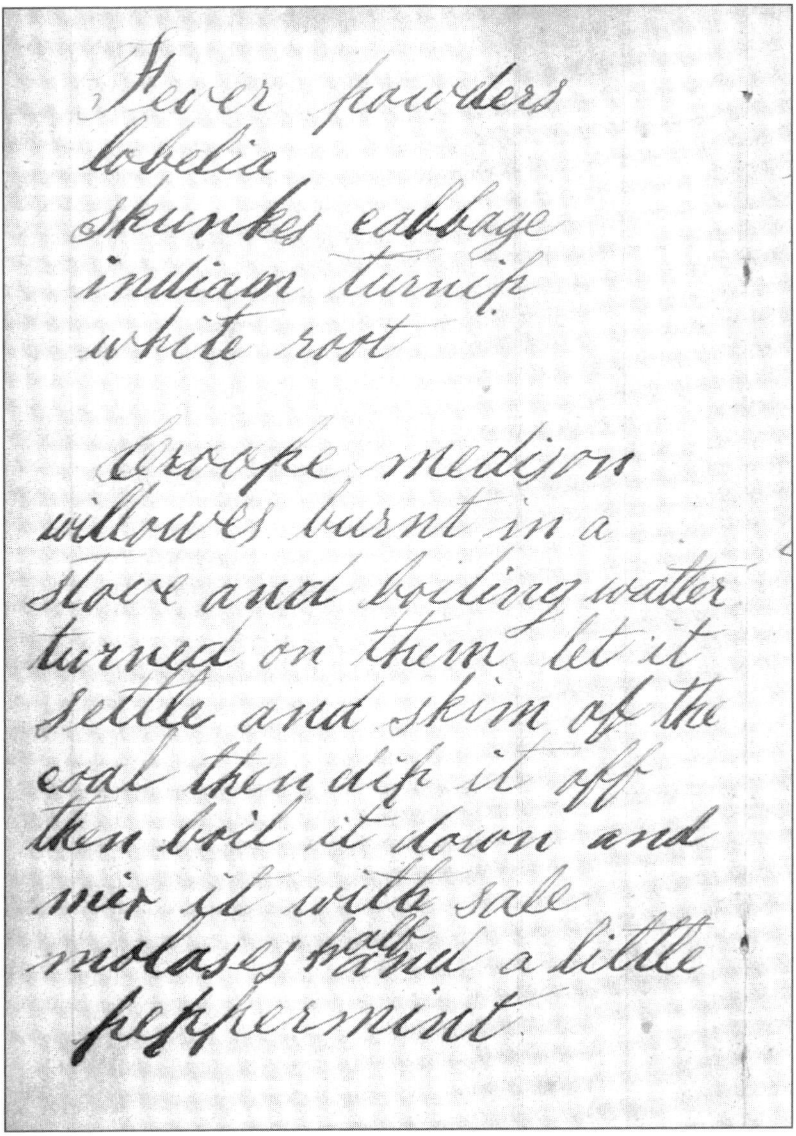

Fever powders
lobelia
skunke cabbage
indian turnip
white root

Croope medison
willowes burnt in a
stove and boiling watter
turned on them let it
settle and skim of the
coal then dip it off
then boil it down and
mix it with sale
molases half and a little
peppermint

Pioneer Medicine
"Fever Powders" and "Croope Medison"
Dr. Levi Cheney Medicine Book, 1860

Mariah Pulsipher Burgess, William Jr.'s wife, recorded life at Winter Quarters in her diary.

> I was living in a leaky log cabin without a floor in November when a daughter was born. I was never able to leave my bed. The baby had to be weaned at three months. I was sick, but my father and husband would not give me up because I had to other little children, Mary Harriet and Carnelia, to look after and care for. They said I should live, so I gradually got better but was very weak. Hundreds of the Saints laid their bodies down there.

Zerah Pulsipher's journal mirrors a similar experience.

> There were not well people enough to take care of the sick and dying. My boys continued to team through the winter till they both got sick. John was laid on the bed and was near the gate of death for a long time, when I was called in to see him breath (sic) his last... I said, "You are not going to die now. I cannot spare you now, you must get well to help us move through the mountains." He immediately began to vomit a large quantity of the most filthy matter I ever saw come from any persons (sic) and go ahead and assist in making roads...

No family was untouched by the hand of death. LDS Church records indicate that from September 1846 to May 1848, disease claimed the lives of 359 residents in Winter Quarters alone.

The Burgess family certainly endured its own agony as pillars of the family succumbed to disease one after the other. By 1849, Perry had lost not only his father, Abraham, but also his aunt, Semantha's sister, Caroline Cheney Pulsipher; his aunt Hannah Burgess Jones; and an uncle, Horace Burgess, a bishop within the Mormon Church. With families being as close-knit as they were on the Mormon exodus, these deaths must have taken quite a toll even on a boy as young as Perry. Life was incredibly difficult, a daily struggle. And until July 1847, the Mormons hadn't any idea where they were going. They just knew where they'd been, and where they didn't want to be.

In the spring of 1847, Brigham Young organized an exploratory company, the Vanguard Company, that would leave ahead of the rest of the Saints and act as a sort of scouting group. They would break and evaluate trails, find water sources, and begin construction once they reached their destination, which by then had been determined to be somewhere in the Great Basin. According to the LDS Church, those in this advance company were handpicked for their skills by Young, with men being assigned roles such as hunter or blacksmith. The group depended more heavily on horses and mules than on oxen in hopes of moving along at a faster rate of speed. The Vanguard Company, with Young as its leader, left Winter Quarters on April 5, 1847, with 143 men, 3 women, and 2 children along with an inventory that included 73 wagons, 89 horses, 52 mules, 19 cows, and 17 dogs. The wagons contained food, cookware, seeds, grain, and farming utensils. The train was then divided into smaller companies, each with a captain. This military-like organizational strategy was one the Mormons would use for later wagon trains as well, and it was a key factor in the successful crossing of the wilderness.

While no members of the Burgess family were in the Vanguard companies, Elam Cheney, cousin of Semantha Cheney Burgess, Perry Burgess's mother, was one of the few Saints to make the exodus to Utah in 1847. His pregnant wife, Hannah Compton, accompanied him on the 1,000-mile-plus exodus. Elam and Hannah arrived in Salt Lake Valley on October 5, 1847, as two of the earliest residents. Their daughter, Matilda Cheney, was born just nine days after their arrival.

The Vanguard Company chose not to follow the already existing Oregon Trail on the south side of the Platte River, and it was a decision that would work in the Saints' favor. Aside from the fact that their enemies were part of the Oregon Trail group that had originated in Missouri, the Saints did not want to compete with anyone for basic necessities such as wood, water, and viable camp sites. With this in mind, they traveled along the north side of the river and blazed what is today known as the Mormon Trail. It would be traversed by another 70,000 Mormons for more than twenty years, until the 1869 completion of the First Transcontinental Railroad.

Throughout the long journey across Nebraska, each group of ten took turns leading the company so that the backbreaking chore of clearing the road could be shared. Those men assigned the task of hunting found buffalo to be plentiful and easy to kill. This unfamiliar meat quickly became a favorite among the Saints, who valued it for its sweet taste. Dried buffalo dung soon became a staple for building fires to cook and ward off the night chill.

The pioneers were impressed by the majestic rock formations they passed in western Nebraska in late May and carved their initials into some of them, thus beginning a long tradition of late 1800s pioneer graffiti. Chimney Rock was especially important to young Perry Burgess and his Cheney uncles, who would carve their initials into that same landmark twenty years later while heading toward the Bozeman Trail during the Montana Gold Rush.

Six weeks after leaving Winter Quarters, the Company reached Fort Laramie, where they were joined by a group of Saints from Mississippi. After replenishing provisions, the advance company crossed the Platte River and traveled the Oregon Trail. Near Casper, Wyoming, the Saints spent four days re-crossing the river using two canoes connected by planks. Recognizing a money-maker when he saw it, Young ordered ten men to remain behind to operate the ferry for all travelers of the Oregon Trail. The money would revert directly back to the Church.

On June 28, the exploratory company ran into mountaineer Jim Bridger near the Little Sandy River. The legendary adventurer was the first white man to set eyes on the Great Salt Lake, and he advised Young of the agricultural challenges of the area. Two days later, adventurer and entrepreneur Sam Brannan arrived with his own group of Saints hailing from New York and bound for California. Brannan tried unsuccessfully to convince Young to join him on his journey to coastal California.

Ignoring both Bridger and Brannan, Young and his company continued on their journey to the Great Basin. Most members of the company had suddenly become ill with fever, hot flashes, chills, and general aches and pains. Some even experienced delirium. In early July, they met up with twelve or so members of the Mormon Battalion who had been let go because of illness. Behind them were another 140 Battalion members as well as the rest of the Mississippi Saints. July 7 found the now larger company at Fort Bridger, where they rested a few days and made moccasins to replace their worn-out boots.

By midmonth, illness became so rampant in the Vanguard Company that it split into three groups. One was sent ahead to clear the trail. Another—the largest—followed, and a smaller group of eight or ten wagons trailed behind with Young, who was too sick to travel.

Over the next ten days, these three groups of Saints made their way over the mountains and into the Great Basin. From the summit of Big Mountain, the pioneers could see the Salt Lake Valley. On July 24, 1847, Brigham Young looked over the valley and said, "This is the right place. Drive on."[6] The first of the Saints had reached their Zion.

As the Mormons began building roads and constructing buildings, Young selected several of the Vanguard Company to return with him to Winter Quarters in August to organize the remaining Saints into additional companies. Subsequent smaller groups, many from Europe, would travel through Winter Quarters on their way west.

The Brigham Young Company was the largest group of Saints to travel together, numbering approximately 1,220 people and 397 wagons upon departure. The final tally of animals included 1,275 oxen, 699 cows, 411 sheep, 605 chickens, 2 beehives, and 1 crow, among others. The company wagons were organized by the elders into four main groups of one hundred each. These groups were then subdivided into smaller groups of ten to twenty. Zerah Pulsipher, Allen Taylor, William G. Perkins, and Lorenzo Snow were designated as captains of the four groups.

Meanwhile, the Burgesses remained steadfast in performing last-minute baptisms before the Saints' departure. Thomas Bullock, the Mormon scribe, records the event as the companies begin to move:

Pulziphers Co starts—Harrison Burgess baptized Theodore Curtis for the remission of sins. & Confirmed him a member— ordained him and restored him to his former standing as a member in the 24 Quo. of 70—by orders of Pres. Young in the presence of William Burgess Sen[ior]. about 1 P.M. (gave him a Certificate for Pres. Young to sign).[7]

Zerah Pulsipher was captain of the first one hundred to leave on June 5, 1848. His wagon train, according to official Church archives, included 156 souls, 51 wagons, 10 horses, 161 oxen, 96 cows, 49 loose cattle, 41, sheep, 22 pigs, 71 chickens, 5 cats, 13 dogs, and 2 geese. Of that company, a smaller group of ten were selected to lead the way under the direction of Captain William Burgess Sr.

Like the Burgess family, the Cheneys found their way to Utah in smaller groups. Levi, Lewis, and Mansel Cheney—along with Seman- tha Cheney Burgess and little Perry—were among the Saints to leave around the time of the Burgess/Pulsipher company. The Cheneys are harder to track because their specific names are not included on any of the official LDS company listings. In most instances, lists of the companies include only the number of "souls," not individual names.

Much of Mormon history is passed down through families and recorded as such. In that way, it is well known that Levi and his broth- ers hauled furniture for Brigham Young along the Mormon Trail. Given that the family was working to make a living, they did not have time to record events in diaries and journals. Records do show that Hurd Cheney, uncle of Levi, Lewis, Mansel, and Semantha, died on August 12, 1861, on his way to Salt Lake Valley.

Hurd would have been mightily disappointed had he realized he was never to reach Salt Lake City. But as history would soon prove, Zion wasn't so heavenly for the Cheney family.

As the pioneers crossed the Great Plains making their way west- ward, they hunted and collected food supplies along the Mormon Trail. Long before white settlement, massive buffalo herds roamed freely across the American West, threatened by few predators. For centuries, Native Americans followed the buffalo herds during hunting season as a major source of food. The Burgess, Pulsipher, and Cheney families of the Brigham Young Company found buffalo hunts both an exciting and a dangerous affair for all involved.

Zerah's son John kept a diary of life on the trail. On June 29 the hunt was on, he wrote:

> Buffalo abounds along the Platt (sic) River in such vast numbers that it is impossible for mortal man to number them— ... Sometimes our way seemed entirely blockaded with them but as we approached they would open to the right and left so we could pass through... We killed what we needed for meat always dividing the meat equally among the different families of the company so that none was wasted.

Charles Pulsipher, John's brother, also recorded his experience with the buffalo.

> I was appointed one of the hunters of the company. My brother John was to help me. We had to get someone to drive our teams, as we would travel out off the road three or four miles to find our meat. We had shot one buffalo down late in the evening and I stayed to watch it while John went for a team to drag it into camp. That country was inhabited with numerous buffalo which stood about the height of a yearling steer. If several of them came together on a man he had better be somewhere else than in their powerful jaws... There were many thousands in that part of the country. A large herd of about 2,000 had been to the river for water and when they saw the white top wagons come along and several men rushed onto them to get a shot at them, they took fright and ran towards the mountains where I was watching my beef. The faster they ran the bigger the herd became, which made a mad stampede, rushing over everything they came to. When they got within a few hundred feet of me I began to be alarmed, and started to run, but saw it was impossible to get out of their reach... I just kept on swinging my hat and shouting until they all had passed by me. I was unharmed. A man said that he heard me three miles away. I assure you I was

Capt. Zerah Pulsipher and Mary Brown

Mormon Immigrant Train, Echo Canyon, Utah - circa 1866

very glad when it was all over. It would take considerable money to hire me to go through an affair like that again.

The company arrived in Salt Lake September 20–24, 1848, with the Burgess and Pulsipher families in particular arriving on September 22. According to John Pulsipher's diary, the distance from Winter Quarters to Salt Lake City was 1,031 miles.

> We arrived at Salt Lake City on the 22nd of September. Were 125 days on this journey. No deaths in our company except the little boy that drowned at the start and to balance against that there was a birth. William Burgess had a son born on the road.

Immediately upon arrival in Salt Lake, the Burgess men—and quite possibly the Pulsiphers as well—set to work milling lumber and shingles used to build the first homes for the Saints. As they had done in Nauvoo and in Winter Quarters, these pioneers made a lasting impact on the lives of their families, friends, and Mormon history in general.

Harrison Burgess, Perry's uncle, also left Winter Quarters, exactly two years to the day after he left Nauvoo. Brigham Young sent him on a mission to England rather than let him remain with his family. His recollections reflect his dismay:

> ...the idea of leaving my family to make their way to the Utah Valley without my company or assistance was a heavy damp on the atmosphere of my feelings. My family, however, chose to undertake the enterprise rather than to have me fail my mission. I accordingly turned my whole attention to prepare everything in my power as comfortable and convenient as I could for my family's expedition and resolved to see them across the Elkhorn River myself... We left Winter Quarters on the 20th of May 1848, had a good journey to the River and crossed over it in safety.

Harrison returned from his mission and journeyed to Utah with a later company. Along the trail, which was shared by gold seekers headed for California, the Saints would find the bones of some of the men who had murdered Joseph and Hyrum Smith back in Missouri.

We often passed the bones of some of the wretches who took part in the Martyrdom of Brothers Joseph and Hyrum. After they had acted in that dreadful tragedy the most of them had started to cross the plains for California in search of gold mines, but they generally had died a most miserable death on the plains as it had been predicted upon their guilty heads... some of these skulls had been kicked along by the passers until they were 2 or 3 miles from where they had been buried as some little stick or board with their name generally marked the hole into which they had been thrown. Thus vengeance over took them speedily.

Other members of the Burgess family made their way to Utah within a few years. Horace Burgess died in June of 1849 in Winter Quarters, most likely of one of the many illnesses running rampant throughout the community.

Elder Horace Burgess
Uncle of Perry A. Burgess, died at Winter Quarters, 1849

Whatever fate lay in store for the Cheneys, the majority of the Saints felt nothing short of exaltation upon finally reaching Salt Lake Valley. Twenty-one-year-old John Pulsipher duly recorded what he found upon reaching Zion, the famous "Old Fort":

> The city at this time consisted of 2 blocks, 40 rods square and a half block 40 by 20 rods, all joining. These blocks were enclosed by joining houses in the form of a fort. These forts were built by the People that came last year, while their numbers were small they built so they could defend themselves against Indians in case of need.

> Besides these forts there was a small saw mill and a corn cracker for a grist mill and a small house by each mill which was the amount of the building in this country at the time of our arrival.

John would eventually serve on the Salt Lake City police force. But for now, he was content—as were most of the others—to bask in the glow of the certainty that they had finally reached home.

Peace for the Saints would not last in the Great Basin. Church policies, federal government pressure, and events like the California Gold Rush would quickly cause divisions among the Saints, eventually resulting in deep rifts in both sides of Perry's family.

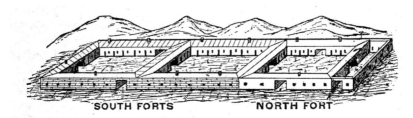

Old Fort, with later addition of 'North Fort' - circa 1849

Sam Brannan
California's First Millionaire

Brigham Young
Leader of the LDS church

CHAPTER 4
California Gold Rush – Family Business Begins

No other period in American history so embodies adventure and folk heroism as does the gold rush era. And no figure in the gold rush epitomizes the quintessential folk hero quite like Samuel Brannan. A true legend in his own time, Brannan was considered many things by many people: multimillionaire, Mormon, leader, builder of empires, manipulator, rebel. He was indeed all these and more, and the adventures of his life fit together to create one of the most remarkable portraits of the nineteenth century.

Two days after the Burgess and Pulsipher families fled Nauvoo for Utah, Sam Brannan pulled anchor in New York and set sail on the *Brooklyn* with a crew of 238 Mormons who were, as Brannan said, "armed to the teeth" ; the group consisted of seventy men, sixty-eight women, and one hundred children. Under the orders of Church Elder Orson Pratt, they were joining the exodus west, out of " Babylon," [1] in search of a new home beyond the boundaries of the United States.

William Mulder and A. Russell Mortensen recorded daily life on board the *Brooklyn* in their book *Among the Mormons: Historic Accounts by Contemporary Observers:*

> There were many rules and regulations for the passengers. Reveille was sounded at 6 a.m. when everyone was to arise from their beds, dress, and wash. No one was permitted to leave their state rooms, without being completely dressed (with coats). After reveille, the corporal would visit every state room and receive the names of the sick and those who could not work. Every state room was to be swept, cleaned, and beds made by 7 a.m. All state rooms were inspected each day to see that they were neat and clean, and that all dirty clothes were removed and put in bags. The main hall must be dusted and cleaned by 7:30 a.m. each morning. The table in the hall was spread at 8 a.m. and at 8:30 a.m., the children ate breakfast first. When they were done, they went back to their state rooms. No children were allowed in the hall before 8:30 a.m. At 9:15 a.m., the men and

women ate breakfast and then retired either to the deck or their state rooms. At 10:00 a.m., the hall was swept clean and all state room doors were thrown open to receive fresh air. From 10–2 p.m., time was devoted to various occupations. At 2:30 p.m., all retired from the hall so that dinner could be prepared. At 3 p.m., the children dined and at 4 p.m., the adults ate dinner. By 5 p.m., the hall was swept clean and the doors of the state rooms thrown open. From 5–8 p.m., the time was spent in reading, singing or other amusements. At 8 p.m., a cold lunch was placed on the table. By 9 p.m., the table was cleared and all were ready to retire for the night. Every Sabbath morning, there was to be held a service on ship, starting at 11 a.m. All were at attend, shaved and washed clean.[2]

Himself an Elder in the Church, Brannan was a logical choice to lead this group of disciplined Saints. Of large stature and even larger personality, Brannan's rough manners belied his generosity and fortitude. He had been publisher and sometime-editor of two important Mormon newspapers, *The Prophet* and *The Messenger*. The experience had him working directly with Joseph Smith's brother, and Brannan developed a reputation as a visionary whose commitment to the Mormon Church was both unswerving and impassioned.

He and his crew arrived in Yerba Buena—present-day San Francisco Bay—on July 29, 1846, almost six months after setting sail. A pit stop in Honolulu to deliver cargo and stock up on provisions allowed Brannan to acquire something else he wanted: weapons. His plan was to take Yerba Buena from the Mexicans. When he and his crew arrived in port with 150 new rifles and ready to rumble, Brannan's eyes mirrored his disappointment. There at the Mexican customhouse hung not the flag of Mexico, but that of the United States. Captain John B. Montgomery had arrived three weeks earlier and unknowingly dashed Brannan's hopes. "I swore at that American flag," Brannan said years later. "I could have torn it down." [3]

Never one to let obstacles keep him from his personal goals, Brannan began publishing his own newspaper, *The California Star*, in

January 1847. By March 20, the name of the town was changed to San Francisco. Brannan used the money and influence of his high-profile position to begin building an empire that soon included a hotel, a flour mill, and several general stores, one of the more successful of which was located in the bustling hub of Sacramento and became known as Sutter's Fort.

In April 1847, Brannan traveled to Utah to meet with Brigham Young. The adventurer tried to convince Young to settle the Saints in California rather than the Great Basin. His argument was based entirely upon the difficulties an agricultural people such as the Mormons would experience in the harsh conditions of the Great Basin area. Young, of course, remained committed to his vision, and the disagreement between the two strong-willed men would not be the last.

As Brannan's wealth increased, his relationship with Young and the Church deteriorated until all ties were severed in 1851. History shows that as he made his way to becoming California's first millionaire, Brannan's interest in the Church weakened while his frustrations mounted at Young's refusal to even consider settling in California. Their relationship was further strained when Brannan refused Young's request to pay the Mormon Church money from his many profits. This conflict would prove to be the final straw that led Young to excommunicate Brannan from the Church. Ironically, upon his death at age seventy Brannan was nearly penniless.

On his way back to San Francisco, Brannan's path crossed that of members of the Mormon Battalion who had chosen to head north from Los Angeles in search of work to pay for the trip back to Utah. These men—among them one Henry W. Bigler—found work constructing a mill for Captain John Sutter in Coloma, along the south fork of the American River. They worked alongside other laborers, including a sizeable population of American Indians.

Sutter hired contractor and builder James W. Marshall to oversee the mill project. Peter L. Wimmer was hired as overseer and his wife, Jennie, worked as housekeeper and cook. What historical accounts of the discovery of gold in California often fail to mention is that Peter and Jennie Wimmer, though not Mormons themselves, had lived among the Mormons in Nauvoo, just miles from the Cheney family.

Construction of the mill began in late 1847, and during the morning of January 24, 1848, Marshall and Wimmer were strolling along the riverbed when Marshall noticed something shiny lying among the rocks and sediment. Stooping to pick up the object, he inspected it and then handed it to Wimmer, who declared it gold. "I would take my pay in that metal," he responded.[4]

Wanting proof, Marshall sent the shiny nugget to Jennie with the instructions to boil it in her kettle of lye. If the nugget lost its sheen, all would know it was not gold. When Jennie was handed the nugget, she took one look at it and pronounced it gold on the spot, no hesitation. Times being what they were, none of the men put much faith in this woman's proclamation. Even Peter, who himself believed it was gold, had his doubts about her certainty.

The next morning, Jennie poured out the lye. There at the bottom of the kettle lay the nugget so brilliantly gold that there was no denying its nature. "Seizing it, she sprang into the cabin, threw it on the table before her husband and Marshall, shouting aloud, as she had from the first, 'there is your nugget, and it is pure gold.'"[5] That piece of gold became known as the Wimmer Nugget.

Mormon laborer and chronicler Henry Bigler kept a diary of his time at the mill, and historians rely on his account as one of the few accurate records of the discovery. Although skeptical of Marshall's claim, Bigler wrote on January 24: "This day some kind of mettle was found in the tail race [the part below the water wheel where spent water flows] that... looks like goald."[6]

Further testing revealed that the nugget was indeed gold. And while Sutter tried to bribe the workers at the mill into secrecy by giving them each a pocket knife, a secret of such incredible magnitude can never be kept long. One of the Wimmer children shared the news with a teamster passing through camp at Coloma, who excitedly

James Marshall and Jennie Wimmer

shared it with someone at Sutter's Fort, who in turn informed Sam Brannan. The newspaperman immediately printed stories of the gold discovery, going so far as to print a special edition that he distributed throughout the East via horseback. The California Gold Rush had formally begun, and by year's end, gold fever had afflicted hundreds of thousands of men and even some women.

Mormon Island

Six weeks after the initial discovery of gold at Sutter's Mill, former members of the Mormon Battalion founded Mormon Island where the North and South Forks of the American River join, between Sutter's Fort and his sawmill at Coloma.

More than one hundred men called the mining town home by the summer of 1848, and Sam Brannan opened a general store there, where he required the miners to tithe one-tenth of their earnings to the Church. At its peak, the town claimed 2,500 residents and eventually included a school, a post office, four hotels, seven saloons, and approximately fifteen other businesses.

The completion of the Sacramento Valley Railroad in 1856 and the resulting establishment of the town of Folsom led to Mormon Island's decline. By 1880, no one lived there, and in 1955, the waters of Folsom Lake flooded the site. All that remains to identify Mormon Island today is a road marker.

The discovery and subsequent media coverage of gold in California changed the course of American history as hopefuls traveled west in search of their fortunes. Seemingly overnight, the state was dotted with hundreds of boom towns and mining camps. San Francisco's population alone increased from 1,600 in 1848 to 25,000 in just one year.[7] Such drastic population swells affected not only the demographics of California, but the economic position of the United States on a global scale. Western expansion and development depended upon

Peter Wimmer
Circa 1855

Jennie Wimmer
Circa 1890

Diarist Henry Bigler
Circa 1897

attracting people committed to prosperity, people who would give their all for even the possibility of striking it rich. Knowing this, newspapers focused their stories on the successes of the few miners who got lucky. Such tales attracted people from as far away as Chile, Peru, and Hawaii.

While California was all agog with gold fever, Utah's Great Basin was in an uproar of its own, for a completely different reason.

When the Mormons reached Utah in July 1847, the territory belonged to Mexico. This was part of the region's appeal: The United States had not proved to be Mormon-friendly in any way, and Young's goal was to lead his people to a place where they could worship and live their beliefs in freedom. Ownership of the territory changed hands with the end of the Mexican-American War and the subsequent signing of the Treaty of Guadalupe Hidalgo on February 2, 1848.

With the signing of the treaty, Utah officially became a U.S.-owned territory. This fact caused some tension among the Mormons in the Great Basin, as the memories of their persecution and torment were still vivid in their minds. But something more serious, more subversive, was at work, and its impact was potent enough to split the Mormon Church irreparably.

Before leaving Nauvoo, some leaders of the Church had begun taking more than one wife. These "sealings" were done with little ceremony or attention, and the idea of polygamy or plural marriage had not yet truly taken hold. Once the Saints reached the Great Basin, however, plural marriage was practiced openly, and not only among leaders.

As the practice became more widespread under the direction of Young, dissent among the Saints intensified. Few families escaped Young's requests that they engage in polygamy, and the Burgesses were no exception. Young offered the widowed Semantha Cheney Burgess into a polygamous relationship soon after the group's arrival in Salt Lake. Both the Cheneys and the Burgesses began to practice plural marriage. Semantha's brother-in-law Harrison—an Elder in the

Church—had already taken his second wife before leaving Nauvoo, and the couple's first child was born in 1849 in Salt Lake. In 1851, they gave birth to the first set of white twin boys born in Utah.

Before a polygamous union involving Semantha could be arranged, she took her son Perry and left Salt Lake, likely with at least one of her brothers. They headed to Jo Daviess County, Illinois, the new home of her father Ephraim. By 1850 Semantha had remarried Dr. Ben White, an adventurous young man who, like so many others of his time, could not resist the lure of the California Gold Rush. That year's census shows her and Perry living in Millville, Jo Daviess County, Illinois, just doors down from her affluent in-laws, who owned department stores in the area until the turn of the century. It is not known how Semantha met or when she married Ben White, but according to the 1850 census, he was not living with his spouse or stepson. In all likelihood, White had already found his way to California in the company of his new Cheney in-laws.

Although Young made a pronouncement in 1852 in which he claimed that Joseph Smith had prophesied and condoned polygamy several years earlier, many Saints doubted the truth of that statement. Plural marriage became the dividing factor of the Mormon Church, with those believing in its prophecy remaining in Utah with Young and comprising the LDS Church. Those who could not abide the morality of polygamy often separated from the Church. The draw of California and the 1849 Gold Rush served as a relief valve for disgruntled Mormons leaving Salt Lake over polygamy and other Church polices. Eventually, some banded together and formed the Reorganized Latter-Day Saints Church, known today as the Community of Christ.

Another family not untouched by the polygamy issue was the Cheneys. At President Young's request, Elam took five wives, among them Margaret Wimmer, niece of Peter Wimmer of Sutter's Mill fame. He even named one of their sons after Peter. Another wife, Talitha, journeyed across the plains to Salt Lake in the same group as Jacob

Bigler, father to Henry William Bigler, whose diary provides the most historically reliable account of the discovery of gold at Sutter's Mill. Between letters sent and received, census records, diary and journal entries, and other historical documents, it becomes clear that the Cheney, Wimmer, Bigler, and Burgess clans forged close relationships that lasted from Nauvoo through Utah and even into California.

Despite Elam's polygamy, the concept did not sit well with most other Cheney family members. It would prove to be, in fact, a major bone of contention, expressed vehemently in letters exchanged between Elam's sister Olive Cheney and his cousin Levi.

Levi was the most outspoken of the Cheneys, and his disdain for polygamy only intensified following offers of plural marriage by Church leadership involving his sister Semantha. Given their outspokenness, the Cheneys were likely branded as "apostates" (those who have abandoned their religion) by local Mormons who did not share their views. Family history tells that the Cheneys, including Levi, Mansel, and others, fled Salt Lake under the cover of darkness one night in 1849. Having covered the wagon wheels and horses' hooves in burlap so as not to awaken anyone, the Cheneys stole away and headed west, joining thousands upon thousands of other hopefuls on the trail to California. Many years later, Levi would recall their parties' absolute fear of being caught or overtaken by the "Destroying Angels," a group believed to threaten apostates and Mormon dissenters. Although Levi and his brothers fared well in Salt Lake as cobblers; like many other Mormons, they were less than impressed with the Great Basin.

Destroying Angels: Early Vigilantes?

In June 1838, Mormons in Caldwell County, Missouri, had founded a fraternal organization of vigilantes known as the Danites. Key players in the 1838 Mormon War, the Danites allegedly disbanded after the Mormon exodus to Utah in 1847. Although the accuracy of that claim is still debated today, the

Danites and their activities remain legendary in Mormon and secular folklore and culture.

Speculation of Danite activity intensified once the Saints reached Utah, and the press frequently accused Brigham Young and Orrin Porter Rockwell of membership in similar vigilante groups nicknamed "Destroying Angels" or "Avenging Angels." Controversy continues to surround them even today.

Arthur Tyrrell was another Forty-Niner who set out to find riches in California, specifically in San Francisco, Sacramento, Nevada City, and Shasta. As was the case for thousands, he left his wife and family behind to answer that siren call of wealth. Ward's Grove, Illinois, was home for Tyrrell, and it was to his family there that he wrote letters detailing his adventures and those of his fellow prospectors.

The Tyrrell family were neighbors of Ephraim Cheney and his extended family, and their neighborhood was just miles away from the home of Semantha Cheney Burgess White and her son, Perry. And while neither Semantha nor the Cheneys heard much regular news directly from their loved ones in California, Tyrrell's letters were filled with news regarding his friends and comrades:

Shasta. Cal. Dec. 17th –52
Friday noon

... as for Mrs. Cheany I have not received any letter from her all I can say about the Cheanys is I saw the youngest one of the two that is out here last Sunday in Shasta he was well and oferd to sell me a sac of flour 50 pounds at 75 cents a pound he was pedling I asked him whare his brother was he said with the pack train comeing up from Colusa I asked whare Ben White was he said hunting that is all I know a bout them but if I git a letter from her I am at her servis and will do the best I can for her according to her instructions She or any of the California widows will find a friend in me...[8]

Dr. Levi Cheney

Lewis Cheney

Uncles of Perry A. Burgess

This letter shines a light on the whereabouts of Ben White, Semantha's husband and Perry's stepfather, as well as on the activities of the Cheney brothers. During the exodus to Utah, the Cheneys ran freight for Brigham Young. It is clear that they found freighting a profitable business, as they engaged in it throughout the gold rushes in both California and Montana.

In addition to personal letters, newspaper articles provide glimpses into the lives of the Cheneys. Just over one hundred years after his departure for California, a 1953 *Boulder Daily Camera* article about Lewis Cheney confirms his participation in the California Gold Rush as well as his business acumen (both as a freighter and a banker). The biographical sketch leaves out just one pertinent fact about Lewis Cheney: his Mormon roots.

Lewis Cheney Had Many Interesting Experiences In The Western States
By Geo. W. Stryker
Boulder Newspaper
July 21, 1953

Mr. Cheney, one of our early eminent bankers, was not a pioneer, as he arrived in Boulder May 10th, 1877. To be a real full-fledged pioneer one must have arrived in the western country prior to 1876.

Born on a farm in Cattaraugus county, New York state April 4th, 1830

While a small boy his parents moved to Stephenson county, Ill., and he worked on a farm. Here without the aide of schools he acquired sufficient information to conduct his own business, as his business increased so did his knowledge. He was educated by the contracts he made in business.

In 1850 he joined the California gold rush, crossing the plains and arriving in California late in the fall of that year. During 1850–51 he was engaged in mining–placer mining–and the results were very satisfactory. The next three years were devoted

Shasta, California - circa 1855

to freighting, (the freight rate was $1.00 per pound) and dealing with livestock.

Returning to Illinois from California
Mr. Cheney returned to Illinois during the summer of 1854, and entered the mercantile business at Lena, Ill. ...

As sketchy and rife with misspellings and misrecorded information as they sometimes were, poll tax and census documents from the gold rush act as a sort of textual snapshot of any given area. According to the 1852 Colusa County, California, poll tax list, Ben White and L. Cheney—which could be either Lewis or Levi—were living there. Levi Cheney and Ben White were both doctors who practiced patent and Indian medicine.

The two companions left California around 1855. It was not White's first trip home, as he and his wife already had one daughter, Adelaide, born, according to census records, some time before 1855. Cheney relocated his family to Springfield, Wisconsin, where their names appeared on the 1860 census. White's daughter, Emma, was born on August 27, 1856, in Ward's Grove, Illinois. Perry was around eleven or twelve years old when his stepfather and his uncles Lewis and Mansel returned home. Given that much of the boy's life had been spent in hardship and in traveling across the country without a father, it is easy to understand how Ben White came to be the only real father-figure to have any kind of influence on him.

For the most recent five of those eleven or twelve years, the gold rush informed young Perry's childhood. At home with only his mother and his stepfamily nearby, he undoubtedly dreamed of adventure as young boys are prone to do, especially when a letter with news would arrive. And when his stepfather returned, Perry undoubtedly heard first-hand accounts of Ben's adventures in the gold rush. Entering his teen years hearing these fortune-seeking tales of peril and hope, Perry understandably matured with a desire to experience his own exploits, to follow his own path. He would be forever intrigued by the lure of gold, and his life's accomplishments would directly mirror that attraction.

tobaco salve
1 plug tobaco boiled in
one quart of watter
chamberlie then strain
and add beeswax and
rosin and tar each as
large as a hens egge
when dun pore it in
watter and worke ~~tare~~
like wax

Notgrass tea will stop
fucking

Pioneer Medicine
"Tobaco Salve" and "Notgrass tea"
Dr. Levi Cheney Medicine Book, 1860

CHAPTER 5
Utah War – Perry's Uncles Go to War

Unlike Perry and his Cheney relatives, the Burgess uncles and cousins never took an interest in gold, nor did they feel the need to escape the reaches of the Mormon Church. They chose instead to follow Brigham Young's instructions to spread out across the territory and multiply in an effort to live their lives in religious freedom. Many of them—including Harrison, Melancthon, and George, along with their respective families—moved to Lehi,[1] Utah, by the year 1851. Lehi incorporated the following year, the sixth city in Utah to do so. A flourishing community from the start, Lehi is still in existence today.

Although the Burgesses never succumbed to gold fever, they did have the good sense to take advantage of the financial opportunities provided by the gold rush. As miners trekked west, the journey was often more harrowing and demanding than they had imagined it would be. To compensate, they would take measures to lighten their loads by ridding themselves of their possessions wherever they happened to be along the trail. The Burgess men would claim those "found" items—which included everything from clothing to tools to mining equipment—and then turn around and sell them. It was easy money that could be made close to home.

Lehi was not the only Mormon outpost of its kind. One of the most significant and famous is Fort Lemhi,[2] Idaho. Fort Lemhi was named in honor of the Lamanites. According to the Book of Mormon, Lamanites were dark-skinned indigenous Americans who engaged in warfare against the light-skinned Nephites. Mormons believed that Native Americans were Lamanites and took it upon themselves to enlighten them with these beliefs. This was not a new mission; Joseph Smith had evangelized to Native Americans for the same reason.

William Burgess Jr. was a pivotal figure in the settlement of Fort Lemhi. In addition to being one of the Mormon founders of the settlement, he took it upon himself to transport with him from Utah the millstones used to construct a grist mill. The value of his ability to

Col. William Burgess Jr. - Utah Territory Militia

socialize with the Native Americans cannot be overstated, especially when his very life and the lives of the other Mormons depended upon developing a level of trust with the Shoshone and the Bannock. William's obituary called him "a peace maker and friend of the red man."[3]

Another figure who would prove prominent throughout Mormon history is Lot Smith. Although well known for his exploits and military daring in the Utah War, Smith proved himself far earlier than that when he was the youngest (at sixteen) member of the Mormon Battalion. Even less well known is the fact that Smith carried mail back and forth between Utah and Fort Lemhi in the summer of 1856.[4]

In May 1855, Brigham Young instructed twenty-seven men—eighteen of them missionaries—to settle among these Indian tribes and bring to them more "civilized" ways in hopes of converting them. Among these men was William Burgess Jr. An October 9, 1855, letter he wrote to Joseph Smith's cousin George reflects the respect the missionaries had for the Native Americans:

> The Indians here are the noblest race I have seen in the west.
> They are very friendly. They are not afraid of a white man, as

some other tribes are. They say the white men are their friends. I think we shall do good work here. We are learning their language as fast as we can. The Indians are very honest here, or have been so far. When we wash we sometimes let our clothes hang out for days, let our tools lie around any way, and Indians coming and going daily. Not one thing has been stolen yet. They abhor a thief, comparing him to a wolf, and they think a wolf is the meanest animal there is... Not one thing has been stolen yet... I wish Christians were this honest.

The trek—known as the Salmon River Mission—was not an easy one; there were no established trails or roads. The group crossed the Bannock Mountains and arrived at what is now known as Idaho Falls on the Snake River. From there they crossed the desert to arrive at a place twenty miles above the confluence of the Lemhi and Salmon Rivers. The men had traveled 380 miles in 30 days, and this spot is where they chose to establish their mission. It was one of the missions farthest from Salt Lake, and more well known than others for having been explored by Meriwether Lewis and William Clark in 1805. The Lemhi Valley was also the birthplace of Sacajawea of the Lemhi-Shoshone tribe. In his letter, William Jr. expressed his appreciation of the land to George:

> We have explored considerable since our last mail and find that there is more land here than we expected. It is our opinion that this valley would be sufficient to sustain as big a population as Davis county in Utah. It is a good country to raise stock, as there is plenty of grass, and the Indians say not much snow here. The valley is from one to five miles wide, 60 or 70 miles long.

Upon their arrival, the pioneers met many Shoshone and Bannock Indians as they were catching and drying salmon. When one of the Mormons explained the purpose of their journey, they were treated politely—albeit uncertainly—and allowed to cut timber for fuel and construction. Although late in the season, some of the men cultivated a tract of land and planted carrots, potatoes, and peas. Others dug an irrigation ditch. Still others built homes and constructed out-buildings. Everyone contributed to the relentlessly long days of strenuous physical labor. For William Burgess Jr., these responsibilities included fishing, as he indicates in his letter to George Smith:

> This is a great fish country in the season. The salmon come up in July in great quantities. They are the best fish I ever saw, I think. The herring come up here in September, red spotted trout come up in August and stay until cold weather.

Those first crops were eventually destroyed by grasshoppers, a disaster that must have all but devastated those twenty-seven men. The physical exertion required to establish Fort Lemhi was staggering. The men would work from sunup to sundown, building, digging, felling trees, and would then take turns standing guard at night. Eventually, mental fatigue would have set in as well. To be in this state of mind and then lose everything to natural disaster would have crushed all but the most dedicated of souls.

Even before the plague, the Mormons knew their supplies were running short. After completion of some houses and a stockade, about half the men headed back to Salt Lake to replenish supplies and bring their families back with them. They returned to Lemhi on November 19, 1855, thereby establishing the first white settlement in Idaho.

The settlement thrived until 1857, when sixty more Mormon settlers arrived and a second, smaller settlement was established just two miles away. This created tension between the Bannocks and the Mormons, as did the missionaries' role as peacemakers in the war between the Nez Perce and the Bannock and Shoshone. In late February 1858, the previously friendly Shoshone and Bannock tribes attacked Fort Lemhi and forced the settlers to return to Utah.

On the surface and judging by the development and early years of Lehi, Fort Lemhi, and other settlements, it would seem that things had finally begun to settle down for the Mormons. Brigham Young had led them out of persecution and into the deserts of the Great Basin, where he had hoped the Saints could live in isolation, free from conflict and crisis. Soon after arriving in Utah, however, the territory came under the jurisdiction of the United States, and almost imme-diately, the country was gripped by gold fever. As thousands of gold seekers headed west, Young's hopes for a life of isolation were dashed.

In response, Young proposed setting up a separate Mormon state, one known as the State of Deseret. He firmly believed that the key to peaceful living lay in the ability to self-govern, in the creation of a leadership of the Mormons' own choosing. The Compromise of 1850, however, kept the Saints under federal control. President Mil-lard Fillmore appointed Young the first governor of Utah Territory. And while this seemed at the time to create a win-win situation, time would prove differently.

The Mormons' lifestyle clashed with that of other residents of Utah Territory. Specifically, their adherence to polygamy caused problems for most of the American public. This, despite the fact that the vast majority of Mormons did not practice plural marriage. Outsiders, or Gentiles, as they were called within Mormon confines, cared not one bit about how many Mormons were polygamists or the reason behind their choices. They found the practice immoral and reprehensible, along the lines of slavery. The Republican Party platform of the 1856 presidential election reflected this attitude as it promised "to prohibit in the territories those twin relics of barbarism: polygamy and slavery."[5]

Wanting to avoid any possible conflict with the Mormons while simultaneously wanting to please the Democrats, newly elected Presi-dent James Buchanan and his Secretary of War, John B. Floyd, chose new, non-Mormon officials for Utah Territory but did so without publicly announcing the decision or informing Young of his removal from office. Instead, Buchanan appointed Alfred Cumming as gov-ernor of Utah Territory and issued general orders on May 28, 1857, for the assemblage of 2,500 troops at Fort Leavenworth, Kansas, to be dispatched to Salt Lake City. These troops would accompany Cumming and quash any rebellion the Mormons planned to initiate.

In hindsight, it is difficult to say how the transition of power from

Young to Cumming might have unfolded had Buchanan not been so easily swayed by territory officials—particularly by federal judge W. W. Drummond, who charged the Mormons with disloyalty and murder and warned him that the Mormons would revolt if forced to follow the leadership of anyone other than Young. Investigation into the situation may have revealed that Young and his followers would offer no resistance. As history shows, however, what is commonly referred to as "Buchanan's Blunder" resulted in misinterpretation owing to lack of communication, and the Mormon community responded as one might have expected them to: with organized resistance.

For all Young knew, the government was coming to wipe out every last Saint. Conflict between Mormons and the American public had been constant even in Salt Lake City; it didn't require much imagination to believe that the United States wanted to get rid of all Mormons once and for all. Newspapers in New York and Washington were demanding federal action with their sensationalism, while Illinois Senator Stephen A. Douglas referred to the Mormon population as a disease when he declared a "knife must be applied to this pestiferous, disgusting cancer which is gnawing into the very vitals of the body politic. It must be cut out by the roots and served over by a red hot iron of stern and unflinching law."[6]

Despite not having been told officially of Buchanan's decision, Young was informed that the federal government was sending troops to Salt Lake. On July 24, a thousand Mormons were celebrating the tenth anniversary of their settlement when Orrin Porter Rockwell charged dramatically into Big Cottonwood Canyon on his horse to announce the impending arrival of federal troops. Young assured his people that this time there would be no fleeing, no turning the other cheek. They would stay. And if need be, they would fight.

Young immediately set to work writing letters with explicit instructions to his followers everywhere. He informed them that all ties with the United States had been severed and that their God-given duty was to protect their religious freedom, regardless of the orders given by any federal agent. He declared martial law and deployed the local militia, the Nauvoo Legion. This militia eventually became known as the Utah Territorial Militia and was the biggest in the country, with more than 1,000 members. William Burgess Jr. was a colonel in the militia and is reported in some sources as a lieutenant at Fort Lemhi, while Harrison Burgess served as a captain and Melancthon, the youngest brother, a soldier. William Sr., though more than willing to serve, was too old to participate in the militia.

It isn't possible to state with unequivocal certainty that the impending conflict came as a surprise to Young. His application for statehood having been repeatedly denied, he had to have been aware that the Saints' practice of polygamy and demand for theocracy were points of disdain for the American public as well as for the federal government. Put in the simplest terms, Mormons were largely viewed as un-American in their values. When mail service to and from Salt Lake was cancelled and word of approaching troops spread, it makes sense that the Mormons assumed the worst. After twenty-seven years of constant persecution, the assassination of their prophet thirteen years earlier, and the murder of Parley Pratt—one of the revered Twelve Apostles—just two months before fresh in their minds, Young and his followers believed the government was coming to hunt them down and murder them all.

John Pulsipher, the esteemed Mormon memoirist and in-law of the Burgess family, recorded this entry in his diary on July 26, 1857:

> ...The News from the States is—that Hell is boiling over, the Devil is mad—The U.S. mail is stopped & an army is coming to kill us.[7]

This belief nurtured in the Saints the attitude that they had nothing to lose. There is no more dangerous enemy than that which embraces death willingly. And yet Young gave strict orders to his men not to shed blood unless absolutely necessary. He and the Legion's commanding general, Daniel H. Wells, told their men:

Let there be no excitement... Save a life always when it is possible. We do not wish to shed a drop of blood if it can be avoided.[8]

It was an order that would be upheld, as history shows that the Nauvoo Legion relied more on its wits than its brawn in the war against the government.

On August 1, 1857, the Nauvoo Legion mustered and began collecting food supplies and weapons. Two weeks later, a reconnaissance unit marched eastward to observe federal troops and protect those Mormons still on the overland road. Other units were sent north while councils were held in Salt Lake in an effort to maintain friendly relations with the Native Americans.

The federal government would have been surprised to discover the organized and determined manner in which the Nauvoo Legion set about preparing for possible conflict. Jesse Augustus Gove, later a notable Civil War colonel, was a captain in the 10th U.S. Infantry during the Utah War. Like his superiors and most, if not all of his comrades, he underestimated the strength and fortitude of the Mormon resistance, as evidenced in this letter excerpt dated September 18, 1857:

We have made 19 miles today. Everybody in fine health. The sun is out, we are quite warm. If the Mormons will only fight, their days are numbered. We shall sweep them from the face of the earth and Mormonism in Utah will cease. Our campaign will then be at an end.[9]

Throughout this bloodless war—the first rebellion in Utah Territory—the purpose of the Nauvoo Legion was simple: Make the federal army's job as difficult as possible so as to slow its progress. The militia wintered in Echo Canyon, the most direct route to the Salt Lake Valley. Here they built fortifications and dug rifle pits along the narrowest sections. According to John Pulsipher's diary, Echo Canyon was the largest camp by mid-November, with 1,600 men.

No strangers to traveling in harsh winter conditions, the Mormons made themselves quite comfortable there in the canyon. Pulsipher and a friend named William Riley Judd built a house, complete with bunk beds.

> Tuesday, November 17—We were so comfortable, we had many visitors--& finally our whole 10th company that we belonged to joined us. We were so comfortable, sheltered from storm and wind, by a good fire—that many others done likewise & this camp, before we left it—became quite a city of Wickeups [single-roomed, domed buildings].[10]

It wasn't enough to construct small shacks; Pulsipher built an oven in his "leisure time."

> November 26—Having a little leisure time today I made an oven to bake our bread in—dug in the clay bank near the fire place in our house—which proved to be a valuable improvement. We could now have light bread baked just right—Ever so much better than the burnt dough that is so common in camp life. Our rations were now too big ...[11]

Federal troops were not so fortunate as to enjoy the comforts of home. Conditions throughout that winter were particularly grueling. About the troops' march to Fort Bridger, which had already been burned by Charles Pulsipher and the other Mormons, Captain Gove reported to his superiors:

> Nov. 6: This morning it commenced to snow and was very cold. ... All day we plodded along with those villainous trains until about 10 o'clock at night, when I got in camp nearly frozen, a more disagreeable day's duty I never experienced ...

> Nov. 12: The thermometer fell last night to sixteen degrees below zero. This temperature in a wall tent without fire is very uncomfortable...

> Nov. 16: The animals are still dying rapidly. They are seen fallen in such attitudes as could only result from the last possible effort of remaining strength to resist the effects of starvation and cold. ... Horses, mules and oxen in some places all lie together ...[12]

The trains Gove refers to in his report were trains of oxen-led wagons loaded with food and various supplies. These were no insignificant wagon trains, but rather carried upward of 5,000 pounds and were led by five or six yoke of oxen. The wagon trains were manned by civilians contracted by Russell, Majors, & Waddell, the premiere freighters of the time. After being bankrupted by the Mormon attacks during the Utah War, the company regrouped and formed the Pony Express, the famous mail carriers throughout the West from April 1860 to October 1861. Freighting in the Utah War was a dangerous undertaking, and the Mormons' strategy for slowing down federal troops often included destruction of their wagon trains. One well-known incident took place in September of 1857 and involved a legend of heroic proportions.

Lot Smith, a rather eccentric and quick-tempered Mormon for whom bravado was in no short supply, was a pivotal figure in the Utah War. His courage is celebrated in Mormon histories, and the train-burning incident near Green River is one in which Smith's intelligence matched his fearlessness.

> ... After traveling 14 miles, we came up to the train, but discovered that the teamsters were drunk, and knowing that drunken men were easily excited and always ready to fight, and remembering my positive orders not to hurt anyone except in self-defense, we remained in ambush until after midnight ...

> ... I arranged my men, and we advanced until our horses' heads came into the light of the fire then I discovered that we had the advantage, for looking back into the darkness, I could not see where my line of troops ended, and could imagine my twenty followers stringing out to a hundred or more as well as not. I inquired for the captain of the train. Mr. Dawson stepped out and said he was the man. . . I replied by requesting him to get all of his men and their private property as quickly as possible out of the wagons for I meant to put a little fire into them...

> While riding from wagon to wagon, with torch in hand and the wind blowing, the covers seemed to me to catch very slowly. ... About this time, I had Dawson send in his men to the wagons,

not yet fired, to get us some provisions, enough to thoroughly furnish us, telling him to get plenty of sugar and coffee. On completing this task I told him that we were going just a little way off and that if he or his men molested the trains or undertook to put the fire out, they would be instantly killed. We rode away leaving the wagons all ablaze.[13]

Colonel W. F. Cody, better known as Buffalo Bill, began his remarkable career as a young man in the train traveling on the Salt Lake Trail. He provides an account of the event from a different perspective. He was riding with the train at the request of the freighters, who had hoped he would provide both an extra hand and protection. Whatever else he may have supplied, his efforts at protection weren't much good against Lot Smith.

> The Mormons, after taking what goods they wanted and could carry off, had set fire to the wagons, many of which were loaded with bacon, lard, hard-tack, and other provisions, which made a very hot, fierce fire, and the smoke to roll up in dense clouds. Some of the wagons were loaded with ammunition, and it was

not long before loud reports followed in rapid succession. ... We learned that two other trains had been captured and destroyed in the same way, by the Mormons. This made seventy-five wagon loads ... which never reached General Johnston's command, to which they had been consigned.[14]

Albert Johnston was an officer determined to rid the world of its Mormons. In another few years, he would become one of the most highly decorated commanders in the Civil War. As it was, he claimed to be willing to sacrifice "his plantation for a chance to bombard the city for 15 minutes" as he rode through the empty streets of Salt Lake City on June 26, 1858.[15]

Bullwhackers

The teamsters who drove the freight wagons were commonly referred to as "bullwhackers" for their habit of whacking the oxen to keep them moving. Some bullwhackers were women, which is surprising, given the fact that bullwhackers were the members of the freight companies who got harassed, beaten, and robbed.

Teamsters in general were considered the lowest rung on the social ladder, primarily because of their appearance. Because of the nature of their business, they rarely bathed, and their clothing and hair were often infested with lice and other vermin. Bullwhackers in general were illiterate, though there were exceptions. For $25 a month, bullwhackers worked long, hard days and more often than not spent their later years suffering the pains of arthritis and rheumatism.

It was not an easy career. Though one thinks of driving a wagon in terms of sitting, bullwhackers did very little sitting. They drove their oxen teams by walking alongside the wagon. Through rain, snow, and other inclement weather conditions, the bullwhacker forged ahead. At night, the ground beneath the wagon served as a bed.

When one teamster—T. S. Kenderdine—applied to work for Russell, Majors, & Waddell on the Utah Expedition train, he asked what the scenery would be like on the trip. Furious, the wagon boss ripped up his application papers, saying anyone who asked questions like that was too smart to work as a bullwhacker. Kenderdine returned the next day dressed in his worst clothes, said nothing, and was hired.[16]

Almost as common as train burnings was cattle rustling. One incident that occurred at Horn Fork in Echo Canyon was so remarkable that it has been written about in several historical accounts and was also recorded in the recollections of Charles and John Pulsipher, Lot Smith, and even Buffalo Bill.

Charles Pulsipher provides arguably the most detailed and accurate account of what happened late on the night of October 13 in Echo Canyon:

> One striking incident that I will mention here. While the soldiers were traveling up Horn Fork our boys saw a good chance to take their [the federal army's] beef stock. We were much in need of beef to feed our soldiers. Three thousand U.S. soldiers were moving in a solid body up Horn Fork and the beef stock was about 1 1/2 miles below the main company, so we thought that a good chance to run them off. Two companies of our boys, 26 in each company—one under Porter Rockwell and the other under Lott Smith— concluded to meet in the same road as they rode along, came over the brink of the hill in plain sight of the camp. They came to a halt before they discovered that the soldiers had stopped for dinner and the beef stock had come up to the rear of the soldiers making it difficult to get them without endangering the lives of our boys. Porter Rockwell, being very cautious, said it was too risky to take them, but Lott Smith, being hungry for beef, and did not know what fear was, said he would do his part and at the time pulled his sword from the sheath and flourishing it over his head said, "Come on, boys."

He dashed down the hill on a charge. Of course all the boys were at his heels. Porter, seeing that Lott was determined, did the same thing, and called for his boys to follow him. Wishing to prove to Lott that he was no coward, he dashed right in between the soldiers and the beef stock in less time than it takes to tell about it, we had the herd over the hill and out of their sight. It was done so quick that they hardly realized what was done until we were out of sight. Well, the first thing for them to do was to call the officers together to hold a council of war. They soon decided to mount infantry on their work mules and follow up the Mormons and get their beef stock back. When they were about settled on this plan, the old colonel said, "Hold on, gentlemen, I have not had any say yet. The Lord inspired me to speak. I want to tell you there is a deep hard plot to decoy this camp away from their wagons. Maybe the Mormons have thousands secreted away and will rush in upon us and cut us all to pieces." So, they took his advice and did not try to follow. We did not have another man within 30 miles of them, and from that time on we had plenty of beef to eat.[17]

Lot Smith's account of the incident is a bit more colorful:

When we arrived within sight of the camp, I discovered a herd of cattle numbering about fourteen hundred head on the bottom lands below. We were on the bluff. I told Porter we would take those cattle. He said that was just like me. ... While he stopped to survey the situation with his glass, I started down the bluff, only about one-third of the men being able to keep up as we rushed down the steep descent. Porter came on in a terrible rage, swearing at me for going so fast, and at the men for being so slow. He wanted me to wait for them all to catch up. There was, however, no time to wait. ... We intercepted [the herd], unyoked the cattle and turned their heads the other way, so that the poor cattle which had been in the rear were now in front ... the enemy refused to take up the gauntlet, and we were compelled to ride slowly away without an encounter. We fell back on Fort Supply, eating beef we had borrowed and sampling some half-cooked government beans. This experiement developed, as never

Burning Government Trains.

" DASHED ACROSS THE BURNING PLAIN."

before conceived in my imagination, the enourmous pressure the human stomach is capable of sustaining without damage, and came very near developing the necessity for some one else to write this sketch. [18]

Of the same comic yet impressive scene, Buffalo Bill Cody said:

> Meanwhile bands of Mormons, under their nimble and ubiquitous leaders, hung on the flanks, just out of rifle-shot, harassing them at every step,... A few infantry companies were mounted on mules and sent in pursuit of the guerillas, but the Saints merely laughed at them, terming them jackass cavalry.[19]

Orrin Porter Rockwell and Lot Smith were rivals who eventually became competitive friends. Both men were devout Mormons, and both would defend their faith and their people with their very lives. Both together and separately, the two lawmen led raids on the federal army throughout the Utah Expedition.

Porter Rockwell statue - Lehi, Utah   Capt. Lot Smith

Although noteworthy for its execution, the Horn Fork event was just one of many instances of Mormon courage and strategy in the Utah Expedition. Militia were known to dress up as teamsters and blend in on federal army routes without ever being discovered for who they really were. The stories that comprise the Utah War are worthy of admiration, yet they have been overshadowed by another conflict that occurred in September 1857, the Mountain Meadows

Massacre. One was tragic, the other impressive. History loves a tragedy.

The winter months of December 1857 to March 1858 brought a halt to the conflict of the Utah War. Brigham Young had written to Thomas Kane of Pennsylvania back in August, asking for his assistance. Kane had some political clout and had already helped the Mormons on their exodus to Utah. Kane offered to mediate between the Mormons and the federal government, but President Buchanan initially rebuffed him. Eventually, he gave Kane unofficial authority to act as mediator. Kane made the 3,000-mile journey during those winter months and arrived in Salt Lake City in February 1858.

Although details of the negotiation are not completely clear, Kane did manage to convince Young of Cumming's appointment as territorial governor. The new governor, in turn, agreed to arrive in Salt Lake without military protection. Young and the followers politely received Cumming in mid-April, a gesture that led to Cumming's decision not to take the hard-line stance against the Mormons supported by Colonel Johnston and others.

> Col. Thos. L Kane an old friend of this people—seeing the situation of things came in haste from Washington to this place & then to the army. He finally got Governor Cuming to leave the army & come to Salt Lake City. And when we found that he would come in peaceably without an army & that he really was sent to be Governor of Utah we were willing to receive & acknowledge him as such.[20]

This truce did little to ease the tensions felt by the Mormons of Salt Lake. They still feared persecution and possible violence. The "war" officially ended on April 6, 1858, when President Buchanan signed a proclamation declaring all Mormons pardoned for their treasons and sedition if they agreed to submit to federal rule. Young accepted the terms but denied ever having rebelled against the United States. John Pulsipher's diary records the event:

> General Johnson the commander of the army also issued a

proclamation & promised to keep the peace & neither molest persons nor property, said he wished to pass thro the city to some out of the way place, where he could locate and wait for future orders. As their feelings are so changed that they are not the hostile army now, that they were when we stopped them—so when they were humbled enough & promised so well. Our boys guarding the road were invited home & the great U.S. Army allowed to come in.

In late June, army troops rode through the streets of Salt Lake City without conflict. One witty *New York Herald* reporter eulogized the war as such: Killed, none; wounded, none; fooled, everybody.[21] Ultimately, the Utah War would be a major stain on Buchanan's record.

By the time the army arrived in Salt Lake, the Saints were gone. Unable to trust the government and unwilling to remain living with the ever-present possibility of violence and persecution, Young evacuated Zion at the end of March so that federal troops could pass through unhindered. The Saints returned within two weeks' time and lived under federal authority.

Charles Pulsipher's diary gives insight into the evacuation of Salt Lake:

> ... although we had declared that if they continued to push their way into our midst, and if we had to give up our homes to them, we would burn everything that we could not take with us leaving the place as desolate as possible. To prove to them that we meant what we said, before leaving Fort Supply, we set fire to the place and rode off by light of it, and thus demolished a years hard labor that I had done in helping to build up that place. We did it cheerfully for the defense of Isreal. When the troops came up to Fort Bridger for supplies and found everything destroyed by fire that would burn and the winter was upon them, they were licked.

Buffalo Bill states:

> In a word, Buchanan and the Washington politicians and the Johnston- Harney army must confess themselves hopelessly

beaten, before a blow was struck. The army was powerless before the people they had come to punish. All that remained to do was forgive the Mormons and let them go.[22]

In 1861, Brigham Young gave orders to the Saints to migrate south to Utah's Dixie, properly known as St. George and believed to be named after George A. Smith, one of the Church's Twelve Apostles. The esteemed leader had a winter home in Dixie, and this migration was part of Young's attempts to expand the Mormon community throughout Utah Territory.

Young called hundreds of Mormon families to Dixie, where they would become involved in the cotton industry. Some families and groups broke off along the way under Young's direction to continue to spread out across the Territory and multiply, a trend that continued through 1862 and was halted by the events of the Civil War.

Burgess family members were among those to heed the call and migrate south. According to his own recollections, William Burgess Jr. wrote,

> In the fall of 1862 we helped build up Southern Utah, then moved to Pine Valley and started the first sawmill in that part of the country. The timber in this part of Utah was very good, so we made lumber to help build the Salt Lake Tabernacle and the great Organ. We were called to this part of Utah by Pres. Brigham Young. We lived there nearly twenty years. We also ran the first grist mill in that part of the country.

John Pulsipher also followed the requests of Brigham and moved with his Burgess in-laws to St. George and Pine Valley. Life in southern Utah was difficult for the residents of Dixie, as they were often under the watchful eye of the Native Americans. According to John's diary:

> We gathered our horses, kept armed herdsman with them days and armed guards at the coral with them at night. This was the heavy expense on us, few as we are—but we are hunting and gathering stock as well as picket guarding, which we were care-

ful to attend to, so that we may not be surprised by any large force. We did not gather our stock any too soon, for the Indians were here spying around every night as sly and summing as foxes. Every morning we would find tracks where they walked or crawled around the coral in the darkness of night, but they could not break the fence or open the gate, so they must try another strategy.

The Pine Valley saw mill was built in 1863 by William Sr., William Jr., Melancthon, and Harrison and was located in the canyon, just under the steep bank north of Birch Flat at the junction of the road to the lake and the main highway. Little could the men have known when they constructed their simple mill that it—and they— would be called upon to contribute their skills to the creation of arguably the most famous musical instrument ever made.

The Tabernacle Organ remains today one of the most impressive pipe organs ever built. The original was crafted in 1867, its 700 pipes constructed of wood, zinc, and alloys of tin and lead. According to *Emery County Pioneer Settlers of the 19th Century,*

> President Brigham Young rode on horseback to Pine Valley where he picked out a large straight tree to make the Tabernacle Organ out of. William [Burgess] and his father and brothers cut down the tree and sawed it in their saw mill. Then it was hauled by ox team to Salt Lake City. It took six weeks to make the trip.

And so the Burgess men, who had contributed greatly to their community in Nauvoo and throughout the Utah War, also played pivotal roles in this most recent relocation to St. George and Pine Valley. Having felled the timber used to build the famous Tabernacle Organ, as both William Sr. and his sons did, and having built one of the first homes in St. George, as Melancthon did, the Burgess family has cemented a place for itself in the annals not only of Mormon history, but of American history.

And that was only the beginning, as young Perry would carry the torch into the next generation.

World famous Salt Lake Tabernacle organ, circa 1860
Organ pipes were cut by the Burgess family
at the request of Brigham Young

Perry A. Burgess, 1860s
Courtesy of Carnegie Branch Library for Local History
Boulder Historical Society Collection

CHAPTER 6
Colorado Gold Rush – Perry Begins to Write

While Utah Mormons were finding a new normal in the aftermath of the Utah War, Perry Burgess was taking his first steps toward a new life with a fearlessness reserved for the young.

By 1859, Perry had spent seven of his seventeen or so years listening to his stepfather's tales of Gold Rush adventure. Apart from those stories, Perry's life was ordinary for a boy living in northwestern Illinois at that time. He grew up surrounded by his Cheney uncles and step-family relations, all of whom lived in either Jo Daviess or adjacent Stephenson County. Later journal entries would show he kept in touch with the Whites, including Mansel Cheney's wife, Polina, indicating the tight-knit bonds that developed over the years.

Life in Millville, Illinois, was not on the fast track. Perry's days were filled with fishing in Yellow Creek with friends, and the most exciting event ever to take place in the region was probably the second of the seven Lincoln-Douglas debates. Abraham Lincoln and Stephen Douglas (the very one who referred to Mormons as a "cancer") debated in nearby Freeport in August 1858. At that time, Millville was the only settlement located between Freeport and Galena.

Although the second debate was a major event in Perry's serene life in that it brought the country's current concerns almost to his doorstep, the seven debates as a whole were pivotal for the nation. Where its focus had recently been on the Utah War and the ongoing issue of Indian relocation, the country now became fixated on the issue of slavery. A new day was dawning, and soon the United States would be embroiled in the Civil War. Individuals and states would choose sides: for or against, North or South.

Cheneys in the Civil War

Although Perry himself felt called to take his life in a different direction and managed to avoid military duty, two of his Cheney uncles—Matthew and Chester—enlisted in the Union

Army on August 15, 1862. Both were members of the illustrious 92nd Illinois Infantry and served throughout the entire war, mustering out on June 21, 1865.

The 92nd engaged in nearly fifty battles and conflicts in the war and was one of the few Union regiments to use the relatively new Spencer repeating rifle, a reliable lever-action weapon that could not be manufactured in the South owing to a copper shortage. This rifle gave the Union cavalry an advantage over its opponent, and the 92nd became part of Colonel John T. Wilder's Lightning Brigade, a unit renowned for its daring exploits.

In addition, the regiment was part of General William T. Sherman's famous Atlanta Campaign, in which the city was captured and burned.

Matthew Cheney sustained injuries during his service in the Civil War and suffered from their effects for the rest of his life, which he spent as a pioneer in Sac City, Iowa. Chester (and their brother Wesley) lived in Sac City as well for a time, but moved to Tologa, Dewey County, Oklahoma, where he lived at the time of his death. Wesley eventually moved to Hobart, Kiowa County, Oklahoma, where he died in 1911.

Perry's every dream must have been heavily influenced by Ben White's recollections. And so it would not, perhaps, have been surprising to his parents that his youthful ambition was to be part of the next gold rush. Little could Perry have known that the next gold discovery would launch the largest gold rush in American history.

The Pikes Peak Gold Rush—later known as the Colorado Gold Rush—began with rumors. In 1848, Cherokee on their way to California by way of the Cherokee Trail discovered gold in a stream in the South Platte basin, which was located at the time in Kansas Territory. Although they did nothing about their find, they shared the discovery with others of their tribe. For ten years, that information was nothing more than that: information.

All that changed in 1858 when Georgia-born William Green Russell, whose wife was Cherokee, got wind of the discovery. Having worked the gold fields in California, Russell had enough experience to know how best to act on the rumors of gold at Pikes Peak. In February 1858, he organized a small party that included his brothers, Levi and Oliver, and six others: Samuel Bates, John Hampton, William Anderson, Solomon Roe, Lewis Ralston, and Joseph McAfee.

As they traveled along the Santa Fe Trail, others—both whites and Native Americans—joined until there were about 104 gold seekers en route to Pikes Peak. Although they traveled together, they were in no way companions but rivals, divided into four basic groups, each intent on being the first to "rediscover" gold in the South Platte basin.

Once they reached Fort Bent, the groups traveled northwest. They reached the confluence of Cherry Creek and the South Platte River on May 23. After about twenty days of prospecting river beds and exploring Cherry Creek and Ralston Creek without success, many of the miners gave up and left. The Russells and ten other men remained and continued their explorations.

The men's efforts finally paid off in early July, when several hundred dollars' worth of gold dust was discovered at the mouth of Little Dry Creek on the South Platte River. The site of the discovery is today in a suburb of Denver called Englewood, at the junction of U.S. Highway 285 and Interstate 25.

Word of the gold discovery spread like wildfire all the way to the East Coast, and by 1859, 100,000 potential prospectors—nicknamed Fifty-Niners—were on their way to the Rocky Mountains. The slogan "Pikes Peak or Bust" was painted on the sides of wagons, letting everyone know they were on a mission. Only half of the hopefuls would ever make it to their destination.

Pikes Peak or Bust!

Although the slogan "Pikes Peak or Bust" was adopted in 1859, gold was not actually discovered near Pikes Peak in Cripple Creek until the 1890s. The mountaintop took on importance because the prospectors knew that if they could see Pikes Peak, they were close to Cherry Creek.

Farther east than any other mountain in the Front Range, Pikes Peak is one of Colorado's fourteeners, or mountains with an altitude in excess of 14,000 feet above sea level. It sits at 14,115 feet (4,302 meters).

Busted!

The Pikes Peak Gold Rush attracted so many people that make-shift camps developed seemingly overnight, just as they had in the California Gold Rush ten years earlier. Some of those camps eventually became Denver City, Golden City, Boulder City, and Idaho Springs. The population increase, which also provided the first major white population in the region, led to the creation of Colorado Territory in 1861, just as the gold rush was ending.

Although Perry Burgess's involvement in the Montana Gold Rush is well known and documented, previous works regarding the Colorado Gold Rush have never mentioned him. In fact, almost his entire life's history prior to 1866 has been virtually ignored or unknown because so few primary sources exist to prove where he was and what he was doing at any given time.

If not for a local Steamboat Springs newspaper—*Steamboat Pilot*—Perry's earlier years might still be a mystery. As it is, Steamboat cofounder and resident Perry was a regular contributor to that newspaper in the late 1890s, just prior to his death in 1900. He wrote a weekly column concerning his adventures during the Colorado Gold Rush and beyond, and a handful of those columns still exist today. The rest were lost in a fire when the *Pilot* offices burned to the ground on May 1, 1909.

More than a writer of recollections, Perry was instrumental in the continued publishing of the *Steamboat Pilot*. In 1896, he helped an old friend and Colorado historian, Charles Leckenby, by engineering the sale of the newspaper to Leckenby and to Perry's son, Bruce Burgess. As partners, the two men bought the paper from Mrs. Jane Hoyle, widow of *Pilot* founder James Hoyle. Under this new ownership, Perry became a featured contributor. His diary entries from the same time frame indicate that while he was writing for the *Pilot*, he was also sending his stories to popular publications like *Harper's Weekly* and *Frank Leslie's Weekly*. Although it would seem that his pieces were never accepted for publication, they were returned to him with suggestions for improvement. Local Steamboat Springs readers enjoyed them as they were, however, even though he never had a byline.

The following 1897 recollection stories regarding the Colorado Gold Rush remain missing: July 28; August 4; August 11; September 1; September 8; September 15; September 21; October 13.

Those for which a copy still exists follow, in order, and are reprinted in their entirety and with all original spellings and grammar.

Across the Big Muddy

Our Pilgrims Are Now West of the Missouri River.

"On Jordan's stormy banks we stand" is familiar as a dear old hymn to every one. We had heard it sung in the little school house and at Camp meetings from childhood, and now, as our pilgrim band of gold hunters were gathered on the eastern shore of the "Big Muddy," gazing down upon and across the seething tide that rolled between us and the long and almost desert waste that had to be crossed ere the golden goal could be reached, some one in our band caught the inspiration and started to sing the song that means so much. Before the first verse was half finished all had joined in, and a wave of simple melody floated across the muddy water that must have astonished the little village of Pawnee Indians whose teepees or lodge could be plainly seen on the opposite shore. They evidently thought that some sacred rite was being enacted, perhaps to soothe the angry god of river before attempting to cross.

We had for some time noticed that some members of our party had been manifesting symptoms of that nightmare of a complaint namely, home-sickness, and here, with Indians in sight and the chilling flood of the Missouri to be crossed, the certainty of hardships ahead, the uncertainty of finding and acquiring golden treasure and the thoughts of a comfortable home and loved ones from whom it already seemed they had long been absent, changed the minds and sentiments of several of our band and they turned back. But while we would have been glad to have their company we were relieved of the incubus, the dead weight of dragging – like a ball and chain – the homesick ones who had lost their first enthusiasm.

A farewell supper was given to our backsliding friends and the next morning the final farewells, hand shaking and "good bye, God bless you," and the deserter's wagons turned about and rolled solemnly toward the rising sun, while the majority continued on toward the sunset.

An arduous day's work found us safely over the river into Nebraska. One day was spent in outfitting, getting what information we could regarding the country ahead of us and getting acquainted with other pilgrims like ourselves. We here admitted several outfits into our caravan, which in numbers and fighting capabilities more than compensated for what we had lost from desertion, and when our line of march was taken up the next morning we numbered eighteen wagons and thirteen mounted men. We could muster thirty five able bodied men, all pretty well supplied with arms and ammunition and a fixed determination to succeed. Five men had their wives and children with them and were going to carve out new homes as well as to look for gold.

Our first camp after leaving Plattsmouth was on Salt creek, where two days were spent in making repairs and giving our loads a general overhauling, casting bullets, washing and mending clothes and letting our stock rest and fill up on the nutritious feed. Salt creek is very deep, narrow and sluggish. Hooks and lines were set and a large mess of fine catfish secured. Several rattlesnakes were killed near camp, and one little boy came running back to camp with the intelligence that a big boa constrictor, such as they had in shows, lay across the road a short distance away. He thought at first it was a fence pole and was going to get it to bring to camp for wood, but on getting near it saw it glisten in the sun and noticed that it was spotted, in fact that it was a "great big snake." Our captain said that it was probably a Bull snake, which was harmless, but often grew to a large size. The lad's father, armed with a shot gun, went back with him to look for the reptile, which had not moved. It lay across the broad gauge wagon road enjoying the hot sun, and was so long that its head and tail were both concealed in the prairies grass on each side of the road. Our friend cautiously advanced and paused a rod from the creature to note its fine proportions. His snakeship was evidently asleep for he remained motionless until a sharp stamp of the man's foot on the ground aroused him, when his shapely head and tapering neck rose slowly from the grass and was riddled by a charge from the shot gun. Then, in its dying struggles the lithe body was rapidly coiled and uncoiled and knotted in many fantastic shapes. After these contortions had ceased the boy put a string around its neck and dragged it into camp where all could see it.

A species of laughing owl inhabited the dense growth of cottonwoods that grew along the creek and made the nights hideous with their clatter, which made one think the inmates of some insane asylum were at large in the forest.

During the day large numbers of tortoises could be seen sunning themselves on logs that had fallen into the water, one end of which, resting on the bank, gave them an easy slope to climb up into sunlight. Gar fish would float by the hour at the surface of the water, being carried lazily around in the eddies. A great variety of waterfowl and land birds were also encountered, among which were black birds with yellow or white spots on their wrings where they are usually red.

During the last day's sojourn at Salt creek one of the men killed a fine buck antelope which gave us an agreeable change of meat diet.

Our captain here instituted a regular system of night herding of the stock and two men volunteered to do this work and be relived from day duty for the time or until it should be found desirable to make a change.

On The Great Plains

Interesting Incidents of the Overland Journey.

Before leaving Salt creek we took on enough dry wood to do camp cooking with until we should strike the Platte again. A three day's ration of bread was baked. We were not yet in the land of aromatic sage brush and our wood supply was only considered sufficient for making coffee and frying meat and potatoes.

The first day from Salt creek was over a rolling, treeless prairie. Camping for night in a shallow ravine, at the bottom of which we found a chain of long, narrow pools of clear water in which were numerous sun fish or "pumpkin seeds," as we boys used to call them. Enough of these were secured for a small fry and just before sun set a small pack of coyotes appeared on the summit of a neighboring swell and gave us a serenade. Not knowing any name for the chain of pools we called the place "Camp Nameless." The next day we journeyed over a treeless, brushless and apparently perfectly level plateau. A blistering wind prevailed which made our faces burn and our lips crack. We had brought kegs of water from a spring that we had passed in the morning, from which we made noon coffee, but our teams had to be turned loose to rest and graze without a refreshing drink that we would have been so glad to have given them. No water could be had for the poor beasts until we should reach the river. The action of the sun and heat on the sandy soil gave a shimmering, wavering appearance to the air near the surface of what then seemed to be a boundless plain. Soon the mirage developed into what looked like countless numbers of cattle and horses; fair, green, wooded islands seemed to dot a blue expanse of water, both of which were inviting and so real that it was hard to believe that it was only an illusion. It recalled tales we had read of the mirage of the great Saharan desert, always receeding as the attempt to approach it was persisted in and finally luring the deluded traveler to a horrible death from thirst, heat and exhaustion. We wondered why our thirsty cattle did not try to reach the cool and refreshing water that appeared to be so temptingly near. The sky, like a great dome of azure, seemed to rest like an inverted bell on the plain that we were in the midst of, looking to be not over two miles on either side of us to where it seemed to touch the ground.

Presently our captain, who was riding perhaps a mile in advance of the train, was seen to halt, turn his horse toward us and ride slowly back to meet his little command. As he got in speaking distance he said that the river was in sight and advised the teamsters to be careful to restrain the cattle from rushing to the water when they should come within sight or smell of it, as they were liable to stampede in that direction and rush down off the bluff, to the almost certain destruction of teams, wagons and the precious loads they carried. He had every horseman ride slowly at the head of the train to prevent such a disaster. The breeze freshened and the cattle scented water before we had got within a mile of the river and quickened their pace considerably. As we neared the edge of the plateau the valley proper came into view and we looked down upon the real broad blue river, with its cool green islands and broad grassy bottom lands, the mirage of which we had recently beheld in the air.

The road down the bluff was quite steep and with loaded wagons pushing from behind and the alluring water acting as a magnet in front, great care was needed to make the descent in safety. The bottom was reached without accident and our captain shouted orders to "drop the log chains and let the cattle go," which was obeyed with alacrity. As the chains were unhooked and dropped each pair of cattle would rush for the water and very soon all the stock was standing knee deep in the edge of the river, taking down long drawn swallows, and as their parched gullets began to cool off their great brown eyes would take on a softer expression and when they could hold no more, deep sighs of satisfaction told a tale of appeased thirst that was very pleasant to witness. We were soon in marching order again and made an early camp where a small brook of icy coldness and crystal clearness came down through a lovely bit of meadow land. We called it "Crystal brook." The youngsters soon discovered that our camp was surrounded by acres of crisp, large wild onions and that tender, pepperry water cresses grew in the brook. But the most important discovery was that schools of "Red horse," a specie of sucker, were laying in the deeper holes along the brook above camp. This discovery was made while gathering dead willows for camp wood. A few gunny sacks were hastily ripped open and the deft fingers of the women soon converted them into a respectable fish seine. It did not take long, with this improvised net, to capture as many of these delicious fish as the entire outfit could use while they could be kept fresh. Sharp knives in willing hands made short work of scaling, cleaning and preparing our catch for the frying pan: fires were kindled and ere long the savory odors of frying fish and boiling coffee mingled with the scent that came from our dutch ovens where the bread was baking, as the lids would be lifted from time to time to inspect the loaves and test the degree of doneness by running a sliver into them or tapping on the crust with the fingers, or both. An arduous day's toil had whetted our appetites to razor keenness and that night we ate by firelight out on the edge of the great plains, a repast that the gods might well envy. After supper pipes were filled with fragrant tobacco and lighted, our night herders rode forth into the dusk to guard our precious stock until summoned the next morning to breakfast and a day's sleep and rest in the wagons.

Rolls of blankets were tumbled out of wagons. The youngsters played hide and go seek in and out of the fitful shawows of tents and wagons and while the beds were being made down a flute and a violin were brought forth and sweet strains of music were wafted out over the great prairie by the gentle night zephrs. We were all glad to be there.

The fires burned out, our wayfarers crawled between the blankets and were soon in dreamland. The quavering treble of the prowling coyote, the hoot of the prairie owl and an occasional snore from some tired sleeper were the only sounds that broke the stillness of the starlight night.

Perry's recollections as a whole shed light on the more mundane day-to-day activities and experiences of the hopeful prospectors and their families, but the astute reader will also realize how much detail each story provides in terms of the gold rush experience in general.

The Things They Carried

Most miners tried to outfit themselves and their caravans with six months' worth of provisions. These they had to keep dry and protected while hauling them over hundreds—sometimes thousands—of miles. In addition to mining implements, professional outfitters of the day suggested that a party of four carry, among other things,

- 1,000 pounds of flour
- 400 pounds of bacon
- 20 blankets
- 6 pounds of nails
- 25 pounds of soap
- 24 boxes of matches
- Coffee mill

*According to 1859 guidebooks

For those traveling west through Kansas Territory, Plattsmouth, Nebraska—which Perry mentions in the previous story—was the last "safe" camp before entering the truly wild frontier. Once Plattsmouth was behind the adventurers, what lay ahead of them was the unknown, inhabited by Native Americans both friendly and unwelcoming.

At the time of the Pikes Peak Gold Rush, six different Native American groups resided in the area that is now Colorado: Apache nation, Arapaho nation, Cheyenne nation, Pueblo tribes, Shoshone tribe, and Ute nation. The Comanche, Kiowa, and Navajo tribes also sometimes extended into the region.

These nations and tribes were constantly at war with one another, but relations between white prospectors and Native Americans were surprisingly peaceful in the early phase of the gold rush, even as travel increased along the South Platte River.

That changed as Native Americans incorporated horses into their culture. The impact this animal had on indigenous cultures cannot be overstated. Horses were trained and fully integrated into Native American culture, and their inclusion allowed tribes and nations to expand their territories while waging more efficient warfare on one another and, eventually, on white settlers who were encroaching upon their land.

Another facet of the culture clash involving whites and the Plains Indians was the variance in priorities among the subgroups of those who lived on the Plains. In addition to Native Americans and gold seekers, the Plains were home to farmers, merchants, ranchers, and freighters. Each had their own way of life and goals, and they were often in direct conflict with the way of life and goals of the others. As the gold rush progressed, so did the determination of each subculture not to lose itself in the big picture. In this way, the Colorado Gold Rush impacted the history of the American West to a degree nothing else ever had or has since.

Perry Burgess had to have known of the dangers inherent in the trek from Illinois to Kansas Territory. After all, not only had he grown up on the stories told to him by his stepfather, Ben White; he himself had spent the earliest years of his childhood en route to Utah, with several stops along the way. This was a boy whose most formative years were molded by persecution, violence, and the instability that comes with a life spent as a refugee. Perry was no stranger to hardship or challenge, and participating in the Colorado Gold Rush combined both.

His next article reflects just such challenge, namely a battle against an unspecified tribe of Native Americans. Close reading suggests they were Pawnee, as another group that Perry's caravan later comes upon—the Sioux nation—was out rounding up the aggressive Pawnee renegades. The Sioux took their peace treaty with white settlers seriously.

An Exciting Time

A Sharp Skirmish With Indians and a Rescue.

There was not a breech loading fire arm in our train, but there were several muzzle loading rifles and some good shots among the men. In those days nearly every American citizen who did not reside in a city prided himself on keeping a good rifle and knowing how to use it. The plains Indians were armed principally with bows and arrows, spears and knives. Very few of them could boast of owning guns and what few they did possess were smooth bore or some antiquated pattern. A mere handful of resolute, cool headed white men could hold ten or twenty times their number of Indians at bay and out of rifle range. Our captain dashed ahead and was soon in the very teeth of the redskins, who were loth to abandon their apparently easy prey and the sight of the rapidly approaching squad of men from our train did not serve to check them. Our captain was seen to suddenly check his horse, raise his big rifle to his eye, a jet of smoke shoot from its muzzle and an Indian threw up his arms and went backwards off his pony. In anticipation of an easy conquest the Indians had not lashed themselves to their ponies as is their custom when a hard battle is expected.

Not being in position to reload, our captain threw down his now empty rifle, dropped his hat to mark the spot and one of his navy revolvers, of which he carried a pair at the pommel of his saddle, was seen to flash in the sunlight as he jerked it from the scabbard. By this time the wagon had met him and the two half grown boys, who at the first alarm had abandoned the loose stock to their fate, had rode past him in the direction of our train and safety. By the time the squad of our men had reached the captain and with a yell charged the redskins, who fell back like a pack of coyotes, and scattered out as they retreated to divert the attention of the white men, who dismounted and while two held all the horses the balance used their rifles with the effect of killing one more Indian and two ponies. The Indians shot arrows as fast as they could until out of shooting distance, but entirely without effect. By this time the fleeing emigrants and the two boys had nearly reached us, as the mules were not allowed for one moment to slacken their speed.

Just then we hear a yell from our men, saw them mount their horses and dash ahead to head off four of five Indians who were making for a place in the road near where the emigrant wagon had first turned about. Our men rode like mad and a few shots turned the Indians. We saw one of our men dismount when the place was reached and lift a bundle off the ground and give it to the captain. Just then the women in the wagon gave a yell that might have raised the dead, and began screaming and wringing her hands, saying: "Mein Gott! Mein Gott! Oo, mein boor leetle Mary. The Indians haf got mein leetle Mary!" She jumped from the wagon and started to run back in search of the lost one, but one of her wooden shoes flew off, which retarded her flight sufficiently to enable some of the men from the train to catch and detain her pending an investigation. The little one was certainly missing and proved to be the bundle the men had driven the Indians from, that we had seen them pick up. It proved to be a flaxen haired, chubby little miss of four summers. It seems that as the wagon was turned around the mules lashed into a gallop, that she had been seated at the hind end of the wagon. She saw the Indians and, young as she was, realized the danger and was watching the devils when the wagon struck a bump and gave a jolt which bounced her out. She said she was not hurt but was "fraid" and lay still waiting for "fader" to come and take her. The eagle eye of our captain detected her at the same time the Indians did, and with his men rescued her as above seen. During the brief and to us and ours, bloodless battle, it was hard to think that the balance could not lend a helping hand, but our captain said we might have a chance to do a little fighting later on.

We were soon over the flurry and strung out in marching order again. As we passed the battle field a halt was made and all hands viewed the bodies of the two dead braves, and a few arrows were picked up. The bows, arrows and knives of the defunct braves were also taken to send back to some meuseum in the east and the dead warriors left for the coyotes and turkey buzzards, provided their comrades did not come after the bodies after we had got out of sight.

The rescued party proved to be a middle age German, his wife and three lusty children. The man and his wife talked very brokenly, but the children spoke English quite plainly.

The man said, "Ve vas go mit Bikes Beak und tig goold und makes putter und cheeses for dem beeples." They took their rescue and the episode which had come so near ending their earthly journey as a matter of fact, but we could not know from their stolid, undemonstrative manner what might have been passing in their minds nor how grateful they might be in their hearts for their timely deliverance.

As the train was taking its nooning that day some objects were seen across the river. The spy glass revealed them to be mounted Indians with pack animals. It took them some time to find a fording place and cross to our side. When across they rode slowly toward us, one at some distance in advance, who, as he got within speaking distance, showed a white cloth and said "How?" Our captain walked out to meet him and while a short parley was being held the two other Indians with the pack animals waited.

Soon the leader gave a signal for them to ride up and they all come into camp. This Indian, who had an unpronouncable name which our captain said meant Swift Antelope, said he was a sub chief of the Sioux tribe. That a large party of them were camped on the Niobrara river, "three sleeps" north.

A lot of the young braves, getting impatient of enforced idleness, the season for buffalo hunting not having arrived, had obtained permission from the head chief to go out and scout and see how many Pawnees they could kill; that the chief had information that they were practicing their deviltry on emigrants and this sub-chief had been sent out to round up and bring back the renegades, who would be punished for any violation

Sioux Chief Running Antelope

of the peace which the head chief wished to maintain toward the whites at the time.

While our callers remained their five ponies were turned loose to rest and graze. The men were made acquainted with the details of the morning's skirmish and treated to a good square meal and then the pipe of peace was filled, lighted and smoked and saddling and mounting their ponies our copper colored friends said good bye and rode on a gallop toward the bluffs, in the direction we had seen the hostiles ride after the fight.

Perry's next article mentions Fort Cottonwood in Nebraska. Fort Cottonwood (eventually renamed Fort McPherson) was situated near a high hill that overlooked a migratory route used by Pawnee and Sioux. The initial purpose of the fort was to escort stagecoaches and immigrant wagon trains across that portion of the Overland Trail between Fort Kearny and Julesburg.

Julesburg, Colorado, was itself a key location for nearly every hopeful prospector because of its location near the junction of several overland routes. Established in 1859 as a trading post and stage station, it was transformed into an important transportation and military center during the following decade. The original Julesburg settlement was destroyed by a fire set by Sioux and Cheyenne in January 1865.

At Fort Cottonwood

What Our Band of Pilgrims are Seeing and Doing.

The only weapons our German proteges had was a small single barreled fowling piece, which the man said he had brought to kill "vild shichens mit," and that it "was no goot to gill beefle oxens nor Indians mit." We made a short drive that afternoon and an early camp and that night, seated around a cheerful camp fire, as some song that carried home sentiments was rendered by our quartette, accompanied by flute and violin, our German friend was seen to take his "'two story" pipe from his lips, look around the snug circle of wagons, then gaze fondly at wife and children and some large tears were seen to moisten his cheeks which were hastily brushed aside as if ashamed of this evidence of weakness. But as the [music] subsided he said to his wife in a voice husky with emotion: "I vas so glad dot ve is all togadder." He was evidently thinking of his little flaxen haired Mary and the narrow escape the child had from being a captive.

Two more uneventful days passed and we laid over a day to rest, shoe cattle, secure a new supply of fresh meat and some fire wood. Our camp this time was perhaps a mile from the hills, on which scattering cedars could be seen. We were near Fort Cottonwood and a detail or squad of soldiers in charge of a sergeant rode out to give us orders not to graze our stock within two miles of the post and to forbid us selling the soldiers any whisky on penalty of having it all emptied out and we detained and heavily fined. Our captain politely thanked the officer and curtly informed him that we were not peddling whiskey, but claimed the right to graze our stock where we saw fit, provided they were not allowed on the meadow land.

Toward night that day an outfit of dilapidated wagons, sorry looking, foot sore cattle and nine very untidy looking men passed us, going eastward. The leader said they had seen Pikes

Peak; been close to it but had seen no gold; that none was being mined and that people there were near starvation. He gave the country a terrible berating and said he was going back to the States, where they raised something to eat and advised us to turn about and return home also.

Our captain said that he thought we had better push ahead and see what was to be seen, as it was just possible that our friends had not had time to explore the whole mountain region or had been misinformed regarding the gold. The greasy, long haired party who acted as chief spokesman of the homeward bound outfit seemed to feel miffed at what our captain had said, and berated us for being bull headed idiots who would not be guided by friendly advice nor believe "Gods truths" when they were told us, and ended his tirade by offering to trade jerked buffalo meat for whisky. This offer being refused, we were told in language more forcible than elegant that they had no use for temperance people where we were going; we could not appreciate the pleasure of traveling with plenty of whisky to stimulate bravery and good fellowship.

Our captain in reply pointed to their skinny, foot sore oxen and suggested, very mildly, that a few day's rest on good feed and some shoes on the tired, worn feet would be a more humane and lasting stimulant to the cattle than the brutal rawhide whiplashes in the hands of whisky and tobacco saturated drivers. This was the cap sheaf, so to speak, and with a parting wish that starvation and other dire calamities might overtake us, they passed and continued their homeward journey.

That morning six of our best shots had gone into the hills to hunt for meat and about the same number had taken axes and a yoke of cattle, with log chains to snake the wood into camp, and gone into the hills after cedar logs. The captain and our blacksmith went to cattle shoeing, with plenty of willing hands to assist in throwing and holding down the animals while the operation was being performed. The stock were herded near the train and the tender footed ones driven into the corral for shoeing and released and turned out with the herd after their feet had received attention.

By noon three snake loads of nice cedar logs had been brought into camp, which was an abundant supply for present needs.

We still continue to keep the night watch at the camp, and each night a sort of breast work is improvised by placing the ox bows two deep around the corral, just inside the circle of wagons.

We travel in sight of bison nearly every day, but as our supply of dried meat still holds out we have not attempted to kill any more.

Our hunting party that set out this morning returned about the middle of the afternoon with the carcasses of two fine white tailed deer and one antelope. Fishing was tried during the day, but with poor success.

The Platte is rising thers days, which means that the snow is melting off the mountains that are yet so many weary miles ahead.

An outfit of three wagons, containing two lawyers and a doctor, with their small families, who are going to the new Eldorado with a view to locating permanently, and who have been detained at the post waiting for reenforcements to make travel more secure, applied this afternoon for permission to join our caravan. They were admitted, and from present appearances will prove a valuable acquisition, socially and otherwise.

Disregarding nationality, being united by common interests and universal brotherhood, and at home wherever night would overtake us, we are a cosmopolitan crowd. We all felt that great possibilities were ahead of us and resolved to make the most of our opportunities.

Our doctor took occasion to overhaul his case of instruments and repack them, and the glittering array of polished steel caused the shivers to creep unpleasantly along the regions of one's spinal column and a fervent hope that none of us would need to have their keenness tried, upon any of our crowd at least.

Perry's next surviving article reflects the level of hope that inspired thousands upon thousands of people to leave the safety and familiarity of their homes in search of gold. After months of marching over vast, endless prairies filled with danger and suffering from uncontrollable factors such as weather and sickness, these weary travelers must have been buoyed by the success stories of those returning from their own adventures.

The overall reality of the gold rush was less heartening, as relatively few prospectors ever found substantial amounts of gold. The mills they built simply were not able to recover gold from the deeper sulfide ores. This problem and the search for its solution led to two of the most prosperous industries in the state of Colorado: gold and silver mining.

Stories of Gold

Returning Emmigrants Tell Stories of the Promised Land.

Another week slipped into the mighty past without anything out of the common happening.

The mock lawsuits which had furnished us with so much instructive amusement had given way to a series of debates in which all hands participated, and it was astonishing how much seemingly forgotten lore, on the various subjects debated upon, our fellow travelers would rake up and drag from the musty vaults of memory. Some of the speeches were of a depth and brilliancy that would have done credit to people who made pretentions to eloquence and scholarly ability. It proved that it will not always do to judge of a man's mental strength or scholarly attainments by the garb he wears; that it is possible for blue denims overalls and jumper and a much worse-for-wear slouch hat to cover a body that contained an intellect that would shine like a star in any social position.

Little flaxen haired, blue eyed Mary was the pet of the entire train. From the day of her rescue our captain had called her

"Dottie," and now all called her that, and not one of our crowd of bearded men but would have laid down his life if necessary to protect her from danger.

A tough looking crew we had become by this time, yet these uncouth exteriors covered spirits as brave as a lion's and as gentle as a dove's; spirits that would give no occasion to insult and woe to the mistaken wight who would offer one. An humble apology or a fight would have been the inevitable result.

We laid over one day each week, or usually every fourth or fifth day, to shoe foot sore stock, make repairs, rest and secure fresh game and fish, and these days always seemed like holidays. They are yet pleasant to call up from memory's storehouse. We had seen no more Indians nor encountered any more bison stampedes, but the second "lay over" day after the stampede mentioned in the preceding chapter, we beheld a sight which quickened our pulses and entirely banished the slight gloom which was caused by meeting that returning outfit which gave the Pike's Peak country such a black eye, as they passed us some days' journey back.

It was this. We encountered another returning party in spring wagons and on horseback, and made our noon camp with them. They were returning to the states to close up business there and bring back families and friends to the "land of promise," as they called the Pike's Peak country. These men had been one year in the new Eldorado and being rustlers, not whiskey soaked idlers, had won yellow wealth from the bosom of mother earth. They carried the precious dust in well sewed bags of buckskin and expibited several thousand dollars' worth which was intended for shipment to the U.S. mint as soon as the party should reach some point on the railroad. The sight was good to look upon, especially as we realized that one dollar in gold was, at that time, equal to two dollars in greenbacks. Not worth two to one, but the shylocks who at the time had Uncle Sam by the throat would, in order to maintain their deadly grip, exchange upon that basis.

Some of the returning party had operated that summer in Clear

Creek canon and some in Gregory gulch, where Central City now stands. In addition to the small bags of gold dust, some pieces of which would equal a grain of corn in size they showed us some rich specimens of quartz in which wire and specks of native gold could be plainly seen, also specimens of pyritous ores and many beautiful quartz crystals which looked to us like glass in different colors.   One man of the party had a small bottle full of garnets, which he called rubies, that he was taking to his wife. From them we learned that no one need starve or even go hungry if willing to work. That nature had provided many wild fruits and berries, that the creeks and rivers teemed with the most delicious fish and the woods were full of deer, elk and fat bear and numberless land and water fowl were to be had for the small trouble of shooting them. Agriculture had not yet been tried, but one man of the party said he could see no reason why many of the valleys should not produce abundant crops, as the soil, climate and water was all that could be desired. He intended coming back as soon as possible with grain and garden seeds and impliments to try to experiment. Another was going to bring herd of cows with appliances for running a dairy, while others were to bring a stamp mill, saw and shingle machinery, etc. The entire party were eager to return and most of them planned to come back yet that season. One of the men remarked that he had more wealth in gold dust than his home and all its belongings were worth and his claim was not a quarter worked out. He said if he could not sell out in the states he would give his home and farm to his poor relations, take his wife and children and get back to his mine as soon as possible.

This brief visit cheered our hearts as we had seen, actually seen, and handled enough gold to make several people well to-do, and when we parted company and again took up our line of march along that dusty highway, it was with lighter hearts and a firmer resolve to persevere than we had heretofore experienced.

The last known surviving recollection of Perry's Colorado Gold Rush experience is aptly titled "Denver at Last." The events he speaks of took place in 1860, a scant two years after the "Denver City" was developed as a mining camp following the discovery of gold. Its founders named it after James Denver, governor of Kansas Territory.

Denver City was a typical frontier town whose location was easily accessible to existing trails. As thousands of prospectors migrated to the region, the town's population increased rapidly. Winters were especially profitable for Denver City, as gold seekers could not navigate the deep snows in the mountains and so had to wait out the cold months somewhere. Since the economy was focused on serving miners, it relied upon gambling, saloons, trading, and livestock.

Denver City was incorporated on November 6, 1861. In 1865, it became the territorial capital and officially shortened its name. Eleven years later, it became the state capital as Colorado was admitted to the Union.

Denver at Last

The Eventful Journey Across the Plains is Brought to a Close.

For a week the weather continued to be very pleasant. About 10 o'clock each forenoon a refreshing breeze would set in from the northwest which seemed to carry with it the properties of health and vigor, which made us glad that we were alive. Sleep was so refreshing and our victuals tasted so good that it was a pleasure as well as a duty to nature to eat, and it was truly astonishing how much grub we could stow away at each meal and suffer no pangs of indigestion.

Each time we had a glimpse of the solemn blue ridge ahead of us it seemed a little nearer and a little clearer cut against the blue sky beyond. At the end of the week we again made a lay-over camp in plain view of it, but by this time we could make out by the aid of the captain's glass the unmelted snow fields, grand stretches of forest and canons deep and gloomy. Yet it all seemed so silent that it was hard to realize that we were not looking at some mighty painting or an illusion instead of a solid fact. Later on, when the tints of autumn had dressed the slopes like Joseph of old, in a "coat of many colors," and we had listened to the "whistle" of a bull elk and startled the solitudes of the primeval forest with the report of our rifles, had toiled up rugged slopes with pick, pan and shovel, a pair of blankets and a little "grub" on our backs, some of us began to realize that the Rocky Mountains were not a myth, but a stupendous reality.

This day, while busy with our cattle shoeing and making repairs, another returning party came along and camped with us. This party also brought good reports, and like the other outfit were going back to the states to sell out, wind up business affairs and return to the mountains. They pointed out to our eager eyes Pike's Peak, Long's Peak, Fremont and Gray's Peaks, the canons of the South Platte and Arkansaw rivers, and the places where Clear, Boulder, St. Vrain and Cache la Poudre creeks came down and emptied into the valley. They gave a more minute description of the various localities where gold and silver had been found, the various processes then known by which the yellow metal was extracted from the gravel and sand and ledges of gold bearing rock. Like their predecessors, they exhibited buckskin bags full of gold dust and rare specimens of gold bearing quartz, and when they finally rolled on and left us, it was with fervent hand shakings and many heart felt wishes, on both sides expressed, of a safe journey and the smiles of Dame Fortune. When we resumed our journey the next day it was with lighter hearts and a firmer determination to win. The hardships thus far met and conquered seemed trivial to us now, mere unpleasant incidents in some dream of long ago.

At the end of another week the mountains seemed to lie almost within speaking distance, yet no sounds came to us from the mysterious solitudes, which we were so soon to find throbbing with life and musical with nature's voices. From this camp we had a first view of sunshine and shadows chasing each other across the tilted up landscape. Storm clouds, blue sky and grand peaks so mixed together that at times it was difficult to separate the solid substances from the evanescent or flitting.

This was to be our last day to lie over for rest and repairs. We knew that we would soon be scattered, some going to one camp and some to another, and decided to celebrate the day in a manner that we could look back to with pleasure. Our hunters left camp early in the morning and returned before noon with an abundant supply of meat.

Stunted red cedars from the banks of an arroyo not far from camp supplied us with abundant fuel, and a little after noon one of the antelope that the hunters had brought in was being barbecued. The contents of the wagons were delved into, each furnishing some toothsome edible which was added to the catalogue of viands, and which under the manipulation of the deft fingers of the ladies of the party, were, as the afternoon wore to a close, skillfully arranged in tempting order for the evening repast. All this made us anxious to see "Gld Sol" sink to rest behind the shadowy ridge ahead, and just as night let down the first dusky curtain and the first note of the coyote quavered out on the evening air we, with brightly blazing camp fires, sat down to a repast that any epicure might envy.

After supper the short evening hours were passed with music of flute and violin and a few songs rendered by the quartette and then slumber sealed our eyelids and our camp was silent.

Three days later we rolled into the village of Denver which at the time did not give promise of so soon becoming a railroad center, a western metropolis and the "Queen City of the Plains."

It is hard to realize that the then embryo has in a brief thirty seven years grown to such mighty proportions and is still growing so much in importance.

We must now leave our pilgrim band and scatter out, each for himself, as such expeditions invariably do, and crave permission to skip over a period of six years, drop back to the old California and Salt Lake crossing of the South Platte near old Fort Julesburg and conduct a similar expedition northward into Montana. The experiences of this expedition will be of a more tragic nature than those we have just finished relating.

And with that Perry leaves Colorado and jumps ahead six years, to 1866 and another gold rush adventure, this time along the Bozeman Trail to Montana. It would prove to be a more violent historical event and one with far-reaching, catastrophic consequences beyond what anyone of the era could have imagined.

Denver, Colorado 1859

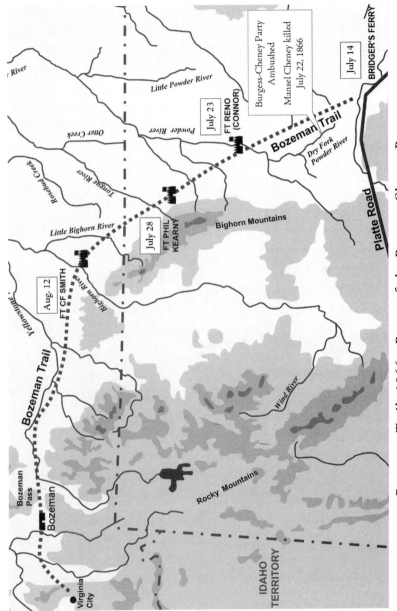

Bozeman Trail, 1866 - Route of the Burgess-Cheney Party

CHAPTER 7
'Bloody Bozeman' Trail
Perry's Montana Diaries & Recollections

On May 26, 1863, gold was discovered in Montana Territory at Alder Creek[1] in Virginia City. As had happened in Colorado and then in Idaho, thousands of hopeful prospectors trekked across the country to find their fortune. One of those hopefuls was Perry Burgess.

Perry began his journey on March 29, 1866, just a few months prior to his twenty-third birthday. Earlier historical references to Perry's gold rush activities indicate that his participation in the Colorado Gold Rush was unknown, yet by this time, he was an experienced—albeit young—Western adventurer.

He hired out to his uncle Mansel Cheney for $25 a month, and left Lena, Illinois, with Mansel, his aunt Paulina, and their three children, Franklin, George, and Mary. From there they crossed the Mississippi River and picked up Mansel's brother Lyman in Sabula, Iowa. Taking two wagons across Iowa, the group crossed the Missouri River into Plattsmouth (Nebraska Territory). There they were joined by another brother, Lewis, his brothers-in-law William G. Blair and Lucien Rogers, and William Blair, cousin of William G. At that point, Mansel and Lewis became business partners and bought 300 head of cattle to join the wagon train. Lewis Cheney began the journey with $10,000 in cash.

In addition to these family members, the following people were recorded as being part of the Burgess-Cheney party:

- Harry Bliss
- "Texas"
- Patterson
- Charlie
- Rudolph

- 9 unnamed drivers/teamsters

- James McGarry, a resident of Jo Daviess Co., Ill. Hired July 28, 1866 by Lewis Cheney at Fort Phil Kearny.

- Thomas McGarry, brother of James, also a resident of Jo Daviess County, Ill., and hired July 28, 1866.

- Lewis Baker, hired along with the McGarry brothers at Fort Phil Kearny.

- Jim Bridger, famous Western adventurer, traveled briefly with the Burgess train.

Perry's group, the Burgess-Cheney train, was led by his uncle Mansel Cheney. A seasoned pioneer, Mansel was the only man in the group to be joined by his wife, Paulina White Cheney, the sister of Perry's stepfather, Dr. Ben White. Beyond his experiences in the Mormon exodus and the California Gold Rush, Mansel and his family had been living in Plattsmouth, Nebraska Territory, as early as 1860, and at Fort Kearney, Nebraska Territory, in September 1864. Mansel and his brothers were experienced in Indian ways and, like the Burgesses, possessed a great deal of confidence when traveling the American West. Furthermore, Paulina was as much a pioneer as her brother Ben, who had spent several years with the Cheney brothers in California.

The Mysterious Frederick Burgess

It is interesting to note that while in Plattsmouth, Perry met up with yet another uncle, Frederick Burgess. His diary reports he had not seen Frederick in twenty-one years, since around the time that Perry's father, Abraham, had died. Other than this diary entry, there is no indication that anyone in the Burgess family ever saw Frederick again, nor is there any record of what became of him. It is quite possible that, like the Cheneys, Frederick struggled with the issue of polygamy within the Mormon Church. Although his brother Harrison and other Saints willingly took on additional wives, Frederick may have been uncomfortable with the practice, enough so that he left the Church and the family behind.

The Burgess-Cheney train was representative of most other trains that traveled the Bozeman Trail. Because few diaries and journals were kept and even fewer still exist—twenty-four are known to historians today—there is no way to know precisely how many women and children made the westward journey on that route. According to historian Susan Badger Doyle, available figures estimate that 20 percent of Bozeman emigrants were women and children.[2]

The members of Perry's party enjoyed close and easy relations, a blessing when people are traveling a great distance together. That said, the train was like other larger trains along the trail in that it frequently broke apart, with smaller groups traveling at different paces. The Cheney party, for instance, was slower than Perry's group because the Cheneys were migrating with 300 head of cattle. Sometimes a few days would separate the groups, but they would eventually catch up to one another at various forts along the Bozeman.

The Bozeman Trail was just one of many overland gold rush trails. When gold was discovered in Montana in 1863, there were only two routes leading to that territory. One followed the Missouri River north before turning west and then south. The other took its followers into what is now western Wyoming and then north through present-day Idaho.

Former prospector John Bozeman and pioneer John Jacobs knew that a more direct route was possible, and traced their trail from western Montana east, past the Bighorn Mountains, where it turned south. At just 500 miles or so, it basically served as a shortcut connecting the Oregon Trail to the gold fields of Montana.

Travel along this corridor established by Bozeman and Jacobs wasn't new. Native Americans had been following the north–south trails through Powder River country since prehistoric times. Explorers, trappers, and traders were also familiar with the trails. What Bozeman and Jacobs did that no one before them had done was to establish a route that was accessible by wagon. Once that goal was achieved, they promoted travel along the trail—which was actually a system of trails—and suddenly the American public at large was made aware of what had been under their noses all along. As for the actual scouting of the trail, Bozeman did very little of that himself. For most of the route, he was guided by local traders or followed other wagon trains.

The Bozeman Trail was used primarily from 1863 to 1866 by those participating in the Montana Gold Rush. It was not used by many; most historical accounts agree that only about 3,500 pioneers traveled this route. What made it better than other overland trails was the fact that most of it provided enough water, grass, and timber. What made it more dangerous than any other trail was the fact that it cut directly through Powder River Basin, the last—and by far the best—hunting grounds of the Northern Plains Indians, primarily Sioux, Cheyenne, and Arapaho.

For this reason alone, the Bozeman Trail—a seemingly insignificant, relatively minor route—did more to change the course of the history of the American West than did any element or event leading up to its establishment.

Bozeman and Jacobs understood the sacredness of the Powder River Basin to the Northern Plains Indians. Bounded on the east by the Black Hills, on the south by the North Platte River, on the west by the Bighorn Mountains, and on the north by the Yellowstone River, the Powder River Basin was a valley rife with bison. Before the Bozeman Trail was even established, the Native Americans noticed a depletion in the abundance of available game as more emigrants traveled the Oregon Trail. To have another route cut a swathe directly through their hunting grounds guaranteed dire consequences.

Just What *Is* the Bozeman Trail?

The Bozeman Trail, commonly nicknamed the "Bloody Bozeman," has a reputation of rather mythical proportions. While it was indeed a more violent route than other overland trails used during the gold rush era, many who followed it did so safely and without tragedy. Regardless of this fact, the Bozeman Trail's legacy is one in which wagon trains carrying white pioneers are encircled by warring Indians on horseback wielding tomahawks and muskets.

A north–south shortcut to the gold fields of Montana, the Bozeman Trail is actually a system of smaller trails that sometimes joins in places and at other times veers miles away from one another. The Bozeman stemmed from the Oregon Trail in central Wyoming, skirted the Bighorn Mountains, crossed a number of rivers including the North Platte, the Powder, and the Bighorn, and then followed a course of mountainous terrain into western Montana.

Eager to show emigrants their newfound shortcut, Bozeman and Jacobs ignored warnings that tribes north of the North Platte River would not be welcoming. On July 6, 1863, the partners, a train of emigrants, and a guide named Rafael Gallegos left Deer Creek Station on the North Platte River and headed north.

The first 140 miles were uneventful. As the travelers reached what is today Buffalo, Wyoming, they were approached by a large band of Native Americans who threatened to destroy the train if it continued on its journey. The emigrants turned around and headed back toward Deer Creek.

After retreating fifty miles or so, Gallegos and two men left the train for the military post at Deer Creek, where they unsuccessfully requested military reinforcements to accompany them on their expedition. Upon hearing that they had been denied assistance, Bozeman took nine men and journeyed through the mountains on horseback. They arrived ahead of the rest of the train, which had taken a circuitous route to the main overland road.

Although this incident may not seem like much given the violence that often accompanied a pioneer–Native American confrontation in the mid-1800s, it was, in fact, a foreshadowing of things to come. Had the prospectors been provided military backup, their strength would have allowed them to fight the Indians. Had that happened, the Plains Indian Wars in the north might have begun that day. Instead, the confrontation raised awareness among the tribes: Emigrants were headed their way in droves, and something had to be done to stop them.

Tensions mounted as emigrant trains successfully traveled to Montana using the Bozeman Trail. There was no turning back now, as the opening of the new route initiated conflict between the federal government and the Northern Plains Indians. Had expansionism not been on the agenda of the federal government, the military presence along the route might have remained nothing more than a safety precaution. As it was, the government recognized their problematic relations with the Indians as an opportunity to take possession of the Northern Plains, and what ensued was an all-out war.

Altogether, approximately 1,500 prospectors with their families and teams crossed into Montana via the Bozeman Trail in 1864. Most contact between pioneers and Indians was peaceful. The brutal Sand Creek Massacre in November drastically changed relations between the federal government and the Native Americans, and the Cheyenne and Arapaho tribes in the south moved north in early spring 1864. There they formed an alliance with noted warriors of the Upper Platte Sioux and the Northern Cheyenne and assembled in the Powder River Basin. Attitudes had changed after the military's unprovoked attack on the Southern Cheyenne camping along Sand Creek in Kiowa County, Colorado, which resulted in the deaths and mutilations of around 133 Indians, 105 of them women and children. The Indians were no longer interested in developing a relationship with white settlers; they were determined to defend themselves and their way of life.

As fear of Indian attack escalated in early 1865, the government closed the Bozeman Trail to emigrant traffic. During this time, the military took action designed to put an end to Indian raids. That summer, Brigadier General Patrick Connor led his troops on what can only be described as a hunting party. His purpose was to destroy any Indians who had been known to attack, while scaring the others into submission. Along the way, he planned to construct two military posts.

Connor didn't bother to determine which tribes were aggressive and which were peaceful, however. He massacred the first Indian village he found, which belonged to the Northern Arapaho. The fact that these peace-loving Indians were not part of the conflict didn't matter to Connor.

While he was leaving a trail of destruction in his wake, another government-led campaign was going on. A civilian party led by James Sawyers was in the Bozeman Trail region with instructions to survey the land and build roads along much of the trail. Miscommunication put the Sawyers party right in the middle of Connor's expedition, and the civilians were forced to fend off an Indian attack that was drawn out for thirteen days. Casualties occurred on all three sides. And though Sawyers declared his expedition a success, his party never did build any roads.

What the battle between the military, the civilians, and the Indians did do was to strengthen the government's resolve to protect emigrants along the Bozeman Trail. With the trail re-opened and spring in the air, emigrant travel along the trail was about to increase as 1866 progressed. While the U.S. government was holding council with the Lakota (Sioux) and Northern Cheyenne at Fort Laramie in an effort to agree on some kind of win-win policy for allowing emigrants to pass through Powder River country, Colonel Henry B. Carrington showed up at the fort with orders to construct military posts along the Bozeman Trail in that region. Red Cloud, a respected Lakota chief attending the negotiations, was outraged that the government would bring in troops to establish a military presence before the Lakota had even agreed to such action. He and his tribesmen left the meeting without ever signing a treaty and with the promise of resistance to emigration. A series of conflicts between the Indians and the government, given the name Red Cloud's War by the U.S. Army, took place from 1866 to 1867. A peace treaty was signed in 1868.

Altogether, the government built three army posts along the Bozeman Trail. The first of these, Fort Connor, later renamed Fort Reno, had been established August 14, 1865, on the banks of the Powder River, near the mouth of Dry Fork Creek. Next came Fort Phil Kearny, which was built on July 13, 1866, near the confluence of the Little Piney and Big Piney Creeks of the Powder River. The last fort, Fort C. F. Smith, was established on August 12, 1866, on the south side of the Bighorn River.

These forts were tantamount to dares for the Northern Plains Indians. By mid-July, the increased military occupation of the trail only strengthened the Indians' determination to prevent pioneers from traveling the Bozeman Trail. Within one week, Indians stepped up their attacks and took the lives of more than two dozen civilians and soldiers. Many more were left wounded.

On July 22, 1866, the Burgess train was the first in a succession of trains when it was ambushed by a party of nine Sioux warriors. It was a prime target, as the wagons of this particular train had scattered, leaving each vulnerable to attack. Worse yet, Mansel and Lewis Cheney had separated from the trains, riding in front of Perry and the boys who were herding cattle. After pretending to be friendly, one of the warriors pulled a pistol from underneath his blanket, and at the age of thirty-two years and four days, Mansel was shot and killed. He left behind his wife Paulina, two young sons, and a daughter. Unknown to anyone in the party—including Mansel and, quite possibly, Paulina—his beloved wife was carrying another child at the time of her husband's murder. Mansel Jr. would be born February 5, 1867, in the

Mansel Cheney Jr.
Born Feb. 5, 1867

Mary Cheney
Circa 1872

Children of Mansel and Paulina Cheney

Montana Territory. In a newspaper article of unknown origin written not long after the tragedy, it was reported that a ring bearing the name Cheney was taken from the body of a dead Indian. Although the ring was returned to the family, no living descendants possess the ring or know of its whereabouts.

The attack on the Burgess-Cheney party was included in the testimony of Colonel Carrington on August 29, 1866. Carrington's testimony was used in official investigations into the Fetterman Massacre at Fort Phil Kearny, one of the bigger conflicts of Red Cloud's War:

> There had been, during the latter part of July, and early in August, up to this date, few other Indian outrages, other than those already named. Mr. M.A. Nye, lost on July 22nd, while encamped near Fort Phil Kearney, four animals. Mr. A. Axe, and Mr. I. Dixon lost each respectively two mules the same date.
>
> On the same date the train of Louis Cheney was attacked at the "Dry Fork of the Cheyenne," and again at "Crazy Woman's Fork," by the Indians, though his train was fully armed, one man killed, horses, cattle and private property destroyed. During the same period there was lost at Fort Philip Kearney seventy head of Government stock.[3]

The rest of the trip to Montana was relatively uneventful for the Burgess-Cheney train. At Fort Phil Kearny, their smaller train had been ordered to join two other larger trains for the sake of safety. According to Perry's diary, they left the fort on August 2, 1866, with 110 wagons, 171 men, 6 women, and 5 children.

What follows here, and in the majority of Chapter 8, is a compilation of the 1866-68 Perry A. Burgess Bozeman Trail diaries and subsequent recollections related to the same time frame. This series of recollections was published in the *Steamboat Pilot* near the turn of the century. As mentioned in Chapter 6, numerous articles remain missing, while all known articles have been included in this work. The reader will find the diary entries interlaced with relevant recollections pertaining to the same events, each denoted by appropriate headings.

"We were told that they wished merely to pass through our country ... to seek for gold in the far west ... Yet before the ashes of the council fire are cold, the Great Father is building his forts among us. You have heard the sound of the white soldier's axe upon the Little Piney. His presence here is ... an insult to the spirits of our ancestors. Are we then to give up their sacred graves to be plowed for corn? Dakotas, I am for war."

Chief Red Cloud, 1866

The authors believe the diary entries provide an interesting outline of events, while the *Steamboat Pilot* essays enhance those accounts through greater attention to detail and a writing style honed over years of observation and experience.

- Recollection -

The Prospector

His Occupation is Not as Dangerous as it Used to Be.

Prospecting in these modern times in the Rocky Mountains, while retaining its old time interest of the love of gain, lacks the spice of danger which, in the early days, gave a peculiar charm and zest to the work. The what was once dangerous and fierce bears and mountain lions have been so nearly exterminated by the modern deadly breech loading rifle that the small remaining remnant have been cowed into a condition of almost abject timidity and are no longer considered as dangerous. "Poor Lo," our red-skinned brothers, have been taken from their former picturesque haunts and are now herded on reservations under guards of armed United States soldiers.

Thirty or more years ago it was different, and the prospector's peril has been graphically illustrated in verse by (we think) the immortal Joaquin Miller.

"A rough wild glen
As dry as bone,
Far from the haunts of men
And home;
The gnarled wood growth
Clings close to the cliff,
Sprouting or dying (or both)
And stiff.
"Tis a cheerless glow!
The chink of a pick

Comes up the rocks now and then,
But quick,
As it came from one
Who struck as he went,
In search of treasure in store,
Intent.
There's a man down there,
And up in the brush
An Indian glides, taking care
To crush
Not a single twig or sprout
'Neath his cat like foot,
But fixes his bow,
From his lookout
To shoot.
He twangs his bow,
And an angry thud
Tells where he draws, by his arrow,
The blood.
There's a grasp of the place in
 The blue faded shirt
And a fall of a pick and a face in
The dirt.
Then a shuffle and slide,
With a step ever light,
The swarthy face comes to the side
Of the white,
There's a clutch in the hair
And a skull laid bare,
And a wild war whoop on the mountain air.
And there,
Alone in the brush
And eternity's hush,
A prospector lies in his blood,
Dead."

"Why does'nt he write?"

It will never be known how many such ghastly tragedies have been enacted, witnessed only by the solemn peaks that towered in silent majesty above the red assassain and his victim. He never returned to the dear ones at home, and, as the days, weeks, months and years were added to time and no tidings reached the far away loved ones at the fireside, longings for his presence at home would give place to doubts, then despair, and finally he would be forgotten and the great busy world would move on the same as before.

Today no such danger threatens the gold hunter, and if he is careful to avoid accidents that are avoidable he is as safe in the woods as he would be in his own dooryard.

We are now in camp at Charley Franz's ranch near Greenville, where we expect in the future to do some prospecting and try to share with Charley and his brother the vast wealth that nature has deposited about their camp.

- Diary -

March 29, 1866 (March 29, 1866.) – The long looked for day having at length arrived, I picked up my dunnage and we viz. my uncle Mansel Cheney, his wife, three children and myself bid goodbye to our friends and started on our journey toward the land of gold. Not wishing to go through on my own hook, I have hired to Mansel for $25.00 per month the through trip to Montana. We start from home with two wagons, one pair of mules to each wagon. To-day we travel to the Mississippi River and stopped for the night at the town of Savannah. The road we traveled over to-day was very hilly, the day was warm and pleasant and the snow, which was six inches deep this morning has nearly all disappeared. At noon to-day I ate a large piece of cake and some apples which my dear, kind mother put in my pocket this morning. I think Savannah is a pretty hard place from the number of doggerys it supports. Distance travelled to-day 27 mi.

March 30, 1866 (Mar. 30.) – We intended to have crossed the Mississippi this morning; but the ice was running so that we could not get over until late in the afternoon, when we were set across to Sabula, Iowa. There we sent for Uncle Lyman Cheney who was superintending a job of chopping a few miles below town. He came late in the evening after I had retired and I did not see him until the next morning, when he made arrangements for joining us at Plattesmouth and going to Montana with us. It seems quite natural for me to make blunders for this morning while harnessing a span of mules I put one of the collars on wrong side to and could not for the life of me tell how the blamed thing was ' til some one modestly suggested the propriety of taking it off and putting it on right side to. We put up for the night at Sabula. Distance to-day 3 ½ miles.

March 31, 1866 (March 31, 1866.) – Hitched up and started on our journey this morning, crossed deep creek at Deep Creek Mills and stopped at Spragueville where lives Dr. Cheney, (Levi) to make him a farewell visit. In the evening I was playing on my violin for their amusement, a few of the young folks came and danced until

12 o'clock. The country over which we travelled to-day was very hilly, destitute of timber and tolerably well improved. The wind blew hard from the N.W. and although it thawed fast was very disagreeable riding. Distance to-day 15 mi.

Dr. Levi, Amelia, Samantha and Hattie Cheney (L-R), circa 1888
Samantha Cheney was named in honor of Perry's mother

Perry A. Burgess, circa 1870

April 1, 1866 (Apr. 1.) – Left Spragueville late in the forenoon and travelled to Mequoketa, put up for the night together with a number of fellow travellers and the evening passed pleasantly away in telling stories and adventures. Country poorly timbered, hilly and not very well improved, weather warm, cloudy and has the appearance of rain this evening. Distance 18 mi.

April 2, 1866 (Apr. 2.) – Rolled out from Mequoketa this morning and travelled to Monmouth. The country along our route was well timbered and watered and tolerably well improved, although hilly. We crossed several fine creeks to-day. The weather was warm, rain a little this morning but clear and pleasant afternoon with the exception of the roads which were very bad on account of the frost going out. Heard frogs croaking for the first time this year. Distance 12 mi. to-day.

April 3, 1866 (Apr. 3.) – Left Monmouth and went to Wyoming, a distance of 8 miles and took dinner with a couple of men who were going out into the western part of Iowa on a trapping expedition, who over took us and stopped for noon. After dinner we hitched up and traveled ten miles, put up for the night at a farm house. The day was pleasant with the exception of a little rain this morning, roads very bad and country, prairie some what rolling and improved. Distance to-day 18 mi.

April 4, 1866 (Apr. 4.) – Hitched up and travelled to Wyoming, passed through the fine, flourishing little city of Aromosa. The roads were very muddy and the country low, level and sandy. The weather was cloudy and uncomfortably cold for travelling. Wind N. W. Saw some men plowing to-day. Distance to-day 17 mi.

April 5, 1866 (Apr. 5.) – Passed through the beautiful town of Marion and also Valley City which is situated on the east side of Cedar river at Cedar Rapids. Country very sandy, the same drifted like snow, in some places around the fences. Crossed Cedar River at the Rapids, went three miles farther and put up for the night at a farm house. The country over which we passed to-day was well timbered, well watered, well improved and some hilly. The day was very cold, froze all day. Wind N. W. Distance travelled to-day 20 mi.

April 6, 1866 (Apr. 6.) – Travelled to-day over a fine prairie country, not much improved and poorly timbered. Put up three miles east of Marenge. Weather cold, wind N. W. Distance to-day 19 mi.

April 7, 1866 (Apr. 7) – Passed through Marenge, took a lunch by the way, afternoon went through Brooklin, crossed the Iowa River near Marenge. Country well timbered and watered, but poorly improved. Day beautiful and roads good, saw many prairie fires burning in different directions. Distance to-day 30 mi.

April 8, 1866 (Apr. 8.) – Pulled out early this morning and passed through the town of Srinell and put up for the night at the city of Newton. The country travelled over was mostly prairie and well improved. The roads were good and the day fine. Distance to-day 32 mi.

April 9, 1866 (Apr. 9.) – Left Newton and journeyed until noon. We then pitched our tent for the first time. The country we passed over to-day was hilly and poorly improved. Passed by two steam saw mills this afternoon. Day was cloudy with rain this afternoon. Dis. 12 mi.

April 10, 1866 (Apr. 10.) – Lay over to-day. I went hunting and shot three wild ducks and a couple of large hawks. Day warm and pleasant. Vegetation begins to start.

April 11, 1866 (Apr. 11.) – Broke up camp, passed through the cities of Mitchell and Des Moines, the capitol of Iowa. It is a large and flourishing town to be situated so far from railroad and steamboat navigation. We saw a house burning out in the country. The weather was fine and the roads good, considering the roughness of the country. I shot three prairie hens to-day. Distance 26 mi.

April 12, 1866 (Apr. 12.) – Travelled to the city of Winterset. The country was hilly and poorly improved but well timbered. Passed in sight of two steam saw mills. The day was cold and windy. Distance to-day 31 mi.

April 13, 1866, (Apr. 13.) – Hitched up and travelled to Spring-ville, Country prairie, no timber and not much improved. Saw large prairie fires burning. Distance to-day 28 mi.

April 14, 1866 (April 14.) – Left Springville, travelled all day over an unimproved prairie country and camped for the night in a piece of woods. Roads good and day cold. Distance 25 mi.

April 15, 1866 (April 15.) – Broke up camp and travelled 15 miles to Louis. Nooned. Hitched up, went 18 miles, stopped for the night at a farm house. Country prairie, not much improved. Roads good and to-day pleasant.

April 16, 1866 (April 16.) – Traveled till noon, eat our dinner and then travelled till sundown and stopped at a farm house for the night. Day very warm and the wind blew furiously all day from the south. Country hilly and people have to dig very deep for water in this part of the state and crib up their wells with flank or sticks, there being no stone. The water is of an inferior nature when they get it, being rily and disagreeable to the taste. Distance to-day 25 miles.

April 17, 1866 (April. 17.) – Hitched up and travelled until three o'clock when we came to the Missouri River, passed through Glennwood 7 miles east of the Missouri. It commenced raining and as we reached the river we were obliged to wait an hour or so until the ferry boat came and set us over to Plattesmouth, Nebr. territory. The river was very swift and muddy and the bank kept dropping down as the currant of water undermined it. At Plattesmouth I was intro-duced to my Uncle Fred Burgess whom I had not seem for 21 years. The country we traveled over to-day was hilly, but well timbered. Distance to-day 20 mi.

Stayed in Plattesmouth 7 days. Was joined by an uncle and a couple of brothers-in-law of his and another fellow viz. Lewis Cheney, Lucien Rogers, Wm. Blair and Wm. G. Blair. Plattsmouth is a dirty place and drinking, fighting, etc. are the principle amusements, there was two shooting brawls during my stay there. At one of them there were 30 or 40 shots fired and no body hurt although one drunken man in crossing the street fell down and scratched his face a little and stoutly maintained that he had been scratched with a bullet or knife but did not know which. Lewis and Mansel Cheney entered into partnership to buy stock together to drive to Montana and hired Lucien and the two Blairs to help drive across the plains

April 24, 1866 (April 24.) – Traded one span of mules for 15 head of cattle and us boys, four of us, started on foot to drive them to Salt Creek where we were to head quarter until time to start across the planes. The cattle were poor and drove easy only they went very slow. So we moved on, each being provide with a hickory staff to support our selves and to use as an argument with our bouvine companions in case they should become unruly. We travelled most of the way over a beautiful rolling prairie which was mostly burned over by prairie fires. There were plenty of ground squirrls along our road and when we became tired we would stop and take out our six shooters and practice shooting at their expense. At noon we were overtaken by Mansel with the team hauling our dunnage and tent together with some provisions for our consumption during our stay at Salt Creek. He also brought some cheese cakes and a bottle of bitters of which we imbibed rather freely and felt much refreshed, <u>very much indeed</u>. After eating and drinking to our hearts content we proceeded on our journey, put up for the night at a dutch farm house, fed the stock hay and corn and having refreshed ourselves with some supper proceeded to fill our pipes, smoked and talked until bed time and then "tumbled in" for the night. Distance to-day 14 mi.

April 25, 1866 (April 25.) – Arose at the invitation of our stolid host, fed the stock, washed ourselves at the little creek that ran by the house and went into breakfast. We dispatched enough sour kraut to astonish a native, we paid our reckoning and our kind hearted land lady having milked our cows (we had two) for us we started on our journey with lighter hearts than stomaches. We travelled over a wild prairie country until noon when we came to a hut and being very hungry and tired sent in to see if they would accommodate us with some dinner which they would not do having no license to feed travellers but we bought a dozen eggs which we ate without the ceremony of cooking.

Proceeded on our journey about a mile farther, came to a place wher they did keep folks and there we got a good square meal. We then went on to Salt Creek, crossed at Salt Creek bridge and stopped at Parkes Ranch where we rested from our labor. We pitched our tent and cooked our first bachelors supper and ate it with as good relish as could be expected considering how it was prepared. Distance 18mi.

Salt Creek is a deep sluggish stream, the current is hardly perceptible and the water in the spring over flows the banks and carries up drift wood which lodges in piles along the shore and is impregnated with brackish water. This decaying sent forth an odor similar to carrion, which if the wind is blowing can be smelled half a mile away and is very nauseous to those who are unaccustomed to it. We thought there must be a lot of dead cattle decaying by the smell that greeted our nostrils as we approached the creek.

April 26, 1866 (April 26.) – We took our little herd out the 26 about a mile and a half below Parks on a large tract of bottom land where the green feed was quite good. This flat contains a little alkali which the cattle lick up greedily. There are also a number of ponds which abound with wild ducks and a number of species of curious snipes, some with white plumage, with the exception of the head and neck which is red. I failed in my many attempts to shoot one, they were so wild.

There were also a species of black bird with yellow spots instead of red on their wings. Rattle snakes and bull snakes are abundant around Salt Creek. We kill some of them every day. Wm.G. Blair, in one day killed a rattle snake and seven snakes of other species. Salt Creek is the home of countless numbers of turtles, some of them very large. Garr and catfish are frequent caught out of the creek. Cattle fatten very fast and the people are very healthy around there. There are two towns started, one at the bridge and one at the ford five miles below. There is a grist mill, saw mill, a couple of blacksmith shops and several stores and salons at the town below. The timber is cotton wood and not very abundant. The fences and houses are built of cotton wood lumber as also the city of Plattsmouth and other towns along the Missouri. Land can be had here by settling on it and a number of farms are under a flourishing condition.

May 7, 1866 (May 7.) – They have bought, drove in, and branded stock so that we now have 58 head to herd. The Cheneys (Lewis and Mansel) have gone back to Plattsmouth to buy up what they can around there and to-day we received a letter from them wanting two of us to come and help drive. Lucien Rogers and Wm. Blair volunteer to go, so Wm. G. Blair and myself are in charge of our little herd. We have to watch them very close for some of them are very anxious to get back to their former master and improve every opportunity of escaping from us. We have one horse to ride between us. The corral into which we put the stock nights is none of the strongest and they break out sometimes nights causing us to crawl out of our nest of blankets and to out to drive them back and fix up the fence again without as much clothes on as we might have if we had taken more time to dress.

May 14, 1866 (May 14.) – Packed up and started on our journey toward the land of gold, we have two teams, one 14 ox team with 4700 pounds of provision and a small trail wagon coupled on behind containing stove, bedding, my chest and other articles and one two mule team hauling Mansel's family and 2500 pounds of provisions. These, together with nine mounted drivers and our 300 head of loose cattle of all sizes completes our outfit. We travelled 7 miles and nooned, yoked up and travelled 8 miles farther and camp for the night. The day was pleasant, the country rolling prairie and no water until night except what we took. Distance to-day 15 mi.

May 26, 1866 (May 26.) – Rained all the after part of last night, did not move to-day. Rain most of the time.

May 27, 1866 (May 27.) – Hail, wind and rain all night, cold. I was out on herd part of the night, very disagreeable. To-day the weather was clear and cold for the time of the year. Took the stock two miles from camp to graize. I saw a number of wolves and shot some sunfish in some little ponds, without any inlet or outlet to them.

May 28, 1866 (May 28.) – Rolled out in the morning, the day was clear but very chilly wind blew hard from N. W. Camp on a little slough where we obtained water. Were obliged to carry wood ½ mile to cook supper with. Lost a yearling out of the herd, supposed to have eaten some poison weed. Distance to-day 20 mi.

May 29, 1866 (May 29.) – Comfortably warm. Passed by Giddings ranch and drink at the spring where he was murdered a few days ago by some teamsters. They had some difficulty about the teamsters driving their stock into the spring, when Siddings ordered them off they shot several bullets into him killing him instantly. The murderers are under arrest and their trial is now going on. Distance to-day 19 mi.

May 30, 1866 (May 30.) – Came in sight of the Platte River to-day at 10 o'clock this morning. The country we passed over yesterday afternoon and this was perfectly level as far as the eye could extend and very sandy. A burning wind blew from the south that chapped our lips and blistered our faces. The reflection of the sun's heat caused a mirage and one could see what appeared to be large streams of water with beautiful islands, groves, etc. Then some times you could fancy you saw countless numbers of horses and other animals all running in the distance. We came down onto the great Platte bottom or valley at noon and stopped for dinner. Have very poor water. After dinner we moved on to Clear Creek (as it is rightly named for the water is icy cold and clear as crystal) and camped. Some of the boys saw some fish (suckers) and we constructed a net out of gunny sacks and caught some for supper. The Platte river is very wide, swift, shallow and muddy. The river is full of beautiful islands covered with cedar and cotton wood trees. Passed several ranches or farms this afternoon. The ground is covered in spots with crystalized alkali, which is white and tastes like soda we used in making bread. Distance to-day 20 mi.

May 31, 1866 (May 31.) – Rain in the forenoon but did not hinder our travelling. We went over fields of wild onions today miles in extent. The road was slippery. We stopped for noon close to the river and intend to lay over the rest of the day. Some of the boys went over on an island and cut some cedar for fire wood. We took a bath in the Platte although the water was uncomfortably cold. Saw a grave by the road but the lead pencil marks on the head board were so obliterated by the weather that we could not make them out. One of the boy: found a couple of "plug" hats which we proceeded to put up and shoot at as a target until the unfortunate hats were sadly riddled with bullet holes. Distance to-day 7 mi.

June 1, 1866 (June 1.) – The country over which we passed to-day was very sandy and those of us who thought it would be pleasant to walk barefoot in the sane were soon convinced of our mistake by having our feet pricked with burrs which lay hidden in the sand. The weather is very pleasant to-day. Distance to-day 15 mi.

June 2, 1866 (June 2.) – Travelled five miles, nooned, took a swim in the river, yoked up, harnessed up and saddled up then rolled out 8 miles farther Camp. Alkali puddles stick, have to watch the cattle to keep them from drinking too much of the water. Grease or fat, bacon is administered to stock that becomes alkalied or get poisoned by eating weeds. The weather is pleasant. Distance to-day 13 mi.

June 3, 1866 (June 3.) – Travelled till noon and laid over the rest of the day. Shod some of the cattle that had began to get foot sore. Found a deep place in the Platte and took a glorious swim, saw prairie dogs and burrowing owls, the first time that we have seen any. Weather beautiful. Distance 8 mi.

June 4, 1866 (June 4.) – Left the bottom and took to the bluffs travelled on a dry ridge all day. Camp at night close to the river. Drove the stock down a very steep bluff to water. We travelled through a very disagreeable rain in the forenoon but the afternoon was pleasant. Distance to-day 16 mi.

June 5, 1866 (June 5.) – Came down upon the Platte bottom a

little afternoon to-day, passed through a little town built mostly of sod and mud. Dead cattle were laying very thick around there. We saw prickely pears growing wild for the first time. Weather cold, with some rain in the afternoon. Distance to-day 20 mi.

June 6, 1866 (June 6.) – Saw the first Jack rabbit or hare to-day and large numbers of dead cattle. Weather lovely. Distance to-day 18 mi.

June 7, 1866 (June 7.) – Saw many buffalo skulls to-day along the road, also many dead cattle. Killed two jack rabbits, wind blew furiously all day, about 6 o'clock P. M. it commenced to storm, hail, rain, and wind. Terrible storm, a perfect tornado and lasted about one hour. Four of us boys who were to herd the stock that night went out with blankets. Harry and "Texas" took the first watch, Lucien and I the second. The night was cold and ran so that we were most chilled through when we went to camp after our breakfast. There was a man caught up with us to-day who had a couple of whiskey barrels which he was taking to Montana. So three of us boys went to him and made known our wishes, he immediately took a long quill out of his pocket, gave it to us and told us to get into his wagon and help ourselves. We took two "sucks" a piece at his old whiskey barrel through this quill, paid him .30c each and went away so joyfull that we forgot all about being wet and cold. Distance 15 mi.

June 8, 1866 (June 8.) – Passed through Kearny and the fort. Kearney City or Doby town is built mostly of sun baked brick. There are many trains of wagons going westward. We saw the skeleton of a buffalo to-day. The head and neck of which had the hair on yet. Day warm and pleasant. Distance to-day 8 mi.

June 9, 1866 (June 9.) – Warm and windy, cloudy. Distance to-day 16 mil. Roads good.

June 10, 1866 (June 10.) – Four of us went out on heard last night. "Texas" and Harry Bliss were to take the first watch, it rained all night, cold, the cattle stampeded so the boys could not find us when it came our turn and we could not tell which way they were, or where camp was, so we were obliged to lay and take it until morning. We were so chilled in the morning that we could scarcely walk when we got to camp a potation was prepared for us which soon warmed us. Rain most of to-day, we did not move.

June 11, 1866 (June 11.) – Warm and pleasant. Moved camp. Distance 17 mi.

June 12, 1866 (June 12.) – Pleasant, saw some swifts or sand lizards. Lyman killed a snake that he called "the shovel snake" from a curious projection of the upper jaw. Distance moved to-day 19 mi.

June 13, 1866 (June 13.) – Shot two jack rabbits, passed a ranch where they had a large pile of dead wolves, that they had poisoned. I should think there was over a hundred. A party of soldiers passed us going west. Distance to-day 18 mi.

June 14, 1866 (June 14.) – This is my 23rd birthday. The gnats and mosquitoes are getting exceedingly troublesome and bite as fierce in the dust and hot sun as in the shade. The mosquitoes rise in clouds from the ground as we ride along, to the great annoyance of the stock as well as ourselves. Distance to-day 20 mi.

June 15, 1866 (June 15.) – Laid over waiting for wagons and men enough to form sufficient company to get by the Fort (Cottonwood). The government requires that all trains passing Forts shall consist of at least 20 wagons and 30 armed men. I took a long hunt after antelope. Saw many tracks but no antelope.

June 16, 1866 (June 16.) – Laid over, some boys went up into the hills after some wood to burn along the road, there being none west of here obtainable for many miles.

June 17, 1866 (June 17.) – Passed Cottonwood, day pleasant. Distance to-day 18 mi.

June 18, 1866 (June 18.) – Travelled 20 mi. Weather fine.

June 19, 1866 (June 19.) – Saw a part of the Winnebago Indians that had been in the employ of the United States to fight the Sioux. Distance to-day 17 mi.

June 20, 1866 (June 20.) Moved 18 miles to-day. Rain in the evening.

June 21, 1866 (June 21.) – Travelled 16 miles. Weather pleasant. Prickley Pears are in bloom. Their flowers are of two different colors, pale yellow and pink. They resemble hollyhock-blossoms in smell and taste. The pods that the thorns grow on are tough and very glutinous and slightly acid to the taste. Cattle can hardly be drove through a bed of them and the sorely inconvenience footmen unless the foot are protected by heavy cowhide-boots. Saw an antelope to-day. Mansel fired a shot at it with his rifle but it was out of reach. They are very wild. Prairie dog villages are scattered thickly along the Platte. Lyman shot one a few days ago. They belong to the Marmot species and as near as I can describe, they are about half way between the common grey ground squirrel and the american ground hog or wood chuck. The burrowing owls that live with them are a queer little bird. They look about the size of a quail, they usually sit on the mounds, near the mouth of the burrow. If you frighten them they will fly to another mound and as they light, have a very amusing habit of facing you and making you a very profound obsience.

June 22, 1866 (June 22.) – Day very hot. Travelled 17 mi.

June 23, 1866 (June 23.) – Travelled to the Ft. Juelsburg. There is a small town building east of the Fort, one and one-half miles. Day very sultry. Distance 15 mi.

June 24, 1866 (June 24.) – Crossed the South Platte river, in company with a freight train which is bound for Salt Lake. Before starting across, were obliged to raise the boxes of our wagons 7 or 8 inches above the bolsters to keep the water from running in and damaging the freight. The river is very swift about one mile in width and the average depth is about four feet. The bottom of the river is composed of quick sand and in going across the wheels of the wagons raise up then drop suddenly down which shakes the wagons as if driving over a log way. It took nearly all day to get the stock and wagons across. The water was cold and to prevent being injured by being in it so long the boys partook of whiskey, some of them rather freeley so that by the time we were all over the stream some were jolly drunk, especially one of them who in attempting to wash his trousers lost them in the water and came into camp presenting a very ludicrous appearance, having only a single garment and that unfortunately extremely short. He was soon provided with another pair of unmentionables and order at length restored. Distance to-day 1 ½ miles.

June 25, 1866 (June 25.) – Pulled out at day break. Travelled till 10 o'clock and camp on Lodge Pole Creek, a fine little stream. Lay over the rest of the day. Rigged some hooks and lines and soon caught several messes of small fish. Shot three hares. Weather very fine. Distance 5 mi.

- Recollection -

Westward Ho!

Crossing the South Platte River in the Early Days.

According to promise we have dropped back to the crossing of the South Platte river and six years of time has been added to the great past. We are in camp at Julesburg and have made the necessary preparations to ford the swift, muddy stream by unloading all the wagons, one at a time, raising the boxes to within an inch or so of the standards and putting blocks of cedar under them and on the bolsters to keep the boxes above the water in crossing. The wagons have been reloaded with a view to keeping the contents dry or protecting the more easily damaged part of the freight. As 133 wagons have been thus treated, most of which were of the "desert ship" order and carried loads of four or five tons each, the task has been great. It has taken five days to do this work and to shoe the tender footed cattle, make repairs, etc.

"We" consisted of a freight train of eighty wagons bound for Salt Lake, a train of thirty-five wagons bound for Helena, Montana,

Julesburg. 1865

Julesburg, 1865

a mixed train of twenty one wagons for Gallatin valley, Montana and our own outfit of two wagons and 450 head of cows and young cattle likewise bound for Gallatin valley.

Our camp presented a very imposing appearance, especially at night, when the camp fires were burning bright, the great circle of wagons with their covers of white canvass, inside this great corral tents of families and the fires of the different messes and the busy crowd made an animated scene that was pleasant to look upon.

As a wagon would be made ready for its trip across the river it would be greased and hauled into position. A sloping chute or roadway was cut down the bank. Eight yoke of strong oxen, together with all the saddle animals, were driven across. A cable of strong log chains, long enough to reach across the river and for some rods out on the opposite shore, were fastened together. The cattle that had been driven over were yoked and placed in position for work and the moving began. A coil of rope was put on the wagon to draw the cable back again. The cable was made fast to the first wagon and the teams on the other shore started. As the cable began to grow taut willing hands pushed the wagon down the incline into the river. The drivers on the other side cracked their whips and the solitary wagon looked lonesome as it went through the seething waters, shaking from side to side as if being driven over a rough logway. It had to be kept moving to prevent going down in the quicksands and being lost. All who have had this experience will readily recognize what we are trying to tell.

Wagon after wagon was transported across the swift, muddy river in this way and as they ascended the opposite bank were hauled around and left in the regular corral forming position, where plenty of help was at hand to unload, put the box back into its former position by removing the blocks from beneath it and reloading, having a care to lay out all articles that had got wet in crossing.

By noon enough wagons had been put across and placed in a semicircular position to make quite a respectable camp, and a rest was taken for dinner. A good many men were continually in the water, which on that 24th day of June was too cold for comfort.

One of the wagons of the train for Salt Lake was loaded with whiskey and brandy. A barrel of whisky was tapped and a bucketful of the liquor set on the river bank at the fording place, in which was a tin dipper, with the invitation to "help yourselves gentleman," an order which a large portion of the men obeyed with an electricity that seemed a trifle inelegant. Some would take a few sips, while many drank too much. By the middle of the afternoon a few were helplessly drunk and had to be cared for. It was interesting to note the effect of the staff on different temperaments. It seemed to strengthen some and nerve them to redouble their exertions, some would become jolly, sing songs, crack jokes and make speeches, some would take a view of everything and weep and lament in a maudlin way, saying we would be killed by the redskins and never see home again, some would be rich, and a few, who were ashamed of their plight, would be sullen and non-committal. A few wanted to fight and one or two tragedies were narrowly averted by cooler and more sober heads.

This days work was terrific and just before sundown the last wagon was put over and rolled up the north bank of the river and took its place in the great corral. A bountiful supper and a good night's repose put everything to rights.

We had not as yet seen a living bison on the trip and very few antelope. A small squad of soldiers told us that we would not begin to find bison until we got to the Powder river and Black hills region. Thus far the only fresh meat we had tasted was jack rabbit, and these had been few and far between.

The next morning we were up early, and by sunrise our two wagons, eleven of the emmigrant wagons and our herd of cows were on the march to reach a place where the feed, wood and water could be found more abundant, in order to rest up a bit and let the stock recuperate. At 10 o'clock we went into camp on Lodge Pole creek and prepared breakfast.

- Diary -

June 26, 1866 (June 26.) – Made a 10 mile drive this morning. Camp. Spent the afternoon shoeing cattle. Patterson gave chase after an antelope but did not get it. The grass along this creek is rich and green. We make only one drive each day and give the stock a chance to feed the rest of the time.

June 27, 1866 (June 27.) – I started out hunting this morning at sunrise and was fortunate to kill a large fat buck antelope a couple of miles from camp. Came back in sight of camp just as the train was moving out and made a signal for some one to come to me. Uncle Lyman came with his pony to take my game and we soon caught up after Mansel met us with my pony. We stopped early so as to have some of the antelope for dinner. It was the first we had and we partook of it freely. Excellent eating. Distance to-day 7 mi.

June 28, 1866 (June 28.) – Lyman and Mansel went hunting to-day. They overtook us late in the afternoon and brought a couple of fawn antelope with them. Distance to-day 15 mi.

June 29, 1866 (June 29.) – Moved 5 miles in the morning. Lay over until three o'clock P. M. Then leave Pole Creek. Travell over a dry ridge. Camp after dark at a pond of water. Lyman went hunting to-day. Killed an antelope. Rain by spells all the afternoon. Distance to-day 15 mi.

June 30, 1866 (June 30.) – Moved 13 miles. Nooned at Mud Springs. Shod some cattle, had a small thunder shower. Some of the boys went after some wood to take with us for to cook with. We rolled out again at dark and went 4 miles farther. Camp. Distance to-day 16 mi.

July 1, 1866 (July 1.) – Passed Court House rock which reminds me of pictures I have seen of the ruins of some ancient castle. Did not go to it, so can not judge the dimensions of this wonderful piece of natures handiwork. We camp to-night on the North Platte river, are in sight of Scotts Bluffs. Can see Chimney rock ahead of us. Distance to-day 16 mi.

- Recollection -

Wild Game
The First Antelope is Brought Down by a Well Directed Shot.

The small boys of the train soon made the discovery that Lodge Pole creek contained many fish, and were soon dilligently at work, some catching bait and some fishing. They secured an ample mess of bullheads, pumpkinseeds, chubs, dace and shiners, the sight of which carried us back to childhood and the banks of old Yellow creek in Jo Daviess county, Illinois, where many boyhood hours had been spent in angling for the very same species that the boys were catching here.

We could see several pair of antelope from camp and after breakfast some men started out to try to kill one. They returned at noon tired and hungry with two jack rabbits. These with the fish gave us a fine supper that night.

While fishing one of the urchins found a human skull in some drift. None of us were able to tell whether the skull had belonged to a red or a white man, but it was buried. The ghastly reminder of our inevitable demise was forever put out of sight.

This little valley and the ravines or gulches which opened into it had evidently been carved by the erosive action of the water from a great mesa or plateau. The hills were clothed with rich grass, which the stock appreciated and they were allowed to rest and graze the balance of the day. In the afternoon other hunters made a fervent but ineffectual attempt to get an antelope. The creatures were to shy.

The next day we were on the march at sunrise and the writer struck out ahead of the train on his first antelope hunt. All hands had become so eager for the taste of venison that a prize had been offered to the first man who should kill an antelope. We rode until we were perhaps two miles ahead of the train. Then turning our pony loose to pick grass until we should return or the train come along, we took it afoot. Climbing a range of low hills two antelope were in sight on the summit of the next ridge. This was our only chance, and aiming at an imaginary spot about three feet above the shoulders of the one that had horns we cut loose. The creature gave one leap skyward and fell. This was the first time we had ever been near an antelope and we gazed with admiration at his beautiful eyes. When a boy we had noted that the antlers of deer were not horn, but an osseous bony structure. We had supposed that antelope were the same, but now we saw that they were actual horns and black like the horns we had seen on bison skeletons that lay thick in places along the road up the Platte valley.

This was our first game larger than a wild goose, and we felt more elated then than we have since when contemplating the carcass of some huge ugly bear that had fallen by well directed shots from our Ballard. As we looked down into the little valley we saw the train was nearly opposite, and waved a big bandana as a signal. A man rode out and caught the pony we had left and we, with our game, soon joined the caravan, which immediately went into camp for the balance of the day, and the enjoyment of the feast we had that evening can be better imagined than described. The discomfort caused by the change of our smoked bacon diet to the intemperate eating of fresh venison was very marked on the following day. But the ice was broken and we had no difficulty from that time on in killing all the meat we needed.

One of our party was an old time plainsman and had been once over the route we were now traveling. He said we had better make easy drives and let the stock have abundant time to rest and eat, as we were nearing a region where feed and water were scarce and of poor quality and where forced drives would be necessary in order to reach camping places where grass and water could be found.

One the 29th day of June we made our last camp on Lodge Pole creek after a five mile morning drive. Journeyed that afternoon over a dry ridge or hogback and travelled until after dark to find water. We camped that night near a marshy pond and the next day moved on to Mud springs where a few soldiers were camped. It rained and we had some very sharp lightning and very loud thunder. Some of the boys went after some wood to take with us and took rifles as well as axes. They returned wet and reported that during the electrical disturbance balls of greenish fire rolled along their rifle barrels and clung to the edges of the axes. We made the first night drive of the journey tonight.

The next day, July 1, we passed Court house rock. None of us took time to visit and examine this strange freak of nature, but it looked from the road like some ruin. It did not require a very great stretch of imagination to see a busy throng of prehistoric men at work with appliances for moving mighty rocks, such as the wonderful ruins of Egypt are made of, from some source unknown to modern man, lifting the great blocks of stone into position by some mechanical power, the knowledge of which is one of the lost arts, and after the great pile was finished to see the throngs of human ants rearing other structures, cultivating their fields, tending flocks and herds and sailing

Chimney Rock National Historic Site

their rude craft, laden with merchandise peculiar to that age, on the waters of the sea that once rolled its flashing waters over the land where we are now journeying. That the sea once covered this land we had ample evidence in the fossil remains of marine animal and vegetable life we encountered. We remembered reading how the material of which Solomon's Temple was built was conveyed by great floats from the quarries where they were hewn to the place where needed for use. From our camp tonight we can see Chimney rock.

- Diary -

July 2, 1866 (July 2.) – Nooned to-day opposite Chimney Rock Wm. G. Blair and myself went out to see this great monument of nature which was 1 ½ miles from camp. This rock seems to be composed of a mixture of sand and clay. Is as near as we could judge 150 to 200 feet in height. Its base covers about ¼ acre of ground. It is in three divisions, or stories, that last or top story is about 15 ft. square and 50 ft. high. I should think that it might be the center of a high hill, the outside of which has been gradually worn away by the action of the wind, rain and floods. There were a great many initials and names cut around its base and we did not fail to leave ours there. A little above where we nooned to-day was a place where some soldiers had entrenched themselves and had a fight with Indians and which must have lasted some time by the amount of cartridge shells that lay on the ground. There was one grave outside the breastwork. Distance to-day 18 mi.

July 3, 1866 (July 3.) – Halted for noon to-day at Scotts Bluffs which seem to be composed of the same material as Chimney rock. They rise abruptly to the height of two or three hundred feet and look grand. After dinner, moved on through a pass, partly natural and partly artificial, camp near Fort Mitchell. Weather pleasant. Distance to-day 17 mi.

July 4, 1866 (July 4.) – I went hunting this morning, saw some antelope after riding 4 or 5 miles, but they were on level ground and I could not get close enough to shoot them. The gnats and flies were very thick and my pony became so restive, that I went back to camp. They were busy shoeing cattle when I got in. We finished shoeing cattle about 10 o'clock, greased the wagons, then made a pail of milk punch to drink. The women prepared a splendid dinner for us. Wrote some letters and pulled out camp at dark. Could see Laramie peak ahead of us to-day looming up like some dark cloud. Distance to-day 7 mi.

July 5, 1866 (July 5.) – Made a 17 mi. drive in the afternoon. Weather pleasant.

July 6, 1866 (July 6.) – Made one drive, camped for the night among a party of Sioux Indians. There were 400 warriors, beside the old men, women and children. They appeared to be very friendly and peacable. The chief together with an attendant, took supper with us. We gave them some bread, molasses and a large quantity of new milk. Played some on our violins for their entertainment. Distance to-day 7 mi.

- Recollection -

The next day being the "Glorious Fourth" we celebrated the forenoon in shoeing some cattle, greasing the wagons and putting guns and ammunition in trim. By noon the women had a holiday dinner prepared, a pail of milk punch was brewed and passed around. By 2 o'clock we were in marching order and the train, like a lazy worm, was crawling along the hot and dusty road again. After an hour's travel we heard a bugle call ahead and a little later saw a line of bluecoats ride into view onto the next ridge. Then some ambulances and government freight wagons appeared. This proved to be a company of Indian cavalry under command of white officers. The officers told us that these were Winnebago Indians who had enlisted in the regular service. That they made the best Indian fighters, that they combined wood, or rather, plains-craft with natural Indian cunning and military discipline. Being well mounted and thoroughly armed, they had great confidence in their ability to fight and were brave in consequence. They considered themselves invincible when pitted against foes of their own race and color. We were further informed that the Sioux and Cheyennes had joined forces and that serious trouble was anticipated. That actual hostilities had not yet commenced but that the military feared that some trifling act might precipitate a long and bloody warfare, and as the whole region was under military law, all parties of white men were commanded under severe penalties not to provoke any Indians they might come into contact with, but give presents when convenient and under no circumstances to make any hostile demonstrations unless attacked.

I will here remark that this proved to be a suicidal policy and cost many white emmigrants and freighters their lives that season. Many a poor fellow laid down his life by the way and filled a coffinless grave that summer in consequence. The whole highway from the head of Powder river to the divide between the Yellowstone and Gallitan valleys was a line of battle. We afterwards learned that if you treat an Indian as a friend and neighbor he attributes your friendship to cowardice, but if you begin by whipping the "supreme stuffing" out of him he regards you as a "big brave chief" and deports himself in conformity to his belief by treating you with great consideration and respect.

Four centuries of contact with the Caucassion has transformed the once brave and generous red man of North America into a cruel, cowardly hyena in human guise. The white man with his cunning and treachery, his insane lust for gold and his superior death dealing appliances has, in his greed to acquire new territory, robbed the poor savage of his God-given hunting grounds and crowded the fast vanishing tribes of red men off the stage of action. For years the government Indian agents have appropriated annuities that should have been paid to the Indian, and the outrage will continue so long as the rotten fabric that we call government places favoritism and imbecility above integrity and capability in its appointment of servants whose duty it is to carry out and fulfill its pledges to the Indian. This treatment of the savage has made him treacherous, has been the cause of numerous outbreaks, wars and massacres in which the innocent have been the sufferers, and has degenerated the Indian to a grade a trifle above the coyote.

The Indian has been over four hundred years on the descending scale. His degeneracy beginning with the advent of the treacherous, cruel, gold worshiping Spaniard.

But to resume our journey, we will say that on the 6th of July we made one drive of seventeen miles and camped for night among a party of Sioux Indians, numbering six hundred warriors with their old men, women and children. On both sides of the river their teepees clustered, a city of leather houses. Vast herds of ponies in charge of herders grazed on the grassy slopes. We had no choice but to camp as we did. Feed and water we must have, and we felt safer in their midst than we would a little distance from them. They greeted us with a pleasant "how" as we drove amount them, which salutation we pleasantly returned.

Shortly after we made camp an old Chief and several head men of the tribe made us a visit, and a general hand shaking and exchange of "hows?" was followed by the old chief pulling from some receptacle beneath his blanket an enormous pipe carved from the sacred pipe stone and asking for some tobacco. One of our boys handed over a small sack and the pipe was filled. Then a match was called for and the chief motioned for us to sit down on the ground. He and his men setting the example we all followed suit. Then he went through some incantation and lighted his pipe, took two or three whiffs and passed it to the next man, who did the same In this manner it passed twice around the circle and when the tobacco burned out it was filled and passed again. When the third pipe full had been exhausted the chief knocked the ashes from it and gravely put it back in the place from whence he had brought it. Then drawing a villainous looking butcher knife from a rawhide scabbard and smoothing a place on the ground he drew with the point of his knife a map of the country. Tracing and naming the rivers, beginning with the North Platte, where we were, he traced the South Platte, then the Republican and Blue rivers. Pointing to the space between the latter streams he said, "Heap buppalo." Then with a sweep of his knife he gave the number of the warriors and said: "All go Republican, heap kill buppalo, get heap meat, heap robe. Heap tight Pawnee. Heap wano me." Then extending his map northward, the Powder, Tongue, Little and Bighorn and Stillwater rivers, Clark's fork, the Missouri and its tributaries, the Gallatin, Madison and the Jefferson rivers. North of these he made a mark in the dust and said, "heap gold, heap white man, do so'" indicating by motions picking and shoveling. Then with a glance at us and our outfits he said, "White braves go there, dig gold." Upon being answered by an affirmative nod the old chief grunted in a self satisfied way, and covering the entire region ahead of us with a gesture of his hand, said "Heap many bad Indian, heap no wano. Crow Indian heap bad, Blackfoot heap bad, heap take scalp whiteman. Me good indian, no take scalp whiteman, me white man's brother."

During our confab crowds of villainous visaged bucks came about and gazed with hungry eyes at our outfits, but when their curiosity would get the better of good manners a grunt and a gesture from the old man would cause them to fall back.

Finally he said "time go sleep" and a few words, which we could not understand, to his men caused all except his attendants to leave us and go to their teepes. We then gave him a sack of flour, several pounds of tobacco, a lot of matches and a quantity of sugar and again shaking hands and saying "how" they went to their quarters and left us alone.

While we realized that we were entirely at the mercy of this vast army of savages and that they could wipe us out of existence with scarcely an effort, not a man, women or child in our train showed the least uneasiness or fear. All went about their customary work as unconcernedly as if Indians were an every occurrence. We ate hearty and slept as sweetly that night as if there had not been an Indian on the continent.

We owed our escape that time to the fact that open hostilities had not yet begun and that this was a great hunting party who had their women and children with them. After breakfast the next morning, while we were getting ready to "roll out" the same chief and attendants called on us again This time they brought presents of beaded and silk worked moccasins, tobacco pouches and other Indian trinkets.

Another hand shaking and "hows" exchanged and we were on the march and in an hour the great Sioux encampment was out of sight and we wondered what next.

- Diary -

July 7, 1866 (July 7.) – Weather beautiful. Moved 8 mi.

July 8, 1866 (July 8.) – Crossed Laramie river at Fort Laramie. We swam the loose stock and crossed the team over a toll bridge. Drove two miles and camp. Tootle and Leach's train from Nebraska City bound for Virginia City Montana also crossed and camped with us. Todd and Parkers train crossed late. Distance 15 mi.

July 9, 1866 (July 9.) – Travelled 7 miles. We are at the Black Cull. Travel in company with Todd & Parker train.

July 10, 1866 (July 10.) – Nooned at Limestone Springs, country very hilly. Feed poor. Cattle dying off at the rate of two or three a day, supposed they are poisoned by weeds. Travelled 18 miles to-day. Weather very sultry. Camped at a small stream called cotton wood. Water very scarce and poor.

July 11, 1866 (July 11.) – Drove 5 miles, nooned on the North Platte. Afternoon passed Twin Springs, where we obtained the first drink of good clear cold water, that we have had for many days. Camp on Horse Show Creek, a pretty stream. Distance to-day 12 mi.

July 12, 1866 (July 12.) – Moved camp 8 miles. Smashed a wheel of our trail wagon and left it ½ miles from where we camp. Laid over in the afternoon, went back after our wagon and repaired it. Took bath in the river. Weather very hot.

July 13, 1866 (July 13.) – Lay over to rest and let the stock recruit a little. Sam Patterson and I went hunting. Saw signs of bear, buffalo, deer and antelope, but did not see any of the animals. I killed a sage hen. We also saw Indian and pony tracks. Found the remains of a wagon, a few barrel, stoves, etc. that had probably been laying there 20 years. They were 10 miles away from the road.

- Recollection -

On the following day we only made one drive of eight miles. The sky was clear and the sun shone hot, making the white snow fields on Laramie mountain, which now loomed up majestically ahead of us, look deliciously cool and inviting. We were eager for a drink of clear, cold water and fancy carried us back to the time at home when we would fill the dipper with snow, then pour in enough water to thoroughly wet it and drink the water as it drained from the wet snow.

The next day, July 8, we passed Ft. Laramie and crossed Laramie river. This stream was high and angry. We crossed the river on a toll bridge, paying villainous exhorbitant toll. The loose stock was driven into the water and made to swim. Before making the cattle take to the water camp was made on the opposite shore and the oxen that hauled the wagons unyoked and turned loose to serve as a decoy for the cattle that were to swim. As the cattle were forced into the river and struck the current it took them off their feet and they whirled on down the river like so many chips of wood. But they swam bravely and about half the herd reached the other shore over half a mile below where they started in. The balance of the herd drifted down and lodged on a low landy island considerably farther down. These had to be got off and started and the writer volunteered to do the work. We wanted a good swim anyway. Divesting ourselves of all clothes except shirt and pants we backed off a rod or so and made a rush and a plunge. The water seemed icy cold, and on coming to the surface we found that our puny efforts did not suffice to keep us from drifting down almost as fast as the cattle had been swept along, and it took all the skill and strength we could muster to keep from being carried past the island. We struck a shallow place and waded ashore among the cattle at the lower end of the island very tired and chilled to the marrow. The sun shone bright and the air was warm and the exercise that followed was of a nature that soon got our blood stirring again.

The cattle were loth to again enter the cold, swift water and it took very active chasing, aided by blows over their backs with a willow sapling, and much vigorous shouting to get them started. When they finally got off we followed, and by the time the cows were climbing the other shore we were there too. One such experience in a lifetime is enough for us.

By the time we had made camp Tootle & Co's train, which we had left at the mouth of Lodge Pole creek, near the crossing of the South Platte, came along and went into camp with us

The officers at Fort Laramie told us that the Indians were peaceable and would not harm us unless we molested them first. We did not quite like the way they looked when telling us to be on the alert and counseling friendship at the same time, and resolved to act as we deemed best for safety and as occasion would demand, and it is just possible that some of us had a premonition of danger ahead. Anyway, we scented enough danger to cause us to agree to travel in close proximity to the more powerful train of freighters

The next day we were in a spur of the Black hills, a desolate, arid, desert like region, and although we were traveling slow and making very short drives our stock began to succumb to the heat, dust, poor feed and water and some poisonous herb or weed, the nature of which we did not know. The alkali in places was crusted thick and made the ground white as snow. Our only remedy for treating poisoned cattle was fat bacon, by liberal doses of which we saved many that seemed hopelessly sick.

July 10th we moved from Limestone Springs and camped for night at a small, nearly dry stream named Cottonwood. The water was very scarce and so strong with mineral salts held in solution that it nearly took the skin off our palates to drink it. Three head of our cattle died at this camp and others are sick. The weather was very sultry and buffalo gnats almost unbearable.

The next afternoon we halted at Twin Springs and had the first cool drink of palatable water that we had tasted for some days. We nooned that day on the North Platte and our poor thirsty animals filled their parched stomachs once more with sweet cold water. We are not making to exceed twelve miles a day now.

On the 12th we had the misfortune to smash a wheel and laid by in the afternoon to repair it. The roads have been very rough and rocky for the past few days and we have passed the wrecks of several nearly new wagons that had been unloaded and abandoned. We found better feed here than we had seen for many miles and decided to remain in camp one day and let the stock eat, drink and rest.

Two of us went back into the hills to hunt and explore. Climbing a lofty point we could see, still farther back, a green valley with a line of green trees and willows running through it. By this time we were very thirsty and the water in our canteens was too warm to drink with comfort. We knew that the green trees and bushes meant water and lost no time in getting down into the little valley, where we found a bed of apparently dry sand. A few rods farther up we came to a clear stream and the long drink of pure water repaid us for the long walk we took to get it. We found on investigation that this tiny stream sank beneath its sandy bed every few rods, also that wild animals, such as bison, elk, deer and antelope, came to this spot to drink. We also saw pony and moccasin tracks in the moist sand and saw where a small fire had been recently made and concluded that a party of redskins had halted here the day before. In the thick willows we saw the first bear tracks we had ever seen. But this discovery, in a sheltered nook, of the remains of a wagon and the bones of horses set us to thinking. The woodwork of the wagon had been burned, leaving only ironwork, which was deeply corroded by years of rust. Near where the wagon had been burned we found the warped and partially decayed staves of a small cask which had been hooped with iron, but the fragments of hoops we found were rust and could be rubbed to a powder between the thumb and finger. The skulls of the two horses and the leg bones that we found were much decomposed and had sunk into the ground so as to be nearly concealed. We could find no writing or other means of identification, but concluded, as this was not over four miles off the old California trail, that this particular wagon had been over taken by winter and had worked back off the road to find shelter and food and the people that were with it as well as the horses had died of slow starvation or had met death at the hands of the merciless red man, who had burned all that he could not carry away, and that this was one of the outfits that dropped out of existence, so far as human knowledge is concerned, and no tidings from them ever reached the home which they had left so long ago. We made a diligent search for something that would give us a clue to the identity of the men who had made their final camp and ended life's journey here in vain, and after eating the lunch we had brought from the train and filling our canteens with water we shouldered our rifles and struck out in the direction of camp and the river, counting ourselves as the only white men who had ever seen the wagon which had for so many years been hid among the willows of the little oasis in this desert of the North American Bad Lands.

- Diary -

July 14, 1866 (July 14.) – Cross the North Platte river at Bridgers Ferry. River deep, swift, and 1/8 mi. wide. We had some difficulty in swimming the stock, but got them over at last. One of the men in Parkers train came near drowning. Distance to-day 13 mi.

July 15, 1866 (July 15.) – Travelled 14 miles. Camp on beautiful ground, feed good, weather hot.

July 16, 1866 (July 16.) – Pulled over some heavy hills. Rain in the afternoon. Distance to-day 15 mi.

July 17, 1866 (July 17.) – Laid over to let the stock rest and recruit. Cattle dying off, one to three almost every day. Weather very sultry.

July 18, 1866 (July 18.) – Left the Platte, travelled up a dry creek six miles and nooned. Water one mile to the right. Moved five miles in the afternoon. Camp, water to the right in pools. No wood. Have to burn sage brush. Rain in the evening. Distance to-day 11 mi.

July 19, 1866 (July 19.) – Travelled 17 miles at one drive. Camp on Cheyenne Creek. Water by digging. Good wood and feed. Fell in with an emigrant outfit of 10 wagons. Day pleasant. A number of our outfit are unwell.

July 20, 1866 (July 20.) – Drove 7 miles. Nooned. Water in pools. Afternoon travelled 9 miles. Water ¼ mile to the left. Do not know the name of the watering places. Distance to-day 16 mi.

July 21, 1866 (July 21.) – Pulled out ahead of Todd & Parkers train. They lay over to make a night drive and travelled 32 miles without water. Camp for night on dry fork of Powder river. Water very scarce. The emigrant outfit were camped there also, having out travelled us. I did not get in camp until dark, having stayed behind with a bull that had given out for want of feed and water. I picked up an Indian arrow to-day by the road side.

- Recollection -

The following day we made the last crossing of the North Platte for this journey. The water was deep, cold and rapid, and it was with much difficulty that the stock were driven in and swam across.

This was Bridgers Ferry and it cost from three to five dollars per wagon to get over, according to size and weight. The boat was a flat, scow like affair built of plank that had been hewn out of cottonwood logs and spiked together and it was astonishing to see so small a craft carry such tremendous loads. This, like nearly all far western ferries in those days, was a rope ferry, and its motive power was the current of the river. One of the men of the freight train attempted to cross on his horse, but his weight was too great and he came within a hair's breath of drowning, as his horse could not keep its nostrils above the water and he had to fall off. Being a poor swimmer and in the cold water he was nearly helpless and it required our united efforts to get him out. His horse, freed of its burden, swam to the other bank and climbed out with the cattle.

On the 18th of July we left the Platte and the old Salt Lake California trail and took the new route, then known as the Bozeman cut-off. The road led us up a dry gulch which we followed six miles. We found a little very poor water in pools but no wood except sage brush. The weather continued to be entensely hot and our stock began to die at the rate of from two to five head each day.

The next day we had to make a forced drive of seventeen miles in order to find a place to camp. We camped on Cheyenne creek, where we found plenty of fuel, but the bed of the gulch was as dry, apparently, as the road, and here we had a new experience. Our thirsty stock went along the bed of the creek with noses to the sand vainly trying to find water and fairly moaning in an agony of thirst.

Murmurs and curses at our ill luck in making a dry camp were going up from the human portion of our caravan when one who had had the experience said: "There is plenty of water here. Get out the shovels and go to work." Suiting action to his words he grabbed a shovel out of his wagon, removed a shovel of sand and the hole thus made began to fill with clear water. The cattle lost no time in improving the opportunity to get a sip of water. All the shovels were soon in use and it took but a few minutes work to give all of them a chance to drink. It was a curious sight to note the change of expression that came into their brown eyes as the long drawn swallows of water cooled their parched gullets, and as one would finish a sigh of satisfaction would be drawn that seemed to come from way down in the bottom of the heart. A few shallow wells were scooped out a little farther up the gulch for use by the train.

The grass was good and, with wood and water in abundance, we soon forgot our trials, especially after we had eaten a hearty supper and lighted our pipes. An emmigrant outfit of ten wagons came in and camped. We shall be traveling companions the rest of the journey and make mention of them occasionally as this narrative proceeds.

July 20th we made two drives, altogether sixteen miles. Found poor water in shallow pools a quarter of a mile from camp. A small squad of soldiers passed us escorting a colonel from New Fort Reno to Fort Laramie. They told us that the next water would be found at Dry Fork, twenty-two miles ahead, and advised us to look out for Indians and be very careful not to offend any that we might meet, as they were yet peaceable but that an outbreak might easily be provoked.

The next day the emmigrant outfit and our outfit pulled out at daylight, leaving the freight train in camp. This was deemed necessary on account of scarcity of feed and water. The sun rose like a ball of fire and as it got up in the sky the heat became terriffic. There was no shade, no water and no rest. We had to make frequent stops as animals would succumb to the heat to revive them. It was very tantalizing to be compelled to keep that dusty, hot highway when we could look at the cool, green mountains on which a few snow drifts still lingered and which looked to be such a short distance away. At 2 o'clock we halted on a high table land, unyoked and turned the stock loose to get a little rest and pick the few blades of grass which existed by some means unknown to us. Improvising a shelter from the sun's fierce rays by making an awning of a wagon sheet, coffee was made with the little water that remained in our kegs, meat fried and bread baked over a meager fire of the few stunted sage brush we were able to gather. While we were at dinner someone was looking up the side of the mountain, saw some object come out of a clump of trees. It galloped across a grassy park and again entered the timber. We all pronounced it a bison but after, experience told us that it was a mounted Indian with a buffalo robe covering his recumbent carcass and the neck and shoulders of his pony. The red devils were then watching our movements as they had evidently been doing for several days and we were entirely ignorant of the fact.

After we finished our dinner a big, innocent, good-natured man whom we knew as Dutch Pete shouldered his rifle and saying that he would walk on slowly ahead, kill some meat and be waiting with it at the roadside as we should come along, stuck out. He looked back and said "Good bye." We all shouted "Good bye and good luck Pete." This was the last we ever saw or heard of the poor fellow. His scalp was evidently dangling from the lance pole of some Indian ere the sun went down that night. After he had gone we yoked up and resumed our weary march.

The cattle soon began to lag and it was hard work to make them go on, even at the slow pace we were making. We soon had to abandon one that refused to move, then another and finally the finest bull we had in our herd refused to go farther and laid down. The owners reluctantly gave the order to leave him and push on and try to save the balance. Personally, I objected and not realizing my great peril told the rest to move on and I would stay with the bull and if he revived I would work him along and try to catch up with the train by dark. I had not rode my pony that day and although she was

"One of the ways into Montana" – *Harper's New Monthly Magazine*, October, 1867

terribly hungry and thirsty she was comparatively fresh. The caravan moved on and I was alone save the bull, my pony and shooting irons. Being ignorant of my danger I had not the least particle of fear. Yet as the train went out of sight behind a rocky ridge I could not repress a feeling of lonesomeness.

I found a few tufts of wild rye grass growing on the north side of a comb or crest of rocks and carefully cutting the same with my sheath knife I divided the grass between the bull and pony. Oh, how I wanted a drink of water. Phantoms of all the cool well springs and streams I had ever seen crowded through my mind in a most tantalizing manner.

- Recollection -

After about an hour's rest, most of which time I and my pony stood so as to keep the rays of the sun off the bull, he seemed to revive, then got on his feet and began to move slowly in the direction the herd had been driven. I followed with an arm through the reins of my pony's bridle. A refreshing breeze came for a moment from the mountain ridge. After an hour of very slow walking we came to a small patch of blue grass which both animals cropped eagerly. We resumed our journey and passed a great pile of rocks. A few rods beyond these I heard a sharp hiss and an arrow struck the hard ground ahead of me. It entered the ground and stood quivering at an angle of about thirty degrees. I instantly had my rifle in position to shoot and keeping thus ready, led the pony clear around the big rock pile, keeping a sharp lookout, but, as I have since thought, fortunately for me I saw no Indians. They were evidently concealed among the rocks and mistock my apparent unconcern and foolhardiness for bravery and dared not show themselves. By this time the bull had got quite a ways ahead of me and when I overtook him we were near the edge of the mesa over which we had journeyed that day. I could see, way down in the valley, the wagons being arranged to form a corral. The train was going into camp and a line of green willows, alders and cottonwoods that ran near where camp was being made told that water had been reached. The bull, now completely exhausted, laid down and I feared he would not get up again. My pony saw camp being made and with ears pricked forward neighed softly in her eagerness to be released. At our parting the boys said that if they found water before I caught up with them they would come back to meet me with a couple kegs of water. Knowing they would not forget, I waited patiently and looked down upon the scene below. I noted that putting up of tents and as dusk came on could see the twinkle of camp fires that were being built. I was in an agony of thirst and time dragged slow. Finally I noted a couple dark objects coming from the direction of camp followed by a trail of dust and knew that relief and water were near at hand. It was a couple of our boys. One had a tin bucket and a three gallon keg of water and the other a five gallon keg. While the bucket was being filled out of the large keg I took what seemed to be the best drink of water I ever tasted. As soon as the bull heard the gargle of the water as it was coming from the keg he got up. The water was divided between the two animals, each having a large pail full. The effect of the water was almost magical. The bull struck for camp almost on a trot and my pony was so much refreshed that I rode her to camp. This camp was on Dry Fork of Powder river, the bed of which was "as dry as a contribution plate" save a tiny rill which issued from the sand a few rods above camp and ran along the surface of a clay bed rock for nearly a quarter of a mile and sank to come to the surface six miles farther down.

A cottonwood tree had been peeled at the place where the road led down into the canon and a pencil written notice told us that water could be obtained six miles down the gulch and that new Fort Reno was eight miles further. The notice further stated that the water was scant in quantity and poor in quality. Our camp this night was particularly pleasant to us, and to be once more among green trees and bushes and to hear the soft music of the tiny little rill of water which trickled down the almost dry bed of the branch of the Powder river was very grateful after what seemed an age of journeying over a hot, arid waste of barren sand, alkali and rocks. The water was clear and cold and although a little tinctured with alkali and sulphur was very refreshing. The pasturage was good in the vicinity of our camp and after our stock had drank all the water each animal could hold they went eagerly for the rich green grass. We found an abundance of dry camp wood, cedar, cottonwood, alders and willows. Our proximity to the mountains made the night air crisp and chilly and we once more indulged in generous sized camp fires.

Fearing a possible night attack from the red skins and hoping to see "Dutch Pete" again, we sat up that night later than usual. But poor Pete did not show up. My experience that afternoon and the arrow I had stuck in my hat band, as evidence, gave us the knowledge that we were in the Indian country and the non appearance of Pete gave us some alarm. Some one suggested that the arrow was shot at me as a joke, to see how badly I could be scared, and that my bravado had kept the sportive brave who shot it from showing himself and being friendly, for fear that I, fool like, would shoot without waiting to learn his real intention towards me. We all fell in with this idea and I really felt ashamed of myself for not having taken this view at the time and sat down and waited for "Poor Lo" to come out and demonstrate his brotherly love for the strange white man, instead of cavorting around the point of rocks with an ugly looking double barreled rifle in my hands and in a position for instant use, and an expression of countenance that betrayed hostile intentions.

It was argued that if I had behaved myself like a Christian, laid down my arms and advanced smiling and empty handed to the rock pile, I might have met some red brothers who would have been pleased to have made my acquaintance and been eager to impart some useful knowledge regarding the country over which we were journeying, water, feed, etc. My self sacrifice and apparent bravery that afternoon had reacted against me and I felt that I had acted the idiot. The idea was also advanced that Pete was being entertained at some Indian camp fire near at hand, and that ere sunrise he would be seen stalking into camp and tell us how royally he had fared on juicy bison steaks, that he had reclined on a couch of the softest and costliest furs and had been lulled into slumber by the simple songs of gazelle eyed, willowy formed Indian maidens. We really began to envy our fellow traveler. But could we have at that time known, we would have seen him enduring the most damnable tortures which the devilish savage could invent, or his body, scalped, stripped and mutilated, lying out in the cold starlight, a grewsome feast for the wolves. As we enjoyed the warmth and light of our camp fires and smoked and chatted, we little thought or knew of what the morrow would bring forth.

- Recollection -

The morning of July 22nd dawned clear and beautiful. The birds sang amid the green trees and bushes and nature looked smiling and happy. Morning did not bring our genial fellow traveler, Pete. In view of the fact that our stock was so near played out and that feed and water would be poor and scarce for some time yet and that the great freight outfits of Tootle & Co. and Todd & Parker were close behind us and would soon be along, it was decided that the part of the caravan which belonged to the crowd that the writer of this narrative was with, consisting of three wagons, of which one was a trail wagon, eleven men, two women, three children, a dozen horses and ponies, a herd of over four hundred cows and cattle and one dog, pull out and try to reach water and feed and let the stock eat, drink a rest a little and then move on and get out of the way so that the outfits that were following could have a chance. The emmigrant train was to remain in camp until 10 o'clock, then break camp and follow. Our wagons rolled out and we drivers of the loose stock followed. Our guns and ammunition, except the revolvers which we carried in holsters, were in the head wagon as we, thinking no danger menaced us, did not care to encumber ourselves with rifles on that hot day. We moved slowly down the dry bed of the gulch, the wagons at times being out of sight as curves in the road ahead would hide them from our view. About 10 o'clock we saw the wagons halt and the oxen turned loose and knew that water had been reached again. At this we ceased urging the herd along and two men rode ahead to hold the herd in check until the work cattle should have finished drinking, be hitched up and get out of the way.

In the meantime we boys amused ourselves by practicing with our revolvers at chipmunks and in this manner our pistols were nearly empty when we saw the oxen being hitched up again. We began to reload our revolvers. Each man carried a powder flask in his pocket as well as a box of caps and bullets to fit his particular make of revolver, although most of us had a Colt's navy. We had become by long practice expert shots and these weapons in our hands were nearly as effective as the muzzle loading rifles of that day were. The wagons went on and the herd was started toward the water. As the wagons went out of sight around a bend in the gulch one of the boys who was looking up the left slope of the canon shouted "Indians" and we saw about twenty five mounted red skins riding down the slope to meet us. They were gorgeous in war paint, red blankets and bright colored feathers, but we noticing that they were empty handed and hearing the friendly greeting of "How, how," supposed of course that they were friendly Indians and made no effort to check their advance. They rode directly to the two men who were in advance of the herd and began shaking hands in the most friendly and cordial manner imaginable. We were completely deceived by this friendly demonstration. One of the red devils suddenly whipped a revolver from beneath his blanket and shot one of the owners of the herd through the head from behind while two others were shaking hands with him. He pitched forward off his horse like a log and then the scene changed.

Bows, arrows and fire arms were suddenly brought forth from beneath blankets and the war was on. For one brief instant we were completely dumbfounded and paralized at the sudden change and the murder of one of us. One moment sufficed to show us the situation and our revolvers were at work. The Indians gave way and fell back like a pack of coyotes, but began to use their bows and arrows and

"A Powwow with Cheyennes"

manifesting a desire to surround us. The main body of them were between us and our wagons, which were out of sight ahead. Our rifles, the women and children and our precious ammunition were in the wagons, which we must reach in order to make a successful stand and save the lives of the women and children. We made a dash through the Indians, who speedily got out of our way seeming to have a much greater fear of a bullet wound than the most cowardly white man would manifest. A pistol shot fired among them would cause them to duck and scatter. As we made the dash they gave way, but closed in behind us and wasted some arrows, but their aim was not accurate and we escaped injury. Their blood curdling yelling was frightful. As we rounded a bend in the canon we came onto our wagons. The drivers had seen the Indians ride down off the bluffs and hearing the firing had wisely stopped. A dozen mounted Indians that we had not previously seen were gathering around, intent on murder and plunder. At sight of us they scattered like frightened sheep and were soon out of sight around a rocky point that ran down into the canon. While we were getting our rifles and ammunition out of the wagon arrows began dropping down on us from the hills and we saw the Indians on foot were thick among the rocks on either side of the gulch. An Indian would pop up and throw an arrow down and dodge back out of sight before a rifle could be brought to hear upon him. These arrows when in the air looked like a small black dot and were easily dodged, yet they came with terrible force. Many of them found lodgment in some large cottonwood trees that we were in the midst of. They would pass with a very unpleasant hiss as they cut the air in close proximity to our bodies. We opened fire on our assailants with our rifles, for which they seemed to have great respect, and thus managed to keep a large circle of the landscape around us clear. Beyond this we did not seem to be doing any good and their numbers seemed to be constantly increasing.

To remain here would be to lose all. To attempt to push on eight miles further to the fort would be virtual suicide as the enemy would follow and pick off an occasional man until we were reduced to a condition that would render the balance helpless, when the yelling savages could close in on what was left and take all without risk to their vermin infested skins.

To remain here, surrounded as we were by rocks, trees and bushes, convenient hiding places for the redskins to shoot from, would be equally hazardous. We had left our dead comrade where he fell and our herd of stock half a mile back and it was uncertain how long we would have to wait before being reinforced by the arrival of our fellow travelers. It took but a short time to decide to turn back and fight our way through until we should meet some of our friends. The wagons were turned about and the retreat began. Our teamsters, unknown to the rest of us, uncoupled and left the trail wagon, which carried our bedding, tent, stove, a sack each of flour, sugar and bacon, a keg of syrup and many other, to us, useful articles. By the time we noticed this we were half way back to where we had been attacked. Not being followed and annoyed by the Indians caused us to investigate and it was then the discovery was made. A howl of indignation went up at our loss and two of us rode back to save the wagon and its contents. Too late, as the little wagon was surrounded by a horde of redskins who were busy with the work of plunder. So intent were they on plunder that we were nearly among them before they discovered us. We were imbued with the spirit of revenge and now was our chance. With an admonition to each other not to waste our ammunition but "shoot to kill," we dashed up revolvers in hand, yelling as hard as the Indians themselves had when we were working in the lead in our efforts to save the women, children and our wagons.

Not a show of resistance was made. On the contrary the redskins fairly fell over each other in their efforts to escape. Those that were on foot were out of sight as quick as if the ground had suddenly opened and taken them in. Those that were mounted could not get so quickly out of sight, as they had to ride directly from us, and they were at our mercy and we made good use of our opportunities. We could not have had better targets. A bullet through the back seemed to exert a more willing influence over "poor lo" than one in the breast.

Mansel Cheney, circa 1865
Leader of the Burgess-Cheney Party
Ambushed and killed by Sioux Indians at the
Dry Fork of the Powder River, July 22, 1866

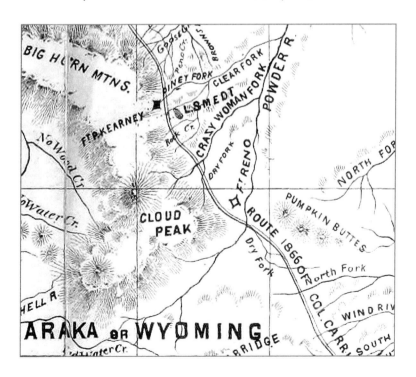

He would simply give a yell, throw up his hands, dropping whatever he had in them, and pitch forward. His pony would round the nearest point and be out of sight. Not one of them fell from his horse, which made us think at the time that they possessed a wonderful facility of gripping the animal with their legs and thus being carried away. Our revolvers were accurate shooting weapons and we were in good practice. Although our shots seemed rapid we took careful aim. Our revolvers were soon empty and we hurriedly reloaded. If our red foes could only have known, we would have been an easy prey. We realized this, and also that the teamsters' act of apparent cowardice had saved us, and our hearts were not so bitter against him. We also felt elated to know that Mr. Indian had paid dearly for his little exhibition of love for his white brother. We further realized that our companions might even now be in trouble and need our aid. We reluctantly left our wagon and its precious load and galloped back to overtake our friends and comrades.

- Diary -

July 22, 1866 (July 22.) – Our little outfit pulled out early this morning in hopes of finding more water and feed, where we could rest awhile. We had journeyed 6 miles down the canyon when we come to some small springs where we obtained a little indifferent water. Mansel and Lewis were in advance of us boys who were driving the herd. A party of nine Indians rode down from behind a hill and rode up to them apparently very friendly and commenced shaking hands with them, when one of the red devils suddenly drew a pistol from beneath his blanket and fired at Mansel who fell from his horse dead. Lewis' horse jumped and ran toward us. We were taken completely by surprise, we had supposed the Indians to be perfectly friendly and had treated them all as such. We were wholly unprepared for such an attack, having no fire arms about us except our revolver and they only partly loaded. We recovered from our surprise, however in a moment and drawing our pistols, charged at the Indians, fired a few shots at them, and drove them off. We then made a dash for our wagons, which were ahead, expecting to find them taken, found them ½ mile ahead. They had seen the Indians ride down off the hill and hearing the fireing, had rightly conjectured the cause, and stopped the teams. We got our guns, gathered the cattle and turned back. By this time we could see 25 or 30 Indians gathering around

"A Peril of The Plains"

the hills. Lyman and Lewis went ahead to turn back some stock that had gone on. The Indians fired arrows at them from the top of the hills, but they dodged them. We fired several shots at them as they would dodge up to shoot arrow from the hill tops. When we got back to where Mansel was killed we found that the Indians had been there and stripped him. They had also shot arrows into some of the stock. When we got back to where we started from this morning we found that the Indians had been there and shot one of their men wounding him badly. When we turned back from where our teams were, the man who was driving the ox team uncoupled the trail wagon and left it. Todd & Parkers train came up just as we got back and after laying out poor Mansel seven of us went back to where we were attacked. We were well armed and hoped to find the Indians, but was fortunate enough to not find them. They had plundered our wagon, taken what things they wanted and destroyed the balance. My chest was in the wagon when that was left. The Indians had torn the cover off from it and taken or destroyed all it contained, my watch, clothing, keepsakes, a small collection of curious petrifications and in fact every thing I had with me except my violin and rifle which happened to be in the other wagon. The clothing all except the blankets of the other boys was in carpet bags and they were also in the other wagon.

Yesterday a man belonging to Parkers train went out hunting, but did not come back and is supposed to have been killed by the Indians. They called him Mountain Frank. Those that went back after the Indians were Lyman, Lewis, Harry, Texas and myself from our outfit and three men from Todd & Parkers outfit. Lyman went around through the hills and saw a lot of clothing, Luciens violin and some other articles which the Indians had left in a hollow. He brought a pair of pants belonging to one of the boys.

When the Indians came up to the emigrant outfit they came in friendly and wanted something to eat. They were given all they could eat, then they wanted some amunition but were refused. They stayed and talked awhile, then rode off and shot a man who was on herd as they went away. The Indians tried to stampede the stock but did not succeed on account of their being so worn down by hard driving without food and water. The arrows that were shot into the cattle went in up to the feather. The Indians captured Mansels pony, also his gold watch and a considerable sum of money, which he had with him.

July 23, 1866 (July 23.) – Started all of us in company. A man rode on each side some distance from the train as scouts. We travelled 12 miles and stopped for noon. Dug a grave and buried Mansel, poor fellow, in as decent a manner as we could under the circumstances. Obtained a little water for the stock after hard digging. Afternoon we moved 8 miles farther on to a small millitary post that has lately been started by the name of Fort Reno, on Powder river, where the poor, tired, thirsty stock could get water in abundance. The soldiers are very much alarmed on account of the Indians and are building a log stockade around the fort. Distance to-day 20 mi.

- Recollection -

It did not take us long to catch up. We found our dead comrade stripped but not scalped or mutilated. The Indians had omitted this part of the program and had tried to stampede our cattle. About twenty head had been shot with arrows in their efforts to make them stampede. The poor cattle were too tired to run and some were already dying of their wounds. We gathered up all of the herd that were able to move, put the body of our murdered comrade in one of the wagons and not meeting our friends, who were then past due, we continued our backward march until we came in sight of our late camp. The emmigrants were still in camp as we had left them that morning. We wondered at this, but soon learned that the Indians had, as soon as we were out of sight that morning, rode into camp in an apparently friendly mood. They had no weapons in sight and said they were "heap hungry" and wanted "biscuits." Our friends had fed them until their paunches were well stuffed, then added some presents. The Indians had shook hands and said "me go now," mounted their ponies and rode leisurely away until about fifty yards from camp, where they halted, drew their bows from beneath their blankets and without warning fired a volley of arrows, back at their benefactors, who stood watching them, then rode away on a dead run.

By the time our friends had recovered from their surprise and got their guns, the redskins had got beyond range of the rifles. A few shots had been sent after them which fell far short and was answered by the Indians with a derisive yell and insulting gestures.

An Indian may be deficient in good manners but he is certainly not lacking when it comes to offering insult and injury and playing hog.

As a result of the "playful" volley of arrows above mentioned, one man was dying from a wound in his stomach and another man who happened to be standing with his back to the reds had an arrow wedged in his spinal column. We took him to the fort where he could have surgical treatment, where he died a few days after.

The dead were laid on a wagon sheet spread in the shade of some cottonwood trees to be prepared for burial in as descent a manner as the circumstances would allow. We intended to take the bodies to Fort Reno for burial. While we were making these preparations Todd & Parker's train rolled in and camped. They had encountered no Indians and supposed that they were still friendly. Burning with anger and a desire to work further vengeance and wanting to see what the Indians had done at the battle ground after we had left, six of us, heavily armed, rode back that afternoon to the scene of the fight. We did not see an Indian, but found that they had carried off or destroyed the contents of our trail wagon.

In a shady place near a small pool of water we found where they had broken the head of the keg of syrup and spilled what they could not eat on the ground. The sugar had all been eaten or carried off, the flour had been scattered to the winds and our blankets carried off. We bitterly regretted that the syrup and sugar had not been well mixed with some deadly poison and our blankets were not reeking with some pesty house infection, such as small pox, scarlet fever or measles. Some of us firmly resolved that if we lived to get out of that place to return as soon as possible, invite an attack and let the redskins capture and treat themselves to a very generous dose of death dealing blankets, sugar, whisky and other delicacies so dear to the red man's heart. How our fingers did itch for more opportunities to pull trigger on other hostile savages.

From this time on our camp was picketed by a lookout post on each prominent hill within hailing distance of camp and when on the march by two men who rode in advance of the train.

This was a sorry night for us. A watch was kept up all night, with our dead and those of us who had lost our bedding made use of gunny sacks and horse blankets and had to borrow from our more fortunate neighbors, covering to keep out the chill night air.

By frequent changing of our pickets and night watch each man had a chance to sleep part of the night and once laid down, the drowsy god did not need wooing, but-soon had us in his mysterious realm.

After this day's experience we gave up looking for poor Pete, it being certain that he had met death at the hands of the red assassains.

We were astir early the next morning and by sunrise we were, like a great funeral procession, moving slowly toward Fort Reno and the land toward which we had so long journeyed. By 10 o'clock the air had grown very sultry and the body of our murdered comrade had become so offenseve that we were forced to halt and bury it. A place was selected under the shade of some stately cottonwoods, the grave was dug deep and a carpet of green boughs carefully laid at the bottom. The body, decently dressed and wrapped in a pair of clean woolen blankets, but, without a coffin, was tenderly lowered into the grave, covered thick with green boughs and the grave filled and rounded up. The lid of a mess box was inscribed with name, age and how he met death. The letters being first cut into the soft pine and then blackened with a lead pencil. The trunk of a small tree was peeled of bark and a note of warning written thereon to put those who might follow on their guard and we moved on and left our comrade in the

Cottonwood trees along Dry Fork of Powder River
This photo was taken 8.5 miles from old Ft. Reno
and is likely the final resting place of Mansel Cheney

slumber of death This was the saddest burial we ever saw. It seemed awful to leave our comrade alone in the wilderness. The occasion was made doubly sad from the fact that his widow and children were along and had to go through the terrible ordeal with the rest of us.

We did not see any more Indians that day and reached Fort Reno, after fording the main branch of Powder river, a little before sundown that evening.

This new frontier post was just being built, the barracks and quarters were incomplete and the plat of ground was as yet only partially surrounded by a stockade of logs set on end in a trench and held by the dirt being tamped in around them.

These were the first buildings we had seen for many a long weary day, and they had, to our eyes, a look of security, restfulness and comfort that made us wish that our journey was ended. We found this little garrison of two companies of soldiers in a state of terror, fearing the Indians would take and burn the fort. Two days before our arrival the Indians had made a descent on the herd, killed and scalped the soldiers who were on herd duty and ran off all their mules and ponies, nearly a hundred head in all. This was a severe blow to the garrison.

As we could get no water after leaving Fort Reno until we should reach Crazy Women's fork of Powder river, and the days were terribly hot, we decided to made a night drive. We succeeded in buying some blankets from the post sutler at an enormously high price, filled our kegs and canteens with water, cooked an extra day's ration of bread, cleaned and oiled our fire arms, refilled our powder flasks, moulded a new supply of bullets and made down our beds for a brief sleep and rest. The stock was herded near the post that night, but they were too weary to be stampeded and there was no danger of any leaving the main herd and straying away.

The different bugle calls that night sounded inexpressibly sweet to our ears, so long accustomed to less musical sounds.

- Diary -

July 24, 1866 (July 24.) – Lay over until 4 o'clock P. M., then drive till 12 o'clock. No water. Distance 12 mi.

July 25, 1866 (July 25.) – Drive 16 miles without water. Camp on Crazy Womans fork, a beautiful stream. The feed was so poor that we were obliged to drive the stock half a mile from camp. Charley, Rodolph, Lyman, Lucien and I were on herd until after the other boys should eat dinner and come to relieve us. Hary and Texas came out. We gave them our guns and started for camp. We had got about half way to camp when we heard the cry of Indians, ran up on a little hill just in time to see a party of mounted Indians coming like the whirl wind into the herd and go away with all our ponies and saddles, except two of the poorest. Harry and Texas fired all the shots they had in their weapons but did not kill any of them, that we know of. We rolled out at 6 P. M. and had gone about two miles, when the Indians drive in our scouts. We instantly corralled the wagons and made preparations for an attack but our red foes did not choose to fight us. A couple of dogs we had with us left us to-day. We think they must have gone back to the Fort. Distance to-day 18 mi.

Lewis Cheney, circa 1880
Lewis Cheney led the Burgess-Cheney party
following the death of his brother Mansel

- Recollection -

We were stiring again at, or a little after, midnight, refreshed ourselves with hot biscuit, coffee and fried bacon and gave the cattle a chance to drink. By this time two of the wounded ones that we had abandoned on the battle ground came along and joined the herd. One of these, a fine cow, we gave to the soldiers, who would try to cure her wounds and keep her for her milk. The other we decided to let follow or not as she pleased and take chances of living. She had an arrow in her side driven in clear up to the feathers. She followed the herd and would be with them each morning and after we had carefully extracted the arrow the wound healed up.

After our midnight lunch the teams were yoked and hitched up and we rolled out. The night was delightfully cool and we made good time.

We halted at daylight on some very fair feed and let the stock rest and graze while our breakfast was prepared and eaten. There was no water for the stock and we used of the scant supply we had brought from Powder river very sparingly to make coffee. It was so cool that the animals had not got very thirsty yet.

The morning was glorious and we were on the march again before the sun had chased the shadows out of the deep gulches.

By 10 o'clock the heat had become oppressive and our thirsty animals were moaning for water and although it seemed heartless we had to keep moving. Water meant life and we must push on and try to reach it. At 3 o'clock that afternoon a line of green was to be seen several miles ahead, at first wavering and indistinct like a mirage. It seemed almost too good to be believe, be we kept on until there was no mistake. It was a line of green willows and we knew that they meant water. The cattle took in the situation and seemed to be imbued with new strength and vitality. They required no more urging. An hour later they were standing knee deep in a clear mountain stream and drawing long cool draughts of water.

The feed had been cropped so close near the creek by other outfits that were ahead of us that we had to drive our stock out to a butte nearly a mile from where we made camp.

Four of us volunteered to guard the herd while the rest got something to eat, which would be the first food we had eaten since dawn that morning. Two others climbed the butte to watch and give warning in case any Indians should be seen. Loading ourselves with firearms we took our stations, tired and hungry. We found that unless we kept walking we would go to sleep in spite of our good resolutions to the contrary. We could see the smoke of the fires at camp where cooking was going on and it seemed to us a long time that we had to wait for our turn to go to camp and break our fast. At last two men were seen coming to relieve us. Four were to have come but from some oversight only two were sent. We turned our arsenal over to them and started for camp. The sentinels on the butte were also relieved.

Everything looked very calm and peaceful on that sultry midsummer afternoon. We could see the great corral of wagons at the creek on one side and a thousand head of cattle quietly grazing at the base of the foothills on the other side. It did not seem as if the peaceful scene could so soon be changed. We started to walk back to camp and just as we reached the foot of the low mesa on which the herd was grazing the cry of "Indians" from the pickets sent the blood surging through our veins and we hurried back up the slope to see a cavalcade of mounted Indians swooping down into our herd yelling and waving their red blankets in their efforts to cause a stampede. They rode through the herd like a whirlwind and not withstanding the fact that our two herders were busy emptying their guns at them they managed to scoop out our ponies as they went past and we had the mortification of seeing them disappear through a low gap in the hills a few moments later, and being unarmed and afoot we were powerless to prevent. This was a bloodless battle with the exception of one cow that one of the boys accidentally shot and killed.

As our camp was too near the dense willows for our safety in case the "gay and festive red man" should take it into his head to attack us from ambush, we decided to yoke up and move on in hopes of finding some suitable place where we could make a stand and fight if necessary. If any more fighting was in store for us we wanted it to take place in the open, or where we, instead of the indians, could shoot from a place of concealment. It was nearly sundown by the time we had got strung out and in marching order again.

We missed our ponies. It was hard work to get the big herd together and drive on foot. Our boots chafed our feet and made us weary. We could see that the road ran over a high treeless ridge.

Two men walked in advance of the caravan to give warning if any Indians should be seen. Every man was ready and anxious for a fight, our guns and pistols cleaned and loaded and kept where instant use could be made of them. Dusk was coming on and we were nearing the top of the ridge when a couple shots fired ahead of us and the clatter of hoofs caused every man to get his shooting irons in hand. The hoof beats grew louder and a band of redskins appeared in a semicircular mass on the summit of the ridge. They were clearly outlined against the sky and as they were not over a hundred yards away they made good targets, even in the gathering dusk. The cavalcade halted right in our teeth, so to speak, and fired a volley of bullets and arrows down on us. They only fired one volley. A hail of rifle and revolver bullets from us spoiled their anticipated pleasure of riding down the line, shooting down the drivers as they passed and capturing and plundering the train. Their shots all passed harmlessly over our heads, not a man, beast or even a wagon received a scratch.

Before the Indians could possibly get out of sight below the brow of the hill we had got in our work in fine shape, two or more hundred shots having been sent after them. We saw that they got out of range very quickly but could not tell what damage they had sustained, as it was too dark to see anything except objects outlined against the sky, but with our first fire their yelling ceased.

The wailing sound of mourning came up from both sides of the ridge, showing that the band, in its frantic effort to escape, had separated. But gradually the sounds came up from the shadowy depth on our left.

We did not know what these sounds meant until a day or two afterwards when the great scout, Col. Bridger, and his half breed attendant joined us and told us that the peculiar noises we described were lamentations at the death of some important man or men of the tribe. The colonel and his man Friday were of a small stature but well knit and wiry built, nimble of motion and keen eyed. They seemed to be able to take in every detail with one sweep of the eye, and we noticed that. Their eyes were continually searching the landscape. The colonel told us to never let any Indians approach in a hostile country.

- Diary -

July 26, 1866 (July 26.) – Drive 17 miles to-day. Passed a place where some unfortunate men had fought a battle with the Indians. There were slight breastworks thrown up with small stones. There were two ponies and a mule lying dead and some bloody garments had been left. Camp for the night at some springs. Water very disagreeable to the taste being strongly impregnated with sulphur and salts, found stone coal cropping out of the sides of the hills in some places.

July 27, 1866 (July 27.) – Moved ten miles, nooned at Rock Creek, a beautiful mountain stream, clear and cold. The stock rushed into it as eagerly as ourselves Drove five miles after noon. Weather very hot. Travelled 15 mi.

July 28, 1866 (July 28.) – Passed Smith's Lake this morning. Did not have time to go and see it. Nooned at Piney Fork, a small Creek. There are large logs and stumps of trees lying in the creek that are pertified, with the gnarls and grain of the timber perfect. After dinner moved to Fort Phil Kearney, a new milliatry post that has just been established. There are 600 soldiers here. There are a number of trains camped here waiting to organize into a large company so that they may safely proceed on their journey. This post is situated on Piney Creek and at the base of a spur of the Wind River mountains. The post is under command of Col. H. B. Carrington. Distance to-day 10 mi.

Hired three men at Fort Phil. Kearney: Lewis Baker, James & Thomas McGarry. There were three trains of us together when we leave the fort: Kirkkendalls' mule train. Tootles ox train and our train, composed of Todd & Parkers train, the emigrant and our outfit 110 wagons.

July 29 – August 1, 1866 (July 29, 30, 31 & August 1.) – Stay over to rest and let the stock recruit.

- Recollection -

The attack had caused us to corral with more than customary dispatch. Not knowing the meaning of the strange sounds which continued to come up from the shadowy depth on our left, we kept the work cattle confined for a time within the narrow limits of our corral of wagons, as we fancied that the doleful bellowing might be a general call to arms and that a vast number of hostiles might swoop down upon us and refuse to beaten off. The moon came up and lent a wierdness to the scene. No Indians showed themselves and the log chains were taken down and the oxen allowed to go out and graze with the loose cattle. Our fighting force was then divided into two squads, one of which was to lie down behind the barricade of ox yokes which had been laid around inside the circle of wagons, while the other squad went on guard until midnight. The writer was in the first watch and we had to keep in motion to stay awake, and even this did not keep us from sleeping. Thinking we were keeping a sharp look out and that the mysterious sounds of night were filling our ears we would stumble over a sleeping cow, go down, get up and look sheepishly around to see if any one had seen us and then resume our walk with a determination to do so no more. This determination would remain and seem to get more firm, when another recumbent bovine would be run against and down we would go again.

Our boots began to chafe our ankles, but this, together with the fact that we could see, hear and think, could not keep us awake all the time.

After what seemed an eternity the member who carried the watch announced midnight, but it seemed too bad to awaken our sleeping comrades so soon and we decided to stay on guard an hour longer. When relieved we laid down and in less than half a minute were locked in a slumber too profound for dreams.

It did not seem as if we had slept a minute, when we were awakened and saw the sun was an hour high. The morning air was glorious. Carefully scanning the landscape around us not an Indian could be seen.

A dead pony lay a hundred yards to our right and the blood on the grass and weeds was evidence that our scrimmage of the night before had been effective.

Circumstances over which we had no control had caused us to make a dry camp the night before, and ere we could make coffee and cook breakfast water had to be reached. This compelled us to yoke up and move on with empty stomachs and call down bitter maledictions upon the innocent head of the noble red man. We could see, down in a gulch ahead, a line of green willows, which meant water.

After a late breakfast we moved on and passed a place where a train had been corralled and had a battle with Indians. Two ponies and a mule lay dead just outside a slight barricade of boulders, which had been hastily built up, and inside lay a blood soaked pair of shirts with a bullet hole through each, which showed that the victim had been shot through, just under the armpits. We learned a few days later that these bloody garments had been worn by the wagon master or captain of the train and that the fight had lasted three days, the captain being the only white man killed.

We made camp that night at some springs, the water of which was villainous with sulphur and other minerals held in solution, but here a fortune was sticking out of the bluffs in the form of a strata of hard, shining coal. This is the third deposit of excellent looking coal that we have seen cropping out of the hill sides since reaching the Powder river country, and we imagined a time which would bring civilization; when the shriek of the locomotive would be heard instead of the dismal howling of wolves and the blood thirsty yell of the lousy redskin.

We were now in a land abounding in very interesting fossils, which we had no time to stop to study nor the means of transportation to carry them with us. Some of us resolved to return at some future date, when it was safe to explore and when we could come prepared to carry away a wagon load of these wonderful petrifactions. Over thirty years have passed since then and monopolistic greed and a mismanaged government has made the masses too poor to indulge in such pleasures and we, being of the common herd, have been reduced to a state of poverty which forbids the hope of ever realizing this rare pleasure that we had for so long a time considered as almost certain.

Nature had for ages been engaged in the work of petrescence in this land of wonders, which was peopled by a race who considered not the rare archeological wonders here disclosed and who were as unappreciative as a drove of hogs.

The next day, July 27, we nooned on the bank of what Col. Bridger told us was Rock creek. This was a most beautiful mountain stream. The water was clear and cold. Here we heard the whispering pines and saw for the first time mountain trout lying in the shady pools. We did not attempt to take any of them, as we did not dare to go far from camp. How restful this beautiful, shady noon camp seemed on the that sultry, midsummer day. We dallied here so long that we only made a five mile drive that afternoon.

The next morning we passed a blue sheet of water that lay to our right. Col. Bridger told us that this was Smith's lake and that wonderful fossil remains were abundant around its shores.

This region showed that at some period in the dim and shadowy past it had been the scene of great seismic activity. It was plain to see that after having been above the surface of the ancient ocean that once covered it for a period long enough to be covered with forests of gigantic trees, the land had been resubmerged. During its second submersion powerful submarine eddies and currents had formed great bars of gravel and boulders which had been torn from the rocky sides of the mountains and deposited where we now saw them. The land had remained under water long enough for the animal and vegetable forms to become agatized and buried in a sedimentary deposit. Since the land had arisen the second time the slow process of erosion had carved ravines and gulches, uncovering and exposing to the view of man all of these wonders. We were told that in some ravine in this neighborhood the erosive process had partially uncovered an agatized forest and that some beast bearing a close resemblance to an elk had been caught in the grand mix up and turned to stone in a standing position among the trees of his native forest and had been uncovered down to where its legs joined its body.

That day the writer picked up at the roadside a small fossil tortoise which served as a pocket curiosity for many days. In shape it bore a strong resemblance to the land tortoise now so common on the prairies of Illinois and Missouri. After our experience at noon that day we could swallow the yarn of the petrified elk.

We nooned that day where a small creek had cut a deep channel through the alluvial formation, and here the process of erosion had uncovered some gigantic agatized trees which bore resemblance to the great redwoods of the Pacific states. The gully down which this little stream ran was bridged in places by these massive trunks, the limbs of which had been broken in fragments and lay thick on the ground where the trees that were once the pride of some mighty forest had stood. We crossed and recrossed the gully on these strange bridges and knew that the trees once lived and grew on the spot where we saw them, but could not guess how many vast eons of time had come and gone since the infant shoots from which these forest giants grew had pushed their tender heads up through the dark mold into the beautiful sunlight.

- Recollection -

That afternoon we moved on and went into camp with other trains on a swell which overlooked a new military camp called Fort Phil Kearney. The quarters were at the time all canvas. Teamsters were busy hauling logs from the hills for building purposes and men were hard at work digging a trench around the grounds in which to place the logs that would form the stockade or enclosure. This new post had a most picturesque location, being situated on the Big Piney, a beautiful mountain stream, surrounded by grassy slopes and pine clad mountains.

Droves of antelope could be seen at any time of the day from the fort, while back in the wooded hills an abundance of deer, elk, bear and sheep were to be found. Coyotes and timber wolves were also very abundant and just at dusk the quavering treble of a coyote was wafted to our ears, followed by others and then the baying of the timber wolves set in. This music swelled in volume as other throats were tuned until the very air seemed to throb and quiver with the ghostly melody. The serenaders seemed to surround our camp and a thousand throats must have been acting in unison to produce such a volume of sound.

"Fort Philip Kearney"

Six hundred troops were quartered here and the commander of the post was a man-much-afraid-of-Indians. In our outfits were 300 private citizens and nearly that number of wagons, but we soon learned that we were to be detained, by military orders, until two companies could be sent to the Big Horn river where they were to establish another fort, when we were to travel together for mutual protection, as Sitting Bull had sent in word that Tongue river would be a dead line over which no white man could pass that season. Consequently it was expected that a large force of fighting Sioux would be encountered at Tongue river and a long and bloody battle would be the result.

To add to the general alarm the squaw and half breed family of French Pete, a trader, came into the post for protection, saying that her husband and four other men had been killed and scalped, their wagons plundered and burned and their stock driven off and that a powerful body of Sioux and Cheyennes were going to stop further travel westward and would "heap kill white man." This tragedy occurred only a few miles from the post and a detatchment of troops were sent out to bury the dead.

This post sported a fine brass band and the music during the different drills and daily exercise was a rare treat. The wolves serenaded us regularly each evening.

A day was set to move on our journey. The night before starting festivities in honor of the two companies who were to go under our protection lasted until late in the evening and ended with a grand serenade. That evening we pilgrims had several large fires of dry pinon logs blazing inside of our great corral of wagons and were visiting and formulating plans for the future. We were eager to be again on the move and to face any dangers that might lie ahead.

The wolves had been unusually persistent in their howling that night, but when the band struck up at the fort and the waves of melody from the brass instruments rolled up the slopes the wolf racket subsided, only to begin again at the end of the piece.

We could not guess whether the beasts enjoyed the band music better than their own or whether it was politeness on their part which caused them to give way to the band. Anyway the howling would cease each time the band struck up. Finally, after a long pause, the ever beautiful "Home, Sweet Home" was rendered. Our camp was just the right distance from the fort to give the music a good effect. The melody carried us back to the old home hearthstone and the voices around our camp fires grew husky with tender emotion as we listened. Rough, bearded giants would hurriedly leave the fires and seek the shadows of the wagons to conceal the tears that could not be kept back, not a few sobbing aloud as they walked away. We never before realized the softening powers of music, but many poor fellows who listened that night to the melting strains of that dear old piece never saw their dear home again.

That autumn an entire company of troops were massacred a short distance from and within plain view of the fort. The soldiers were eager to go to the rescue of their comrades but the craven colonel who was in command ordered them to remain inside the stockade, his excuse being that he dare not weaken his forces for fear the post would be captured. Thus the brave men were compelled to witness the butchery of their fellow soldiers and were not permitted to try to save them. The massacred company had that morning started out to perform some labor outside the enclosure and while at work had been surrounded by a band of Indians, who kept circling around them on their ponies and as the circle narrowed the deadly arrows got in their work on the defenseless soldiers. Not a man of that ill fated company escaped.

The Custer massacre a few years later was enacted in this same region, as well as other deadly conflicts between the white and red men. The contemplation of these bloody encounters calls to mind the appropriate lines, which we quote:

"Hollow ye the lonely grave,

Make its caverns deep and wide,

In the soil they died to save,

Lay the brave men side by side.

Side by side they fought and fell,

Hand to hand they met the foe

Who has heard his grandsire tell

Braver strife, or deadlier blow?

Pile the grave mound broad and high

Where the martyred brethren sleep,

It shall point the pilgrim's eye

Here to bend and here to weep."

During our sojourn at Fort Phil Kearney our stock had become rested and saucy. We had bought a new outfit of ponies and blankets and had put wagons, clothing, arms and ammunition in good order and now felt ready to meet any emergency.

After the exercises at the fort were over the camp fires were again encircled to take the go-to-bed smoke and complete plans for the morrow. The two companies of cavalry with its train of freight wagons and ambulences were to take the lead. Kirkendall's mule train next, then the great ox trains of Tootle, Hanna & Co and Todd & Parker were to fall into line, while the smaller trains of freighters and emmigrants with the loose herds were to bring up the rear. Two or more mounted men from each outfit were to ride at each side of the mighty caravan, well back in the hills, while three or four men were to ride behind the whole column to guard against surprise. With the completion of these details those who were not on guard duty knocked the ashes from their pipes, sought their blankets and were soon oblivious to mundane affairs.

Fetterman Massacre at Fort Phil Kearny, December, 1866

- Diary -

August 2,1866 (August 2.) – Leave Fort Phil. Kearney, travel three miles and camp. We now number 110 wagons, 171 men, 6 women and 6 children in all.

August 3, 1866 (August 3.) – Moved four miles, camp on a small stream called Peam Creek. Passed the place where a French trader and four others were murdered a short time ago by the Indians. They had been buried so shallow by the soldiers that they had been uncovered by the wolves or other wild beast and were partly decomposed. Some of the men covered them again.

August 4, 1866 (August 4.) – Travelled 8 miles. Camp on Tongue River, were joined by two companies of soldiers who were going to the Big Horn river to establish a new millitary post. Two men went hunting this evening and killed a buffalo and an antelope. Saw to-day where a wagon had been captured by the Indians, plundered and destroyed.

August 5, 1866 (August 5.) – Drove eight miles, saw many buffaloes at a distance. Met an old school mate by the name of Aron Bailey. Weather lovely and the best of feed and water for the stock. Cattle beginning to look well again. Country hilly, Mountain scenery splendid.

August 6, 1866 (August 6.) – Drove seven miles, nooned on South fork of Little Horn river. Camp at night eight miles farther at [illegible] Creek. This would be a splendid country for farming and stock growing. Distance to-day 15 mi.

August 7, 1866 (August 7.) – Moved 20 miles. Camp at Little Horn River. Buffalo very numerous. Some of the men killed them and left them lay without even cutting off a piece of flesh. I think that they should not kill any more game than they want to eat. Lyman killed one, the hams of which will be as much fresh meat as we will want for some time. Where we nooned to-day, we saw where a man that was killed by Indians out of a train a few days ahead of us, had been buried in a very shallow grave, some of the men shoveled more dirt upon the grave to keep the wolves from devouring the corpse.

August 8, 1866 (August 8.) – Nooned after a drive of 8 miles at North fork of Little Horn. Moved five miles afternoon camp. Could see the hills and beautiful prairies dotted over with buffalo on all sides as far as the sight could extend. One huge bull ran through the train to-day and forfeited his life by the means. Travelled to-day 13 miles.

"Splitting the Herd"

August 9, 1866 (August 9.) – Drive 18 miles to-day. Were delayed and made a dry camp 5 miles from Big Horn river. Day pleasant, country beautiful. Buffaloes very abundant. The men shot them for mere amusement.

August 10, 1866 (Aug. 10.) – Drove one mile in the morning and stop for breakfast at a small creek, saw some beaver dams, rain till about noon. Rolled out after dinner, drove four miles farther, and camp at the Big Horn river. This stream is deep, swift and about 250 yards wide. Distance to-day 5 miles.

Texas shot a buffalo calf to-day, which was very fine eating. Saw large banks of stone coal a short distance from the road to-day.

August 11, 1866 (August 11.) – Lay over, try to find a place to ford the river in vain. A man, belonging to Kirkendalls' outfit was drowned. His body was recovered after two hours search. His watch was still running and his six shooters were found to go every barrel, after having lain so long under water. The name of deceased was McGear. Found graves of men that had been killed by Indians.

August 12, 1866 (August 12.) – Moved five miles up the river to the Big Horn Ferry. The soldiers have selected this spot to build the fort. They are going to call it Fort C. F. Smith. There is a few wagons and men on the other side of the river. They are a part of a train that had most of their stock run off by the Indians a few days ago. The rest of the men having gone on to Virginia City after more stock to take the rest of the wagons through. The ferry boat here is a sorry affair. It is constructed of rough planks hewn from cotton wood logs, corked with rags and barely large enough to carry one wagon. Lyman and some others went at work to repair it.

- Recollection -

The next morning was fair and full of promise. The bugle calls at the post aroused us at dawn and we were soon as busy as a colony of ants. The cooks prepared breakfast and the herders brought in the stock. No one was idle, yet the sun was two hours high when the vast concourse of wagons, drivers and stock began to leave camp and string out in the order agreed upon the night before. "Large bodies move slow" and with us the trifling accident which would cause one team to stop would detain the entire column, as it would not do to leave any behind in this dangerous locality. These delays were so frequent that we only made three miles that day.

The next morning we reached the place where French Pete and his men had met death. The very air reeked with the odor of carrion. The soldiers who had been sent out to bury the dead had buried the corpses so shallow that the wolves had uncovered them and eaten a portion of the bodies. What remained was in an advanced stage of putrescence and the odor was horrible. We reburied the bodies and covered the grave with large flat stones to prevent the wolves from again getting at them. The ground in this little park where the killing had been done was strewn thickly with broken bottles, cigar and tobacco boxes, as well as other wreckage. We also saw many patterns that had been cut out of pasteboard by Pete's squaw and grown daughters. These were evidently intended to lay off fancy work on moccasins, gun cases, quivers, garments and other articles which the squaws are so deft at making of buckskin. We picked up and carried away several of these strange patterns as relics, but finally lost them.

We were glad to finally move on and leave this grewsome spot behind us. We only made four miles that day and camped on a small creek which the soldiers said was Peam creek, which was crossed in many places by fresh bison trails. As yet we had seen no signs of redskins. We considered this an unfavorable omen, as we reasoned that they had concentrated at Tongue river or some point ahead and were lying in wait for us. No doubt they were watching us and our strength alone kept them from appearing. We knew in all reason that not an Indian would show up except enough were back of him to give us serious trouble.

The next day August 4, we reached Tongue river, crossed and went into camp. Everything was peaceful and no Sitting Bull or Spotted Tail was there to dispute our right to be there by giving us battle. We did find the remains of another wagon which had recently been captured, but no dead bodies. If any killing had been done the wolves and vultures had obliterated the evidence.

The sight of a thousand armed warriors swooping down upon us would have been a welcome one.

A few bison were seen peacefully grazing on the hills and a few bunches of antelope regarded the long string of covered wagons with evident curiosity. A bison and an antelope were killed that evening and divided up so each mess or party had some for supper that night.

In this fair valley we noted flowers and plants that we used to see growing on the prairies of northwestern Illinois. They had been friends of ours from our earliest childhood and we felt as if we had found some old home acquaintances.

The eight miles we traveled the next day was through a most beautiful region of fertile land, grand scenery and a country fairly teeming with noble game. We were getting accustomed to traveling in a large body and could make greater distances with less troublesome delays than when we left Fort Kearney, and in the next two days we got over thirty-five miles of road and camped the night of August 7 on the Little Horn river, or "Little Big Horn" as it is called. Bison and antelope were as numerous in this region as cattle and sheep would be in some thickly settled neighborhood in the States.

At our noon camp we reburied the partially decomposed remains of a man who had been killed in a fight that some train ahead of us had been engaged in.

We reached the turbulent Big Horn river on the 10th. The next day we laid by and vainly tried to find a place to ford the river. In the attempt to cross on a mule a man named McGee, belonging to Kirkendall's train, was drowned. His body was in the water two hours, yet his watch did not stop and every chamber in his revolvers fired at first trial.

We found near the river the graves of more men that had recently been killed by the Indians.

That night as we gathered around our camp fires we could not refrain from speculating on the vast wealth which might be lying up in the mountains and which man could not at that time prospect for. Of the rare richness and beauty of the valley, its adaption to agriculture and stock growing, which but for the blighting influence of the red man would soon be covered with fields of grain and thickly dotted with happy and prosperous homes.

Every attempt to find a fording place failed. The river was too deep and swift, so the next morning we moved five miles up the river where an abandoned boat was found. This was a very clumsy affair constructed of heavy plank hewn from cottonwood logs and was so leaky it had sank to a level with the gunwhales. This had once been the rope ferry but the makers had taken the rope when they left. Although the boat was new the planks of which it was made had been roughly hewn, so the joints were a poor fit and water ran in faster than it could be dipped out. We happened to have three or four old Mississippi river raft men in the crowd who volunteered to raise and calk the boat and make it serviceable. This was our only chance to cross and although the task seemed hopeless it beat trying to build a new craft or waiting for the water to go down so that fording would be possible. The boat was dragged out by two yoke of oxen, turned over and our river men began work.

We noted a train corralled on the opposite bank. No stock was to be seen and but few men were visible. Finally a couple of men got into a dugout which they had concealed in the willows and paddled over to see us. The swift current carried them rapidly down but we ran along down the bank to aid them and as they neared our side one of them threw us a rope and we drew them in and helped tow their craft up stream to be ready for their return trip. The train had crossed about two weeks before on the ferry. After crossing and corralling they had been attacked by the Indians who ran off all their stock. This left them in a bad box, but the biggest part of the men had started for Virginia City to procure more stock and were expected back in ten days.

It took our men the balance of that and all of the next day to get the big boat in shape and hew out oars.

The following morning some oxen and mules were forced into the river and made to swim across. A set of harness, an ox yoke and

Kirkendall Train, Montana, 1869
The Burgess-Cheney party joined with the Kirkendall
and other trains during the summer of 1866

some log chains were sent over in the dugout and the work of crossing was begun in good earnest. A big freight wagon was rolled onto the boat and it was shoved off. Four men propelled the craft with side oars while another worked a stern oar. In spite of the herculean efforts of five powerful men at the oars the boat drifted down nearly three-quarters of a mile before it reached shore.

- Diary -

August 13, 1866 (August 13.) – Kirkendalls' train crossed the river; four of his mules were drowned in swimming across.

August 14, 1866 (August 14.) – Tootle and Leach's train crossed over.

August 15, 1866 (August 15.) – Our train crossed. Had considerable trouble in swimming stock; but got them over safe. We worked hard all day. Were obliged to partly unload the heavy freight wagons and carry over on a couple of dugouts that were fastened together. Other trains coming up. Three hundred wagons waiting to get across. Some of the men prospected a little for gold; but could not raise the color.

August 16, 1866 (August 16.) – Roll out early this morning. One of Parker's wagons broke down and we were obliged to lay over to mend it. Met some men with stock going back to Big Horn after the wagons that had been left there. Camp on a small creek. Do not know the name. Day pleasant. Rain after dark. Drove ten miles to-day.

August 17, 1866 (August 17.) – Travelled twelve miles Roads bad. Day pleasant.

August 18, 1866 (August 18.) – Moved eight miles. Camp on a small creek near Prior's Gap. One of the men in Kirkendall's train was seriously hurt by a wounded buffalo to-day. He had one arm and a leg broken and several ribs broken also.

August 19, 1866 (August 19.) – Passed through Prior's Gap. Nooned at a creek which we call Beaver Creek, from the number of dams which these industrious animals are constructing across. Camp for the night at another creek where the beavers are doing much work. The weather is pleasant. Distance travelled to-day is 14 miles.

August 20, 1866 (August 20.) – Passed over 14 miles of our road to-day.

August 21, 1866 (August 21.) – Nooned to-day at Clark's fork. Lyman killed a fat buffalo heifer. Camp for the night at Rock creek, a beautiful stream two feet deep and one hundred feet wide. While crossing Clark's Fork a dutch man drove his wagon a little below the ford where the water was deep enough so that it ran into the wagon bed and damaged his load some. Clark's fork is 50 yards wide and three feet deep.

August 22, 1866 (August 22.) – The emigrant outfit and our outfit, 13 wagons in all, left Todd & Parker's train this morning and pulled out ahead. Drove 18 miles.

August 23, 1866 (August 23.) – Travelled 15 miles. Crossed the south fork of Great Rosebud. This stream is clear, swift, four feet deep and 50 yards wide.

August 24, 1866 (August 24.) – Moved ten miles. Nooned at Still Water, a beautiful stream, clear as crystal and cold as ice. It is four feet in depth and 150 feet wide. Hitched up after dinner and travelled twelve miles. Camp on a high ridge near a pond where we obtained water. Weather cool and beautiful. Distance to-day 22 miles.

- Recollection -

A yoke of oxen towed the craft up to a point a half a mile above camp and it was towed back and another wagon rolled on and sent over. This operation was continued two days, during which time all the small outfits and Todd & Parker's train had crossed. Here we decided to part company with the big mule and ox trains and after swimming our loose stock across we struck out ahead, nearly fifty wagons strong.

A minister, a southern man, accompanied by a little son and a colored driver and servant, becoming disgusted at the profanity of the masculine portion of the various outfits said that our wickedness would certainly bring Deific vengeance down upon us and like Sodam of old the Almighty would destroy us and all who remained with us, root and branch; that the same Power which overwhelmed the hosts of Phario would save him and his and he would put trust in God and leave us poor sinners to our fate.

There was serious talk of compelling him to travel under our protection, but, to our shame, the argument that we were in a free land and every man had a right to do as he pleased was allowed to prevail, and our clergical fellow traveler, his innocent boy and servant were allowed to pull out alone. As his lone vehicle went out of sight over a swell in the prairie another big dispute arose among us over the question of whether horsemen should overtake and compel him to desist from his rash purpose, but those who argued personal freedom and those who wanted to see the experiment of Deitic protection tried prevailed and he was allowed to proceed. This was the last we ever saw of any of that outfit in life. We shall hereafter tell of their fate.

What a wonderful land we were now journeying over, with game on every side.

This first morning one of the great wagons in the freight train broke down and we all laid by to repair it. That day we met the men who had been sent out from the stranded train returning with stock, they having had good luck and were returning much sooner than expected, which would be a pleasant surprise to their comrades.

On August 17 the trains we had left at the Big Horn caught up and we were again strong in numbers.

The next day we camped at a small creek near Priors Gap and that afternoon one of Kirkendall's men was butted off a ledge of rocks by a wounded bison. The poor fellow was, as he expressed it, "badly broke up in business," having one thigh and several ribs broken. In the absence of a surgeon his damaged framework was patched up and bandaged as carefully as the circumstances would allow and a place smoothed off on a big load of freight and the poor fellow was compelled to ride over those jolty roads in that manner. He begged piteously to be shot and have an end put to his sufferings or to be left at the roadside a prey for wolves, but his prayers were unheeded and he was hauled along. Of course, his bed was made as soft and comfortable as possible, but nothing that we could do could prevent the jolting. At the first settlement he was left with a ranchman and a man was sent to Virginia City for a doctor. By the middle of winter he had entirely recovered and was a strong, healthy man

On the 19th we passed through Priors gap and nooned on a small stream which came down a rather steep gulch. This stream had a high beaver dam across it every few rods, which from a distance resembled a gigantic stairway leading up the gulch. The water in the pools between each dam was muddy from the night work of these industrious creatures. This was a very interesting sight to most of us, who had never seen such a thing before.

The following day we nooned at Clark's Fork, a beautiful little stream, and camped at Rock creek for night. In fording a German got below the right fording place and into deep water. We rescued him without further damage than the wetting of his load.

Bison meat had become a drug with us and a juicy antelope was a great treat.

By this time we had become weary of traveling in so vast a procession and not having seen any signs of Indians since leaving the Big Horn, on the 22nd we pulled out ahead, thirteen wagons strong, and felt more freedom and could travel much faster.

We passed through the beautiful valleys of the Great Rosebud and Stillwater and smaller streams without incidents worthy of note and on the 24th camped for night on a high ridge near a small lake, where we obtained water.

The next morning, after we had got strung out it line of march, someone looked back and discovered what we all supposed to be a large body of mounted Indians. We thought that they had massacred all the outfits behind us and were coming after our scalps. Our few wagons were hurriedly corralled as compactly as possible, guns and revolvers got ready, ammunition passed around, and without hoping to get out of this dilemma we made a firm resolve not to allow a man, woman or child to be taken alive, but to all die at our posts fighting like men. The helplessness of our situation seemed to make all of us more brave and determined. Escape by flight in a body would be out of the question and not a man entertained the idea for a moment of making a run and escape by himself. No, we would all die together and make each life cost the Indians dearly.

The oxen were unyoked and let go The herd of loose stock was also left drift on at will, but we tied our ponies to the wagons. They would be a witness to the impending struggle. The foe was getting nearer. We were fast getting tired of suspense and were eager to have it out with them, when one of the emigrants, remarking that he would have a good look at the red devils, got a spy glass and mounting his wagon looked through the tube. He jumped down off his wagon laughing like a maniac and throwing down his glass he began to dance, hold his sides and fairly scream with laughter. He was unable to articulate a word but continued his insane actions until two men caught and held him. Then another man took the glass and looked. He too, suddenly lost his reason and power of speech. We thought that these two poor fellows had escaped the terrors of the massacre in losing their reason. Another man looked and he too, went daft. He tore off his hat and shouted "Hurrah for General Jackson." By this time lunatic No. 1 began pointing back and shouting "Elk! Ha, Ha! Elk; not Injuns."

By this time they had got within range of the unaided eye and then we all went crazy. The reaction was tremendous. A keg of whisky was fished up out of one of the wagons and with a tin cup was passed around. None refused to drink that time. The oxen were soon in the yoke and we, with light hearts, were again on the march.

While hitching up, the great band of elk, yet a quarter of a mile distant, turned and disappeared down into a gulch and we saw them no more.

We pushed ahead and about an hour later were at the edge of the great plateau and looking down upon a beautiful valley through which the Yellowstone, flashing in the autumn sunlight, wound in out through cottonwood groves like a great shining serpent.

We could see a smoke curling up from a grove at a point where we thought the road would strike the river after leaving the bluff. We thought it might be the camp of our preacher friend, whose smouldering camp fires we had passed daily since he had left us at the Big Horn, and were little prepared for the grewsome sight that we were soon to behold.

- Diary -

August 25, 1866 (August 25.) – Moved ten miles. Came down upon the Yellowstone river. Nooned. This morning we saw a large band of elk running numbering as near as we could judge 500. They were a long way off. We at first thought they were mounted Indians and were considerably alarmed until a spy glass showed us our mistake. Where we struck the Yellow stone, we found a Minister, his little son, and a driver that had left the train at Big horn and gone ahead, murdered by the Indians. They were scalped by the red devils, their stock run off and the contents of their wagon destroyed. They had not been killed long for their camp fire had not gone out. We moved eight miles up the river in the afternoon. Day very pleasant. Distance to-day 18 miles.

August 26, 1866 (August 26.) – Nooned at Boulder creek. Moved ten miles farther. Camp. Saw written on a tree at Boulder, that Sawyer's train had been attacked by the "reds" and lost 8 mules. Distance to-day 20 miles.

August 27, 1866 (August 27.) – Moved six miles to the ferry and lay over the rest of the day. Some of the boys captured an old horse that bore marks of severe riding and whipping. He had probably been in the hands of the redskins.

August 28, 1866 (August 28.) – Tumbled out of our beds this morning at three o'clock. Yoked and hitched up and got the start of all the rest of the other outfits in getting to the place of crossing. Were ferried over and got the stock across after considerable delay. Ate our breakfast at noon and proceeded on our way rejoicing. Two miles from the ferry we cross a small creek. Water cold. Two miles farther on, came to another small creek. Was very thirsty just then. The water looked so clear and good that I immediately dipped up a cup full and come near burning my mouth with it. It was so hot. Went two miles and camped on a beautiful little stream called Orange creek. Moved six miles to-day.

- Recollection -

As stated in the preceding chapter the view we had of the upper Yellowstone valley was grand. A panorama of solemn, tree clad mountains, sublime in their apparent eternal stillness, grassy and graceful undulations of foot hills, bits of charming mesa land and the beautiful green valley with its willow marked creeks that made distinct lines of darker green to mark their course from the mountains to the flashing river. A sort of mellow early autumn haze seemed to rest over all the scene, but not dense enough to impede the vision.

The descent into the valley was long, steep and rough. The thin column of smoke that we had noted from the bluffs was still rising from a grove of Balm of Gilead trees, but aside from the murmur of the river all was silent. We should have been glad to have heard the sound of the voices of our friends who we felt must have their camp in that pretty grove. Upon entering the grove to greet them we did not see any one stirring and noticed that their light spring wagon had been stripped of its canvas cover and the bows were twisted and broken.

A friendly "hello there" brought no response, and on approaching the wagon and smouldering fire the bodies of the preacher and his little son, stripped, scalped and mutilated were discovered lying on the ground. Each had over a dozen arrows in their breast and their scalps had been cut in pieces the size of one's finger nail and scattered all over the ground. There was no signs of a struggle, so it was evident that no resistence had been made. The horses, harness, bedding and all articles of cloth had been taken, but the flour, canned goods and camp utensils had been scattered and broken up.

The bodies were yet warm and the wagon had not been set fire to, so we thought the Indians had been frightened at our approach, stopped their orgies and either fled or at that time might be lurking in the woods watching our movements.

Not finding the body of the colored man at camp we hoped he might have escaped. His body was soon afterward discovered lying face down in the edge of the river with a willow fishing rod in his hand. He had been fishing and was shot in the back and instantly killed. It was evident that he never knew what killed him and the red devils did not think it worth their while to strip and mutilate the body or perhaps they had not got through with their innocent pastime at camp to attend to the colored man before being frightened off at our approach.

This episode, while not reflecting on prayer and faith, proved that one should watch as well as pray, and illustrated the wisdom of one of the revolutionary commanders in telling his soldiers to "trust in God, but keep their powder dry."

That nooning was taken up with the sad task of burying the bodies of our late fellow travelers in one large coffinless grave. None of us knew the names of the dead nor the address of any living friend to whom we could communicate the sad ending of their earthly pilgrimage, so all we could do was to bury them as decently as possible, write all we knew of them on a stake and leave them in natures great purifying laboratory to be changed back into the elements of which all living bodies are built up and which is the only resurrection known to science.

That night from our camp on a beautiful creek we saw a grey horse come leisurely down from the foothills and go to grazing on the bottom land about a mile from camp. An examination revealed marks of severe usage and evidence of great fatigue. The theory that he was an old Indian pony, broken down by hard service was advanced and accepted as the probable solution, and as he was knee deep in the best of feed we left him unmolested. At this camp we saw a notice on a tree that a train ahead of us had been attacked and lost eight mules.

On August 27 we went into camp at the crossing of the Yellowstone, where we found quite a number of outfits waiting to cross. The river was too deep and swift to attempt to ford with wagons. The travelers had been detained by the breakage of the rope cable that controlled the ferry boat, which like all ferry boats west of the Missouri river, was a rough, clumsy affair. We also went into camp and waited. This was in the forenoon and by night the trains we had left behind came rolling in. One of the wagons that we found in camp here contained a family. They had a cage which was divided into two compartments, one of which held a pair of pigs and the other a trio of chickens. These were turned loose to exercise and the grunting of the pigs and chatter of the chickens carried us back to childhood. It did us good to watch and listen. A whole circus would not have been half so entertaining as were these never-to-be-forgotten sounds of the farm. We were pleased to note that their long journey had not changed their instincts or habits. The pigs rooted in the dirt the same as pigs do that have never traveled. The two hens scratched and pecked like ordinary home raised fowls. The rooster had lost none of the gallantry common to his kind, and when he strutted and crowed cheer after cheer went up from the great crowd of men who were watching and admiring him.

Three young men had charge of the boat and dwelt in a barricaded log cabin at the eastern end of the ferry. Their little cabin was a perfect arsenal of guns and revolvers, all in perfect order and kept loaded for instant use. They had not been molested, and while their position was dangerous, at $3 and $4 per wagon they were fairly coining money.

It was thought that the river would go down so that fording would be safe within a month, when the boys would tie up their boat and go to the settlements or return to their homes in the east.

In view of that fact that such a vast concourse of wagons were waiting to be set across the river, a meeting was held to decide what trains should go over first the next day. As all hands were eager to get over, it was finally decided that the first outfit to be ready the next mourning should have the first use of the ferry. We being with the emmigrants and having so cumbersome a herd of loose stock, made up our minds to be the first to cross and get out of the way of the freight outfits. That night there was much spinning of yarns and singing of songs at the various camp fires, so it was after midnight when people began to leave the fires and seek their best of blankets.

Our part of the caravan, reasoning that if we laid down we would over sleep, did not go to bed. On the contrary we began to cook breakfast. The first streaks of dawn caught us finishing breakfast and by daylight we had our oxen hitched up and the first wagon at the crossing ready to be rolled onto the boat. We routed out the slumbering ferry men, who cursed a little and grumbled a whole lot at being aroused so early.

While the wagons were being ferried over the loose stock was driven into the river and made to swim across. The train of emmigrants were out of the way by the time the other outfits had begun to prepare breakfast. We now realized that we were out of danger of an attack from Indians and with this feeling we began to relax our vigilance.

The road left the river and led over low foothills and mesas, a beautiful region. About two miles from where we crossed the river, we came to a small creek of crystal clearness. The day was sultry and all hands were thirsty. Here was a chance to get a drink. The first fellow to dip his tin cup into the limpid rill, took a hasty sip, remarked that the water was just splendid but that his thirst was gone. He threw the water out of his cup and moved on. It was lucky for him that he did so, as a moment later a dozen cups of water were lifted to thirsty lips and as hastily dashed out. The water was scalding hot and the first man who tasted it had a good joke on the balance of us and had also escaped a good wallowing by moving out of the way. He looked back in time to witness the discomfiture of his comrades and uttered a yell of delight. This creek must have issued from some hot springs up the gulch, but we did not take time to search for its source. The next day we made our noon camp on the river again and spent nearly the whole afternoon in climbing a great hill, to come down again and make our night camp in the valley close to the river.

- Diary -

August 29, 1866 (August 29.) – Came onto the Yellowstone River again after an 8 mile drive. Nooned. Started again after dinner, spent nearly all the afternoon climbing a mountain. Struck the Yellowstone again in five miles. Camp. Mosquitoes very troublesome. Distance to-day 13 miles.

August 30, 1866 (August 30.) – Travelled ten miles up the river and nooned on 25 yard creek. A cold storm of rain and snow set in. We left the river and after a four-mile drive camp.

August 31, 1866 (August 31.) – Moved ten miles. Went upon the divide between Yellowstone Valley and Salida Galletin Valley. Begin to come into civilization once more. See men travelling the road alone and unarmed.

September 1, 1866 (September 1.) – Moved 15 miles. Came down into Gallatin Valley. Saw people haying and harvesting. Nooned at Couvier's Mills, near Bozeman City. Afternoon moved ten miles down the valley. Camp at Middleton on Middle Creek. The crops look fine and farmers are very busy harvesting. Two of the hands left to-day. Day cool and pleasant. Distance to-day 25 miles.

September 2, 1866 (September 2.) – Lay over in the forenoon. Bought some new potatoes. Three of the boys left the train. In the afternoon drove twelve miles. Cross the West Galletin river. The Galletin is 75 yards in width and three feet deep.

- Recollection -

Wild redtop grass in the river bottom grew dense and rank, and directly we made night camp mosquitoes came forth from the dense growth in swarms and gave us great annoyance.

The morning of August 30 was misty but warm. We traveled up the valley and nooned at 25-Mile creek. The temperature began to fall and a drizzling rain set in, which soon turned to snow. Although it was disagreeable, a snow storm in August was a new experience to all of us, and we rather enjoyed the novelty.

The storm ceased by the middle of the afternoon and we moved four miles up the valley and camped. As we were making camp we saw a horseman coming down the valley at a gallop, leading an extra animal. He rode up, dismounted and changed his saddle to the extra horse. He proved to be John Reshaw, a half breed Indian scout, and was at the time in the employ of the United States in that capacity. He had agreed to ride back into the Indian country until he met Tootle, Hanna & Co's, freight train or learn its fate and convey the intelligence back to Virginia City, where the firm had stores. As the train was long over due the partners in Virginia City had become alarmed and took this means to learn the fate of the train. We told him that the missing train was coming a few miles back. He rode on, met the train and returned, bearing a letter to the Virginia City branch. He was our guest that night. He was feeling good at the ease with which he had earned his $500 fee, which he said he was to receive for the job. He had the dash and daring of the typical Indian scout without appearing foolhardy. In deportment he was a perfect gentleman. His skill as a rider and shot was almost phenomenal. He had caused many a hostile savage to bite the dust, and while they feared him more than a whole regiment of soldiers, they were continually trying to entrap him and get his scalp.

We feel justified in devoting so much space to a man we were glad to know and who was such a prominent figure in the early history of Montana. His wife, a beautiful half breed, and their pretty little daughter had a home with a Frenchman named John Maryville, who had a ranch near the junction of Spanish creek and an arm of the Gallatin river.

A large and very interesting book could be written of the adventures of Scout Reshaw without artificial tinting or doing any violence to the truth. The plain bare facts would be intensely interesting. We never heard him relate his own exploits, but got them from others who had personal knowledge of them.

The same evening a ranchman from the upper part of Gallatin valley, with flour and supplies for the ferryman, camped with us. Here was a citizen alone and unarmed, peaceably traveling the roads with no fear of Indians. He told us that harvest was in progress in his part of the valley, which seemed strange to us, who had been accustomed to harvesting grain in the summer, say July and August. And we were almost in a region where people were doing this work surrounded by hills capped by newly fallen snow.

That night, for the first time on that long journey, we let the stock herd themselves, and all laid down to sleep. While gathering the stragglers up the next morning, an Irish lad saw his first elk. He said "it was the divil for sure, and had the top of a dead tree upon the head of him and at first he thought it was a mule trotting off with trees on his head."

After a fifteen mile drive we nooned on the summit of the divide between Yellowstone and Gallatin valleys, and meeting several people going over into the Yellowstone country to prospect or hunt, we realized that our tribulations were over.

That afternoon we reached the settlement at the upper end of the Gallatin valley. The city of Bozeman then consisted of four one-room, one-story mud-covered log cabins. Work had been begun on a flouring mill.

As our caravan, in descending the divide, came in sight of the fields of grain, the cabins and fences, the boys went fairly wild and cheer after cheer went up. One of the more enthusiastic put his hat on the end of a teepee pole which he had picked up by the roadside and waved it aloft. But as the hat had, become dilapidated by a summer's wear, the pole slipped through a hole in the top and refused to be held aloft.

We saw grain shocks and hay cocks with hay on the north side of them, but what made our mouthes fairly water was the sight of a large patch of potatoes and a field of excellent looking cabbage. Twenty five cents per pound for the cabbage and 20 cents for the potatoes was willingly paid. The cabbage was crisp and Oh how good! The potatoes were large and smooth skinned and burst their jackets while being cooked, disclosing the mealy interior of snowy whiteness. For many long months we had tasted nothing in the line of "garden truck," and that night our stomachs were too small to hold enough to appease our craving for vegetables. At this point over half of the boys found work with the ranchmen and were paid off and left.

This broad and fertile valley was beautiful beyond our power to describe and the crops of grain and vegetables were abundant and of a quality which surpassed anything we had ever seen.

This fair valley caught many a pilgrim whose destination had been the gold fields, but who could not withstand the temptation to take a quarter section of Uncle Sam's fertile acres as a gift and settle down to improve it.

In those days times were good. The farmer could turn his produce into gold, which was then the currency of the Territory, at good prices. Flour was then $25 per sack, but soon came down to $10, potatoes soon came down to 5 cents per pound and other vegetables in proportion. Butter and eggs were in demand and for a long time held the price of $1.50 per pound for butter and $3 per dozen for eggs. Farm hands received from $40 and $60 and board per month, while $6 per day was the wages in the mines. As before stated, gold dust was the currency of the country and was current at $18 per ounce, while "mill retort" passed at $14 per ounce. At every store and nearly every ranch cabin was to be found a "blower" and magnet for cleaning dust and scales for weighing the same.

One of the territorial offices was that offices of sealer of weights and measures, which to be legal had to bear his stamp or brand.

Within a year the government had established Fort Ellis just above Bozeman and the place had grown from four mud covered log huts to a little city of 1500 people, with nearly all lines of business fairly represented. The nearest postoffice was at Helena. 85 miles distant. From this city the stage lines radiated in various directions. These delivered mail at the different settlements for 50 cents a letter and 25 for a newspaper. But as times were good and everyone had money, it did not seem so very much of a hardship to pay these seemingly exhorbitant prices. In fact everyone was glad to hear from home and friends at any price. This same portion of Gallatin valley has, since the days of which we are writing, gained a world-wide reputation for the high grade of malting barley which it produces.

Here was an earthly paradise, a valley nearly a hundred miles broad and watered by the clearest of creeks and rivers, while back in the hills all kinds of wild game was to be found in abundance.

- Diary -

September 3, 1866 (September 3.) – Travelled 25 miles down the valley. Rain in the evening. Camp at Galletin City. Galletin City is composed of a small tavern and grocery combined and a mill, which is building. There are some fine ranches around and tolerably well improved. Here the Galletin, Madison and Jefferson rivers come together and form the Missouri.

September 4, 1866 (September 4.) – Crossed the Missouri at Gelliers ferry. The hands were paid off and left.

September 5, 1866 (September 5.) – Day over. Weather fine.

Missouri River headwaters crossing

September 6, 1866 (September 6.) – Moved two miles up the Jefferson to an empty cabin. This we will fix up and probably spend the coming winter in it.

Galletin valley is twenty miles in width and 40 miles in length. Is settling very fast. It boasts of being the most productive valley in the territory. There is one grist mill and one saw mill completed and now in operation and two other grist mills are being erected in this valley. Wages are now and will be during harvest $3 per day or $50 per month. The valley is well watered by the purest of water and timber handy. We see grass fed stock here as fat as any of the stall fed that we ever saw in the states. The prices of groceries and provisions are moderate. Flour $20 per sack, potatoes 6c per pound, cabbage, onions, beets, turnips, etc. are from 10c to 20c per pound. Bacon, sugar and coffee, 70c and other things in proportion. The money circulation is principally gold dust. Greenbacks are worth 80c on the dollar.

Table of Distances miles

From Savannah Ill, to Des Moines, Iowa.............................. 216

" Des Moines, Iowa to Platts mouth,Nebr.................... 170

" Platts mouth to Salt Creek.................................... 38

" Salt Creek to where the road comes to the Platte River..... 67

" the first striking of Platts to Fort Kearney................ 110

" Fort Kearney to Ft. Cottonwood............................ 76

" Ft. Cottonwood to Ft. Juelsburg........................... 120

" Ft. Juelsburg to Ft. Mitchell at Scott's Bluffs............ 130

" Ft. Mitchell to Fort Laramie................................ 60

" Fort Laramie to Bridgers ferry on the N. Platte............. 52

" Bridgers Ferry to Fort Reno............................... 110

" Fort Reno to Fort Phil Kearney............................ 73

" Fort Phil Kearney to Ft. C. F. Smith....................... 96

" Ft. Smith to Clark's Fork.................................. 65

" Clark's Fork to the Ferry of the Yellowstone Valley.......... 90

" Yellowstone Ferry to Bozeman City, Galletin Valley........ 58

" Bozeman City to Galletin City.............................. 35

" Galletin City to Virginia City, M.T.......................... 65

1633

- Recollection -

We traveled leisurely, taking plenty of time to look at the valley with a view to finding a suitable place to winter the stock. We reached Gallatin City the 3rd day of September. At that time Gallatin City consisted of a small log house one and one-half stories in height. This building was made to do duty as a hotel, general store and what was termed a postoffice. This meant a distributing point for mail that was brought from Helena and Virginia City and left to be handed out to parties for whom it was intended upon payment of 50 cents for a letter and 25 cents for a newspaper.

It was quite a trading post for the tribes of friendly Indians, the Flatheads, Bannocks and Nez Perces, that migrated to the Yellowstone country in the fall to hunt and trap and back in the spring to summer quarters. They bartered furs, robes and buckskin for needles, thread, calico, tobacco, groceries and ammunition.

Here the Missouri river is formed by the Gallatin, Madison and Jefferson rivers uniting. Of these three noble streams the Madison is the largest and carries the largest volume of water. At this point one Judge Galliger had a rope ferry.

We had not as yet found a suitable place to winter, but had found a bit of bottom land that had a heavy growth of grass that was yet green. We made a note of this and crossed the river that afternoon and moved two miles up the Jefferson to an abandoned cabin and made camp.

The next day we explored a triangular tract of country known as the "Basin," lying between the Jefferson and Crow creek valleys, and finding all the requisites, wood, water, game and grass, to recommend it as a desirable location to spend the winter, we decided to settle down for the present.

Having been told that it was rare to see the ground whitened with snow, that stock kept fat all winter on the rich bunch grass that covered the hills and seeing that people did not pile up great ricks of hay to feed out during the winter, as they do in most countries, we felt secure on that score. But thinking that some of the cattle might get feeble before spring and need feeding, we got out the two sythes that we had brought so many miles and the cutting and piling up of a small rick of hay was our first work. Save for what we fed to horses belonging to visitors who stopped at our domicile that winter the stack was not disturbed. It probable rotted down, as both horses and cattle refused to eat it unless they were shut or tied up and starved to it. They preferred the freedom and rich feed of the range.

After the hay was put up an addition was duilt to the cabin, an outside cellar constructed and filled with vegetables and a large pile of dry wood drawn up for winter.

We soon made the discovery that great colonies of beaver had habitation along the valley. The Jefferson river ran by a few rods in front of the cabin and the foothills commenced a quarter of a mile back. Through this space ran a large slouhg that had evidently once been a river channel. The beaver had taken possession of this and made extensive ponds and near each pond was a beaver house con-structed of sticks and mud.

These houses were built on the back near the deepest water in the pond, where great quantities of green trees were felled and cut into sizes that made them convenient for the beavers to drag to the water, dumped in and sunk as accumulations of the green wood added weight to the mass. An old trapper told us what we afterwards found out by observation, that these caches of green wood were the beaver's winter's supply of food, that the mud and stick houses on the banks were hollow and that a passageway led from the rooms in the house to the deep water that contained the cache, and the animals would bring sticks up from their cache into the house when hungry, peel off and eat the bark and carry the peeled sticks back and leave them in the water.

One day when at the river we saw five otter sporting in the swift current in shape they resembled gigantic lizards. By keeping entirely motionless we had the pleasure of watching them a long time. It was truly wonderful to witness. They seemed to handle themselves as easily as fish. They could swim with incredible swiftness and, like a hawk in the air, hold themselves motionless in the swift current.

Another day while out looking after the cattle we had our first experience with mountain sheep. Four immense old rams were crossing from one range of hills to another, and as they came into view we dropped behind a big clump of sage brush. They were new creatures to us, but by the time they got within a hundred yards we knew from descriptions we had heard that we were actually looking at the mountain sheep of North America. As they were about crossing the trail that we were skulking on, our rifle was raised and aiming as near as we could at the head of the leader, we pulled the trigger and the foremost ram fell with a broken neck, and we had secured without an effort one of the most wary game animals in the world, and one of the largest and fattest of the species. His head adorned as it was by immense horns, seemed out of proportion to the size of the neck and body. His legs were also much heavier built than those of a deer or antelope. It was all that two strong men could do to lift him into a wagon.

Now that we had time to look about us, and not being compelled to keep such a strict vigilance over our precious scalp locks, we found our part of the Territory a veritable wonderland.

The great bear tracks that were everywhere to be seen in the moist places in the valley reminded us forcibly of the account of the killing of an immense grizzly bear by members of the Lewis and Clark expedition in our readers at school.

Our cabin was on the west bank of the largest river in the world, as the Jefferson is considered the principle tributary of the Missouri, which is the principle arm of the Mississippi, and by many said to be the Mississippi river proper, which rises within one mile of the springs which form the head of the great Columbia or Oregon river, and has an uninterrupted flow to the Gulf of Mexico, a distance of 4,194 miles.

CHAPTER 8
Montana Years – A Trapper's Diary & Recollections

On September 3, 1866, the Burgess-Cheney party reached the Gallatin Valley in Montana. By that time, several other members of the train had dropped off and gone their separate ways. Perry and all the Cheneys remained together and spent the bone-chilling Montana winter in cabins in the valley. Lewis hired his nephew to herd cattle until the spring of 1867, at which time Lewis returned to Lena, Illinois, and Perry entered into a business partnership with his uncle Lyman. Their endeavors were multifaceted as they worked together as trappers, prospectors, and wholesale wild game suppliers to local restaurants and then took odd jobs working farms and gold fields.

Although some of the party's members were never heard from again, history has remembered the names of others:

Lyman Cheney: Lyman remained in Montana with Perry, and the two spent those years hunting and prospecting. After his adventure in Montana, Lyman may or may not have returned to Lena with Perry, but he eventually settled in Tomichi, Gunnison County, Colorado. In the spring of 1877—just one year after Colorado's statehood—Governor John Routt designated Gunnison as the county seat of Gunnison County and appointed Lyman Cheney and W. W. Outcalt as the first county commissioners. By 1885 Lyman was living by himself as a rancher; he died of pneumonia on January 17, 1887.

Lewis Cheney: Lewis returned to Lena in the spring of 1867 and took with him his brother's widow, Paulina, and her four children. He sold his home the following year and moved to Missouri, where he began a successful career in banking with his nephew Perry.

Paulina White Cheney: Paulina returned to Lena and never left again. She married William Clement around 1870 and together the couple raised her four children from her marriage to Mansel Cheney and two more—Caroline and Charles—of their own. Paulina died on July 8, 1899.

Mansel Cheney Jr: Mancil, as he liked to spell his name, was a mystery to historians until now. He was never mentioned in Perry's diary or in any other book about the Montana Gold Rush, and it seems no one even knew he was conceived or born along the Bozeman Trail. Mancil was raised by the only father he ever knew, William Clement, a local cigar dealer. He grew up in Lena, Illinois, in the close-knit family setting his siblings and cousins also enjoyed. Relatively little else is known about Mancil. He married Mary Gordelia Lapp on December 28, 1887, in Stephenson County, Illinois. He and his wife had children, and according to various censuses, they remained in Illinois for most of their lives, with a brief sojourn to Wisconsin in the first decade of the twentieth century. Mancil made a living as a machinist. Sadly, it would seem he never knew even the most basic information about his biological father, as he nor his family were able to give Mansel Sr.'s place or date of birth to any census takers.

Mary Cheney: Mary, daughter of Paulina and Mansel, was born in Nebraska Territory's Fort Kearney (not to be confused with Fort Phil Kearny along the Bozeman Trail) on September 12, 1864, which made her not quite two years old when her family began its journey along the Bozeman Trail. Mary married George Harry McCulloch of Huntingdon, Pennsylvania, on February 11, 1884. The couple produced two sons and a successful machine shop and called Stephenson County, Illinois, home. Mary died on June 21, 1903, in Freeport, Illinois.

Franklin Cheney: Franklin, son of Paulina and Mansel, was born February 25, 1860, in Lena, Illinois. He married Alice Long on July 6, 1877, and the couple had four children. Franklin most likely died in Akron, Summit County, Ohio, on a date that is unknown.

George Cheney: George, eldest child of Paulina and Mansel, was born October 29, 1856, in Lena, Illinois. George married a woman named Cassie and, according to the 1900 census, lived with her and their three children in Leadville, Colorado. The 1930 census shows them living in Glenwood Springs, Colorado. George's death date is unknown.

William Blair: William returned to his 150-acre farm and his wife in Ward's Grove, Illinois, after his six-month journey west. His death date is unknown.

William G. Blair: William G. was the brother of Lewis Cheney's first wife and at eighteen, the youngest hired hand to join the Burgess-Cheney train. He set out to return to his home in Jo Daviess County, Illinois, almost immediately after reaching Montana. His death date is unknown.

James McGarry: James was one of those rare prospectors who actually remained in Montana mining gold. He died in January 1919.

Thomas McGarry: Thomas left Montana for Nebraska. The 1870 census has him farming and living in Omaha with his second wife and six children. By 1900, he is a widower. Thomas's death date is unknown.

For a man in his early twenties such as Perry, the Montana wilderness must have been a veritable wonderland of outdoor activity. He remained there until July of 1868, at which time he booked passage on the steamer *Urilda* out of Fort Benton bound for Sioux City, Iowa.

Steamboat travel on the upper Missouri was inherently fraught with danger, primarily snags, boiler explosions and frequent Indian attacks. If steamboats were not well maintained and carefully watched, pressure would build up in the boiler. Next to explosions, Indian attacks posed the greatest risk to steamboat travelers. Shortly after leaving Ft. Benton the *Urilda* met the steamer *Zephyr*, struggling to make its way upstream to reach the fort. Because of the *Zephyr's* inability to power upstream, a decision was made to switch cargo, passengers and crew between the two ships. The *Urilda* would return to Fort Benton and the *Zephyr* would turn about, and head back east. The *Urilda's* crew were unwilling to return and following a short mutiny on board, the crew were convinced to finally board the *Urilda* and head back into Indian country. Perry and his group joined the *Zephyr* and completed their journey onward to Sioux City.

The *Urilda* finally met her demise in 1869, when she struck a snag and sank in just twelve feet of water. The steamboat was carrying soldiers who had been discharged from the forts along the Upper Missouri. Fortunately, no lives were lost.

After arriving in Sioux City, Perry traveled on to Lena, Illinois, where he was warmly welcomed by family. As for Lyman, there is no way to be certain of his next move. Perry's diary indicates that he invested in a restaurant and bakery in Montana, but there is no mention of his leaving for Lena with Perry. We do know Lyman was living in Gallatin in 1873, but his whereabouts between 1868 and 1873 remain a mystery.

Perry didn't remain in his hometown for long. Soon he traveled to Missouri, quite possibly to work with his uncle Lewis Cheney, who had opened a bank in Holden in July 1868, just one month prior to Perry's return from the West. There is no diary of his years in Missouri, which does not mean such records never existed.

As some of Perry's recollections in this chapter do not relate to specific diary entries, there is a more general placement of the recollections within the diaries.

- Diary -

September 6, 1866 (September 6.) – Lewis Cheney offered me $40 per month in gold, board included, to stay and herd stock until spring, which I accepted. He also hired Jas. McGarry for the same purpose. We went at work dilligently and soon had a cabin rigged up. We cut and stacked some hay. We stay two weeks in this cabin, when Lewis found a better place to winter four miles farther up the river and we moved up there, built a corrall and branded the stock. Cut some more hay and built a cabin. I procured some traps and caught a few beavers and some other furs. Have killed some antelope and other game and now this 25th day of November, 1866, "Jim" and I take the wagon, cooking utensils, provisions, bedding etc. and moved out ten miles into the hills, between Boulder Creek and Galletin City to herd the stock. Camp at some springs. Call this Buffalo Bug camp,

Remnants of Gallatin City Hotel
Gallatin City Hotel was built circa 1867
Missouri Headwaters State Park

The area to the right of the road sign is the
approximate location of Perry's "Buffalo Bug Camp"

from a number of trees of that species growing around. The cattle are getting fat very fast. The weather is beautiful. We have 8 ponies to herd with, so that we have a change of horses as often as we wish.

- Recollection -

The settlers in the valleys raised grains and vegetables, the latter finding a ready market in the different mining camps at prices which, to a new comer, seemed exhorbitant. The grain was principally wheat, which, when converted into flour, sold readily at good prices.

A very few ranchmen were fortunate enough to own one or more cows and a few chickens, and with butter at $1.50 per pound and eggs at $3 per dozen it paid immensely to keep the means to produce these commodities. Very little attention was paid in those days to raising hay or oats, as there was little market for either. Hard wood and iron were in such demand and commanded such prices that many old wagons, after having withstood the long plains journey, were sold to the repair shops for more than they had cost in the States when new. Freighting was a great business in those days, and several large outfits employed many men and made money in bringing supplies from Salt Lake and other points into the mining towns. During the navigation season, June, July and August, vast quantities of merchandise was brought in from Fort Benton, which was then the head of navigation of the Missouri river and where the light draft steamers of the upper Missouri trade discharged their cargoes. During those months enough merchandise was hauled in and stored to keep the stocks of the retail merchants throughout the Territory until navigation should open again. Times were good then and everyone who had a disposition to work could find ready employment at good wages, and no one need go without the comforts of life for lack of the means to purchase them and although one did not hear much about law, life and property were more secure than in any other locality we had ever known.

Previous to our arrival a certain class of bad men had terrorized

Helena Montana, 1870

the orderly element to such an extent that the territorial laws were entirely ignored and the officers were completely helpless and power-less to protect life or property or maintain order. In this emergency the peaceable citizens, unable to stand it any longer, organized a vigilance committee. These men had "spotted" the most desperate of the thugs and murderers and at a given time caught and executed, by hanging or shooting, the worst and compelled the rest to leave. The effect was like oil upon the troubled waters and a great peace settled down over the land. The mere mention of the vigilantes was sufficient to terrify the would-be evil doer into a good citizen.

The following year we spent considerable time in Helena, the metropolis of Montana, on business, and although saloons and gam-bling houses were thick and open at all hours of the day and night and on all days in the week, and no city government existed except the unwritten laws which it is natural for men to observe, we never saw any acts of rowdyism or violence. There was no yelling or random shooting in or near town. In fact, any gross breach of decorum or order at the time would have entitled the perpetrator to a drumhead trial in Judge Lynch's Court, where exact and impartial justice would have been meted out and from which no appeal to a higher tribunal could have been taken. Everyone did as they pleased, and so long as he did not trespass upon the rights of others it was well. One felt absolutely secure whether in cabin or camp or in the densest throng in the crowded streets of the city, or even in a gaming house full of bearded miners and freighters. During our stay in the Territory only a few cases of crime made severe punishment at the hands of the committee necessary, and but few were notified to behave or make themselves scarce. The vigilantes' work was done quietly and without noise or bluster, but work once done did not require being done again, and no good citizen had cause to fear molestation at their hands

A very pleasant custom which existed throughout the Territory in those days was hospitality among all classes. This trait was practiced to the extent that it was considered a disgrace to fasten the door of tent or cabin when the owner had occasion to be away, for fear that some one might come along hungry. While we were there the rule was, if hungry, to enter any camp or cabin and help yourself in what you wanted to eat (in absence of owner) and leave a note or tell the next nearest neighbor what you had done.

Another noble spirit, which is so often manifested in frontier life, was that of helping the unfortunate The following incident will illustrate: A young man, a mere lad, had come from Missouri to find work and make a raise. He had left a widowed mother, for whose sake, more than his own, he had made the venture. He found work in Grizzly gulch and the first day part of the bank fell on him, breaking a leg. He was cared for by a committee of miners, a doctor set the broken limb and that night the miners called a meeting and voted to give the lad the next day's "clean up." The yield proved to amount to nearly $3,000, and this was put in the bank and a New York draft bought. In a few days the lad was around on crutches. Another meeting of the miners was called and the next day the lad, with his draft in his pocket, was put aboard the stage for Fort Benton, where he caught a returning steamboat, and in due time was with his mother with enough to put them on their feet financially and provide for future necessities.

In those days the average prospector's knowledge of valuable ores was confined to free milling rock, that is, quartz showing particles of native or metallic gold to the naked eye or that which could be crushed in a mortar and the gold it contained disclosed by panning.

We often encountered "blossom," which name was applied to the surface croppings of a lode or vein, a sample of which would be broken off and carried to camp, and no matter how rich it might have proved by the tests of a fire assay or smelting, if, when crushed and panned, a good showing of free gold was not obtained, the prospect would be abandoned as worthless. A few small specks of gold would not satisfy and we would move on.

Modern concentrating and smelting was unheard of then and assaying was not known among us prospectors. We had vague ideas of chemical laboratories in the great cities of Europe and America, where rocks could be analyzed at a tremendous expense and the amount of precious metals contained in them determined, but we had never heard of any process by which invisible gold could be extracted from rock and made available. We can now look back over the ground and see ledges that were rich in copper, lead and silver, judging from their green, yellow and red colors caused by the oxides of those metals, and they may have been rich in gold, but we could not get satisfactory results by crushing and panning and passed them by.

Ignorance may, in some cases, be bliss, but in our case, possessing that qualification in such a lamentable degree, it had the effect of keeping us in poverty, a state from which we have never been able to emerge "even unto this day."

In those days the study of animal and vegetable life interested us vastly more than the study of rocks. There was a peculiar fascination in noting the pathetic efforts of nature to repair a wounded plant or animal.

Virginia City, Montana Territory, circa 1866
Final destination of the Burgess-Cheney party

Virginia City, Montana - Due to preservation efforts,
Virginia City remains much the same as it did in 1866

Placer mining was more in favor in in those days than lode mining, for the reason that it was so simple as far as our observation extended. A clean up was made at the close of each day's work. The product, carefully panned, dried and weighed, gave the miner daily knowledge of what he was making.

As stated in a former chapter, gold dust was the currency of the country at $18 per ounce. A pennyweight was 90 cents and a grain represented a value of 3 3/4 cents. A customer would go into a store and buy a bill of goods amounting to say $20.75 and hand the merchant his buckskin sack of dust. The merchant would weigh out in payment of the bill 23 pennyweight and 1 1/2 grains, and this completed the transaction.

This was in the days when letter postage was three cents for each half ounce or fraction thereof The first letter we got at Helena was marked, "due 3 cents" We tendered him our buckskin sack and he weighted out a grain of dust and handed over the letter.

- Diary -

December 2, 1866 (December 2.) – There are plenty of antelope, hare, and sage hens in this locality. I usually take my rifle out with me and shoot all the game we want. Very fine sport.

To-day, we move camp three miles nearer the Jefferson. We camp at the mouth of a large rocky canyon and call the camp Cottonwood. There is a huge cottonwood tree standing along here alone. For firewood we have plenty of dry cedar. There are some warm springs one and one-half miles above here coming out of a large flat where most of the cattle stay of their own accord. Weather fine.

December 20, 1866 (December 20.) – I have been in camp along seven days, Jim being gone to Virginia City where he was sent to help drive some stock, which some parties had purchased. The ground is bare and the weather still continues fine. Have shot three antelope since we moved camp.

December 24, 1866 (December 24.) – Killed an antelope and wounded a mountain sheep. Commenced snowing to-day. Snow three inches deep to-night and coming thicker, growing cold.

December 25, 1866 (December 25.) – Quite cold to-day. Went down to the cabin. Snow six inches deep. Got back to camp at sundown.

December 26, 1866 (December 26.) – "Jim" went down to the river to look for stock.

December 27, 1866 (December 27.) – Very cold. "Jim" froze some of his fingers and toes while coming back to camp to-day.

December 28, 1866 (December 28.) – Rode all day looking up the stock. 29th and 30th the same.

December 31, 1866 (December 31.) – Very cold. So cold that we could not ride and had to take out afoot after the stock.

January 1, 1867 (January 1, 1867) – Very cold. Took a hunt to-day and killed an antelope. Came in camp after dark. Found "Jim" there with supper ready. (The snow is at present six inches deep, very cold and cloudy, northeast wind.)

January 2, 1867 (January 2.) – Were hunting cattle all day. Weather moderate. (cold west wind in morning and from the north in the evening.)

January 3, 1867 (January 3.) – Went down to the cabin and back to camp. (Moderate. West wind.)

January 4, 1867 (January 4.) – Gathering in the herd and choreing around. (cold, S.E. wind Blew hard all day.)

January 5, 1867 (January 5.) – I killed two sage hens and an antelope. (Cold, N.E. wind.)

January 6, 1867 (January 6.) – "Jim" and I butchered a beef. "Jim" went down to the cabin. (Moderate S.W. wind.)

January 7, 1867 (January 7.) – James came back with a team after some game and beef. Went back to the cabin. (Cold N.W. wind.)

January 8, 1867 (January 8.) – In camp all alone. Look after the stock. Found them all. (Still and cold.)

January 9, 1867 (January 9.) – The stock, all except 60 head, went off last night. Could not find them. (Still and cold.)

January 10, 1867 (January 10.) – Hunted all day for the cattle and could not find them. "Jim" came back to camp. (A slight fall of snow this morning. Wind blew heavy all day from S.W.. Thaw a little.)

January 11, 1867 (January 11.) – Cold as greenland. Did not get far away from camp to-day. (Snow fell six inches and wind furious from the north all day. Cold as Greenland at dark.)

January 12, 1867 (January 12.) – Went down to the river in search of missing stock. They were not there. Stay at the cabin to-night. (Clear and very cold.)

January 13, 1867 (January 13.) – Went 7 miles up the Jefferson river, where some herds are being kept; but our cattle were not there. Struck across the mountains for camp and found 60 head of them. Drove them to camp. (Cold in the morning, but warmer at night. S.W. wind all day.)

January 14, 1867 (January 14.) – Saw over 100 head of the stock to-day. I killed an antelope. Came in camp after dark. "Jim" was there ahead of me and had supper ready. Just as we were sitting down to eat, a furious storm of wind and snow drove us away from our comfortable fire to take shelter in the wagon. (Wind heavy from S.W. all day, at dark suddenly changed to north. Cold snow fell all day.)

January 15, 1867 (January 15.) – James went down to the cabin after "grub." (Cold. Snow all day by spells, N.W. wind.)

January 16, 1867 (January 16.) – Was hunting, shot a deer and some grouse. (Morning cold, evening more moderate, thawed some. S.W. wind heavy.)

January 17, 1867 (January 17.) – Went down to the cabin to write some letters. (Thawed very fast all day, S.W. Wind.)

January 18, 1867 (January 18.) – Came back to camp. Saw 120 head of the cattle. I was hunting the stock and James went down to drive up some cows. (Snowed a little, warm S.W. wind.)

January 19, 1867 (Jan. 19th) – (Snow in the morning, N. wind blew hard all day.)

January 20, 1867 (January 20.) – I found 22 head more of the missing stock and killed a deer. "Jim" came back to camp. (Cold, a little flurry of snow in the evening, north wind.)

January 21, 1867 (January 21.) – So very cold that we stay close to camp to-day. (Very cold, clear and still.)

January 22, 1867 (22nd.) – (Cold wind N. blew all day.)

January 23, 1867 (January 23.) – Looking up the stock. (Intensely cold north and northeast wind.)

January 24, 1867 (January 24.) – We went to the cabin to-day. (Snow one inch, still bitter cold.)

January 25, 1867 (January 25.) – I went over the river to buy some ammunition. Shot some grouse. (very cold, no wind.)

January 26, 1867 (January 26.) – Came back to camp alone. "Jim" stayed at the cabin to get up some wood. Killed an antelope and some sage hens on the way to camp. (A slight fall of snow last night, north wind in morning and west wind in evening. More moderate.)

January 27, 1867 (January 27.) – Was hunting to-day, killed an antelope. Come to camp an hour after dark. Built a fire, cooked some supper, ate it, picked my teeth, took a huge chew of real natural leaf and feel 50% better than I did an hour ago. Take out my violin and play a few tunes, then return to "my virtuous couch". (Moderate, snow a little at dark, N.W. wind.)

January 28, 1867 (January 28.) – I killed an antelope. Jim came back with the team. Moved down to the river. (S.W. wind. Thawed rapidly. Prairie dogs out to-day.)

January 29, 1867 (January 29.) – James went to get a tooth

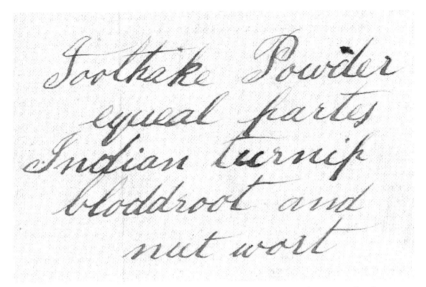

1860 Cheney Family remedy for "toothake powder"

extracted. I was looking after the cattle. Brought in an antelope. (Warm and springlike.)

January 30 – February 3, 1867 (January 30, 31 & February 1, 2, & 3.) – Looking after the stock. (30 – rained a little in the morning, snow at night, wind S.E. and S.W. 31 – Pleasant in the morning, afternoon the wind blew hard from the west. Thaw all day. 1– Pleasant, west wind. 2 – Pleasant, thawed all day. W. wind. 3 – Warm and springlike, S.W. wind.)

February 4, 1867 (February 4.) – Stayed at the cabin. (Cold N.W. wind blew all day.)

February 5-7, 1867 (February 5, 6, 7.) – Was looking for the stock. (5 – Cold. Heavey west wind all day. 6 – Moderate snow all day with a few intermissions. N.W. wind in the morning and N.E. wind at night. 7 – Cold north and N.W. wind.)

February 8, 1867 (February 8.) – James who has been sick with a swolen face ever since he had his tooth pulled has recovered sufficiently to accompany me on a tramp after the stock to-day. (Cold. N. wind.)

February 9, 1867 (February 9.) – Moved up to camp Cotton-wood. Took the ponies with us. (Cold N. wind.)

February 10, 1867 (February 10.) – Went over towards Boulder; found no stock. (Cold.)

February 11, 1867 (February 11.) – Gathered up 125 head of cattle to-day. (Cold.)

February 12, 1867 (February 12.) – Found 5 head; drove them to the herd. Had company in camp to-night. (Moderate, S.W. wind.)

February 13, 1867 (February 13.) – Went to the cabin and came back around through the mountains. Found no stock. Cold day for riding. (Cold. N. wind.)

February 14, 1867 (February 14.) – Saw 131 head of stock to-day. (Very cold. N.E. wind.)

February 15, 1867 (February 15.) – Took some provision and bedding and started for Crow Creek 15 miles distant. Looked among different herds of stock; but found none of ours. Put up for the night, with four men who were staying in a cabin. Two of them were violin-ists. We amused ourselves by playing, singing songs, telling stories etc. until past midnight, then retired. (Cold wind, S.E.)

February 16, 1867 (February 16.) – Took leave of our agreeable hosts this morning. Rode over a large tract of country, looked among different herds; but with no success. Got back to camp after dark. Rode 50 miles to-day. Crow creek is a fine mountain stream 15 feet wide and one foot deep. It has a valley 10 miles wide and 20 long and is a fine place for farming and raising stock. It boast of quite a settlement. Saw a pet elk, moose and buffalo to-day that are owned by Messrs. King & Gillette. Prospectors are finding fine gold bearing quartz and some placer diggings on this creek. (Cold. High wind from the N.W.)

February 17, 1867 (February 17.) – Found 4 head of our strays to-day.

February 18, 1867 (February 18.) – Started for Boulder Creek;

but could not find the pass through the mountains and came back to camp. (Moderate.)

February 19 – 20, 1867 (February 19 & 20.) – Looking after the stock. Weather very cold. (19 – Extremely cold. Heavy wind from the north all day. 20 – Calm and very cold.)

February 21, 1867 (February 21.) – Went to Boulder and back the 22nd and found no stock. Boulder is a fine stream 30 feet wide and 2 deep. The Valley through which it runs is narrow; but is considerably settled. They are mining for gold 40 miles above its mouth. (Cold N.W. wind)

February 22, 1867 (22nd) – (Pleasant in the morning. S. wind at noon suddenly changed to north, and was very cold at night.)

February 23, 1867 (February 23.) – Went down to the cabin and back at night to camp. (a little more moderate.)

February 24, 1867 (February 24.) – Went to upper Boulder. Distance 25 miles. (Cold N. and N.W. wind.)

February 25, 1867 (February 25.) – Came back to camp, after looking among all the stock we could find and asking every person we saw. This trip is of no avail. James went to cabin to-night. (Cold, heavy N.W. wind. At sundown snow falling thick and fast. At dark clear and calm.)

February 26 – 27, 1867 (February 26 & 27.) – Driving the stock together. Have 151 herd. Have company to-night; two men from Crow Creek hunting stock and a man from Boulder to buy stock. (26 – Warmer, S. wind. 27 – Cold north wind.)

February 28, 1867 (February 28.) – Cold. Snowed hard all day. Our visitors still remain with us. (N.E. wind. 28 snow hard all day and cold as Greenland.)

March 1 – 2, 1867 (March 1 & 2.) – Riding after the stock. (1– Cold. Wind N.E. 2 – Cold and snow. A very little wind, E. & N.)

March 3, 1867 (March 3.) – Help start off some cattle that a man had bought. My eyes are very weak and painful. Cannot see well. (Clear and cold.)

March 4, 1867 (March 4.) – Am so blind that I am obliged to remain in camp. "Jim" saddled the horses and piloted me down to the cabin. Am told by a man and his wife that I am snow blind. Could not see to fix my victuals at the table. They put the "grub" on my plate and cut it into mouthfulls as they would for a yearling child. (Same.)

March 5 – 6, 1867 (March 5 & 6.) – Blind as a stone; kept close in a dark room. My eyes were very painful. (5 – Snow. N. wind, very cold. 6 – Very cold; calm.)

March 7, 1867 (March 7.) – Recovering a little. (Clear, still and cold.)

March 8, 1867 (March 8.) – Almost well. Can go out of doors by wearing gogles. Went to camp. (Little warmer and S.W. wind.)

March 9, 1867 (March 9.) – Hunted all day for the mules and ponies. Could not find them. Did not get into camp until after 10 o'clock. The weather grew extremely cold. We unsaddled our horses and left them and hurried to camp afoot. "Jim" froze one of his toes. (Morning pleasant. Evening cold.)

March 10, 1867 (March 10.) – Found the ponies. Took them down to the cabin. (Pleasant. Thaws very little where the sun strikes. Fair.)

March 11,1867 (March 11.) – Hauled some wood and hay. Almost froze. Weather extremely cold. (Coldest weather we have had yet. N. wind blow hard.)

March 12, 1867 (March 12.) – Hauled wood. Colder still. (Colder, N. wind.)

March 13, 1867 (March 13.) – Chored around a little. Cut some wood. (Calm and very cold.)

March 14, 1867 (March 14.) – Sat by the fire. This is the coldest weather I ever witnessed. (Moderate, calm.)

March 15, 1867 (March 15.) – More moderate. Went to camp. Looked after the stock. Found two head frozen to death. (Morning pleasant, afternoon heavy snow, storm, N. wind.)

March 16, 1867 (March 16.) – Looking up the stock. Found one more of them frozen to death. (Clear and cold.)

March 17 – 18, 1867 (March 17 & 18.) – Gathering in the herd. (17 – Cold E. wind. 18 – Moderate.)

March 19 – 21, 1867 (March 19, 20 & 21.) – Same. (19 – Very cold N. wind. 20 – Cold snow all day, N. and N.E. wind. 21 – Snow all day, very cold N.E. wind.)

March 22, 1867 (March 22.) – Went down to the cabin. (Cold, clear.)

March 23, 1867 (March 23.) – Went hunting. Killed a deer. "Jim" and I went visiting in the evening. Had a gay time. (Same.)

March 24 – 25, 1867 (March 24 & 25.) – Was gathering in the stock. (24 – warmer, thaw a very little, N.W. wind. 25 – Clear and cold.)

March 26, 1867 (March 26.) – Drove down to the cabin. (Moderate, S.W. Wind.)

March 27, 1867 (March 27.) – Went up the river after strays. Found (4) four. (Thaw a little, S.W. wind.)

March 28 – 29, 1867 (March 28 & 29.) – Hunting for stock and driving in the herd. (28 – Clear and calm. 29 – Cold. N. W. heavy wind.)

March 30, 1867 (March 30.) – Started for Crow Creek. Stopped with some freighters. (Still and cold.)

March 31, 1867 (March 31.) – Hunted all day around amongst the different herds. Found one head. (Thaw some, snow in the evening.)

April 1, 1867 (April 1.) – Came back to the Stone Ranch. (Moderate, S.E. Warm wind. Afternoon commenced to rain, but turned to snow)

April 2, 1867 (April 2.) – Went Home. (Moderate, S.E. Warm wind. Afternoon commenced to rain, but turned to snow)

April 3 – 4, 1867 (April 3 & 4.) – Went around gathering up the stock. (3 – Cold N.W. wind. 4 – Moderate.)

April 5, 1867 (April 5.) – Went down to the cabin. (Warm and pleasant.)

April 6, 1867 (April 6.) – Went to Boulder, found one yearling. (Pleasant S.W. wind.)

April 7, 1867 (April 7.) – Came back. Moved the wagon down to the cabin and quit camping out. (Cold, snow, N.E. Wind.)

April 8, 1867 (April 8.) – Went up the river. Did not find any stock. (Clear, still and warm.)

April 9, 1867 (April 9.) – Found five head; one of them was dead. (Warm/ S.W. wind.)

April 10 -12, 1867 (April 10,11,12.) – Went to Boulder, searched the valley all over, found none of the stock, and come back home. (10 – Same. Snow commences going. 11 – Very warm, snow almost gone. 12 – Warm, grass begins to start in the lowest valleys.)

April 13, 1867 (April 13.) – Found five head more. (People begin to sow wheat, very warm S.E. Wind.)

April 14, 1867 (April 14.) – "Jim" was paid off and left. My wages was raised to $70.00 per month. Went to Page & Salsbury's camp and looked through herd. (Calm and warm.)

April 15, 1867 (April 15.) – Went to Crow Creek, hunted through all the herds in that valley which took me two days. (Cold wind, N.)

April 16, 1867 (April 16.) – (Cold, rain in the evening, turn to snow.)

April 17, 1867 (April 17.) – (Pleasant.)

April 18, 1867 (April 18.) – Went to Hoobern's camp. (Warm, S.W. wind.)

April 19, 1867 (April 19.) – Found one steer. (Cold, some rain.)

April 20, 1867 (April 20.) – Came home. (Rain in the evening, cold N.W. wind.)

April 21 -24, 1867 (April 21,22,23,24.) – On herd. (21 – Cold, snow and freeze all day. N. wind. 22 – Cold N.E. wind. Snow a little. 23 – Cold, snow, N.W. wind. 24 – Cold W. wind.)

April 25, 1867 (April 25.) – Uncle Lyman came down from Galleten Valley to visit us. He took my rifle out and killed an antelope. (Pleasant.)

April 26 – 30, & May 1, 1867 (April 26,27,28,29 & 30th. May 1.) – On herd. The herd is sold, and delivered. There are six or seven head still missing and I will have to take a look for them. (26 – Warm wind, S.W. 27 – Colder, N. wind. 28 – Cold, freezes all day, N.W. wind. 29 – Warm and pleasant. 30 – Warm N.W. wind. 1 – Warm, Calm.)

May 2, 1867 (May 2.) – Went across the Missouri River to look for stock; could not find them; came back. (Cold, N.W. Wind.)

May 3, 1867 (May 3.) – Took my rifle and went hunting. Killed an antelope. (Very warm.)

May 4 – 7, 1867 (May 4,5,6,7.) – Hunting for the stock. Could not find any of them. (4 – Pleasant. 5 – Warm wind and vegetation finally starting. 6 – Warm S.E. Wind. 7 – Warm and beautiful.)

May 8, 1867 (May 8.) – Packed up and started for Helena City. Drove twenty miles to Crow creek to camp. (Warm and beautiful.)

May 9, 1867 (May 9.) – Drove thirty miles, camp at Beaver Creek. Beaver Creek is one rod wide and 15 inches deep; a swift mountain stream. (Warm, S.W. Wind.)

May 10, 1867 (May 10.) – Went into Helena, fifteen miles farther. Was surprised to see such a fine city as Helena is out in this wilderness. It is ahead of many of the cities in the states.

May 11, 1867 (May 11.) – Went around through the town to see the lions.

May 12, 1867 (May 12.) – Was paid off. Bought a mule team. Lyman came to Helena. He took half interest in the team and we entered into partnership. (Cold, snow fell four inches last night.)

May 13, 1867 (May 13.) – Times being rather dull, we start out on a hunting expedition. Met our old fellow traveller "Texas", asked him to join us, which invitation he complied with. Borrowed a rifle for him at the Spokane house. Camp on Beaver Creek for the night. Lyman killed some plovers on the way. (Cold.)

May 14, 1867 (May 14.) – Shot a few grouse to-day. Moved four miles up Beaver Creek. Musquitoes large as snipes give us the benefit of their music, and also present their bills for our consideration. (Warm, S. Wind.)

May 15, 1867 (May 15.) – Killed some grouse. Lyman shot a mountain sheep. The mules ran off last night. Found them at noon to-day. (Sultry.)

May 16, 1867 (May 16.) – Moved camp five miles farther up. Killed some grouse and an antelope. (Pleasant, N. W. Wind.)

May 17, 1867 (May 17.) – Snowed a little all last night. One of the mules got loose and ate up a pan of dough that we had mixed up to bake for breakfast, spilled our salt and raised Ebenezer generally. The snow falling on our bed made the blankets seem to have increased wonderfully in weight and thickness. We got up, after Lyman had built a fire, shook the snow off our bedding, cooked and ate breakfast, then went into the wagon to avoid the storm, which lasted till 10 o'clock. We then moved eight miles and camp near the Spokane Mt. I killed five grouse and a deer. Came into camp after dark, found supper ready. "Texas" had been and procured a bottle of stomach bitters, which we proceeded to drink "for the stomache's sake." (Cold, snow fell three inches last night, and snow most all day.)

May 18, 1867 (May 18.) – Snow hard all day. Move camp to Spokane Creek. (Cold. Snow fell all day, N.E. wind.)

May 19, 1867 (May 19.) – Clear and cold. Shot some grouse. (Clear and cold.)

May 20, 1867 (May 20.) – Went to Helena and sold our game and purchased a supply of provisions and amunition and started out on another hunt. (Warm and pleasant again today.)

May 21, 1867 (May 21.) – Camp on Beaver Creek for noon. After noon went 20 miles farther and camp on Crow Creek. divide. (Pleasant W. wind.)

May 22, 1867 (May 22.) – Crossed Crow Creek. Camp up in the hills. (Sultry. S. wind.)

May 23, 1867 (May 23.) – I shot two antelope and lost them both. Lyman had the same luck with a deer and elk. (Warm N.W. wind.)

May 24, 1867 (May 24.) – One of the mules ran off last night, and I was all day after her. Found her at Galletin City. Rode 60 miles to-day. Came in camp after dark. (Warm.)

May 25, 1867 (May 25.) – Moved camp 15 miles up into the mountains. Lyman shot an elk. Commenced snowing at sundown. (Warm forenoon, cold in the afternoon, rain.)

May 26, 1867 (May 26.) – Snow by spells all day. Lyman is unwell, has a lame back. I was hunting to-day, shot an elk and a deer and four grouse. Was out very late. Came to camp in time to enjoy a huge fire that Lyman had built to show me the way in. (Cold, snow and rain all day.)

May 27, 1867 (May 27.) – Hunted to-day. Lyman shot two grouse and two wolves. I shot two mountain clump feet. (Snow and rain most all day, N.E. wind.)

May 28, 1867 (May 28.) – Killed a deer, three grouse and one clump feet. Lyman killed two grouse and two wolves. (Same.)

May 29, 1867 (May 29.) – Lyman killed an elk and two grouse. I shot three grouse. (Cold.)

May 30, 1867 (May 30.) – Killed five grouse apiece. (Warm and pleasant again.)

May 31, 1867 (May 31.) – Lyman shot an antelope and three grouse. I shot two wolves and two grouse. (warm, S.W. Wind.)

- Recollection -

Near the beaver slough mentioned in a previous chapter was a bog. An old horse belonging to one of the settlers had got mired and died at this place. In crossing to go to the hills to look after the stock one morning we noticed that the carcass of the dead horse had vanished. Curiosity prompted us to investigate and we found that a bear had dragged it a short distance, eaten a hearty meal and covered the remainder with leaves and brush.

That night and for several succeeding nights we spent the fore part of the night in a cluster of alders with our rifle watching for bruin to return to his feast. During these vigils we saw no bear, but learned much of the habits of the sagacious and industrious beaver and were well repaid for our trouble in the knowledge thus gained.

Coveting the hides of these inoffensive creatures we sent to Helena and bought some traps. The first night we had the traps out we caught three lusty fellows and were very much surprised to find them so much larger than they had looked when working in the water by moonlight.

We had often read of the tail of the beaver being considered a great delicacy by old hunters and trappers who had served the Hudson Bay company. The tails of those that we caught were black and scaly and the skin seemed to be a part of the tail which under the skin was a snowy whiteness, resembling fat but having the consistency of gristle. Knowing no way of removing the skin except by peeling as you would a potato, and not knowing how to cook them we did not venture to eat any of them.

A few days later a party of Flathead Indians came in on a hunting expedition. By this time the magpies and wasps had eaten nearly all the flesh off the beaver carcasses but had not molested the tails. They were given to an old Indian and he drew out his knife and severed each tail at a single stroke, knowing the exact spot to cut to strike a joint. We remained in ignorance of the toothsome qualities of this strange edible until the next autumn.

We were on a trapping expedition up the Gallatin the next fall and were entertaining at our camp a couple of prospectors who had just come to the valley to get supplies. Seeing us skin some beaver and carry the carcasses a short distance from camp and throw them away one of them said: "Heavens man, do you throw away the best eating in the world?" Upon being told that we had never tried and did not know how to prepare them one of them told us to attend to cooking our bread, coffee and potatoes and he would fix up the best dish we ever tasted.

He cut off the tails as deftly as the Indian had done, ran a sharpened stick into one and held it over the fire for a moment. The black, scaly skin loosened and puffed up like an angry toad. This he peeled off, leaving the fleshy portion as white and clean looking as a skinned trout. As each tail was thus prepared he put it into a pan of clear cold water. Then he placed the lid of our extra dutch oven on the coals as if preparing to bake bread. While the oven was heating he drew his keen hunting knife several times across the tails until they were gashed on both sides a half an inch square. Then placing them in the oven he covered the lid with live coals. When they began to crack and pop he took off the lid and seasoned with pepper and salt. Four men stowed a beaver tail under their jackets that night and we never threw away another beaver tail.

In those days the sparkling Gallatin, Madison and Jefferson rivers were teeming with trout and greyling. When nicely cleaned, rolled in flour and slowly fried to a light brown hue they were beyond comparison as an article of diet and two of us would frequently get away with two frying pans full of them in addition to the usual allowance of fried potatoes, hot biscuit and strong coffee at one meal.

A continual out door life with lots of pleasant exercise in the shape of agreeable work gave us muscles like steel and stomachs like an ostrich. No matter where we made camp, whether on mountain, foothill or valley, good mother nature had provided flesh, fowl or fish of the choicest varieties which required but small skill and trouble to secure, to satisfy appetites always whetted to razor keenness by the glorious air and scenic surroundings.

It astonished us to witness the suddenness with which new towns would spring into existence, flourish awhile and decay. To illustrate. In the spring of 1867 we went leisurely from Gallatin City to Helena We traveled slow, making frequent camps to prospect, hunt and enjoy the scenery   At the beautiful little valley of Crow creek we camped two days, during which time we walked up into the foothills to look around. We dug a prospect hole in the main gulch, where it issued from the mountains, and brought a small sack of dirt to camp, which we carefully panned without getting a color. We decided there were no placers there, without taking the trouble to pan the swales and lower gulches further down. We passed on to the city. Within a week after our arrival in Helena rumors of the finding of placers of marvelous richness on Crow creek came thick and fast. The stage coaches were loaded daily with miners and sporting men from Helena to the Crow creek El Dorado. Some of the great freight outfits were actively at work hauling supplies into the new camp and portable saw mill was among the first heavy freight to go from the vicinity of Helena. As we had so recently prospected the main gulch, which should in all reason have supplied any gold that washed down from the mountains and found no gold, we were incredulous and did not join in the stampede. A week passed and as the demand for labor in the mines about Helena was very limited, a couple of us concluded to go back to Crow creek partly out of curiosity and partly to penetrate the mountain region further up, to prospect and hunt. It was an easy two days drive, but we overtook and picked up two men on the way who, too poor to go on the stage, had shouldered their blankets and camp kit and were trudging afoot. We took them and their belongings into our wagon, much to their relief, and found that they were very pleasant company.

Arriving at the new camp, which was named Radersburg, we were astonished to find a small city had sprung into existence where two weeks before we had hunted antelope and sage hens. Here were shops and stores, saloons, hotels and gaming houses in full blast and the mines a little further up. A small ditch had been taken out of the creek and lower down this ditch was divided into several branches, each to supply water to the little draws or gulches which erosion had carved over the surface of the mesa where the camp was located. A placer claim was limited to the width of the draw and 150 feet in length. This was the rule adopted by the miners who decreed that the claims should be small to give everyone a chance to take a claim. The majority rule was supreme and no one was permitted to, hog more than he needed, which was as it should be in all lands and places.

- Recollection -

The auriferous character of these small gulches, so far from the base of the mountains proper, was discovered by the merest chance. A man who was improving a ranch down in the bottom turned his work oxen up into the low foothills to graze nights. The night before the discovery it had rained violently. In the morning the ranchman went up on the mesa to get his oxen and was noticing the black sand and curious pebbles that the water had disclosed as it rushed down these slight gulches. In one place he noticed some yellow particles and was about to pass on when the thought struck him that it might be gold, and it was gold. Our friend did not drive his oxen back to the yoke and the plough that day. He picked around until noon in the sand and gravel of the small gulches with his pocket knife, and when he went to dinner he left a claim stake up on the mesa and carried with him nearly a teaspoonful of yellow grains and small nuggets, the exhibition of which electrified his few fellow settlers. The first work after staking the claims was to get water onto the ground to work with.

The surveying of a ditch by aid of a square and common spirit level was a short job. Two yoke of oxen, a plough and two men with shovels made short work of constructing a ditch, which, owing to its great fall, did not have to be deep or wide to have a great carrying capacity. In the mines, in each gulch where mining was in progress, a string of fluming or sluice boxes ran. The first and sometimes the second claim to take water from the ditch paid a royalty to the owner, $1 per miner's inch per day. The claims lower down paid from $5 down to $1 for the use of the same water. This diminutive ditch was a real bonanza to its owners. The rent was paid daily by claim owners who used the water.

The news of the discovery spread like wild fire, the only difference being that a prairie fire only travels in one direction. Like a fire it gathers volume and fierceness as it travels.

We had hardly had time to unharness, unsaddle and picket our animals when we saw a man coming toward us. When he got within speaking distance he called out, "Hello pards, do you want work?" While he was negotiating with us we saw two more men coming and visitor No. 1 called out to them: "You're too late, fellers, I have the first claim on these men by right of discovery." The conference ended by our agreeing to go to work for our first caller at sun down. His claim was but a few rods from our camp.

As the sun went down we were on hand. Our employer told us where to dig and marked the boundaries of the pay streak by driving some stakes into the ground. He explained that pay was all through the dirt from the surface to bed rock, which was about five feet. He told us we could be guided by the demands of our stomachs as to when we should "knock off" and eat our midnight lunch, and showed us how to keep the flume clean with a sluice fork and then left.

We had no light except the stars and we worked hard and steady until we got very hungry, not caring to waste the time to fill our pipes, as we would have done otherwise. It seemed to us that to honestly earn such enormous wages we must not waste a minute Hunger finally overcame conscience and laying down our tools we went to camp, kindled a fire, got supper, filled our stomachs and then our pipes and went back to work. Being very tired it was a great temptation to roll up in our blankets and sleep the rest of the night.

It seemed a very long time before the rosy dawn tinged the eastern sky and just as the sun peeped over the hills and gladdened the landscape with his cherry smile our employer came over and told us to knock off. As he approached the pit where we were working he expressed surprise at the amount of dirt we had put through in one night, which he said was twice as much as any other shift had handled in the same length of time.

We went to camp, ate breakfast and then laid down and tried to sleep. Our aching muscles and blistered hands and the attention of one or two blue-bottle flies that persisted in tickling our noses had the effect to drive sleep from our eyes, and after repeated and vigorous slaps at our tormentors and sundry exclamations not to be found in modern catechisms we gave up the attempt and busied ourselves about camp until noon. Two other tenderfeet came along in time to partake of a good dinner with us. They were hunting work and we decided to surrender our job to them.

After dinner we took them to the mine, introduced them to the owner and told him that we would have to quit work until we could strike an easier job. He protested vigorously, but finally submitted to the inevitable and employed the men we had brought. Twelve dollars in gold dust was weighed out to us and placed in the company sack.

We went back to camp, took our rifles and prospecting pick and started up toward the mountains to see what we could find, thinking perhaps we might stumble onto the lode or source of all this placer gold. Within and hour after leaving camp we had killed two fine fat antelope. One of us went back to camp to get a pack animal while the other picked around among the rocks.

Before sundown that evening we had got our game into camp and sold it to a man who was running a boarding house. He paid us six dollars a piece for them. Thus we had made as much out of a few hours of pleasant recreation that afternoon as we had out of a long night's toil in the pit.

The weather was very warm in the valley and the pure white snow on the range above us looked cool and inviting. Neither of us had had any real mountain experience up to that time and before going to bed that night we decided to hitch up early the next morning and try to find a pass so we could get our wagon and belongings up into the mountains.

Both of us were good shots and fond of hunting and we argued that we could penetrate a promising field for prospecting and at the same time load our wagon with meat, which we would take to Helena. Before dark we had taken a sort of survey of the lay of the ridges and gulches and concluded that we could make it all right.

We were up ahead of the sun the next morning and soon had our breakfast cooked and disposed of, our pack animals saddled and our mules harnessed and hitched to the wagon. The morning was bright and glorious. We traveled very slow, with frequent stops to rest the train and to prospect. In our ignorance we believed that gold bearing ledges could only exist in the granite formation up in the rugged mountains, and that morning we innocently crossed, in the low foothills and not three miles from our night's camp, the source of all the gold that the placers contained. This was a vein of honey combed iron rust and cropped out of a contact between shale and quartzite on an almost level mesa and quite a distance below the mountains proper. This vein was discovered by an old man, who ground a piece of the float and panned it, getting a result which fairly staggered him.

At noon we halted at a large spring, surrounded by a cluster of large willows and silver spruce. While eating a cold mist came down from the hills and the air grew chilly. We saw that in order to get onto the slope above us we would have to do a little grading. This took us about an hour, when we hitched up and resumed our climbing. The mist kept growing more dense, and as we neared the first drifts of old snow new snow began to come down this was a new experience to us, a snow storm in June was certainly as novel as it was unpleasant, and although it was yet early in the afternoon it seemed to be getting dusk. Our partner suggested that we had better prepare to camp, but as the ground over which we were traveling was very sidling he walked on ahead to what seemed to be the top of the divide to see if a more suitable place to camp was not near at hand. While he walked on we blanketed the mules and pack horses, as they had begun to shiver with the cold.

We watched our partner gain the summit and take a long look beyond. Then ducking his head he started back toward the wagon, and while he hurried toward the wagon as fast as his bent over attitude would admit, he made violent gestures to keep quiet and not advance.

- Recollection -

He hurried down to the wagon and reported that just over the summit was a large expanse of park or prairie with large drifts of last winter's snow still lingering in the groves of timber and on the north slopes of the low swells or ridges which ran through it, that the feed was splendid and lying on a bare place he saw three large animals, which he thought must be elk, although in the fog they looked as large as elephants. He suggested that we immediately unhitch, picket out our stock and try to get one or more of the large animals.

His suggestions were acted upon and the result was an elk. They proved to be three bulls, which at that time were wont to feed in those high grassy parks. Their antlers were merely soft, fuzzy clumps.

After the killing we went back to camp and got an axe, our knives and a shovel, returned to our game, skinned and quartered it, dug a pit in the nearest snow drift and buried it.

We took the head to camp and the next day made a pit roast of it.

An abundance of dry pine and aspen wood was very near camp and the first work after dressing our game was to back down a large supply of it for night use and build a big fire. Then with pick and shovel we leveled a place for camp, pitched our tent and carried into it our rolls of bedding.

After we had eaten supper more logs were piled on our fire and we laid down on the grass near it to talk over the day's adventures, and just as dusk was coming over the land the long drawn wail of a timber wolf apparently near our meat cache, made us aware that we must devise some means for its protection if we wanted to find it safe the morning. Taking our axes and an old coat we went to the snow drift in which it was buried and at the edge of the snow made a large fire, by the light of which we cut and covered the place over our meat with pine boughs. Then we rigged up a scarecrow from the old coat and returned to camp. This was our first big game and we did not want to lose it.

By this time it had grown quite. We returned to our camp fire, dried our wet garments and went to bed.

When we awoke the next morning the fog still hung thick over the land. Our partner had a rheumatic stitch in the small of his back, which, much to his displeasure, prevented him from taking a hand at exploring that day. We decided not to move from our present quarters until we had finished getting a respectable load of meat for the Helena market. After breakfast I dug a pit in which to roast our elk head and brought down a fresh supply of dry wood. While doing this work we kept hearing sounds that came seemingly from all directions. It was, as near as we could describe, like the beating of a muffled tom-tom, and for our lives we could not even guess at the distance it might be from us. We had never read nor heard of any beast inhabiting the wilds of North America having such a voice as that. We determined to investigate and find out what it was. Some of the sounds seemed to come from the pine forest which extended down almost to camp, so leaving our partner to get the pit hot we cautiously entered the woods. Keeping our rifle ready for instant use, we made frequent stops and looked and listened intently, and finally discovered what it was that produced the mysterious, gnome-like sounds. It was the male of the Dusky grouse. They were so adundant that every mossy log or granite boulder seemed to hold one. From where we made the discovery we could see by looking sharp seven or eight fine fellows, and they did not seem alarmed at our presence. A shot from our rifle and grouse No. 1 fell fluttering and headless. Five more shared a like fate, and then fearing our partner might be alarmed at so much firing, we gathered up our half dozen birds and went back to camp, where they were buried in the snow with our elk meat.

By this time the pit in which the head was to be roasted was nearly red hot. The head was placed in the pit on a bed of hot ashes and coals, lightly covered with sods and a large fire built over it.

Our partner's back required attention, so we scraped some tears of balsam and spread on a piece of cloth. This improvised plaster was heated and placed over the seat of the pain and a strong decoction of sage administered. A boulder was heated and placed at his feet and another at his back He was soon sound asleep, and we put in the afternoon at keeping a fire going over the pit and digging to bed rock in two of the small gulches near camp and panning for gold, of which we could not raise a color.

By 4 o'clock that afternoon our invalid was up and said he felt as well as ever and was hungry as a bear. We removed the fire and ashes from our roast and while the contents of the pit were cooling, prepared bread, potatoes and coffee. The head was carefully lifted out of the pit and laid on the clean grass. The skin readily peeled off, disclosing the flesh, tender and juicy. This, shredded and seasoned with salt and pepper, was delicious.

As it was not quite sundown we started out after supper to examine our surroundings. We found that we were at the summit of a spur of what we then knew only as the Crow creek mountains.

This was an immense rolling prairie nearly surrounded by primeval forests The wood lands and prairie were distinct. Arms of the grassy park extended in different directions between patches of forest. To the North an unbroken forest of dark green pines could be seen, and the roar of Crow creek as it rushed through its narrow cannon came faintly to our ears on the evening breeze. We found abundant evidence of the existence of bison, deer, elk, antelope and bear, some of the latter, judging from the size of their tracks, were frightfully large. We saw a small bunch of antelope and saw trails of the mountain sheep.

We could find no evidence of man's presence. No tracks of horses, wagon wheels or human foot prints greeted our eyes and we failed to find even an axe mark on any trees. Evidently we were the only human beings to penetrate this grand bit of mountain vastness for many years. One of the objects of this evening's stroll was our desire to penetrate further into this glorious wilderness and spy out a way to make a road for our wagon.

At the approach of dusk we saw many deer and a few elk come out into the openings and noted the gaunt forms of timber wolves sneaking about in the trees.

It was an hour after dark when we reached camp. Our stroll had made us hungry, and the coffee pot was put on the fire, some meat warmed up and we ate our second supper that night before going to bed.

- Recollection -

The next morning was clear and bright and we had breakfast and left camp early. The business of the day was to look up a permanent camp for that summer, as we had come to the conclusion that we could find no place which would suit as well as this. It was a veritable hunters' paradise, and there was none to dispute the right of territory with us.

We hunted in a northerly direction, where we noted a high comb or crest of rock that stood above the forest clear cut against the blue sky. The air that morning was charged with the health giving breath of the pines and balsams.

We had only gone a short distance from camp when we saw a wolf trot across an opening, and halt at a pile of rocks to look at us. This proved fatal to the creature, as at the crack of one of our rifles it dropped. It proved to be a she wolf of the timber species and she had her lair and family of puppies in this rock pile. As we approached, three puppies that had come out of the den to meet their mother scampered back. They looked innocent and pretty, but realizing the fact that these playful little whelps would grow into savage wolves, the hungry maws of which it would take many young deer and elk to keep filled, and that it was a duty we owed to nature to destroy them, we sat down and watched. Soon a black nose and a pair of shiny eyes emerged from the dark den, followed by the fuzzy body of a baby wolf. As it came out into the light a bullet tore its head off clear back to its shoulders. This was continued until seven young ones with heads torn to rags lay beside their mother. This evidently took the entire family, as no more came out while we were wiping out and oiling our rifles.

Soon after leaving the wolf den we came to a deep wooded gulch which must be crossed before we could reach our main objective point, the high crest of rocks. We had reached the bottom of the gorge, taken a drink from the clear little stream that ran through it and were about to climb the other slope when a magnificent buck jumped up almost from under our feet and bounded up the slope we had just descended. When about fifty yards away he stopped to look back and fell with a bullet through his shoulders. After he was dressed and hung up we resumed our journey and soon crossed a trail where a large flock of sheep had very recently passed, heading for a high timbered point where we could see large rocks standing among the trees. Our partner, being the sheep hunter, proposed that we part here and meet at the crest of the rocks, he taking the course the sheep had gone.

About an hour later we heard his rifle speak twice and knew in all reason that his shots had not been wasted. A few minutes later we surprised a small congregation of roosters of the Dusky grouse species that were having some sort of a meeting, the nature of which we did not have time to enquire into and they did not wait to explain, but took wing directly we came upon them and lodged in the tops of the nearest trees, skulking as close to the limbs as they could and holding their heads and necks in a horizontal position, which made more difficult to use as a target than it would have been if they had held their heads up. After alighting among the branches they sat as motionless as stone images. Here was an opportunity to try our skill and secure some nice game. Our old muzzle loading rifle was a veritable "hair splitter," and our eye and nerves were in perfect condition. Nine shots were fired skyward and eight headless grouse lay at the foot of the trees as a result. The birds were gathered up, drawn and hung up in the dense shade and out of the reach of prowling animals of carnivorous propensities, and we again cleaned and oiled our rifles and resumed our walk toward the crest. Upon reaching the place we found our partner awaiting our arrival.

Here was a beautiful mountain park of thousands of acres of rolling meadow and forest, moss grown and hoary with age. This lofty comb of rocks formed the dividing line between a grand old forest and a flower decked prairie, and from the pinnacle of the crest we could look down upon a great panorama of lovely scenery, in which lower ranges of mountains, great prairie-like mesas, systems of foothills and green valleys with creeks and rivers flashing in the bright sunlight like threads of tarnished silver were to be seen. The air was wonderfully clear and we could see across to the lofty cluster of peaks a hundred and fifty miles distant that like mighty sentinels guard the Yellowstone National Park, where the Yellowstone, Madison, Big Horn and Snake rivers have their birth and from which the Shoshone Wind river and Madison ranges radiate. The sight was truly wonderful, and if we had had no other object in view, what we could see from this lofty position would have more than repaid us for the time and toil expended in getting there. On the north side of the crest and extending into the forest was a mighty drift of snow which was been brought by the winds of ages from the great prairie and deposited here. This snow bank was almost as solid as marble and as near as we could judge was fifty feet deep where it joined the wall of rock. Age and pressure had converted it into a miniature glacier.

Here was an ideal place for a summer's camp. In fact in beauty and convenience it exceeded any pictures that our imagination had drawn of romantic and picturesque grandeur. When considered in regard to convenience, the mighty snow drift, at the edge which we would establish our camp, could be tunneled into and a room excavated in which to pack our game. The finest mountain pasture in the world extended east and south of camp for miles. Unlimited wood for fires or building extended a long distance to the north and west of camp and we were in the very heart of the best hunting and prospecting region on the continent, and being at the edge of perpetual snow the purest and clearest of water was abundant on all sides.

The next thing to be looked up was a pass to get our wagon to this particular spot. Our partner had killed two rams that forenoon which, with the buck and grouse and the meat we had buried in the snow bank near camp, would make a small load.

In going back to camp we followed an open glade down toward the settlement in Crow creek valley which led into a large gulch of easy grade, which we followed to a point where a wood road came up from the mining camp and found that with very little work we could open a fair road to the place we selected for our permanent summer's camp

Night was coming on and we struck for camp, taking the nearest course across the country. In a small grassy opening we ran onto an elk, a solitary bull. He was soon down, his entrails removed, the carcass spread open to cool and a jacket hung over it to keep wild beasts away. By this time it was getting quite dark and we hurried on, reaching camp an hour later very tired and hungry.

Our stock, which we had that morning hobbled and turned loose, except one pony that was picketed where she could help herself to both grass and water, were looked after first and found to be all right. Then no time was wasted in building a fire and cooking a supper such as none but those situated as we were might indulge in. While we cooked, ate and smoked that evening our tongues were busy discussing the events and adventures of the day. Our strong, hot coffee had rested us and made us wakeful, and it was near midnight when we left our pleasant fire and went to bed.

We worked hard the next day getting the game out of the woods, skinned, quartered and packed in snow   We did not hunt that day but about sundown beheaded a few innocent grouse. At dusk we greased our wagon and made ready to pull out for Helena on the morrow.

- Recollection -

The next morning was clear and bright. We were astir at dawn and by the time the sun was two hours high were starting for the city with a load of game. In packing our wagon an extra wagon sheet was spread over the floor of the box, then a layer of spruce boughs, then a layer of snow and then a layer of meat. This was covered with more snow and spruce boughs and we had enough birds and quarters of meat to make one more snug layer, which was covered with snow and a thick layer of boughs. On top of this we spread our tent and then put on our our bedding and camp kit.

When we got down into the valley we found the weather very warm and feared that the snow would melt and the load get damaged before we could get to market. The roads were good and mostly down grade, so we had no trouble in making good time without urging our team.

We did not halt for dinner until we reached Beaver creek, about 1 o'clock. We were driving past the ranch of Col. Vaughan, an old Indian agent and perhaps at that time the oldest man in Montana.

Although past the four score and ten mark he was hale and vigorous, both physically and mentally, and a hard worker. The old man was out irrigating his garden, but seeing us he dropped his hoe and ordered us to halt   Then hurrying along he threw open the gate and bade us drive in. After a hearty hand shake he turned in to help unhitch our mules and ordered his man to hurry up and get us some dinner. We protested that we must not wait long, but be getting on. He said we were on his domain and must obey his commands, which were to turn our mules into his pasture, go in and rest and accept his hospitality that noon.

Having had previous knowledge of the old Colonel's weakness for mountain mutton, we had that morning put the haunches of a fine sheep in our wagon in a convenient position to get at. To witness the old man's childish exhibition of delight at the small but unexpected remembrance many times repaid us for the small donation. Having had over fifty years experience as Government Indian agent and post trader his reminiscences of the frontier, extending over an ordinary lifetime, were deeply interesting. He had a large chest full of Indian handiwork and curios, including a full suit and regalia of an Indian chief, made of the finest broadcloth and the softest of buckskin, elaborately ornamented with various colors of silk and bead work by the deft fingers of his squaw wife, who at that time was, with their family of half breed children, living in St. Louis Mo., where the children were receiving an education.

The venerable colonel exhibited his portrait with this same suit on with its necklace of huge bear claws, his war lance and bow and quiver. He had an insatiable longing for youth and the chance to live the old life over again.

One entertainer made himself so very interesting that the afternoon had more than half gone before we took our departure. We camped that night at Spokane Creek.

The next afternoon we drove into Helena. Stopping in front of a restaurant we enquired if the proprietor wanted some game. He said yes: all we had if it had been nicely handled. We found upon inspection that very little of the snow in which we had packed the meat and melted and an arctic wave came from the wagon as the cover of canvas and boughs were removed. Our restaurant man said he had been wanting just such a layout, as people from the States had begun to come up from Fort Benton. He made us an offer that fairly took our breath, it seemed so generous. He said he wanted all the game we could bring that summer and for elk, moose and bison he would pay 10 cents per pound for fore quarters and 12 1-2 for hind quarters, for sheep, deer and antelope a shilling a pound for the entire carcass, 25 cent for bear, 50 cent a pound for trout and 75 cents each for grouse and rabbits.

Our load brought nearly $150 and we purchased a generous supply of provisions, ammunition and other things we needed and drove back to the Prickly Pear and camped.

As we would necessarily have to spend several days in putting the place we had selected for out camp in order, we were eager to get back. At noon the next day we arrived at the place where our previous survey had told us to turn off from the main gulch and going into camp prepared for the work.

After fortifying our stomachs with a hearty dinner, the pick, shovel and axe were called into play and by night we had built two log bridges over narrow but deep gulches, cut a roadway over the point of a wooded ridge, rolled aside some large boulders and done some grading, so that we could drive our wagon within a mile of our intended summer home. During that afternoon we had several fine opportunities to have killed some noble game, but as we had left our shooting irons at camp the game we saw escaped molestation.

While we worked that afternoon we talked the situation over and made a solemn resolution and agreement to kill nothing but the males of game animals and birds while we should hunt that summer, and also to avoid as much as possible the wounding of any game to let get away and die in the woods or fall prey to wolves and other carnivorous beasts. During the entire season these resolutions were faithfully adhered to, and we also religiously refrained from killing young game birds or animals or any creature that we could not make use of.

That night we returned to camp very tired and hungry, which made us keenly appreciate a good supper, our after supper smoke and our soft bed of warm blankets.

The next afternoon we had our wagon and belongings in the woods on the north side of the crest and at the edge of the eternal snow drift, and as the sun was setting we killed two fine bucks almost in camp.

It took half of the next day to drive a tunnel into the snow bank and excavate a room large enough for a refrigerator in which to store meat, and it took five days to accumulate a large load of meat, which included one small black bear and a bison, and it took three days more to get our game to market, convert it into gold dust and get back to camp again.

We had not as yet found any axe marks, prospects holes or any other evidences of former human occupancy of this charming bit of wonderland. We made frequent visits to the top of the forest to feast our eyes on the wonderful panorama heretofore made mention of.

We noted that Crow creek ran through a deep canon about a mile north of camp and could hear it roaring very plainly. The thought of trout came to us, and as the waters were going down we put in a day exploring the canon. That night we returned to camp with as many brook trout as we could well carry and had other sport to talk over as we sat at our evening meal of trout and fried sheep liver.

While busy fishing that day we heard the rocks rattle on the opposite slope and saw a fine stock of sheep coming in our direction. Our rifles, which were handy, were secured as quietly as possible, but although we were screened by the thick fringe of alders and mountain maple that grew along the creek, our slight movement caught the always keen eyes of the sheep and they started to retreat, but too late to save their bacon- or mutton, rather. Our rifles spoke and two rams fell and rolled down the slope until they lodged against some large rocks.

We had taken care of our sheep and resumed fishing, when a brown bear was noticed turning over logs and boulders. It took us some time to catch on to the fact that the powerful beast was searching for worms and insects. We kept very quiet and watched bruin until he worked over into a draw out of sight. Now was our chance to get within range and we hurried up the slope as fast as possible. The beast had either heard or scented us, for when we came in sight of him he was sitting up on his haunches as straight as a stump. We had then got within seventy-five yards of him. He sat motionless and watched our movements while we prepared to shoot. We both took aim at his breast and on a word from our partner both rifles cracked almost in unison and our ben fell like a log. A few movements of the great paws and bruin had passed in his checks.

- Recollection -

We had learned from experience that carniverous beasts are instinctively afraid of being led into a trap and are by nature suspicious of human kind, and that the hanging of a garment or even a handkerchief over the carcasses of animals that the hunter has killed and cannot carry with him, will protect them for a reasonable time from prowling beasts, unless sore pressed with hunger. In absence of a garment to hang up, to singe the hair in places with a match and place a light covering of limbs or other rubbish over the carcass will answer the same purpose. The creatures will think a trap has been concealed.

Acting on this knowledge; we dragged the dead bear and sheep down by the creek where the shade was dense and where some old snow still lingered. The carcasses were placed side by side and the whole covered with green spruce boughs. By this time the sun had gone below the western ridge and we had got tired of fishing.

So putting our catch in our sacks with a liberal allowance of fresh green grass to keep the trout cool and sweet, we shouldered our rifles and fish sacks and climbed back up the mountain to camp. A big buck got up in front of us when half way back to camp, to fall again with a broken neck before he had made a single jump from the bed where he had been lying. We, while eating our supper that night, felt that we had enjoyed a fine day's profitable sport, especially as we had devoted the day principally to fishing.

We agreed not to kill any large game the next day. We would pack to camp and care for the game we then had in the woods, and perhaps behead a few grouse late in the afternoon.

The next morning as we were eating breakfast we heard one of our mules, which was grazing in an open glade in plain view of camp, give a snort and saw that all our stock was looking in one direction. Grabbing our rifles and investigating the cause, a stately bull elk was seen, with head erect and nose in the air, regarding our animals with as much curiosity was they were regarding him. He received a bullet just back of the shoulder, but did not flinch nor apparently stir a muscle. Thinking that from some unexplained cause we had failed to hit him we were about to try again when the creature began to look skyward and step high with his fore feet, as if tying to climb an imaginary hill. A moment later he stood up on his hind legs and fell over backwards and with scarcely a struggle was dead.

This little episode and what we had eaten completely took our appetites, so our unfinished breakfast was carried into the tent and put in the mess box and we went at the day's work before us. The elk was first to receive attention. He was dressed where he fell and conveyed to the cold storage department a quarter at a time and stored away. Then saddling our pack animals we led them down into the canon where our bear and sheep lay. It took two trips to get them and our buck into camp.

We had seen many grouse in the past two days, but had no time to bother with them. All we now lacked of having another load of meat were a few grouse, so the next day the large game was ignored and we gave our undivided attention to grouse. Twenty-seven of these fine game birds lost their heads that day and were stored in the snow before sundown that night, and neither of us had been over a mile from camp that day.

The next day was put in at mending, moulding bullets, writing, putting things in order and resting. We loaded our wagon about sundown for another trip to Helena.

We had, during our brief occupancy of this beautiful spot, discovered a number of places where Indians had camped. Judging from the piles of hair they must have been hunting parties who invaded this region in the autumn and killed large numbers. As we did not find any evidence of such occupancy near our camp, we did not have any particular fear of molestation although we did not feel exactly safe. We kept a continual watch over our territory to see if fresh pony or moccasin tracks could be seen or any column of smoke which would mark the location of a camp, but without detecting any tangible evidence of such occupancy.

We did get one scare a couple of weeks later which sent the blood tingling through our veins and surging through heart and brain and then receded with a suddenness that made our tongue dry and our hands and feet grow cold. This sensation was followed by a wave of what we will call foolhardiness that tightened our sinews and made us feel like we could, single handed, vanquish any number of the painted warriors.

That morning we had agreed to hunt in seperate directions and not return to camp until about sundown. Our partner went north from camp, while we struck out south. We had put in a hard day's work and been very successful. We were returning to camp and had just started to ascend the last hill between us and camp. Hearing the muffled voice of a dusky grouse we looked about and saw one executing some sort of a war dance. We watched the bird until he subsided and became motionless, then raised the rifle to take off his head, but just as the trigger was about to receive the pressure that would do the work a faint breeze came from the direction of camp and it brought sounds like the distant yelling of savages. The grouse was not harmed, for we knew we had only five or six bullets left in our pouch, and holding our powder horn, which had been worked down to semi-transparency, up against the setting sun, we could see that no more than three or four charges remained in it. Here was a pretty kettle of fish, so to speak. Alone, hungry and tired, with the prospect of a long running fight on our hands and our ammunition exhausted. We had a double barreled rifle which contained two shots, and at our belt the trusty Colt's navy which contained five shots. The first impulse was to make tracks for the nearest settlement. The next feeling was one abject shame at our temporary attack of cowardice. Our partner, our faithful team and pack animals and our camp would thus be left at the mercy of the redskins. Just at this moment the breeze freshened, and with it a succession of the most blood curdling yells and screams, in which we fancied we heard the voice of our partner calling for help. That sent the blood surging through our veins and made us feel as brave and strong as a lion. Hurrying to the shelter of a row of pines that grew along a rocky ridge that ran in the direction of camp, the late tired feeling having entirely left us, we trotted briskly up the slope, forming plans as we ran. The plan was to hurry to camp as fast as possible, meanwhile keeping out of the open country and in the pines. We fully expected to have our camp in possession of redskins and they reveling in plunder they would be taking, and our partner killed and scalped or being tortured, which was a maddening thought and nerved us to redouble our exertions. But nature would assert herself and compelled us to halt twice on the trip to gasp in a few deep breaths of the crisp air of evening which a few moments before had seemed so refreshing, but now it seemed to lack the life giving and refreshing power to reduce the action of our heart, which was now fairly smothering.

The summit of the crest stood out plain against the sunset tinged sky and we were pleased to note that no sentinel was posted on it.

If we could only reach the fringe of young pines that grew along the ridge of which the crest was a part, unobserved, we could look right down onto camp and from our concealed position could, with our seven shots, do terrible work on the unsuspecting savages. We could then dart into the forest, now filled with the gloom of approaching night, and take chances of escaping to the valley. We counted on killing at least seven Indians and rattling the balance so badly that they would think more than one man had attacked them and that when they stampeded to cover it would give us an opportunity to escape.

As we reached the small green pines our breath was nearly gone from our great exertions. Dropping to the ground we listened as well as we could but not a sound came up from camp. We crept on hands and knees as softly as possible toward the edge of the ledge or crest of rocks.

In this manner we gained the last green bush, and cautiously parting the branches with the barrel of our rifle, peered down onto camp.

- Recollection -

Our camp was exactly as we had left it that morning. Nothing had been changed. There was the wagon, the tent and the cooking utensils, but no Indians, no fire nor no partner. It looked terribly lonesome down there. We again listened long and eagerly, looked all around and then clambered down as quietly as possible, took along drink from the small rill that issued from the snow drift, filled and lighted our pipe and sat down on the log by our fireplace to think.

Nothing at the time could have convinced us that we had not heard the yelling of Indians and our partner's call for help. He had not returned to camp, although it was now getting dusk and we had both agreed that morning at parting to be in camp at sunset. It now seemed clear to me that the Indians had got him, but had not found our camp yet. We could conjure up no other solution that seemed in any way plausible. But we had heard no shot fired and could not understand how so wary a man, one who had had his share of Indian fighting and experience, could have been taken alive without a struggle in which his deadly rifle would have played a part. We dared not build a fire, as it would betray the location of camp and place us in a position of great danger. Suspence and the sense of loneliness was becoming unbearable, and we got up to make a cautious circuit of this particular forest to see and hear what we could, when we heard the cracking of dry twigs under a human foot and saw our partner, rifle on shoulder, coming into camp. As he came up, a warning "hist" from us put him instantly on his guard. We sat on the log together and whispered the experiences of that day and the evening. Both had had a big day's tramp with good success, and as both were safe and our camp unmolested, neither could account for the yelling. Then the thought came to us to see if our stock had been disturbed. We both went to the place where our stock usually grazed but could not find a hoof of them, and then we concluded that the Indians had captured and taken off our stock and had missed us and our camp

We had that day killed nearly a load of meat, which we wanted to get into our ice house the next day, but without our animals we would be helpless.

By this time, hunger had got the mastery over us. We must have some food and rest. We wanted our stock back and revenge burned fiercely in our breasts. We would cook, eat, fill our bullet pouches and powder horns, get our shooting irons in perfect order and when another morning dawned would find the trail, follow it until we overhauled the red thieves, watch them go into camp, kill as many as we could, recover our own animals and secure as many of theirs as possible.

It was late that night when our arrangements were completed and we lay down to sleep. Slumber did not have to be wooed that night. We were very tired and as soon as we had drawn the cover of blankets over our weary bodies we lost all track of mundane matters.

Our mate was first to raise his head from its pillow of coat, boots and guns the next morning to look about. It was just daylight, and he gave a yell which made us think that the barbed point of an arrow had entered his anatomy and brought us out of bed with a suddenness which entirely deprived us of our customary spell of stretching and yawning to get fully awake. It was not the stimulating effect of a deadly arrow that brought forth that yell. It was the welcome sight of our mules and ponies grazing in the accustomed park and not fifty yards from camp. But what was the explanation of the screaming of the night before? Our partner advanced the theory that it was the screaming of a cougar or mountain lion. We accepted the solution and a great sense of relief was experienced, which our partner said was equal to getting religion, and again we were compelled to agree with him, as we had never had any knowledge of that blissful sensation further than witnessing the antics of people at camp and revival meetings who claimed to have then and there found grace, but we supposed, like the dutchman, that it must have been "very pleasant."

Before sundown that evening the game killed the day before was snugly stored in our great refrigerator.

While enjoying our after supper pipes as we lounged on the thick, soft carpet of pine needles, we agreed to devote the next day to exploring some of the great stretch of forest that lay north of Crow creek.

We got an early start that morning and saw many things of interest that day. Although we had our rifles with us, we did not molest any deer or elk that day. We struck Crow creek canon at the edge of the mighty forest and a couple of miles higher up than either of us had been before. Walking out to edge of the mesa, which terminated in a rocky precipice that formed the east wall of the canon, we could look down upon the tops of lofty pine trees which grew at its base. While thus looking and listening to the music of the creek and the singing of the breeze among the pines, and at the same time trying to spy out an easy path to descend to the bottom of the canon, the long drawn howl of a timber wolf came from the depths of the forest. Our partner put his hands to his mouth and sent back an exact duplicate of the dismal wail. This was answered by the beast and again by our partner, whose power of mimicry seemed perfect. We could note that each howl from the wolf was nearer and more more distinct, until finally it seemed to come from the foot of the ledge of rocks on which we were standing Our partner, with rifle cocked, peered cautiously down and then raised his rifle. An instant later it was discharged, filling the tree tops beneath us with a dense smoke and sending a report crashing into the timbered hills, the effect which was grand. When we reached the bottom of the gorge there lay the body of the yellow eyed, gaunt bodied wolf with a bullet hole squarely in the centre of his forehead. His lips had drawn apart, disclosing a hideous set of fangs that had probably torn the quivering flesh from many an innocent fawn, but would certainly do so no more.

Near where the wolf lay, we found the carcass of an elk which had lain covered with snow and ice all winter. Bears had dragged it out and eaten part of it.

We worked our way up the stream until we came to a tree that had fallen across the creek, on which we crossed into a green glade. Here we noticed some trees which had been felled several years, but what particularly excited our curiosity was the fact that they had been cut down with an axe, not an Indian's hatchet, and they had been felled in such a manner that a sort of avenue was opened which led into the dense forest. As Montana had at the time only been occupied by white men scarcely three years, we conjectured that probably five or six years before some renegrades or outlaws or some hardy explorers had taken refuge here from the Indians. We carefully looked for some evidence that would make known the identity of the men who had sojourned here. We followed the opening that some white man's axe had cut to a rude domicile that was fast going to decay and had been built of logs, flat stones and dirt over a mass of lava which had served for a bench and table. The roof had long since been crushed in by snow so that the opening that had once served as a doorway was nearly closed by the debris of the fallen in roof. A half hour's work with our hands removed enough of the ruins so we were able to crawl in.

In the niche in the rock at the back end of the cabin we found some iron spoons, knives and forks, badly corroded with rust. With hands and feet we scraped away the loose dirt and found the smooth dirt floor and covered by a flat slab of rock we found some tin plates and cups. In one corner we noticed a sort of mound which we thought must be a grave, but on scraping off the dirt which had fallen on it from the roof and removing some bark which lay underneath the dirt we found two canvas wagon covers, snugly folded and underneath these were a frying pan and cast iron dutch oven.

- Diary -

June 1 – 2, 1867 (June 1st and 2nd) – Went to Helena and sold our game. (1 – Very warm. 2 – Sultry)

June 3, 1867 (June 3.) – Started out on another hunt. Camp at the half way house 15 mi. from town. (Warm wind.)

June 4, 1867 (June 4.) – Camp on Crow Creek. (Cold, N. Wind. Snow in the evening.)

June 5, 1867 (June 5.) – Move ten miles up toward the mountains. (Cold, heavy N.W. wind all day.)

June 6, 1867 (June 6.) – Did not hunt. (Cold.)

June 7, 1867 (June 7.) – I killed an antelope and a grouse. (Warm and pleasant.)

June 8, 1867 (June 8.) – Lyman started out to find a better hunting ground and away to get up on the main range. (Sultry.)

June 9, 1867 (June 9.) – Lyman came back at noon to-day. He shot an elk, antelope, mountain sheep and wounded a bear while he was gone. We hitched up and moved ten miles up into the mountains. (Very warm, S. wind.)

June 10, 1867 (June 10.) – Moved five miles farther up camp. Shot five grouse. Went after the game that Lyman killed yesterday. (Warm, rain in the afternoon.)

June 11, 1867 (June 11.) – Hunted all day. Was caught in a snow storm. Took shelter under a large fir tree. Built a fire and waited until the storm was over, which was about two hours. I killed four grouse and Lyman one. (N. wind, very cold, snow.)

June 12, 1867 (June 12.) – Killed a deer a piece and some grouse. (Cold N.W. wind.)

June 13 – 14, 1867 (June 13-14.) – Stormed, did not hunt. (13 – Cold, rain, N. & N. W. wind. 14 – Cold. Snow and rain all day.)

June 15, 1867 (June 15) – Lyman shot an elk. I shot five grouse. (Rain in the afternoon.)

June 16 – 18, 1867 (June 16, 17, 18.) – Snowed and rained all the time; Killed only a few grouse. (16 – Same. 17 – Snow and rain, N.E. wind. 18 – Forenoon, snow and afternoon rain. Wind from all points.)

June 19, 1867 (June 19) – I stayed in camp to-day. Lyman killed a bison and a grouse. (Morning pleasant, afternoon rain and hail. N.E. & S.E. wind.)

June 20, 1867 (June 20.) – Stayed in camp to-day and fixed up our things. (Warm and pleasant. W. wind.)

June 21, 1867 (June 21.) – Started for Helena with our game. Moved at Crow Creek. Lyman went to market and I started in a different direction to look for stray stock. (Cold and rain in the evening. N. W. wind.)

June 22 – 30, 1867 (June 22,23,24,25,26,27,28,29,30.) – Have been hunting for stock and found only one head. Could not sell him for what he was worth, and left him in the herd. Came back to Crow Creek and met Lyman just going up into the Mountains. He had with him Charlie Williams. (22- Warm. 23 – Sultry. 24 – Very warm, S.W. wind. 25, 26, 27, – Same. 28, 29, – Cold and beautiful. 30 – Sultry wind from S. E.)

July 1 – 14, 1867 (July 1st to July 14th.) – Was hunting a little and was prospecting for gold. We found no gold to pay; killed a deer, three antelopes and twelve birds, and this day, (July 15) we are back in the mountains to take another hunt. Lyman killed one sheep; Camp to-night at Onion Springs. (1 – Cool and pleasant. 2, 3, 4, 5 – Very warm. Wind S.W. & W. 6 – Cooler, rain in the afternoon. 7 – Cool. 8 – Same. N.W. wind. 9 – Warm. 10, 11, 12 – uncomfortably warm. 13 – Cooler, rain a very little. 14 – Sultry wind.)

July 15, 1867 (July 15.) – (Cool, N. W. & W. wind.)

July 16, 1867 (July 16.) – Shot three grouse apiece. (Cool, N. W. & W. wind.)

July 17, 1867 (July 17.) – Stayed in camp. (Rain, cool.)

July 18, 1867 (July 18.) – Killed two antelope and some grouse. (Cold, rain in the forenoon, and snow in the afternoon. Snow all night.)

July 19, 1867 (July 19.) – I killed two grouse and Lyman killed one grouse and a clumpfoot. (Clear and cool.)

July 20, 1867 (July 20.) – Hunted hard all day. Shot five grouse. (Warm.)

July 21, 1867 (July 21.) – Killed one grouse apiece. (Very warm. Wind mostly S. W.)

July 22, 1867 (July 22.) – Lyman shot three grouse, and I shot two. Lyman wounded a bear. We followed his tracks till after sundown, but did not get him. (Very warm. Wind mostly S. W.)

July 23, 1867 (July 23)- Lyman shot a mountain sheep. I killed a deer. (Very warm. Wind mostly S. W.)

July 24, 1867 (July 24.) – Stayed in camp until afternoon then went out and killed six grouse each. (Very warm. Wind mostly S. W.)

July 25, 1867 (July 25.) – Make some elk skin ropes to picket our stock with. I killed two grouse and Lyman one. (Cold, N. wind.)

July 26, 1867 (July 26.) – I went down to the valley to-day after some flour and killed five grouse and a hare on my way back. (Warm, S. wind.)

Trappers' Cabin, *Harper's Weekly*, 1890, drawing by Charles Graham

July 27, 1867 (July 27.) – Lyman killed three grouse. I killed one. (Cool, rain.)

July 28, 1867 (July 28.) – Lyman killed an antelope. I killed seven grouse. (Very cold, for summer, froze hard all night. N. wind.)

July 29, 1867 (July 29.) – (Clear and pleasant.)

July 30, 1867 (July 30.) – Killed three grouse each. (Sultry.)

July 31, 1867 (July 31.) – I went down to the valley after provisions and killed twelve grouse on the way. Lyman killed three grouse. (Sultry.)

- Recollection -

Although these articles had been carefully put away and well covered to keep them dry, the iron utensils were considerably rusted and the wagon covers mildewed. We found in another corner of the cabin the broken tree of a pack saddle, from which the leather and irons had been removed and evidently put on a new tree. We searched every nook in and about the place for some scraps of paper or some writing that would lead to the identity of those who had built and occupied the cabin, but could not discover any, not even a pencil mark on the trees or logs.

From the methodical manner which things had been left, it was clear that the owners had left with deliberation and the intentions of coming back. The elk and deer bones that lay scattered about showed that plenty of fresh meat had been eaten. We were finally compelled to leave the forest cabin, with its mist of impenetrable mystery.

From the number of well worn trails we knew that the forest was fairly teeming with bear, bison, moose, elk and deer, but as enough game could be found near our camp to satisfy our needs, we did not molest the game we saw that day. The creatures did not seem to realize that we were members of the destructive human race, as they did not manifest much fear at our presence among them.

We were in the edge of a primeval forest of many thousands of acres in extent, practically untouched by the hand of man. A veritable Eden where the lover of nature could almost hold converse with the Creator. On this day the beautiful "God's First Temple" came to us with a force that made us appreciate as never before the depth of meaning hidden in that poem.

> "Here are seen
>
> No traces of man's pomp, or pride; no silks
>
> Rustle, no jewels shine, nor envious eyes,
>
> Encounter; no fantastic carvings show
>
> The boast of our vain race to change the form
>
> Of thy fair works. * * * Here, its enemies.
>
> The passions, at thy plainer footsteps, shrink,
>
> And tremble, and are still."

Another day when we each hunted in seperate directions our partner came to camp at sundown with the skin of a cougar hanging over his arm. He had that morning seen the creature sneaking across a grassy park near camp and had to follow it nearly all day before getting a shot. This, he claimed, solved the mystery of the yelling near our camp that has been mentioned in a former chapter.

On the night of July 16 that summer the northern and eastern sky was fairly ablaze with Aurora-Borealic fire It was one of the grandest displays of northern lights we had ever witnessed The next day a high gale prevailed from sunrise until sunset. Old Boreas was that day sweeping a grand march for the gods, his harp strings being the tossing tree tops of the grand old forest. The accompaniment was the crashing of trees as they were uprooted and hurled to earth by the fierce blast. A few of these fell in such close proximity to camp that a feeling of fear mingled with the feeling of awe and grandeur which our surroundings inspired. To guard against our camp being smashed by one of the falling giants, our axes were plied with vigor until the cleared space was far too wide for a tree to reach across.

When we awoke the next morning a dense fog hung like a pall over and around us. The report of a rifle sent sound waves crashing among the peaks and woodlands around us, that rolled majestically back and seemed to awake thousands of echoes that had long slumbered in the woods and among the crags. As we were eating breakfast a sharp peal of thunder startled us and it was repeated by the echoes until it died away in a sullen roar, and then a rain almost as fine as mist set in. This made us hurry a few arm loads of wood into one corner of the tent. It began to get chilly and the large brands from our fire were placed near the door of the tent and fresh log added. We soon had a good fire blazing so near the tent that its glow made the interior very pleasant. The misty rain soon turned into snow and the flakes fell so thick we could not distinguish objects a few rods away. This was in the month of July.

By noon the pine boughs were bending beneath the weight of moist snow that clung to them. Six or seven inches of snow lay on the ground and it was still coming down thick and fast. As the fire would burn down one of us would don a rubber coat and go out and put on a fresh log. Owing to the warmth which came inside the tent from our fire, the snow melted as it fell on the canvass, otherwise it would have weighted our cloth house, caused it to sag and perhaps break down   Our enforced idleness did not prevent hunger, and as the noon hour approached the lantern was lighted and carried into the cold storage room, where some large slices were cut from the ham of a mountain sheep to try and a piece taken from a yearling buck to roast that afternoon. Biscuits were made, coffee put to boil and when the time arrived for the biscuits to be done two frying pans of nice steaks were placed on the coals. Our table was a piece of canvass spread on the tent floor. A can of peaches was opened and that noon we reclined on our blankets after the custom of the far east, while stowing away our vian's

After eating all we could "chamber" the roast was put in one of the Dutch ovens and coals heaped on the lid and raked around it to cook for supper. It still snowed thick and fast. Near sundown it began to grow colder and lighter. The sun set clear, but what a changed appearance the landscape had taken from the way it had looked the day before. By the time it was dark one tent was frozen as stiff as a board. The snow was a foot deep and it really looked like midwinter. Surrounded as we were by dry logs it was small trouble for us to scrape off the snow, chop into convenient lengths and pile up a good supply for night and morning use, and the light and warmth of the fire which was kept burning until bed time at the open door of our tent made the interior very cozy and pleasant.

It froze quite hard that night and the snow having been soft and moist when it fell, was crusted quite solid. The morning was fairly dazzling, so much so that we spent another day at camp to save our eyes. The day was devoted principally to mending clothes, making bullets, cleaning and oiling guns repairing the harness and attending to many small details that in pleasant weather had been put off. Late in the afternoon a couple of fine bull elk came into the little park where our stock grazed and were killed, skinned, quartered and stored in our snow cellar by dark. This completed our sixth load, which the next day was on its way to market. In order to illustrate how one may almost have a fortune in his grasp and miss it, we will state that on this trip to Helena, night overtook us at a small creek between Spokane and Prickly Pear creeks and perhaps three miles from where it emptied into the Missouri river. The ground on which we camped was virtually a rolling prairie and we were not over two miles from the base of the mountains. Noting the next morning that the ground was largely built up of granite pebbles and bowlders, among which quartz pebbles were liberally sprinkled, we decided to give our team a rest and put in the next forenoon prospecting. The weather being cool, we had no fear of our load spoiling by reason of half a day's lay over. We set to work early the next morning with pick, pan and shovel. We began to find gold in the grass roots and at a depth of six feet we came to bedrock, where we got from eight to ten fat colors to the pan. And right there was a placer mining proposition which any experienced miner would have eagerly snapped up but we, greenys that we were, did not consider the fact that the gravel would get richer as we got to the source of the gold, and that it could be easily traced to its source in the hills above us. We were then making money and had a sure thing. In order to prepare for mining we would have to spend some months in preparations, during which time no income would be realized, so we hitched up and went about our business, leaving a nice fortune.

A few years later some parties who possessed more sense than we did, found a large rich lode sticking out of the hill a short distance from where we had prospected, and immense fortunes were realized from the discovery.

- Diary -

August 1, 1867 (Aug. 1.) – I shot a deer. Lyman killed seven grouse and caught a mess of trout. (Clear and calm, and very warm.)

August 2, 1867 (Aug. 2.) – Lyman killed a deer, and I killed one grouse. (Clear and calm, and very warm.)

August 3, 1867 (Aug. 3.) – Shot one grouse each. (Clear and calm, and very warm.)

August 4, 1867 (Aug. 4.) – We went fishing. Caught thirty-five fine trout. (Clear and calm, and very warm.)

August 5, 1867 (Aug. 5.) – Loaded up our game, packed snow all around it, and started for Helena, camp at Antelope Springs. (Clear and calm, and very warm.)

August 6, 1867 (Aug. 6.) – Drove into town and sold out our load. (Clear and calm, and very warm.)

August 7, 1867 (Aug. 7.) – Strike out on a hunt again. Camp on Spokane Creek. (Clear and calm, and very warm.)

August 8, 1867 (Aug. 8.) – Hunted in Spokane Mountains. I killed three grouse. (Cooler, N. W. wind.)

August 9, 1867 (Aug. 9.) – I went to Baker's ferry after the mare.

August 10 – 11, 1867 (Aug. 10. 11.) – Caught some fish. Lyman killed a grouse, I killed three. (10 – 11) – (Sultry S. W. & W. wind.)

August 12, 1867 (Aug. 12.) – Lyman shot a wild goose, and four grouse. I shot two grouse. (Sultry S. W. & W. wind.)

August 13, 1867 (Aug. 13.) – No game. (Cooler, rain a little.)

August 14, 1867 (Aug. 14.) – Stayed in camp and caught twenty pounds of trout. (Cooler.)

August 15, 1867 (Aug. 15.) – same. (Rain, Cooler.)

August 16, 1867 (Aug. 16.) – Lyman shot nine grouse and I killed three. (Sultry.)

August 17, 1867 (Aug. 17.) – Lyman killed six grouse and I killed nothing. (Hot. S.W. wind.)

August 18, 1867 (Aug. 18.) – I killed an elk and three grouse. (Hot. S.W. wind.)

August 19, 1867 (Aug. 19.) – Killed two grouse. (Hot. S.W. wind.)

August 20, 1867 (Aug. 20.) – Went to Helena. Bought some traps. (Hot. S.W. wind.)

August 21, 1867 (Aug. 21.) – Came back. (Cooler, N. wind.)

August 22, 1867 (Aug. 22.) – Went hunting, killed three grouse. (Warm.)

August 23, 1867 (Aug. 23.) – Concluded to stop hunting for this season, and will go to trapping soon. We have passed the summer in a very agreeable manner, and I have made some money. We hitched up and go to Crow Creek and camp. (Cooler, rain afternoon.)

August 24, 1867 (Aug. 24.) – Drive as far as the Basin, (my old herding ground) and camp. Lyman killed an antelope. (Very warm.)

August 25, 1867 (Aug. 25.) – Went to Jefferson camp at Joe Millers. (Very warm.)

August 26 – 28, 1867 (Aug. 26, 27, 28.) – Got up as far as Middle Creek, caught all the trout we wanted to eat. Killed some ducks and caught a mink. (Very warm.)

August 29, 1867 (Aug. 29.) – Went up Little Galletin, twelve miles. Some men prevailed upon us to help them harvest a few days. (Very warm.)

August 30 – 31, 1867 (Aug. 30. 31.) – Harvesting. (Cool and pleasant.)

September 1, 1867 (Sept. 1.) – Lyman went up into the mountains to see if there was any game to be found. Shot a grouse. (Sultry.)

September 2, 1867 (Sept. 2.) – A whole wagon load of us went to election at Bozeman. (Sultry.)

September 3, 1867 (Sept. 3.) – Work in harvest in afternoon. I went down to the Creek, (Little Galletin) and set a few traps. (Sultry.)

September 4, 1867 (Sept. 4.) – Caught one beaver, also killed a fine fat deer on my way to the traps. (Sultry.)

September 5, 1867 (Sept. 5.) – Caught a beaver and a mink. (Sultry.)

September 6, 1867 (Sept. 6.) – Caught a beaver. Lyman commenced building a boat to use while trapping this fall. (Sultry.)

September 7, 1867 (Sept. 7.) – Lyman finished the boat. (Cool.)

September 8, 1867 (Sept. 8.) – Went to Middle Creek and set a few traps. (Cold.)

September 9, 1867 (Sept. 9.) – Caught a mink. Went over to Cottonwood, fourteen miles, this afternoon and came back to camp. (Cold.)

September 10, 1867 (Sept. 10.) – Caught a marten. Went up to the mountains after pitch to stop the seams of our boat with. Dressed some buckskins. Caught a lot of trout, etc. (Pleasant. W. wind)

September 11, 1867 (Sept. 11.) – Caught a mink. Moved five miles down the creek. (Pleasant. W. wind.)

September 12, 1867 (Sept. 12.) – Procured a scythe, and looked for some long hay to cut. (Cool N. E. wind.)

September 13, 1867 (Sept. 13.) – Lyman went to help a man harvest. I stayed at home and cut hay. (Cool N. E. wind.)

September 14, 1867 (Sept. 14.) – Lyman came back this morning with the intelligence that a man by the name of Davidson, who was living 2 1/2 miles below here had been murdered last night. Lyman had been called with others to search for the body, (the murderers having carried it off). They found the body at daylight, out in the field. Mr. Davidson was intending to start this morning for the states, and it is supposed had considerable money with him. He appears to have been killed with a hatchet. His head was horribly smashed to pieces. (Cool, rain.)

September 15, 1867 (Sept. 15.) – We went to the house of the murdered man, saw him dressed and put into his coffin. It is not known who the murders are. (Cool, rain and snow.)

September 16, 1867 (Sept. 16.) – Lyman went to help a man harvest to-day. I remain in camp and cut hay. (Cold, rain and snow.)

September 17, 1867 (Sept. 17.) – Went over to Little Galletin, caught one mink. (Clear and cold. High north all day.)

September 18- 22, 1867 (Sept. 18,19,20,21,22.) – Working at Hay. (18 – Cold, snow and rain, N. wind. 19 – Cold. North wind. 20, 21, 22 – Warm and pleasant.)

September 23, 1867 (Sept. 23.) – Working at Hay. Went to Little Galletin. (Warm and pleasant.)

September 24, 1867 (Sept. 24.) – Moved to West Galletin. Calked and pitched our boat and launched it. (Rain in the evening.)

September 25, 1867 (Sept. 25.) – Moved down to Galletin, five miles. (Showery.)

September 26, 1867 (Sept. 26.) – (Warm.)

September 27, 1867 (Sept. 27.) – Moved seven miles farther down, set some traps. (Sultry)

September 28, 1867 (Sept. 28.) – Caught one mink. Moved. (Cold, N. wind.)

September 29, 1867 (Sept. 29.) – Caught one mink, moved down to Swany. (Same.)

September 30 – Oct 2, 1867 (Sept. 30 and Oct. 1 & 2.) – Caught only one beaver. (30 – Same. 1, 2 – Cool weather, lovely, W. & N. W. wind.)

October 3, 1867 (Oct. 3.) – Moved eight miles farther down river. (Cool weather, lovely, W. & N. W. wind.)

October 4, 1867 (Oct. 4.) – Caught a beaver. Moved five miles down; saw a large party of Indians going to the Yellowstone. (Cool weather, lovely, W. & N. W. wind.)

October 5, 1867 (Oct. 5.) – Caught two beavers. Moved three miles farther down. (Cool weather, lovely, W. & N. W. wind.)

October 6, 1867 (Oct. 6.) – Caught three beavers. (Cool weather, lovely, W. & N. W. wind.)

October 7, 1867 (Oct. 7.) – Caught one beaver. (Cool weather, lovely, W. & N. W. wind.)

October 8, 1867 (Oct. 8) – Caught a mink. (Cool weather, lovely, W. & N. W. wind.)

October 9, 1867 (Oct. 9.) – Came back from Crow Creek. (Cool weather, lovely, W. & N. W. wind.)

October 10, 1867 (Oct. 10.) – Moved Camp over to Jefferson, and set traps. (Cool weather, lovely, W. & N. W. wind.)

October 11 1867 (Oct. 11.) – Caught four beaver. (Cool weather, lovely, W. & N. W. wind.)

October 12, 1867 (Oct. 12.) – Lyman killed a mink. (Warm like summer.)

October 13, 1867 (Oct. 13.) – Caught a beaver. Lost a trap. (Warm like summer.)

October 14, 1867 (Oct. 14.) – Caught two beaver. I went to Boulder. (Warm like summer.)

October 15, 1867 (Oct. 15.) – No Game. (Warm like summer.)

October 16, 1867 (Oct. 16.) – I went hunting; killed an antelope. (Warm like summer.)

October 17, 1867 (Oct. 17.) – Caught a Catamount. I went hunting again. Killed an antelope and a bear. (Warm like summer.)

October 18, 1867 (Oct. 18.) – Caught an Otter. Moved over the Jefferson. (Cool. Rain a very little N. E. wind.)

October 19, 1867 (Oct. 19.) – Moved up the Madison ten miles. (Cold, snow, same in the afternoon. N. wind.)

October 20, 1867 (Oct. 20.) – Moved up fifteen miles farther to

Cherry Creek Camp. (Pleasant. Very cold nights.)

October 21, 1867 (Oct. 21.) – Set out the traps. (Pleasant. Very cold nights.)

October 22, 1867 (Oct. 22.) – Caught four beaver. Moved camp five miles up the creek. (Pleasant. Very cold nights.)

October 23, 1867 (Oct. 23.) – Caught a beaver, but he escaped, and took the trap also. (Warm and pleasant.)

October 24, 1867 (Oct. 24.) – Caught two beaver. Lyman went farther up to look for game. (Warm and pleasant.)

October 25, 1867 (Oct. 25.) – Caught one mink. Moved back to the mouth of the creek. (Warm, high S. W. Wind all day.)

October 26, 1867 (Oct. 26.) – Caught two mink. (Warm until 6 o'clock P. M., when the wind suddenly changed to north and blew furiously. The weather grew cold and commenced snowing at dark.)

October 27, 1867 (Oct. 27.) – Caught one mink and two beavers. Moved down to Madison five miles. Lyman shot a swan. (Snow fell four inches in depth, last night. To-day it is clear and cold.)

October 28, 1867 (Oct. 28.) – Snow fell four inches deep last night. Caught two mink. I killed an antelope. (Same.)

October 29, 1867 (Oct. 29.) – Caught one beaver. Three Flathead indians stay with us to-night. (clear, Moderate.)

October 30, 1867 (Oct. 30.) – Caught one mink. Moved down three miles. (Pleasant.)

October 31, 1867 (Oct. 31.) – Caught one mink. Stayed in camp. (Warm, high S.W. wind all day. The snow is all gone.)

November 1 – 6, 1867 (Nov. 1, 2, 3, 4, 5, 6.) – The weather has been cold and stormy. Have caught two mink and two beaver, and to-night we camp at Stones' ranch near Galletin City. (1 – Cold wind. N. E. snow, most of the day. 2 – Moderate. 3 – Pleasant. 4, 5, 6 – Cloudy and cold wind. N. and N.W.)

November 7, 1867 (Nov. 7.) – Set out traps. (Cold.)

November 8, 1867 (Nov. 8.) – Caught three beaver. The stock ran off. (Cold.)

November 9, 1867 (Nov. 9.) – Found them at 2 P.M. Caught four beaver. (Cold.)

November 10, 1867 (Nov. 10.) – Caught one beaver and a muskrat. (snow a little.)

November 11, 1867 (Nov. 11) – Caught three beavers and two muskrats. (warm and pleasant.)

November 12, 1867 (Nov. 12.) – Caught one beaver. (warm and pleasant.)

November 13, 1867 (Nov. 13.) – Caught three beaver. (warm and pleasant.)

November 14 – 18, 1867 (Nov. 14, 15, 16, 17, 18.) – Caught only three beaver and one mink. (14 – warm and pleasant. 15 – cold rain and snow. Wind N. E. 16 – clear and cold. 17, 18 – warm and pleasant.)

November 19, 1867 (Nov. 19.) – Caught one beaver. Moved ten miles down the Missouri to Horse Shoe Bend. Moved one mile farther down and set traps. (warm and pleasant.)

November 20 – 26, 1867 (Nov. 20, 21, 22, 23, 24, 25, 26.) – Have caught a beaver. The river is freezing so hard that we cannot do much more at trapping. (20, 21, 22 – warm and pleasant. 23 – snow a very little. 24 – snow four inches deep. 25, 26 – clear and cold.)

November 27, 1867 (Nov. 27.) – Stormy. At work making picket ropes. (clear and cold.)

November 28, 1867 (Nov. 28.) – Stormed all day. Keep in camp. (snow a little.)

November 29, 1867 (Nov. 29.) – Went up into the mountains sixteen miles to take a few days hunt. (clear and cold.)

November 30, 1867 (Nov. 30.) – (clear and cold.)

December 1 – 3, 1867 (Dec. 1. 2. 3.) – (cold wind N.W.)

December 4, 1867 (Dec. 4.) – Disgusted with hunting went back to the river, we killed only a sheep, couple of antelopes and a deer; a few grouse. Lyman froze one of his toes Dec. 1st. (cold wind N.W.)

December 5 – 6, 1867 (Dec. 5, 6.) – Cold and stormy, did not move. (5 – warm. Wind S. W. snow almost all disappears. 6 – cold wind N. W. heavy.)

December 7, 1867 (Dec. 7.) – Went to Galletin City. (cold wind N. W. heavy.)

December 8, 1867 (Dec. 8.) – Moved over the Missouri to Jo Millers'. Lyman went up Galletin Valley. (warmer.)

December 9 – 10, 1867 (Dec. 9, 10.) – Rain. (9 – pleasant. 10 – warm. Rain all day.)

December 11, 1867 (Dec. 11.) – Moved to Cottonwood Springs. (warm.)

December 12 – 13, 1867 (Dec. 12, 13.) – Killed eight sage hens and a few hares. Went back to Jo Millers'. (12 – rain in the afternoon. High S. E. wind all day. 13 – colder. Snow at evening.)

December 14, 1867 (Dec. 14.) – Moved to Galletin Valley, fifteen miles. (warm and pleasant. Rain at night.)

December 15, 1867 (Dec. 15.) – Moved up to Middle Creek. (chilling wind. N. W. Blow hard all day.)

December 16 – 18, 1867 (Dec. 16.17.18.) – Cold. Remain at Dogtown. (16 – pleasant. 17 – cold. Snow falls 5 in. deep. 18 – clear and cold.)

December 19, 1867 (Dec. 19.) – Went up Middle Creek five miles to a deserted cabin where we intended to camp the winter. (Very cold wind N.)

December 20, 1867 (Dec. 20.) – Went hunting; killed some grouse.

(same.)

December 21, 1867 (Dec. 21.) – Went up in the mountains after some timber to build a sled with. (same.)

December 22, 1867 (Dec. 22.) – Cut and hewed out the timber. (warmer.)

December 23, 1867 (Dec. 23.) – Came back. Hauled some hay and commenced fixing up for housekeeping. (thaw fast, rain a little.)

December 24, 1867 (Dec. 24.) – Finished rigging up the cabin. (warm.)

December 25, 1867 (Dec. 25.) – Lyman went to Bozeman. (cold, N. wind.)

December 26, 1867 (Dec. 26.) – Went to Middleton. Bought a fat hog. (cold wind N. W.)

December 27, 1867 (Dec. 27.) – Went down the creek. Bought some flour and vegetables. Ground our axes, etc. Lew Baker came to visit us. (pleasant.)

December 28 -29, 1867 (Dec. 28, 29.) – Made a sled. (28, 29 – very cold.)

December 30, 1867 (Dec. 30.) – Went to Dogtown to get our sleigh ironed. (very cold.)

December 31, 1867 (Dec. 31.) – Went to look for a good place to get wood. (moderate.)

January 1, 1868 (Jan. 1. 1868) – Went to Middleton to attend a shooting match. (pleasant.)

January 2, 1868 (Jan. 2.) – Went to borrow a log chain and shovel. (cold wind N.W.)

January 3, 1868 (Jan. 3.) – Chopped wood. (cold.)

January 4, 1868 (Jan. 4.) – Hauled wood. (<u>very</u> cold wind N.)

January 5 – 6, 1868 (Jan. 5. 6.) – The weather is so cold that we stay in the cabin to-day. (5 – <u>very</u> cold wind N., 6 – the same.)

January 7, 1868 (Jan. 7.) – Went to Bozeman City after some provisions. (the same.)

January 8 -9, 1868 (Jan. 8. 9.) – Went to Middleton after straw. Hauled wood. (the same.)

January 10, 1868 (Jan. 10.) – Chopping and hauling wood. (the same.)

January 11, 1868 (Jan. 11.) – Chopped wood and commenced setting a pit. (the same.)

January 12, 1868 (Jan. 12.) – The stock ran off; could not find them. (the same.)

January 13, 1868 (Jan. 13.) – Found the stock seven miles away. (moderate.)

January 14, 1868 (Jan. 14.) – Hauled wood. (same.)

January 15, 1868 (Jan. 15.) – Hauled wood and worked setting coal pit. (pleasant.)

January 16, 1868 (Jan. 16.) – Hired one "Bill" Olmstead to work for us; finished setting coal pit, and commenced covering it. (pleasant.)

January 17, 1868 (Jan. 17.) – Lyman went to Dogtown to help a man make some sleds. Bill and I worked covering coal pit. (pleasant.)

January 18, 1868 (Jan. 18.) – Working at Coal pit. (pleasant.)

January 19, 1868 (Jan. 19.) – Same. (pleasant.)

January 20, 1868 (Jan. 20.) – Went to Dogtown. Middle Creek String Band met. (snow a little.)

January 21, 1868 (Jan. 21.) – Hauled some wood and a load of hay. (snow, wind N.W. and N.E.)

January 22, 1868 (Jan. 22.) – Went to the mountains after timber to build a bridge with. (pleasant.)

January 23, 1868 (Jan. 23.) – Lyman went to Middletown with

a load of logs. Bill and I chopped wood. (pleasant.)

January 24, 1868 (Jan. 24.) – Bill and I went to the mountains after a load of timber. Left Bill there to get out timber and came back alone. Lyman set fire to coal pit. (warm, wind S. W.)

January 25, 1868 (Jan. 25.) – Stormed hard. Bill came down from the mountains. (cold very cold wind N. E. Snow all day.)

January 26, 1868 (Jan. 26.) – Lyman and Bill went to Dogtown. (clear and cold.)

January 27 – 31, 1868 (Jan. 27. 28. 29. 30. 31.) – Walling coal pit and hauling timber.   (27 – clear and cold, 28, 29 – moderate, 30 – pleasant. Slight breeze from the N. W., 31 – cold wind N.)

February 1 – 2, 1868 (Feb. 1. 2.) – Hauling timber. (clear and cold.)

February 3 – 10, 1868 (Feb. 3. 4. 5. 6. 7. 8. 9. 10.) – Working at various things. (3, 4, 5, 6 – clear and cold, 7 – warm. Wind S. E., 8 – cold wind N.E., 9 – extremely cold wind N., 10 – clear still and very cold.)

February 11, 1868 (Feb. 11.) – Commenced raking out coal and hauled hay. (moderate.)

February 12, 1868 (Feb. 12.) – Set another coal pit. (warm wind S. W.)

February 13, 1868 (Feb. 13.) – Worked at covering coal pit. (warm. Snow melting away fast and musquitoes and flies are flying in the air.)

February 14, 1868 (Feb. 14.) – Lyman took a load of coal to Bozeman. I finished covering coal pit. (warm and spring like. The ground is almost bare again.)

February 15, 1868 (Feb. 15) – Set fire to the new pit. (warm and spring like. The ground is almost bare again.)

February 16, 1868 (Feb. 16.) – Worked at raking out coal. (warm and spring like. The ground is almost bare again.)

February 17 – 18, 1868 (Feb. 17. 18.) – Lyman went to Dogtown to work on the bridge. I traded off my rifle for furs to a man from Galletin. (17- warm and spring like. The ground is almost bare again. 18 – cloudy and warm.)

February 19, 1868 (Feb. 19.) – Bill went to Bozeman with coal. (warm and pleasant.)

February 20, 1868 (Feb. 20.) – Worked at raking out coal. I traded my violin for a watch. (warm and pleasant.)

February 21, 1868 (Feb. 21.) – Bill went to Bozeman with coal. Lyman came back from Dogtown. (warm and pleasant.)

February 22, 1868 (Feb. 22.) – Lyman went to Bozeman. I hauled logs. Bill chopped wood. (warm and pleasant.)

February 23, 1868 (Feb. 23.) – It snowed, so we did not work. I traded my six shooter for wheat. (warm. Snow all day. Wind S. E.)

February 24, 1868 (Feb. 24.) – Dressed some buckskins. Hauled wood and raked coal. (cool wind N. E.)

February 25, 1868 (Feb. 25.) – Bill went to Bozeman with coal. Lyman went to Dogtown.

February 26, 1868 (Feb. 26.) – Bill hauled wood. Lyman and I raked coal. (moderate.)

February 27, 1868 (Feb. 27.) – Raked coal. (warm.)

February 28, 1868 (Feb. 28.) – I went to Bozeman with coal. (warm.)

February 29, 1868 (Feb. 29.) – Setting another pit and raking coal. (cold. Snow by spells all day. Wind N. E.)

March 1, 1868 (March 1.) – Lyman and Bill went to Dogtown and I set out some pits. (forenoon warm. Afternoon cold with heavy N. wind.)

March 2, 1868 (Mar 2.) – At work setting coal pits. Bill quit work. (cold wind. N. W.)

March 3, 1868 (Mar 3.) – Hauling wood and setting coal pits. (heavy west wind warm.)

March 4, 1868 (Mar 4.) – Caught a mink. Lyman went after some antelope. Hauled straw. (snow fell to the depth of 5 inches last night. Warm.)

March 5, 1868 (Mar 5.) – Did not work. (snow fell 15 inches deep last night and snow all day. Cold wind N. E.)

March 6, 1868 (Mar 6.) – Shoveled snow and tinkered about the cabin. (clear and cold.)

March 7, 1868 (Mar 7.) – Hauled straw and commenced covering coal pit. (cold. Very foggy all day.)

March 8, 1868 (Mar 8.) – I went to Bozeman with a load of coal. (clear and pleasant.)

March 9, 1868 (Mar 9.) – Set fire to coal pit, hauled hay and raked over some coal. (clear and pleasant.)

March 10, 1868 (Mar 10.) – Lyman went to Dogtown. (warm wind S. W.)

March 11, 1868 (Mar 11.) – Watching coal pit. (warm wind S. W.)

March 12, 1868 (Mar 12.) – Set out some traps. (warm wind S. W.)

March 13, 1868 (Mar 13.) – Watching coal pit. Lyman shot two antelopes. (cold wind N.W.)

March 14 – 15, 1868 (Mar 14. 15.) – Watching coal pit. (14 – cold wind N.W., 15 – pleasant.)

March 16, 1868 (Mar 16.) – Lyman went to east Galletin. (pleasant.)

March 17 – 19, 1868 (Mar 17. 18. 19.) – Watching coal pit, and knitting a net. (17 – warm high S. W. wind forenoon. Snow and turns cold at night with wind N. W. 18, 19 – warm. Wind S. W.)

March 20, 1868 (Mar 20.) – I went to Bozeman. (warm. Wind S. W.)

March 21, 1868 (Mar 21.) – Raked coal. (warm. Wind S. W.)

March 22, 1868 (Mar 22.) – Went to Dogtown, with coal and caught beaver. (cold. Wind N.)

March 23, 1868 (Mar 23.) – Raked out coal. (warm rain in the forenoon. Cold and snow at dark. Wind S. E. and N. W.)

March 24, 1868 (Mar 24.) – Same. (cold snow fell 4 in. last night and snow a little most all day.

March 25, 1868 (Mar 25.) – I went to Bozeman with coal.

March 26, 1868 (Mar 26.) – Went to Dogtown with coal. (warm.)

March 27, 1868 (Mar 27.) – Raked coal and caught a mink. (warm.)

March 28, 1868 (Mar 28.) – Lyman went to Bozeman with coal. (warm.)

March 29, 1868 (Mar 29.) – Lyman went to Dogtown with coal, caught a beaver. (warm.)

March 30, 1868 (Mar 30.) – Set up, covered and put fire into a new pit. (cool.)

March 31, 1868 (Mar 31.) – I went to Bozeman with coal. (warm and spring like.)

April 1, 1868 (April 1.) – Chored around the house. (cold. Heavy N. E. wind all day.)

April 2, 1868 (Apr 2.) – Hauled a load of coal to Bozeman, finished our contract, and settled. (pleasant. Wind N. E.)

April 3, 1868 (Apr 3.) – Hauled coal to Middleton, finished our contract with C. Austin. Come home, rigged our wagon and things, and prepared for breaking up housekeeping. (warm. Grass begins to spring out of the ground and people are commencing to plow and sow.)

April 4, 1868 (Apr 4.) – Moved Lyman up into the mountains, then went down to Middleton. (warm. Wind S. E.)

April 5 – 10, 1868 (Apr 5. 6. 7. 8. 9. 10.) – I was at Middleton. (5 – pleasant. Cool at dark. Wind E. and W., 6 – cloudy. Cold. Rain a very little. High S. W. wind all day. 7 – Warm, S. W. & N. E. wind. 8 – Warm, wind W. 9 – Cool., rain, some wind, N. W. & W. 10 – Cool, wind W.)

April 11, 1868 (Apr 11.) – Came up to the mountains to-day found Lyman alright. He had completed our trout net and had killed an antelope, caught one beaver, one fisher and one martin. (Snowed an inch last night, pleasant to-day.)

April 12, 1868 (Apr 12.) – (Warm, S. W. wind.)

April 13, 1868 (Apr 13.) – Hitched up this morning and moved down the creek five miles. Set some traps. (Cool, wind W., cloudy in the morning.)

April 14, 1868 (Apr 14.) – Went to Middleton, Bozeman and Ft. Ellis; bought a supply of groceries and provisions. (Very cold, freezing all day. Snow fell an inch deep this morning. N. wind blew hard all day.)

April 15, 1868 (Apr 15.) – Set out a few traps, caught some trout. I made a pair of mitts. (Cold, wind, N. & N. W. heavy.)

April 16, 1868 (Apr 16.) – Lyman went to Mosses store. I remain at home, do some washing and mending, caught some fish and a beaver. (Cold, wind, N.W.)

April 17, 1868 (Apr 17.) – Lyman came back. We went at work to drain Middle Creek. (Cold and blustering wind, N.W.)

April 18, 1868 (Apr 18.) – Completed our dam across the Creek and turned the water into another channel and caught a lot of trout that the water, in fallin, had left on the ripples. (Froze hard all day. Wind, N. W.)

April 19, 1868 (Apr 19.) – Caught some more trout and opened the dam to let the water back into the creek. Had some company to-day at dinner. (pleasant, clear, wind heavy from the S.W.)

Bridger Canyon, near Fort Ellis, Montana

April 20, 1868 (Apr 20.) – Went to Ft. Ellis, took some fish. The soldiers were paid off a few days ago and a lot of them had been down town, (Bozeman) and got drunk, and were being punished. Some were carrying poles, some bags of stone some were put astride cannons, some were in the guard house chained. Yesterday nineteen of them were made to strip and from three to five pails of ice water was poured over each of them. Caught one beaver. (Pleasant forenoon, afternoon cold wind, N. W.)

April 21, 1868 (Apr 21.) – Packed up and left our winter quarters, went to Middleton, sold our portables and started for Spanish Creek. Traveled eight miles, stopped at Salters Ranch for night. (Cold, rain and snow. Wind, N.E.)

April 22, 1868 (Apr 22.) – Pulled out at 8 o'clock this morning, moved eight miles up the Galletin. We passed over some very bad pieces of road where we were obliged to hold our wagon to keep from turning over. We moved to-day one mile below the mouth of the Spanish Creek. After dinner we hitched up and moved eight miles up Spanish Creek. Spanish Creek is a beautiful stream, clear and cold. It is fifteen feet wide and one foot deep. (Warm and pleasant.)

April 23, 1868 (Apr 23.) – Lyman set some traps and went over to west fork of Spanish Creek. Lyman shot the grouse. (same.)

April 24, 1868 (Apr 24.) – Caught two mink. Lyman shot two grouse. I went up the gulch to set some traps. (same.)

April 25, 1868 (Apr 25.) – Caught two martin, sunk a prospective shaft on a bar, did not get to bed rock on account of water. Could not find gold. (same.)

April 26, 1868 (Apr 26.) – We gave chase after a bank of Elk. They were so shy that we could not get a chance to shoot any of them. Prospected the rest of the day for gold. (same.)

April 27, 1868 (Apr 27.) – Went to South Fork and set some traps, killed four grouse. (Sultry, cold at sundown.)

April 28, 1868 (Apr 28.) – Caught one beaver. Snow fell three inches last night. Lyman went after some elk but did not get any. Killed five grouse to-day. (Snow fell three inches last night. Cold to-day.)

April 29, 1868 (Apr 29.) – Caught one beaver. Took up the traps. (Cold, wind N.W.)

April 30, 1868 (Apr 30.) – Moved down to the Galletin River camp. Lyman killed an elk. (Cold, wind N.W.)

- Recollection -

While recalling reminiscences of frontier life of over a quarter of a century ago, it will not be amiss to recall some incidents that are forgotten by most of the early settlers of Montana, but which should be written as part of the early history of that now thriving and beautiful commonwealth.

Early in the fall of 1866 rumors came to the settlements of the discovery of rich placers on Salmon river in Idaho. The infection, if we may call it so, was very contagious . It seemed for a time as if Montana would be speedily depopulated. Although winter was near at hand and nearly everyone was well fixed, the greed for gold drove people nearly crazy. Reports from Idaho of the wonderful richness and extent of the alleged new Eldorado continued to come that exceeded the wild tales in the Arabian Nights. Many were of so extravagant a nature as to brand them as wild fiction, yet they were eagerly gulped down by the over credulous, and still further magnified by lively imaginations until a large portion of the people of all callings, trades and professions went fairly wild.

Many considered themselves fortunate in being so near the wonderful gold fields that if they hurried they could get in and secure rich claims before the tide of humanity would pour in from the states. We did not get the fever. Montana, with its vast and varied resources, was good enough for us. Business men hired teams and men at enormous expense, loaded wagon trains with goods, ranchmen gathered their moveable effects, miners formed into companies and started, in many cases leaving comfortable homes and paying jobs.

Winter overtook them enroute and some wisely turned back, but others struggled on until they met those who had been first to start, had reached the goal and were trying to get back again. These reported that the whole thing was a fake. They found no gold and no employment and starvation stared them in the face if they remained Many were in sore need, being without food or suitable clothing. A large percent of the stock died of starvation and many of the humans fell by the wayside, and those who did get back were glad to regain possession of their old homes, and vowed never to take the stampede craze again unless the objective point should be the moon.

That same winter, but near the close of the season, a rumor was started that the Indian tribes that frequented the region at certain times to hunt, were displeased and threatened an outbreak against the whites. At first, it was a mere rumor, but it gathered strength with age. The rumor, like a stampede craze, spread from cabin to hamlet and from hamlet to town, gathering in terror as it spread, until it hung like a hideous nightmare over the land and included the Bannocks, Flat Heads, Shoshonnes, Nez Perces, Crows and Blackfeet. It was even rumored that runners had been sent out from these friendly tribes to hold council with their mortal enemies, the Sioux and Cheyennes, to induce them to join in a general massacre of the whites. A mere hint or conjecture as to what might happen, was repeated as a well authenticated bit of news. It was finally arranged, in imagination, that the attack was to be made simultaneously in all the settlements at the time in the spring when the hunting parties from the various

Fort Ellis, Montana
"On the Bozeman Trail, near the present city of Bozeman.
The arrival of a military escort at the Fort."
The Bozeman Trail, Hebard and Brininstool

tribes should return from the winter's hunting ground. All the Indian tribes of America were supposed to know exactly when and how the attack was to take place, and as many as could were going to rush in eager to secure one or more scalps while the performance was on. The number of available warriors that each tribe could muster, all fierce, well armed and fairly spoiling for a fight, was magnified into twenty times the actual number.

Here were a few thousand white men cooped up as it were, hemmed in by impassable ranges, with no soldiers but the mere handful (six companies) of troops at Fort Ellis, near Bozeman. Time would not wait, but was fast bringing the day when the homes would all be burning, the inhabitants killed and scalped, and perhaps roasted and eaten, any way they would all miss a Christian burial, which was so much coveted that it seemed as if some would take the matter into their own hands and commit suicide in order to get the much desired Christian burial in advance, and thus cheat the poor Indian out of a part of his legitimate pastime, and the coyotes, foxes and buzzards out of a toothsome repast.

Meetings were held in the various settlements to devise ways and means for protection and defense, and the majority decided in favor of block houses of green logs, to be large enough to hold the inhabitants with provisions to last through a protracted siege.

Much bravery was shown at these meetings and an expressed willingness to work diligently until places of refuge were provided. Work was actually begun in some neighborhoods, but green logs were heavy to handle and nearly every one found work of their own that must be done and "Zion languished," so to speak. Finally the excitement died out, and when the bands of hunters migrated back through with a triumphal display of Sioux scalps, neatly tanned, hooped and swung, like banners, from poles, the people had come to the conclusion that our Indians were all good and did not covet any white man's scalps after all. Thus a black ghost of vast proportions and hideous mein vanished and passed away without a struggle or a groan.

During all this fear and excitement the sun rose and set with its accustomed regularity, the constellations did leave their old time positions and no blood could be seen on the moon

- Diary -

May 1, 1868 (May 1.) – Moved down to Middletown. (Warm and pleasant.)

May 2, 1868 (May 2.) – Went to Bozeman and Ft. Ellis. Sold our team to Wilson & Rich. (Same.)

May 3, 1868 (May 3.) – Delivered the team to-day. I am sick to-day. (Cold, rain and snow.)

May 4, 1868 (May 4.) – Sick to-day. Lyman went to Ft. Ellis. (Clear and cool.)

May 5, 1868 (May 5.) – Went to work making shingles. I am better to-day. (Pleasant.)

May 6, 1868 (May 6.) – Work at making shingles. I am sick again to-night. Have a slight attack of the Mountain Fever. (Warm until three o'clock P.M., the wind sprung up from the N. and blew cold.)

May 7, 1868 (May 7.) – I am sick to-day, have a high fever. Lyman is making shingles. (Cold, snow a little.)

May 8, 1868 (May 8.) – I am better to-day. (Warm.)

May 9, 1868 (May 9.) – Lyman is sick to-day. (warm and beautiful.)

May 10, 1868 (May 10.) – Lyman went to Bozeman. (warm and beautiful.)

May 11 – 12, 1868 (May 11. 12.) – We are not able to work. (warm and beautiful.)

May 13, 1868 (May 13.) – Hired a man to move us to Galletin City. (warm and beautiful.)

May 14, 1868 (May 14.) – Crossed three forks and stopped at

Joe Miller's ranch. Lyman has an attack of Mountain Fever and is very sick. (Cold, rain at night. Wind N.)

May 15, 1868 (May 15.) – Lyman is some better to-day. (Cold, rain, wind N. W.)

May 16, 1868 (May 16.) – Lyman is improving. (Warm and pleasant.)

May 17, 1868 (May 17.) – I went to Horse Shoe Bend, but could not cross the river. The river is raising rapidly. (Sultry with occasionaly showers, wind. S.W.)

May 18 – 21, 1868 (May 18. 19. 20. 21.) – Bad weather, lay still. Lyman killed a beaver the 18th. I went over the river yesterday and brought some medicine back for Joe Miller, who is somewhat indisposed. (18 – Showery. 19,20, 21 – the same.)

May 22, 1868 (May 22.) – Helped Joe work at a new string of fences, which he is building. (Cloudy and cool.)

May 23, 1868 (May 23.) – Went to Radersburg on Crow Creek, a mining camp that has sprung up within six months, containing 100 or more buildings. The town is not very lively on account of the scarcity and high price of water.

Met Geo Roush and partner. The first time I have seen them since I left the states. Did not retire to rest until the light of the morning of the 24th had almost appeared. The town contains a number of dry-goods and clothing stores, Grocery and provision stores, one gambling house, a large number of drinking saloons and two barber shops and two chinese laundresses; also one blacksmith shop, one meat market, one drug store, one Jeweler shop and two physicians. (Cloudy and cool.)

May 24, 1868 (May 24.) – Came back to Three Forks the roads were muddy on account of the heavy rain last night and this forenoon. (Cold, rain all night, last night and until noon to-day. Wind N.W. blew quite hard.)

May 25, 1868 (May 25.) – Went up the river and Bostwells ranch this morning and prospecting this afternoon. (Rain in the forenoon.)

May 26, 1868 (May 26.) – Went to Bed Rock, in two different shafts, but only raised two colors. Black gnats very troublesome to-day. (Clear and warm, pleasant, wind, N. W.)

May 27, 1868 (May 27.) – Lyman went to HorseShoe Bend to-day. I helped Joe haul rails. (rain last night , and this morning.)

May 28, 1868 (May 28.) – A man came along to-day in great haste, in search of a great favorite race nag that was stolen from Radersburg last night. Lyman came back from the Bend to-day. (Showery wind, S.W.)

May 29, 1868 (May 29.) – Lyman traded his rifle for a revolver. ((Cold wind, N. blew hard.)

May 30, 1868 (May 30.) – Was tinkering around at various things. Prospecting. (rain, cool.)

May 31, 1868 (May 31.) – Kept the Sabbath. (Showery.)

June 1, 1868 (June 1.) – Footed up to Middle Creek, (28 miles) and was very tired at night. (Wind, N.W.)

June 2, 1868 (June 2.) – Went to Bozeman City, settled up accounts with several men. Times very dull. (Wind, N.W.)

June 3, 1868 (June 3.) – Finished settling and came back to Middleton. (Wind, N.W.)

June 4, 1868 (June 4.) – Rain. Remain at Middleton. (Rain.)

June 5, 1868 (June 5.) – Bid our friends "Goodbye" and came back to Joe Miller's. (Pleasant.)

June 6, 1868 (June 6.) – Hired our baggage hauled and struck out for Helena; camp at Crow Creek.(Sultry.)

June 7, 1868 (June 7.) – Lay over. Lyman bought into a Bakery and Restaurant. (Same.)

June 8, 1868 (June 8.) – I bought Lyman's share of the furs and we dissolved partnership. (Rain.)

June 9, 1868 (June 9.) – Started again for Helena, Camp on Warm Spring Creek. (Showers.)

June 10, 1868 (June 10.) – Went to Beaver Creek. (Hot.)

June 11, 1868 (June 11.) – Camp on Prickley Pear. Rain. (Rain)

June 12, 1868 (June 12.) – Went to Helena, found Lyman there. Stored my furs and made arrangements to go back to Radersburg with Lyman. (Sultry with showers.)

June 13, 1868 (June 13.) – Started for Radersburg at 3 o'clock P.M. Stop for night at the Half Way house. (Hot.)

June 14, 1868 (June 14.) – Arrived at Radersburg at 4 P.M. (Hot.)

June 15 – 16, 1868 (June 15. 16.) – (Hot.)

June 17 – 18, 1868 (June 17. 18.) – (Rain at intervals.)

June 19, 1868 (June 19.) – (Pleasant.)

June 21 – 22, 1868 (June 21. 22.) – (Wind and rain.)

June 23 – 25, 1868 (June 23. 24. 25.) – (Sultry forenoon, cold and rain in the afternoon.)

June 26, 1868 (June 26.) – Have been stopping at Radersburg since the 14th. (Sultry.)

June 27, 1868 (June 27.) – (Showery.)

June 28, 1868 (June 28.) – Start to Helena with some men that are on their way to the States. Camp at Spokane House. (Showery.)

June 29, 1868 (June 29.) – Got to Helena at noon to-day. (Same.)

June 30, 1868 (June 30.) – Went to Montana City and back. Make arrangements for going to Fort Benton. (Same.)

July 1, 1868 (July 1.) – (Pleasant.)

July 2, 1868 (July 2.) – Start for Benton at 2 P.M. Camp at Cold Springs to-day. Pleasant, traveled seventeen miles over rough hills and hilly country. (Pleasant.)

July 3, 1868 (July 3.) – Traveled twenty miles through a steep rocky canon, crossed little Prickly Pear eighteen times. Camp at Dearborn River. Day, warm and country hilly. (Pleasant.)

July 4, 1868 (July 4.) – Drive fifty miles. Camp at Sun River. Roads good. Country hilly. Day cool and pleasant. (Pleasant.)

July 5, 1868 (July 5.) – Drive forty miles over a beautiful country, rolling prairie and level table lands. Day cool. (Pleasant.)

July 6, 1868 (July 6.) – Drive twenty-eight miles to Benton. Roads good. Day hot. (Sultry.)

July 7, 1868 (July 7.) – Started for the states. Took cabin passage on board the Urilda of pittsburg, Pa. left Benton at 3 o'clock P.M. The Urilda has on board thirty-five passengers. Cabin thirty, Deck, five. Three of our passengers are ladies. My room-mate is one Christopher Lapp of Freeport, Ill., a huge good natured fellow. The Urilda is a fast runner. Several shots were fired to-day at some mountain sheep, or American gorillas, but none were killed. (Sultry.)

July 8, 1868 (July 8.) – Passed Camp Cook at daylight this morning. Saw two immense herds of buffaloes and two flocks of wild sheep to-day. A great many shots were fired at them as we passed, but none of them was killed, that we could see. Stopped at a deserted cabin and took in a supply of ice. Saw the grave of Chief Little Arrow, and six other indians. Passed Ft. Hawley at 3 P.M., stopped at Ft. Miscelshell at sundown. Took another passenger. Ran aground at dark, got loose and tied up for the night.

July 9, 1868 (July 9.) – Passed large herd of Buffalo. Some of them were swimming in the water and came near being run over by the boat, one fine young bull was killed and brought aboard.

At noon to-day we passed a cabin, saw some men lying dead around it. They had probably been killed by indians. The boat did not stop to look at them. Ran aground at 1 P.M. at Cow Island. Was fast a couple of hours before we got off. Tied up at dark.

July 10, 1868 (July 10.) – Passed the mouth of Milk River at 4 A.M. Saw large herds of Buffalo and other game.

July 11, 1868 (July 11.) – Saw lots of indians. By Camp Beaufort, took another passenger.

July 12 – 19, 1868 (July 12. to 19.) – Nothing occurred worthy of note except we changed boats and were delayed three days in doing so. Arrived at Sioux City 4 P.M.

July 20, 1868 (July 20.) – Landed at Sioux City one day, then started home. Arrived at Lena, Ill. July 22nd at dark. Saw Uncle Lewis and a great many old acquaintances. Found by inquiry that my relatives were all well.

July 23, 1868 (July 23.) – Waited all day at Lena; but none of my old neighbors came.

July 28, 1868 (July 28.) – After waiting till 10 o'clock to-day my folks came after me with the team. We were all rejoiced very much to find each other alive and well.

- Recollection -

Having for a long time taxed the patience of our readers with reminiscences of a long journey across the plains, and incidents of a residence in fair Montana, we will review some of the experiences of the homeward journey and bow ourselves out and down, with as much grace as could be expected of an old veteran of the frontier. The weight of more than half a hundred years, a good share of which time has been spent on the frontier, in hard work and great exposure, has whitened our locks, dimmed our vision, dulled our hearing, sapped our powers of endurance and stooped our shoulders. We still love nature in all her moods, love to live over again the old life which had so many charms and to fight, in memory the old battles over again.

While life lasts camp fire recollections will continue to be pleasant.

Five of us chartered an outfit, consisting of the proprietor, a pair of large strong mules and a three seated spring wagon. The passengers were a middle aged German, a slight built, pale looking young man with a hectic flush and a consumptive cough, a man who stood six feet three in his stockings, with brawn and bone enough to correspond with his height and a voice like a two year old bull, yet with a disposition kind, and like most men of gigantic build, gentle and winning. A man who had been a lumberman in the pine regions of Wisconsin, an agreeable fellow when sober, but a terror when full of liquor, as we afterwards found out; and the writer. We were to pay the owner and driver of the vehicle $25 each, which included baggage, etc. We "chipped in" and bought flour, hams, tea, coffee, sugar, cheese, crackers and some canned goods, and each man furnished his own matches, tobacco and blankets. We had no tent, as the weather was very pleasant and we all preferred to camp and sleep out of doors. Our immediate destination was Fort Benton, the head of navigation at that time of the Missouri river, where we hoped to meet, and take passage for St. Louis, one of the miniature steamers which plied between St. Louis and the towns and posts on the upper part of the river. We bade good bye to the acquaintances we had formed in Helena.

There were so many small details to be looked after that we did not get out of Helena until 2 o'clock. We traveled seventeen miles that day over a hilly country. The weather was very fine and the scenery pleasant. The afternoon was quickly away and before night we, who had all met that morning as strangers, felt tolerably well acquainted. The first hill of any magnitude we came to we passengers jumped out to walk up it, and thus spare the mules. The small man gave out and had a violent fit of coughing, so the driver had to stop and let him get in and drive the team, while he got out and walked. We learned that afternoon that the invalid had come to Montana a year before, with some money and good health. He had gone into partnership with some other fellows to take and improve a ranch. They found a suitable location, built a house, procured implements and teams and were making good headway when one afternoon one of the partners went to kill some meat and sighting a large grizzly bear, shot and wounded the beast, which ran into the jungle of bushes and ascaped. The hunter found and killed his deer and got it home. The next morning the work oxen were missing and our invalid friend started to look for them, taking his rifle along. In following a trail through the willows he saw a large fresh bear track and got his rifle into position for instant use and continued following the trail. Soon a monster bear, presumably the one his partner wounded the day before, rose up in the path in front of him. He remembered poking his gun at bruin and pulling the trigger, and that instant a blow from the bear's paw sent his rifle flying from his grasp, then a slap aimed at him and he awoke with the bear standing over him and crunching his limbs. He had the presence of mind to feign death and bore the terrible torture in silence. Finally the bear turned him face down and began a systematic crunching from his heals up to his head The last thing he knew the bear was biting his head, and as his skull would slip through the creature's jaws the noise was like the loudest thunder and all kinds of brilliant fire seemed filling his eyes. Then came a blank space, a state of oblivion, which lasted nearly three months. Toward noon that day, and when his partners had become alarmed at his protracted absence, the truant oxen came to the cabin, and then his partners started out to look him up. They found him where the bear had left him, literally chewed to pieces. He still breathed and they carried him carefully to the cabin, removed his blood soaked clothes and arranged his broken bones as best they could in absence of a doctor, none being available. They expected him to die and for days and weeks watched and tended him tenderly, feeding him spoonful rations of broth and doing the best they could. He began finally to mend, his broken bones to knit and, after weeks of weary watching and tender care, the sufferer gladdened their hearts by asking if he did not get badly hurt by a bear, was it not another day now? Did he finally find and drive home the oxen? and other questions pertaining to their daily routine of life. Nature, ever ready to repair damages, had knit together the ends of the broken leg and arm bones, but unaided by surgical skill had made a sorry job in fixing the fractured ends squarely together. The result was that each mended fracture was an osseous knot or bunch which, in our friend's then emaciated condition, could be seen and felt very plainly. Where the wounds had been torn and healed, white scars were left in evidence. It was impossible to examine these evidences without a deep feeling of pity for the unfortunate young man and a desire to do all in one's power to help him. When he was able to be up his partners took him to Helena and a doctor. They paid him back the money he had put into the partnership, which had not already been lived up, and this soon went for living and medicine. He was told by his doctor that the terrible strain on his vital powers had exhausted what had once been a large stock and that he could never hope to be well again and advised him to send home for funds to return with. On account of his parents being old and poor he declined to do this and secured an easy position at one of the mines   He held his place until he had earned enough to buy a suit of decent clothes and have enough to take deck passage on a boat for home, which he hoped to reach in time to visit a little while with his father and mother before the end came.

By the time a camping place was reached that night he was very tired. He insisted on doing his part of camp work but was voted down and almost forced to take a much needed rest.

That night after supper the proprietor of the rig proposed a little game and suiting action to his proposal spread a blanket on the ground near the fire. It was to be a small game and for a starter each member of the party put his jack-knife into a "pot" and fifty matches were counted out to each, and the man who finally got all the matches was to take all the knives. It was what our man called "freeze out." The matches gradually worked our way and as one after another would get froze out he would fill his pipe and look on. Before beginning the game our invalid's bed had been made down and he settled for the night.

By the time a sleepy feeling had began to be manifest the last match had been added to the pile in front of the writer and the knives were ours. We put our knife back in its accustomed pocket and told our companions to do likewise.

The frying pan and coffee pot were called into use and we partook of another supper. The sick man was asked to partake, but all he wanted was a drink of cold water. We found him bathed in a profuse night sweat and regretted our inability to do more for him than to give him a drink.

- Recollection -

Our man routed us out early the next morning with the remark that if we hurried and eat our breakfast we could have a little game of poker while his mules were eating their breakfast. To please him we hurried. He proposed putting our revolvers into a pot and playing freeze out for the pile. He was fairly wild to gamble, and the poorest player in the party, but as none of us wanted to lose our shooting irons his proposition was declined and when we gathered around the blanket which served as a gambling table, matches were used as chips and they represented a cash value of 5 cents. No money was put up and we agreed to settle balances when Fort Benton should be reached. At the close of each game on the trip-morning, noon and night-we had a sort of reckoning and an account was kept by each player of how the balances stood. It only took a few games to put the proprietor in debt to his passengers. The $25 which each was to pay at Fort Benton had been absorbed in the game and he was owing more or less to each player in the party. Our consumptive friend did not play.

Our second day's journey was down the valley of the Little Prickly Pear, which stream was forded eighteen times that day in going twenty-five miles. The next day was the Fourth of July and we made fifty miles and camped on Sun river. Here was a small town, a trading post, the building of which were adobe with mud covered roofs. Here was a village of white men who had Indian women for wives and many pretty half breed children played about the buildings. We were now within seventy miles of Ft. Benton, which we reached the second day after leaving Sun river. The last halt we made before reaching the fort our man called our attention to the fact that, with the exception of our invalid, we had won from him the price of our transportation and had placed him in debt to us from ten to fifty or more dollars each, that he had nothing except his team and rig to pay us with and that he had a wife and children to support, and depended upon his outfit to earn a living. He stated he had lost fairly, but having a mania for gambling he had brought this condition of depleted finances upon himself, that if he was well out of this scrape, he would forever let gambling alone Four of us at once decided to forgive his gambling debt to us and to pay him the full amount he was to receive for conveyance. Our German fellow traveler was very angry and said he would have his money at any cost.

When the fort was reached all but the German settled up with our man as we had agreed, which brought tears of thankfulness to his eyes. We shook hands, bade him good bye and left he and the German at the wagon. As we afterwards learned, the German drew his revolver and demanded payment. This was witnessed by a post sentry who gave alarm, which so frightened the German that he skipped for the hills, although the country was said to be infested with hostile Blackfeet.

Just then the hoarse whistle of a steamer was heard around the bluff. In the bustle which followed our German was forgotten. The small cannon in front of the barracks was hurriedly loaded and just as the smoke stack of the steamer appeared around the bend the gun was touched off. The salute continued until the boat tied up at the wharf. We were lucky once more. As the river was falling and navigation would soon close for the year, we were afraid we might have to wait several days for a boat and might get none and have to return to our old haunts. While the cargo was being discharged, we concluded a bargain with the captain for passage to St. Louis.

The boat was the Urilda, a small upper river steamer. In our haste to secure staterooms we had neglected to look after our invalid, whose vitality was fast ebbing away. As soon as we had taken possession of our rooms and put our luggage therein, we looked after the sick man and found that having only funds enough to pay for deck or steerage passage to the nearest port to his home, he had paid for this sort of accommodation and was quartered down among the colored roastabouts and a couple of horses that were being taken to some post down the river. This would not do, as he was too weak and fragile to last many days, even with the best of care.

Three of us went to the captain and explained the situation. He kindly made an offer to throw off $10 from the regular rate of $80 for cabin passage and to deduct the money that our friend had already paid. The three of us paid the difference and went down to the lower deck, where we found our friend making down his bed of blankets. The colored man who was to carry his dunnage to his room was at our heels. We told the invalid that we had come to see if he was comfortably located but must object to his making camp in that place He looked mystified and a trifle displeased. We told him we had been plotting with the captain, who had ordered his presence above and the grinning darkey would carry his baggage to a room off the cabin which would be his roosting place while the voyage lasted.

The young man protested vigorously at first, saying he had paid for as good accommodations as he could afford and did not want to impose on his friends nor incur any indebtedness. We told him that it was a matter of duty on our part and if our positions were changed we should expect him to do the same by us, that it was all paid for and we would feel hurt if he refused to accept and that he could repay us at any future time he might be able to do so. It was finally settled that way and we had the satisfaction of seeing him comfortably settled. We then went to the post commander and explained the case of our German friend and got his promise not to have him molested so long as he did not make any more bad breaks. We then tried to locate him in the hills where he had gone, but failed to find

Fort Benton - *Harper's New Monthly Magazine*, October, 1867

him, and as dusk was coming on we went back to our new quarters.

It took until nearly midnight for the boat to get unloaded and ready to start back down the river the next morning. We were up at dawn and out looking for our German friend, but found him not. The boat was to untie and start on her homeward journey at 8 o'clock. Opposite the boat's office was a very tidy barber shop with one chair, and next to the barber shop was an elegantly furnished saloon where modern drinks were dispensed. Somewhere under the deck was an ice and cold storage room   The dining hall, which ran the whole length of a cabin, was tastefully decorated and everything above and below was scrupulously neat and clean.

The morning of our departure the captain informed us that it was against the rules of the boat to permit gambling but the passengers who wished to play could put up small articles as stakes, such as watches, guns, rings, pipes and the like. After what seemed the most elegant, elaborate and toothsome repast we had ever partaken of had been served, the boat's bell began to ring, the small cannon which the night before saluted the craft as she hove in sight again pooled forth its thunder, the gang plank was drawn aboard, the cable cast off and the bow of the little steamer began to swing toward mid-stream, a little bell tinkled up in the pilots house, was answered down in the engine room, the machinery began to throb, the great paddle wheel to revolve and we were finally started.

- Recollection -

Once in the channel and under a full head of steam our brave little Urilda fairly flew. Hills, groves, bits of green meadow land and other objects flew by so rapidly that it made one's head whirl to try to keep watch of the scenery along the shore. Having in mind the well being of our German friend who had so hastily struck out ahead the night before, our eyes were busy scanning the landscape in hopes of seeing and rescuing him. Finally we were gladdened by seeing him nearly a mile ahead waving his coat to attract our attention. At the moment of discovery we, with the captain, were on the cabin roof of the pilot house and had been looking at the bullet and arrow marks inflicted in the wood work by ambushed Indians during the up trip. When we saw the German's signal, the captain was hurriedly made aware of the nature of the case and informed that another passenger wanted a berth. He said it would be $10 to make a landing and we said all right. The pilot made his wheel spin like a revolving squirrel cage, another tinkle of the bell and the engines slowed down and the boat turned her big nose in toward the shore, but the current was swift and we seemed to be going past the waiting man, who, directly he noticed that his signal was answered had ran down to the edge of the water. Another tinkle of the bell and the engines were reversed and the big paddle wheel began to tug up stream with the strength of a hundred giants, while the craft continued to swing nearer shore, which she finally struck with a bump that nearly floored us. As the boat touched the bank, the gang plank was shot out and dutchy, who had evidently feared we would miss making the landing and had ran along the shore like a quarter horse, hurried aboard and the boat was soon scooting along down the channel again as if no stop had been made.

The scenery along the river was grand, being made up chiefly of very lofty and steep hills that looked like clay. Trees and bushes were to be seen growing on the nearly perpendicular slopes and startled flocks of mountain sheep were often seen in seemingly inaccessible places. Some of the passengers who had rifles shot at some of them in the vain hope of killing one, but they were fortunately beyond the reach of bullets and we were glad to see them escape injury.

Just before dinner time we could see a heavily timbered bottom ahead, and as we drew near, ricks of cordwood and a couple mud covered cabins could be seen. This was a wood yard which had been cut and piled during the winter. There was also a supply of ice here. The place was deserted, as with the approach of spring the owners had embarked on a flatboat for the nearest military post for protection from the Indians. We tied up here. The plank was again run out and the mate, with note book and tape line, sprang ashore and began to measure a pile of the wood, while the deck hands and passengers, like a swarm of ants, were soon busy carrying it aboard and cording it up again on the boat's deck convenient for the firemen or stokers to shove into the greedy furnaces. The pressure of steam was high and twice during our brief stop the valve opened and the pent up steam escaped with a roar like thunder. A ton or two of ice was taken aboard and were soon racing down the "Big Muddy" again.

The day was sultry and our active exercise made us perspire freely and had sharpened our appetites for dinner. We noted that day numerous beaver cuttings along the banks of the river and passed two large houses of these creatures. We also saw several muskrats swimming These as the boat approached would dive gracefully and be gone. Also several broods of young geese and ducks, which in their efforts to outrun the boat would make the water fairly fly, but they, like the rats, would dive and disappear as the boat overhauled them.

Toward sundown a large cinnamon bear was seen quite a distance ahead clumsily ambling up a gulch from the river. The sounds of the boat's engines reached him just as several rifles were about to be aimed at him.

He sat up to see what it all meant, and as he got a glimpse of the steaming terror that was sweeping down in his direction so rapidly, half a dozen jets of fire and smoke spurted from the muzzles of as many rifles, the sharp reports of which were echoed back from the hills and bruin "hit the high places" with astonishing agility, unharmed, as the bullets all fell short and kicked up the dust, probably fifty to one hundred yards on our side of the game.

A part of the furnishings of the boat's cabin was a rack containing about twenty-five or thirty loaded guns A good supply of cartridges were kept within easy reach and the passengers were told to make good use of these in case of an attack. We enjoyed the view of the scenery from the pilot house and it seemed marvelous to us that a young man should know so much of a river that was so little navigated. He would point far ahead and say, "there lies a dangerous snag," or "there lies a sand bar just covered with water" etc.

It was considered dangerous to run at night on account of snags and sand bars, which it took a practiced eye to detect in broad daylight. The boat tied up at dusk where the land sloped gently up from the water's edge to a high ridge or swell. Scattering cottonwoods grew on the swell near the river, and there being no underbrush to conceal a lurking foe, made us safe from an attack.

Before daylight the next morning steam was up and at dawn we were swiftly gliding down stream, passing Camp Cook at sunrise. The bluffs grew higher and more abrupt and the river more narrow and swift. It was all channel now. Soon after breakfast the canon widened and at each shore, at the foot of the bluffs was a narrow strip of green meadow. Both sides of the river were fairly black with bison. Being alarmed at the sight of the steamer and the hoarse whistle which the engineer blew the terrified animals attempted to scale the bluffs, which were too steep. Then the black rolling mass on either side of the river began plunging into the swift water thinking to escape by swimming across. The engineer shut off steam and allowed the boat to drift with the current and just as the two herds of bison met in mid stream the boat was plowing through the struggling mass of terrified bison. It was a grand sight and nearly every passenger was down on deck. By kneeling down and reaching over we could put our hands on the great animals as the boat pushed them aside and drifted by. A fat young dry cow was shot, hauled aboard, skinned, cut in pieces and stowed in the boat's refrigerator.

Five beautiful calves were seized and hauled aboard alive and unhurt, and tied with shoft ropes to give each brown beauty a little freedom to exercise. They were gamey young bovines and would fight anything that had motion. The little rascals would fight until the object of their wrath would get away for fear the calf would injure itself. We also saw many flocks of mountain sheep scrambling up the steep sides of the lofty clay hills. Juicy bison steaks were served at dinner and supper. Passed Fort Hawley at 3 p m. Touched at Fort Muscleshell and took on another passenger near sun down. Stuck on a sand bar near dusk which hindered us an hour. When we got off the boat was tied up for the night.

- Recollection -

The next day we met the Zephyr, a little steamer of fourteen inches draft. She was hopelessly stalled, as her engines were not strong enough to propel her up stream any further.

The two captains held a consultation and an agreement was made for a transfer of both passengers and freight, the Urilda taking the Zephyr's load to Fort Benton and the Zephyr to take the Urilda's load and turn about and return to St. Louis. The passengers exchanged places then and there and both crews of deck hands were put to work exchanging freight and baggage, which it took that night and the next day to accomplish. Then the crew of the Urilda struck or mutinied and refused to work the boat, saying that they only signed for one trip to Benton and did not intend to again run the gauntlet of the upper Missouri. One darkey said that it would take until the watermelon season was over at home to climb the river again and others said they were afraid of the Indians and wanted to get home. The captain appealed to the post for help and a squad of soldiers came aboard and told the hands that the entire region was subject to military law and that his orders were to order the men to go to work and see to it that his orders were obeyed. He told the men that he hoped they would obey, as he disliked to use harsh measures and that it would be better to go to work peaceably than to be punished and compelled to work. The crew held a short consultation and then each man grabbed something to fight with and huddled together in the after part and one big brawny fellow, as black as ebony, announced that they would fight and die before they would submit to the outrage of being forced back to Fort Benton.

Things began to look serious. The soldiers were ordered to fix bayonets, which they did. It looked like blood was going to flow. The Urilda's captain called the sargeant aside and begged him to take his squad back to the post and wait until morning and in the meantime he would try to persuade the hands to take the boat back to Benton. The captain mingled with the men and reported to his passengers that some would submit peaceably, but that others could not be moved.

At sunrise the next morning the sergeant and his soldiers came aboard and after a short consultation with the captain he ordered them to go to work. About half of them obeyed, the others sullenly refused. Then with fixed bayonets the soldiers surrounded the incorrigible ones, when cords were tied around their thumbs and drawn up and fastened so the men had to stand on tip-toe to relieve the strain on their thumbs. This seemed very cruel and we wanted to rush in and cut them down. They were told that they would be released when ready to give in and go to work, and not until then. They soon began to weaken and as a man would promise to go to work he was released. Finally they all gave up and the Urilda, under full head of steam, began to creep back up the river, and our Zephyr to glide swiftly down towards home.

By this time our bison had all been consumed and we had to come to eating ham again until a fort was passed, where a beef was procured. We were now fairly out of the mountains, although both Indians and bison could occasionally be seen from the boat. We had also reached a point where the channel was so well known that we ran nights as well as days, only stopping when necessary to wood up.

One day we passed an Indian cemetery, the graves of which were in the air. Four tall post set in the ground supported a scaffold which held the dead body. Some of these scaffolds had fallen down, the post having rotted off. Some leaned badly, while others had the appearance of being recently put up. The captain declined to stop the boat to give the passengers a chance to go ashore, examine the place and perhaps secure a few relics. A few turkey buzzards were wheeling at a dizzy height above the place and three or four of these scavengers, gorged to a stage of sleepy inactivity, were roosting on the scaffolds, which furnished the grewsome repast, too disgusting and horrible to think of.

Our little old man, that we noted in a preceding chapter, explained some strange superstition of the tribe that disposed of its dead in this manner, but whose name we have forgotten, and also of another tribe that practice cremation, usually by burning the remains in and together with the hut in which the deceased dwelt.

After twelve days' journey on the river, which had carried us through a large part of Montana and the Dakotas, we became very tired of that mode of travel, and when on the 19th day of July the boat tied up at Sioux City, Iowa, and we realized that here was a terminus of a railway which would take us home in twenty-four hours, the temptation was too great to be resisted. We bade our captain, pilot and friends good bye and walked ashore and put up the night in a hotel, and the next day was spinning over fields and meadows in a different sort of a conveyance, and that night we slept in a town where as a boy we had bartered rabbits and prairie chickens for jack-knives and ammunition.

We had got home safe and sound after running the gauntlet of so many hundreds of miles of dangers and adventures and best of all, we missed very few faces that we had known and loved in childhood. Death had been kind to me and mine.

And now, thanking our readers for their kindness in traveling the "rough and rugged road" with us, that we have tried to make plain and interesting, we will say good bye.

Product & Live-Stock Show - Holden, Mo.

Bank of Holden, Holden, Johnson Co., Missouri (building on right)
Organized by Lewis Cheney & I. M. Smith

History of Johnson Co., Missouri, 1881

Bank of Holden-This bank was organized May 15, 1872, from the firm of I. M.
Smith and Louis Cheney, private bankers. ...Their building is situated on the corner of Market and Second St. It is a large brick structure, 48x80 feet, two stories
high, with an elegant stone front. ...They do a great banking business of discount
and deposit, and engage in no outside speculations. They buy and sell exchange
and government securities, make collections and execute financial orders here, in
St. Louis and in New York. ...Since 1878, they have declared annually a dividend
of from 14 to 15% after paying all expenses. Their stock is worth 30% premium
and is difficult to be obtained at that price. They have on hand deposits of nearly
$400,000, and their business is constantly increasing. The gentlemen engaged
in this bank have long been before the public, and thoroughly known as men of
first- class business qualities. Their future efforts in this business cannot fail to
continue to bring the desired reward.

CHAPTER 9
Missouri Banking – A Change in Careers

Perry Burgess didn't remain in Illinois for very long. Uncle Lewis had already established himself in Missouri as a businessman and banker, and it is quite probable that Perry joined him out of sheer lack of viable options. Whether his departure was part of the plan or merely a whim, Perry left Illinois for Missouri in 1868. He settled in Holden, a town located in Johnson County. It was a region he was familiar with, as it was just south of Independence, the Saints' Zion.

Perry was met by Lewis, who had just recently entered into a partnership with Israel Martin (known as I. M.) Smith and opened a private bank called Smith and Cheney, of which Lewis was president. The organization would be incorporated as the Bank of Holden in 1872. Smith was no rookie in the world of banking, as he and fellow banker Spencer Rising had formed a partnership and opened a banking house in Lena, Illinois, in 1867. According to an 1868 *Lena Star* story, Lewis had just returned home from a business trip to Missouri, most likely to scout for land for the opening of his new bank. He left Illinois permanently for Missouri no later than July 1 of that year. Soon after, Perry arrived.

Smith and Cheney apparently knew their business thoroughly and built a strong foundation because, until 2008, the Bank of Holden was the oldest chartered bank in the state of Missouri. At that time, the institution merged with First Central Bank, and Lewis Cheney's portrait still hung on the wall 140 years after the bank opened its doors for business. It seems he had found his calling, an idea supported by the *Holden Republican* in a September 1877 article that stated, "The financial advancement of Mr. Cheney in itself indicates a man of great executive and financial ability. He is a gentleman, affable and courteous. He stands high in community as a citizen, and is ever ready to stand by Holden and her interests."

Whether he knew it or not, Lewis Cheney was embarking on what would become a lifelong career in banking when he opened Smith and Cheney in 1868. He chose his business partners carefully and wisely, forming trusting relationships with peers whose persistence and willingness to take risks matched his own.

Native New Yorker I. M. Smith was one of Lewis's primary partners. They had met in Lena, Illinois, in 1867 and, together with Lewis's father, Ephraim Cheney, and Perry's mother, Semantha Cheney White, moved to Holden, Missouri.

Smith remained a partner in the Bank of Holden for just five months after it was incorporated in 1872. At that time, he moved to Texas, where he opened more banks. He continued his pattern of moving every few years and opening banks throughout the decade. Both Boulder, Colorado, and Kansas City, Missouri, were home to Smith's banks. Smith eventually became an officer of the First National Bank of Kansas City, one of the largest institutions in the state.

James McClure was another partner of Lewis's in the Bank of Holden. Born into meager circumstances in Kentucky in 1842, McClure came to Holden, Missouri, in 1867, by way of Colorado. He and his wife had spent several years there, where McClure invested successfully in the cattle business. He had in fact the distinct honor of transporting the first trainload of cattle and sheep from Pueblo via the Atchison, Topeka, and Santa Fe Railroad. McClure maintained his business interests in Colorado even while living in Holden. He would eventually partner with his civic-minded brother, William H. McClure, and build the McClure House, also known today as the Strathmore Hotel. Built in 1872 in Cañon City, it is believed to be the oldest building in Colorado used continuously as a hotel. The McClure House is included in the National Register of Historical Places.

McClure was a man to be reckoned with, and many had tried during those years in Cañon City. He was something of a legend in his own era, and by the time he set foot in Missouri, he had already chased Mexican horse thieves across the prairie and successfully retrieved the horses with the help of two men, one of whom had served with the

James E. McClure
Circa 1890

Israel M. Smith
Circa 1880

infamous Quantrill's Raiders. Although his clothes were riddled with bullet holes, McClure suffered no injuries in the ensuing shootout.

The daring McClure eventually returned to Colorado, and in 1885 moved to Montrose, where he established himself in the banking business. In addition to his banking interests in Missouri at the time, his friend Perry Burgess was also president of the Bank of Montrose. McClure bought out Perry's share. This business endeavor added yet another link to the chain of McClure's Wild West adventures when, one evening in mid-1890, the bank president was held up by two gunman on his way into town. Rather than throw his hands up in surrender, McClure grappled with both men and somehow managed to get them to jail. When he wasn't diffusing criminal activity, McClure maintained a high profile in public affairs. He served as mayor for several terms and sat on the state legislature in 1897.

John Cope invested in the First National Bank of Holden in

1872 upon its incorporation. Cope had been in the milling business with John Conner, Lewis Cheney's son-in-law, but he sold his share of the business and used those monies to fund his new investment. Cope was elected cashier of the bank, a position he held until Lewis moved to Boulder.

With no known banking background or education, Perry learned the ropes and developed what clearly became a keen business acumen. Both he and Lewis used their banking knowledge to successfully invest in real estate in Holden, and there was eventually a subdivision—Cheney Addition—named after Lewis.

Lewis Cheney was no longer the poor farmer he had once been. During the Mormon exodus and continuing through the various gold rushes, he used his business skills to operate a successful freighting company, which allowed him to save money, while investing thousands of dollars in government bonds. When he opened Smith and Cheney, it was with an initial investment of $15,000. Using the Consumer Price Index, that would be equal to roughly $234,000 in the current American marketplace.

Because of his wealth, Lewis had made a name for himself almost immediately upon moving to Missouri. His life there wasn't all good fortune however. On August 31, 1869, his beloved wife, Margaret Blair, died and left him to care for their four young children. Tragedy struck just as his career and business interests had peaked in Missouri. Margaret's death was followed by the death of their youngest son, Lewis or Louis (also known as Frankey), in late 1871, and of his father, Ephraim, in September 1872.

Ephraim, along with Ben White and his wife Semantha and their two young daughters, moved to Holden shortly after Margaret's death to help care for Lewis's four children. Unlike Harriet and her son Levi Cheney, the Whites never moved back to Illinois, but spent the remainder of their years in Missouri. Upon his death, Ephraim still owned property in Illinois as well as in Missouri, and his obituary indicates that he remained faithful to his Mormon/RLDS heritage until the day he died.

Lewis Cheney, widower, circa 1870
Children (L-R) - Emma (oldest), Lewis Jr., Nettie, and Ida A.
Lewis Jr. (on lap) died approximately one year later

Ever dutiful to his family, Ephraim took care of his son Mansel's children in his will, leaving them money to be distributed throughout their lives. He, along with Lewis's wife, son, and daughter Ida were buried together in the family plot at the Holden City Cemetery.

According to a Johnson County estate document regarding Ephraim's death, most of the Cheney family had relocated from Illinois to various regions of the West by 1873. Levi Cheney, the executor of Ephraim's estate, and his mother Harriet as well as Emma S. White, daughter of Ben and Semantha White, all lived in Johnson County, Missouri. Lyman Cheney lived in Gallatin City, Montana, while his brother Richard Cheney lived a miner's life in Black Hawk, Colorado. Ben White had moved to the town of Butler, in Bates County, Missouri, as the Civil War was coming to a close. The town, which had been destroyed in the war, was being rebuilt half a block from its original location. In 1866, Ben White "was the first to erect a business—a mercantile store located on the northeast corner of the square."[1]

Bates County had a rich, if tragic, history, especially during the Civil War years. In 1861, the Bates county seat of Butler was a prosperous, bustling town of nearly 1,000 residents. Because of its border location, however, the county—and Butler in particular—fell to renegade bands of lawless thugs on both sides of the war. For the first two years of the conflict known as the Missouri Border War, Bates County was a war zone. Missouri itself was the site of 1,100 of the 6,600 battles fought in the Civil War.

Some of the most brutal tactics involved a group of guerrilla fighters known as Quantrill's Raiders. Organized in 1861 and led by William Clarke Quantrill, this band of about a dozen men harassed Union soldiers and sympathizers to the point that the Union declared them outlaws. To the Confederacy, those outlaws were heroes. Quantrill's men included outlaw brothers Jesse and Frank James as well as their partners Cole and Jim Younger, another set of siblings. The Raiders were often led by infamous fighters like Dave Poole and Joseph Lea.

By 1863, Quantrill had hundreds of men at his disposal. On August 21, he led 450 raiders into Lawrence, Kansas, home of the Free Soil senator James Lane. The senator escaped the vigilantes, but 183 men and boys of the town did not. Much of the city was burned to the ground in the massacre.

On August 25, 1863, Union Army General Charles Ewing responded to the attack by issuing his infamous Order No. 11, which called for the evacuation of four Missouri border counties—including Bates County—within fifteen days. Those who could prove their loyalty to the Union were permitted to stay within the region but had to relocate to outposts. Those whose loyalty was in question were forced to leave altogether. Either way, the end result was the same. Ewing's men burned the entire region, and Bates County became a veritable ghost town, its 7,000 to 8,000 residents homeless. The county had become the epicenter of violence in a state that had already endured unimaginable destruction. It would be a veritable wilderness until shortly after the war's end.

What *Really* Started the Civil War?

Although the first shots of the Civil War were fired at Fort Sumter, South Carolina, on April 12, 1861, many historians and laymen agree that the bloodiest war in American history actually began with the Border War that Horace Greeley of the *New York Tribune* called "Bleeding Kansas."

Hostilities between Missouri and Kansas had raged almost since Kansas was opened for settlement in 1854 with the signing of the Kansas-Nebraska Act on May 30. The conflict was played out in a series of violent events between 1854 and 1858. Anti-slavery Free Staters and pro-slavery Border Ruffians fought over whether Kansas would enter the Union as a free state or a slave state.

Abolitionist John Brown, who lived just fifteen miles outside Butler, defied his movement's stance of pacifism and encouraged violence as an appropriate response to Southern aggression. After spearheading several conflicts throughout the Border War that ended in fatalities, Brown was captured and hanged in 1859 for his attempt to incite a slave rebellion at Harpers Ferry in modern-day West Virginia. His activities are considered key events in the start of the Civil War.

As residents slowly filtered back into Bates County, newcomers also found their way to the scorched and decimated area. A new and improved Bates County was built, and the town of Butler became its pride and joy. The new Butler flourished as a major hub for freight-pulling mule trains throughout the 1860s and 1870s. Until the first railroad ran through Butler in 1879, coal was hauled via mule trains for distribution throughout the territory.

Butler stood out from other cities of its time in that it was the first established city west of the Mississippi River to get electricity. This honor was due in large part to the efforts of Captain F. J. Tygard, who lived in Butler and knew the area well. With the city's financial backing, Tygard founded the Brush Electric Light and Power Company of Butler, Missouri. Tygard was the company's secretary and treasurer, and according to the Butler, Missouri Chamber of Commerce, the lights were first illuminated on December 6, 1881.[2] Legend has it that curious residents of Kansas City would endure a train ride to Butler just to see the lights first-hand.

According to the 1883 *History of Cass and Bates County*,

> There are four burners on the cupola of the court house, which afford ample light for not only the large public square and the streets adjacent, but these illuminate the town generally, or wherever their rays penetrate without obstructions or intervening houses. This light on the court house is a conspicuous object of attraction, and may be seen the darkest night at a distance of twenty miles. The city pays $900 a year for the four lamps. The M. E. and Baptist Church edifices are lighted by this light,

as is, also the Bates County National Bank. Beside the church buildings and the bank, twelve business houses are illuminated by it. The expense to the city is more than it would be for the ordinary street lamps (oil), but the difference in the light more than compensates for the greater cost.[3]

This distinction earned Butler the nickname "The Electric City," and according to the American Public Power Association, Butler's electric power system is believed to be the oldest "in continuous operation in the United States, established before Thomas Edison started his Pearl Street station in New York, and still operating proudly as a municipal."[4]

F. J. Tygard did more than found Butler's electric company. More than a decade earlier, when the private bank of C. B. Dunbaugh & Co. of Butler failed in October 1870, Lewis and Perry opened the Bates County National Bank—the one mentioned in the quoted excerpt above—which was the only bank in Butler for several years. Lewis was president and Perry vice president. Tygard was initially a partner in that bank and was listed as a director, but by July 15, 1871, Perry had taken over as president, and Tygard was named vice president. By the time the Bates County National Bank failed on September 20, 1906, Tygard was president. Unfortunately, he was found guilty of fraudulent activity causing the bank's demise and served five years in the state penitentiary for his crimes.

Another key figure in the life of Perry Burgess was William E. Walton, great-uncle of Sam Walton, founder of the Walmart discount retail store chain. William's mother was Louisa Jane Turley. The Turleys were from Boone's Lick, Missouri, and from a young age were closely associated with Kit Carson. Jane's own uncles could boast that, for a time, they had shared their home with the legendary pioneer. Later in life, Louisa's uncle Jessie Turley was contracted by Carson to write his first biography. Born in Cooper County, Missouri, on August 31, 1842, William himself was the eldest of nine children.

LEWIS CHENEY, Prest. P, A. BURGESS, Vice Pres. F. J. TYGARD. Cashier,

BATES COUNTY NATIONAL BANK.

SUCCESSOR TO BATES COUNTY BANK.

CAPITAL PAID IN - $50,000.

Authorized Capital - $200,000.

DIRECTORS.

J. M. SMITH,	*LEWIS CHENEY,*	*ELLIOTT PYLE,*
W. T. SMITH,	*PHILLIP GLESSNER,*	*F. J. TYGARD,*
	P. A. BURGESS,	

BUY AND SELL EXCHANGE, GOLD AND SILVER COIN,

Government Securities, Notes, Stock,

BONDS AND COUNTY WARRANTS,

DRAW AT SIGHT IN SUMS TO SUIT.

Bates County National Bank advertisement, 1870

In his adult years, Walton was a settler of Bates County and a chief banking competitor of Lewis and Perry. As president of the Missouri State Bank and the Walton Trust Company of Butler, William enjoyed the clout his title and social standing brought him. Even so, Lewis and Perry became friendly with William, and Perry especially would maintain a strong and lasting friendship that would, in due time, leave its mark on Colorado history.

In regard to Bates County, and to Butler in particular, Walton's influence as an early settler was so profound that he was asked to contribute to a book titled *The Old Settlers' History of Bates County, Missouri: From Its First Settlement to the First Day of January, 1900* by S. L. Tathwell. His account includes a discussion of the heated political climate of Bates County around the time of the Border War:

> There was much bitterness in politics then. The republicans called the southerners "Rebels." The southerners called the

republicans "Radicals." Neither side showing much liberality. We had not then learned this truth—that each man's peculiar views are the natural outgrowth of his environments—that education and surroundings in youth largely moulds and shapes opinions.

Had Jeff Davis been born and raised in Maine he would doubtless have been an abolitionist, and John Brown if born and brought up in South Carolina would in all probability have been a secessionist.[5]

For men coming from such humble Mormon origins, Perry Burgess and Lewis Cheney had managed to find themselves in the center of a fascinating world as settlement of the wilderness began, one town, one county, at a time. To be associated—indeed, friends—with the likes of take-no-prisoners James McClure and the esteemed Walton family as they successfully opened one bank after another served only to underscore their place in America's Western history.

Although Perry's banking endeavors must have kept him busy, he found time for other activities in those Missouri years. He married Annie Mapes on October 29, 1870, in Stockton, Illinois, and the couple eventually had three children: Bruce, Helen, and Emma.

Perry also enjoyed a keen interest in inventions, and was granted several patents before the turn of the century. In 1872, he applied for a patent for an improved window-blind stop. Other inventions included a fly trap and a cleaner for a flume (an open channel or trough that diverts fluids).

Perry and Lewis maintained a partnership that took them both out of Missouri and into the bustling town of Boulder, Colorado, located in the foothills of the Rocky Mountains. Here the two men would prosper as they opened more banks while investing in both mining and real estate.

In the meantime, however, Perry began making summer excursions from his home in Missouri to the mountains of Colorado in the company of his good friend William Walton. What motivated the men to make this journey time and again? What were they searching for?

The answer is simple, and it is one that applied to thousands of men whose spirits could not rest while the world around them grew—acre by acre, building by building—as America's wilderness territories were claimed and developed. It was the lure of the West that called to Perry.

And what he found on his travels—and gave back—only adds to the vibrant, exciting history of what we now know as Steamboat Springs.

William E. Walton
Great-uncle of Walmart founder, Sam Walton

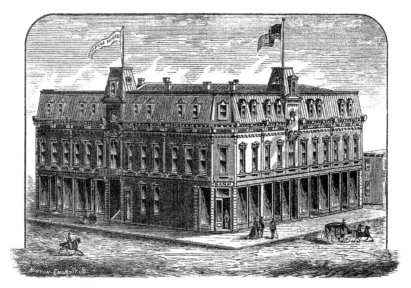

Walton Opera House - Butler, Missouri

History of Cass and Bates County, **1883**

THE OPENING OF THE OPERA HOUSE.

The most imposing event that ever occurred in the history of Butler was the opening of the Opera House, which took place on the evening of December 11, 1882.
A large number of persons were present from a distance. ...At half-past 8 o'clock
the magnificent room was filled from top to bottom with an audience anxiously
awaiting the commencement of the evening's programme. ...The mayor came
forward, and being introduced, addressed the house as follows :

LADIES AND GENTLEMEN: Seventeen years ago the spot now occupied by the
city of Butler was a wilderness ; what had but a short time previous to that period
been a thriving village, was by the ravages of a cruel war destroyed, its happy homes
made desolate, its places of business plundered and given to the flames, and its
people banished, shedding bitter tears over their ruined firesides.

How different the aspects of things to-day! Where but a few short years ago man
was afraid to meet his fellow man unless heavily armed; where weeds had taken the
place of flower gardens; where even many of the old landmarks had disappeared, we
now see a city of 4,000 souls, its people prosperous and happy in the consciousness
of safety to themselves and their loved ones.

Grim visaged war, with all its attendant horrors, has disappeared, the pioneer with
his gun and axe has set his face towards the setting sun, and in their wake have
come churches, school houses, the arts and sciences, poetry, printing, music and
the drama—in a word, civilization.

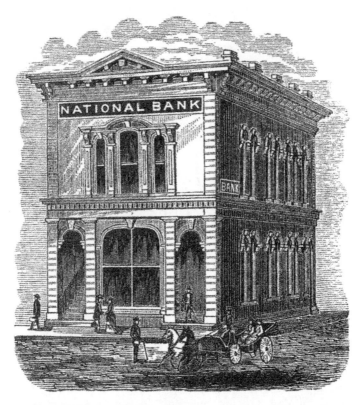

Bates County National Bank - Butler, Missouri

Bates County Democrat, Sept. 23, 1871

On Thursday last, N.W. Britton, Esq., of St. Louis, Inspector of National Banks for the State of Missouri, quietly and unostentatiously visited our town and proceeded to the Bates County National Bank, where he presented to Messrs. Burgess and Tygard, the Vice, President and Cashier of that institution, his credentials as Inspector of National Banks for the State of Missouri, and immediately proceeded to examine the books and papers of the bank. After a thorough and rigid investigation the Inspector complimented Messrs. Burgess and Tygard upon the correctness of their books and accounts, adding that the Bates County National Bank was in as good a condition as any similar institution in the State of Missouri. …Messrs. Burgess and Tygard, ever since their establishment in the banking business, in Bates county, have had the confidence of the people, and the rather unexpected visit of the Inspector, his rigid investigation, with its satisfactory results, is a very substantial assurance that that confidence has not been misplaced.

Bank of Holden - Holden, Missouri
When photographed, the Bank of Holden
was the oldest state-chartered bank in Missouri

Bank of Holden pamphlet, 1902

In 1873 the great panic occurred, strewing the country with financial wrecks. The Bank of Holden and one in Warrensburg were the only ones left in the county. The country was comparatively new, the territory large an increasing demand for money called for a larger capital and on August 1st, 1878 it was increased to $100,000. In 1893 another panic swept the land, although not so disastrous as that of '73, great damage was wrought. Securities of all kinds depreciated greatly and a feeling of distrust so pervaded the entire country as to almost call in question the stability of government bonds. The Bank of Holden, like other strong institutions was well prepared, but even better than the gold in its vaults was the confidence of its patrons and the public, which enabled it to pass though the crisis unscatched and continue on the even tenor of its ways.

'Little Cabin', one of the first two cabins built in Steamboat Springs in 1875
Loaned to the Burgess Family in 1881
Courtesy of Tread of Pioneers Museum, Steamboat Springs, Colorado

CHAPTER 10
The Founding of Steamboat Springs

Perry Burgess was one of the West's earliest Renaissance men. He was a man of minimal education and vast experience, a do-it-yourselfer who never let lack of training or knowledge hinder his progress. By the mid-1870s, Perry had already been a frontiersman, a prospector, and a successful banker. And yet he was about to embark on a new and exciting chapter of his life, one with consequences even he could not have foreseen.

Perry was among good company when he—along with his traveling companion and fellow banker William E. Walton—crossed paths with a young Civil War veteran named James H. Crawford in 1874. Crawford had been making excursions throughout the West for two years in search of what he considered the ideal site to settle and raise his family. He and his wife, Margaret, left Sedalia, Missouri, on May 1, 1873, with their three children—Lulie, Logan, and John, ages six and under—and several other families. Traveling by ox team, the wagon train arrived in Denver on June 4. After several days' rest,

James H. Crawford, 1902   Margaret Crawford, 1870
Courtesy of Tread of Pioneers Museum, Steamboat Springs, CO

the adventurers resumed travels until the road ended. They found themselves in Empire, a tiny town near the mouth of Berthoud Pass.

Crawford left Margaret and the children in Empire for the summer while he continued his scouting mission in the area that today includes Granby, Dillon, Hot Sulphur Springs, and Kremmling. When he had determined that he had not found "home," Crawford returned to Empire to collect his family and head to Golden, where they spent the winter.

The search for suitable land continued the following summer as the Crawford family became the first people to forge ahead on barely cleared wagon road over the Rocky Mountain range. They were not traveling light. In addition to the heavily loaded wagon, their provisions included eight cows and calves, a pair of mules, and several horses. Dodging underbrush when possible and making pit stops to remove it from their wagon wheels when not, it took the Crawfords a month to reach Hot Sulphur Springs. There they built a cabin, intent on spending the winter months in relative comfort. Comfort was a luxury, however, and for the first month, it rained every day. The makeshift roof made of tree bark did not hold up well, and the Crawfords were unable to stay dry. All three of the children suffered scarlet fever in their new home. That rustic cabin was the first building in the new town, and more settlers drifted in as the summer progressed.

Crawford and several companions left again in June. His destination this time was the Yampa Valley. With its beautiful Yampa—also called Bear—River, which dominates the valley, it was the most welcoming sight Crawford had yet seen on his expedition. The rich land was covered in tall grasses and sheltered by a canopy of aspen trees and magnificent evergreens. Wild game populated the rolling hills while streams abounded with fish and waterfowl. And though Crawford could not have known it at the time, the area was rife with more than 150 mineral springs. In fact, Steamboat Springs got its name when French fur trappers visited the area in the 1860s and found a hot spring near the Yampa River that made an interesting "chugging" sound, one similar to that made by a steamboat. From that point on, trappers, miners, and guides came to call the area Steamboat Springs. Those springs—and one called Strawberry Park Natural Hot Springs in particular—would eventually become major tourist attractions for people across the globe.

One pioneer who had a true appreciation for the Yampa Valley region was C. C. Graham. A neighbor and longtime friend of the Burgess family, Graham was a writer whose observations helped preserve the rich historical legacy of early Steamboat Springs. He wrote regularly about the wonders of this area in 1888. In one article penned for the *Breckenridge Journal* in which he extols the natural abundance of the Yampa Valley as it relates to raising cattle and horses, Graham wrote:

> Hay has to be provided for the winter months, which is cut from the natural meadows that abound in the valleys and draws. Buffalo, elk or evergreen, wire and rice, are the principal upland grasses, while redtop, bluejoint and slough, make the meadows below. These grasses are all nourishing and nutritive, evidenced by the general appearance and good condition of stock on winter feeding or summer grazing. Horses find good living on the uplands much longer than cattle, and will wander away from bay corralls to the winter grasses among the hills, after the snow has obtained a depth of from one to two feet.[1]

Such pristine natural resources and abundance of wildlife provided all a settler could hope for. It was pioneer heaven, and James Crawford recognized it as home.

Crawford staked his claim near Steamboat Springs by burning the side of a tree to indicate his intention. As aspen leaves turned from green to gold with each passing day, the young pioneer built his claim cabin's foundation before returning to Hot Sulphur Springs and his family.

Conventional history has it that it was during this fall excursion—

most likely on the way home—that Crawford met up with Perry Burgess and William Walton. In fact, Crawford's granddaughter, Lulita Crawford Pritchett, recorded the meeting in her book *Crawford Pioneer Tales*:

> Burgess and Walton had met Pa on a trip to Colorado in 1874, had been fired by his enthusiasm and strongly attracted to the Yampa Valley, and had arranged to join his project. Both were interested in Missouri banks.[2]

And while this scenario is quite likely, there is one other viable possibility that brought the men together. Sedalia, James Crawford's hometown, is not far from the Holden, Missouri, banks owned and operated by Perry Burgess and Lewis Cheney. Some members of the Crawford family were involved in the banking business as well, and so it is possible that Perry already knew James Crawford before "bumping into" him on his own excursions into Colorado. Whether they were acquainted through business or through a mutual interest in land exploration, it seems plausible that Perry knew of the glories of Yampa Valley before leaving Missouri with William Walton and setting up camp in what would soon become officially known as Steamboat Springs.

Back in Hot Sulphur Springs, Crawford received word that his intended home in Yampa Valley was at risk for claim jumpers. Winter being what it was—and still is—in the Rocky Mountains, Crawford was unable to return to the valley with any degree of safety. Snow was heavy—several feet in places—and blizzards were frequent and harsh. Crawford set out in Spring of 1875 in the company of a friend, Lute Carlton. Even then, the journey was fraught with danger as the two men and their horses slowly trudged through snow drifts.

Fortunately, there was no evidence of claim jumpers along the Yampa River springs or at Crawford's cabin foundation. Nonetheless, the young pioneer was not going to leave anything to fate. So to make his claim even more obvious, Crawford added to the cabin foundation and cultivated a small garden in which he posted obvious signs indicating which seeds were planted in each row. Satisfied that he had done all he could,

Crawford and Carlton returned to Hot Sulphur Springs.

During the Summer of 1875 James Crawford brought his wife Margaret to see Steamboat Springs and to camp there. Upon riding into the valley for the first time, Margaret fell in love with the location and could envision its possibilities. The family immediately set to work making the claim cabin a real livable cabin. This cabin would become known as "Big Cabin." "Little Cabin" was also constructed in 1875 by Sandy Mellen and Charlie Mayo, hired by James to live in Steamboat Springs and protect his homestead claim.

The Crawfords left their temporary home in Hot Sulphur Springs for good in 1876 and made the slow trek to Yampa Valley. Without so much as a trail to help ease the heavy wagons and livestock over the mountain terrain, the journey required determination and commitment, both of which Crawford had in spades.

Crawford was granted the first land patent in 1879, for 160 acres. The next four patents—also for 160 acres—were not granted until 1882, and those were extended to Perry Burgess, William E. Walton, William Mellen, and Charles Mayo. All these early settlers were able to choose the location of their property.

Today much of the downtown Steamboat district, including Lincoln Avenue, consists of the original land grants of Crawford and Walton. Perry Burgess's property was located below town, directly across from the Steamboat Springs Cemetery, running along both sides of the Yampa River.

Grants were issued under the Land Act of 1820 and the Homestead Act of 1862. While the land itself was free, each man paid a $200 filing fee, and the grants were not without stipulations. Each settler had to live on his land for five years before receiving the patent. Civil War veterans could subtract the number of years served from the five-year requirement, and that became the required length of stay. Under this provision, Crawford received his patent earlier then Perry and the others, and that took into consideration the fact that the paperwork alone took two years to be processed. All filers agreed to make improvements to their land one way or another, through farming or some other means.

As visually stunning and teeming with natural resources as the new homestead was, life in Yampa Valley wasn't without its troubles. Before the Meeker Massacre of September 1879 in which Ute warriors killed settler Nathan Meeker and seven others who were trying to force them out of their nomadic way of life, the valley had been a favorite hunting ground for the Utes, who camped there by the hundreds each spring. Although most of these Indians were friendly, there were always the restless individuals who could—and sometimes did—cause conflict simply because it could be caused. For those first years, the Crawfords saw more Native Americans than they did white settlers, and they were never completely free from fear of attack. All that would change by the turn of the century, but it was an unsettling fact of life in their new wilderness home.

With the building of that first claim cabin, thirty-year-old James Crawford founded Steamboat Springs. Perry Burgess and William Walton shared Crawford's vision of the Springs as a summer resort when they visited the valley in the summer of 1875. While camping there with their wives and the Crawfords, the men were impressed with what they saw. Walton especially recognized the potential of what he was looking at, having made several trips to European spas and resorts over his lifetime. A 1911 article in the *Steamboat Pilot* featuring Walton reported:

> Mr. Walton said he knew the waters [of the springs] must contain medicinal properties of value, but he was unable to find a bottle in which to take some of it back to civilization. Finally on his return he filled two pickle jars with the water and when he got to Denver had the first analysis made of these springs.[3]

The article neglects to report that Perry Burgess and Walton took that water sample together, and when testing proved it to be healthy, both men invested in the development of Steamboat Springs, imagining it eventually as a world-class spa and resort that would attract people from across the globe. Crawford, while definitely the first man to settle permanently in the region, did not have the money necessary to do much more than build his cabin at that point. Perry and Walton provided that financial backing. Their investment, coupled with Crawford's commitment and leadership—he served as the first county judge and first mayor—allowed Steamboat Springs to flourish.

Crawford's vision of the Springs as a booming mountain town led to the formation of the Steamboat Springs Town Company, a promotional organization that included the likes of such influential men as A. E. Lea, J. P. Maxwell, A. J. Macky, and Lewis Cheney. Each was a prominent businessman in Boulder, and all recognized the value of developing the exquisite Yampa Valley area not only as a resort, but as a mining region rich in coal and gold. Routt County promoter C. C. Graham expressed it in this way:

> Among the great mining resources of Colorado, which are every day advancing in points of discovery and increasing wealth, Routt county forms no inconsiderable part. Lying beyond the borders of easy exit, and outside the bounds of public transportation, extensive bodies of mineral remain unproductive and undeveloped, vast fields are yet unexplored and no doubt contain a store of some kind of mineral wealth. So far little has been done outside of gold mining and gold prospecting, which have met with certain and increasing success, but as transport means increase and capital and labor are encouraged, the wonderful advantages will be made known in the inexhaustible mineral wealth of Routt county.
>
> It is said and truthfully that coal is intrinsically more valuable than gold. Routt county possess large quantities of both these precious commodities, but coal in the largest and most wonderful extent. Coal is known to exist over an area of 1200 square miles within its borders, and shows a diversity of qualities unsurpassed that meet the requirements of all the uses of man.[4]

The area also boasted a seemingly endless supply of timber and building stone. Truly, at that time, there was nothing one couldn't find in the Yampa Valley.

Steamboat Springs: What's Not to Like?

Yampa Valley was a slice of unadulterated heaven for nineteenth-century pioneers. By the late 1800s, it had earned itself a reputation as one of the most beautiful places in the state of Colorado.

Historian and promoter C. C. Graham could not say enough about the place, and in an 1888 article for the *Montezuma Millrun*, he promoted Steamboat as "a romantic and blissful retreat surrounded with pleasurable objects and necessary advantages to promote health, comfort and contentment, a refuge for rest and retirement, a resort for pastime and pleasure, and a sanitarium for the weak and invalid. Such conditions and attractions will soon popularize among the public and the seekers will build a town,—a city in fact foremost among the healthful and grand resorts of the Rocky mountains of the west."

In his article, Graham made it a point to let readers know that the natural springs—of which there were more than forty at the time—were exceedingly refreshing and beneficial to one's health. "By chemical analysis these waters are found to contain potash, soda, magnesia, lime, sodium, iron, silicic acid, phosphoric acid, alumnia, manganese oxide, impregnated with many kinds of gasses. Their curative and healing powers are undoubted."

Graham accurately predicted that Steamboat Springs would one day be the "principal public resort of the west."

By 1876, Perry Burgess, William Walton, and Lewis Cheney were spending summers in the Yampa Valley. The area was teeming with Native Americans, and the men lived harmoniously with them. This is partly due to the fact that most of the Utes were friendly, but one cannot undervalue the experience each of the men had as pioneers. With their Mormon background, Perry and Lewis were especially seasoned, having spent their childhoods under constant persecution and in survival mode. Compared to the Joseph Smith era and then the Mormon exodus years, living among Indians probably didn't cause them more concern than any other hardship or possible threat.

Lewis was by this time remarried. He and Sarah Ann Milner had married on January 18, 1871. By the time Lewis was traveling to Steamboat Springs, Sarah had given birth to two of the three children she would have with her husband. The Milner connection would prove fortuitous for Perry, who eventually opened a bank with Sarah's nephew, F. E. Milner. Milner also established the first general store and hotel in Steamboat Springs while running the town's post office.

Unlike his nephew Perry, Lewis had not previously visited Colorado. That changed in 1876, however, in all likelihood because Perry shared his excitement over the Yampa Valley region and wanted Lewis to experience it for himself through the eyes of a possible investor.

A *Lena Weekly Star* newsbyte dated June 23, 1876, provided this announcement:

> Lewis Cheney, Esq., Holden, Mo., in a letter enclosing $2 for the Star, writes that times are good there, wheat never looked better. He intends to start for the mountains about the first of July, to rusticate three or four months.

This seemingly insignificant blurb clarifies Lewis's whereabouts and puts him in Colorado with Perry and William Walton during the summer of 1876. While in Colorado, the bankers relied on their partners to run their Missouri banks. By the time Colorado earned statehood on August 1, all three men had interests within its boundaries. Lewis and Perry had their sights set on opening banks in the burgeoning town of Boulder, while Walton invested in real estate. Despite his social standing and the obvious respect he had earned in the valley, Walton was never a permanent resident. After spending just two summers in the Springs, he sold his property in 1877 and returned to Missouri. Walton would not return to the area for thirty-four years. Out of respect for his two partners, James Crawford named Burgess and Walton creeks in their honor. Today, the Steamboat Springs Burgess Creek district is located near Mt. Werner and is close to all major lodging and ski facilities. Multiple roads, a ski lift, and landmarks continue to carry the Burgess name.

Waiting on the Railroad

Almost from its founding, the town of Steamboat Springs counted on two things to ensure prosperity: mining and the railroad. Neither expectation played out the way either residents or investors hoped it would.

Experts of the day forecast great finds of both oil and coal in the Steamboat Springs area. Although coal mines did open and provide hundreds of jobs, the industry never expanded to the proportions everyone had expected. The same held true of oil drilling. The area opened up several productive oil wells, but there was never a major discovery. To be fair, even if the experts *had* been correct, prosperity depended upon railroad access to this isolated area.

Residents and investors had every reason to believe the railroad would come to Steamboat. It reached nearby Wolcott in 1888; surely the track would be extended. And it was, but not for another twenty years. In 1908, the Salt Lake and Pacific Railroad finally came to town and with it an influx of tourists and an increase in mining. Even so, economic prosperity never reached the levels the mountain town's residents had been encouraged to envision.

It wasn't until the 1960s that Steamboat Springs became a popular destination for tourists, but it wasn't mining or healthy water that brought them in by the thousands. It was skiing. In the twenty-first century, Steamboat is nicknamed Ski Town, USA, and is world renowned for its first-class facilities.

The year 1876 is key in the history of Colorado, but also in that of the settlement of Steamboat Springs. Although mail was not delivered to the region during that time, frequent trips were made to Wyoming to pick up mail for the residents of Bugtown, the nearest settlement (25 miles away) to Steamboat Springs. During one of those runs, a package for James Crawford was picked up and delivered.

Inside that package was an 8' x 14' bunting flag, a gift from Perry Burgess and William Walton. Bunting is a loosely woven fabric ideal for flag production because of its ability to retain color and resist fading. The thoughtful present gave Crawford an idea.

Though many versions and reports of the story exist, none is so detailed or vivid as the one provided by James Crawford's granddaughter Lulita Crawford Pritchett in her book *Crawford Pioneer Tales*. Originally typed in 1977, the "book" was photocopied five times and given to her cousins as a Christmas present. In 2005, the manuscript was copyrighted by the Lulita Crawford Pritchett Estate and published under the same title.

In the excerpt here, "Pa" refers to James Crawford while "Ma" is Margaret. Lulita chose to keep these titles because most of the pioneer stories she retells in her book were handed down to her from the point of view of her mother or her aunt or uncles.

James Crawford had the foresight to use the gift in an act of good will, one he hoped would ease the concerns and fears of the Indians as one wagon train after another of white settlers inevitably encroached upon their land.

> Pa could sympathize with the red men. He knew they had often been badly treated. He also knew that nothing could stem the westward tide of settlers and that fair arrangements must be made to accommodate both red men and white.
>
> As the Fourth of July approached, he thought how he could let the beautiful new flag speak for him of the good will he bore his dark-skinned neighbors. He decided to have a flag raising. Selecting a tall lodgepole pine, he chopped it down, trimmed and peeled it, and planted it solidly halfway between the Iron Spring and the claim cabin.

He invited the only other white people in the valley — three young men, Mike Farley, and Charles and Owen Harrison — who had recently staked claims a few miles up the river. And he invited the Utes.

On the morning of the Fourth the Indians were the first to arrive. As curious as children, they squatted about the pole and the cabin. When Mike Farley and the Harrison brothers had ridden in, they, together with Pa and Ma, Lulie, Logan, and John, marched down the gentle slope to the flag pole with considerable formality, Pa leading the way and carrying the large flag. There he and Ma unfolded the bunting so all could admire the red and white stripes and the blue field in one corner. In that field were 37 stars — one large one in the middle, two circles of smaller stars around it, and a star in each corner.

The Indians began to withdraw, muttering among themselves. No doubt they had observed flags waving at forts and agencies and were suspicious that new restraints were about to be put upon them. Pa sought to assure them that here on Bear River the flag would watch over both red men and white. Having fought under that banner three years in the struggle to preserve the Union, his feeling for it was deep. His earnestness spoke better than his attempted use of sign language or the few Indian words he knew, and soon the Utes gathered close again.

Now it was time to run the flag up the pole. But the halyards refused to work, and the rope, being new, kinked in the wooden pulleys Pa had made, and strenuous efforts only seemed to make things worse. The flag stood at less than half mast and would go neither up nor down. The pine pole, being peeled, was so smooth that it was thought impossible to climb up and adjust the knotted ropes. Pa's grand celebration seemed in danger of collapsing. With great dignity Yarmonite stepped forward. "Injun fix um," he announced. He called his nephew, Pahwinta, a fine lad about fifteen years old, who "cooned it" up the slick pole and removed the knots and kinks so that the flag was sent to the top, spreading to the breeze, to the great delight of all, even

Steamboat Springs Town Co. (present day Lincoln, Avenue)
Steamboat Springs founder James H. Crawford (center)
Courtesy of Tread of Pioneers Museum, Steamboat Springs, CO

'Flag of the Town Company'
A gift to James H. Crawford from Burgess and Walton
Courtesy of Tread of Pioneers Museum, Steamboat Springs, CO

the Indians, who, having assisted in the raising, lost all reserve and danced and shouted.

When Ma walked back to the cabin, the squaws with their papooses trailed after her, sure of a sweet treat.

It was a good thing that neither the Indians nor the Crawfords could see ahead a few years to the Meeker tragedy. Now, looking back nearly a century later, we can only be saddened by that chapter in Colorado's history, and by the larger tragedy across the land — the broken faith, the misunderstanding, the mismanagement that separated red men from white. But in that summer of 1876 and in the three summers following, the old Yampa Valley was mother to both, and there was room enough for all.

The flag flew its welcome there for many a year till it wore out. It was the first thing a traveler from any direction could see, and many were the joyous shouts up and down the trails as roving prospectors, trappers, or home seekers sighted it. When at last it had to be retired like an honored soldier, the colors were still bright though some of the threads had broken.

There was good feeling at Steamboat Springs after the flag raising. The Ute braves sometimes helped Pa bring in his horses. The squaws gave Ma wild raspberries on big, clean thimbleberry leaves, and showed her how to dig Yampa roots and pound them into meal to thicken soup or gravy. Charlie Yarmonite, the chief's son, and Logan hunted chipmunks together, with bows the chief made for them, using sharpened sticks for arrows.[5]

James Crawford could not have predicted that the Fourth of July flag-raising would become an annual tradition, but that is exactly what happened. An 1886 *Steamboat Pilot* article mentioned the "flag of the Town Company" being raised at its annual Independence Day celebration.

Lulita Crawford Pritchett was one of those rare people who, like Perry Burgess, seemed to understand the value of history even as it was being made. Without her dedication to preserving her family's stories and legends, much of what is known about James H. Crawford, the history of Steamboat Springs, and Western pioneer life in general would be forgotten to the ages.

Altogether, Lulita wrote nine books, including two novels. She composed more than one hundred poems and eighty-four stories and magazine articles. Many of her stories appeared in *The Denver Post*. Whether recording events as they actually happened or preserving the events and culture of a bygone era in the way of historical fiction, Lulita's efforts comprise a substantial portion of Colorado's historical archives.

Lulita's writing was not limited to history or nature, nor was it aimed only at an adult readership. She wrote at least fifty Western romances from 1930 to 1956, and during that same general time frame published nearly two dozen stories for young adults. For the latter, she won several awards from the Denver Woman's Press Club.

She came by her writing naturally, as her mother Lulie kept a diary throughout her childhood and like Perry, detailed many early aspects of Steamboat life. Lulita died on February 11, 1991, but her writings cemented her place in American pioneer history.

Although they might not have realized it, this period in Perry Burgess's and Lewis Cheney's lives was another turning point. As successful as they had been in Missouri, what lay in store for them in the newly created state of Colorado provided even more opportunity for success. Colorado was growing fast, but few people recognized the significance of Steamboat Springs and the Yampa Valley.

What follows is the diary kept by Perry Burgess during his 1880 Steamboat Springs prospecting trip with James Crawford and other mining partners. The diary ends when Ingram Starkey, a partner and shareholder in the Bank of Holden, Missouri, appears to betray the group. According to Burgess, they call Starkey in a room and 'Mr. Crawford "goes for him."' Burgess calms the dispute and sends a letter to Capt. F. J. Tygard, another business partner and president of the Bates County National Bank of Missouri, in an attempt to resolve the issue.

- Diary -

The following is an account of each day's travel and work from the time we left Boulder until we started for Georgetown after supplies.

May 26, 1880 (May 26, 1880.) – Started from Boulder at 9 AM. Our force is composed of seven men viz Jas H Crawford, A. Shippy, Jas. F. Burgess – Mrs. C. B. and Bruce are to accompany us as far as Georgetown – Camp for night on South Boulder in a furious snow storm.

May 27, 1880 (May 27) – nooned at Central City. Camp for night at Lawson in Clear Creek Canon – day cold with snow and rain

May 28, 1880 (May 28) – reached Georgetown at 8 AM – bought supplies

May 29, 1880 (May 29) – Our wives start back to Boulder on cars – We load up our supplies and roll out – Camp for night five miles above Empire – a courier comes along about 11 PM with reports of indian depredations and Massacres in North park. He is going by order of the Governer to warn settlers and find out the true stat of affairs – He asks for company as far as Hot Sulphur Springs and Starke goes with him.

May 30, 1880 (Sunday May 30) – Ate an early breakfast and pull out at 6 AM. Cross the main divide at 10 AM – had hard work shoveling through snow and holding wagon from turning over road very bad Noon at an old cabin down on the west side of range – and camp for night at head of Middle park 12 miles below the summit of the pass began snowing hard at dark – all hands very tired

May 31, 1880 (May 31st) – Snow is about five inches deep is cold and gloomy Our stock ran off found them at 10 AM. – Moved to Chamberlain's ranch 16 miles and camp – Roads muddy and bad – Crawford and Brooks each killed a grouse today

June 1, 1880 (June 1st) – Broke camp at 8 AM. Moved to Hot Sulphur Springs Halted to hear, rest and write letters, then moved on to mouth of Corrall Creek and camp – I killed three grouse and a jack rabbit today –

On the Plains of Middle Park, Colorado - 1880
Near Hot Sulphur Springs

June 2, 1880 (June 2nd) – Travelled 20 miles   Camp on the Muddy

June 3, 1880 (June 3rd) – Continuing to hear bad reports concerning Indians, and Mr. Crawfords brother who should have been in from cattle camp a week ago not having come. Crawford and I conclude to leave the outfit and ride into the country ahead of us – Starke and Shippy accompany – rode 20 miles and lunched, then rode two miles further. Met Crawfords brother who reported all things quiet – Had seen no Indians – Rode back to our camp on Muddy – Crawford killed a deer today we saw a great many of them – are terrible tired

June 4, 1880 (Friday June 4th) – Got a late start – camp for night at foot of Gore range on eat side – Starke killed a deer this morning and Crawford killed a beaver near camp at dark

June 5, 1880 (June 5) – Snowed last night all hands prospected today – Commence the mens wages

June 6, 1880 (Sunday June 6th) – Got an early start, packed our saddle horses Crossed Gore range – Nooned on Rock Creek in Hills park – I struck out prospecting at noon and after a hard march found the boys in camp at head of Egeria park – I staked two claims today and brought in samples of one

June 7, 1880 (June 7th) – Garbarino and I remain in camp make a small coal pit – balance of force go prospecting – The boys report some finds and bring in samples of ore – Crawford brought in samples of ore.

June 9, 1880 (Wednesday June 9th) – Work at assaying – balance go prospecting – I killed a fine buck near camp before breakfast. Crawford brought in some fine looking ore

June 10, 1880 (June 10th) – Starke and I go prospecting – the balance of force move camp 20 miles to Roaring fork of Bear River – The formation at this camp is eruptive

June 11, 1880 (June 11th) – Brooks goes to Crawfords cow camp after some horses and camp articles – Crawford and I follow up the

Modern day Yampa River near Steamboat Springs, Colorado
Was also known as Bear River

stream to base of flat top mountains and prospect for placer diggings – Shippy and Starke prospect in a westerly course. Bradley goes to sinking on a bar in a big gulch near camp – find nothing

June 12, 1880 (June 12th) – Prospect and hunt find no mines – a colt gets drowned

June 13, 1880 (Sunday June 13th) – Moved camp to Oak Creek and camp

June 14, 1880 (June 14th) – Moved camp to Bear river. Had a hard days work in fixing roads – digging and prying out of mud holes and finally had to unload our wagon and pack through mud and water on out backs – Crawford killed an antelope before breakfast and Starke a deer on the road

June 15, 1880 (June 15th) – Had to make a road at one point on the river, got stuck in the mud several times – Only made four miles. Camp at ford Prospect in the afternoon but find nothing – Got mail today

June 16, 1880 (June 16th) – Made a raft and crossed all our effects on it. Swam the stock – Had a terrible hard days work and went to be tired wet and cold –

June 17, 1880 (June 17th) – Moved camp to an island ½ mile below the springs (Steamboat) and lay over the balance of the day to rest and dry our bedding and effects – I have a terrible headache

June 18, 1880 (June 18th) – Moved camp to Elk River and go to prospecting for placer gold – results encouraging

June 19, 1880 (June 19th) – Moved camp to fine spring built a coal pit and got it burning – Part of the force went to prospect in the mountains brought in samples of good looking ore at night – River high and raising – Have several samples of ore ready for assay

June 20, 1880 (Sunday June 20) – Rain nearly all day – watch coal pit hunt some and write letters

June 21, 1880 (June 21st) – Prospecting continued by balance of force – Garbarino and I set up furnace – Work at assaying

June 22, 1880 (June 22) – Work at assaying – Boys prospect for lodes

June 23, 1880 (June 23rd) – Prospect our placers – Make a raft but fail to cross the river on it, current too swift

June 24, 1880 (June 24th) – Leave Garbarino and Brooks in camp to look after things and start up the river on horseback with pack animal camp 15 miles above, near Reeds ranch. The formation from Steamboat Springs to this place on east side of river is metamorphic and looks very fine with patches of float quartz in places

June 25 1880 (June 25th) – All hands strike out prospecting – killed a deer – Crawford and Starke start in evening for the Hahns peak mines and to get mail   found good looking float

June 26, 1880 (June 26th) – Crawford and Starke return – Send Bradley back to camp at wagon after more provisions – The balance of us prospect

June 27, 1880 (Sunday June 27th) – Moved camp 4 miles in a S.E. course – Prospect and stake two good looking lodes. Eat a late dinner – move five miles – Crawford killed a big elk and we camped

June 28, 1880 (June 28th) – Move camp two miles to Big Creek and all hands prospect – find nothing

June 29, 1880 (June 29th) – Shippy and Starke take some grub and start east toward snowy range – Crawford Bradley and I prospect back toward Elk river – Found and staked two lodes – ate a late dinner and returned to camp at wagon

June 30, 1880 (June 30th) – Prospect on river – Work at assaying Crawford and I ride to Springs to stay all night

July 1, 1880 (July 1st) – Cross the river and prospect North side for placer gold in forenoon, in afternoon go down the river on North side and prospect – Starke and Garbarino kill a deer

July 2, 1880 (July 2nd) – Build another coal pit, work on claim near camp Shippy starts to Troublesome after mail – Mr. Hunt a Boulder county smelter is here prospecting and visits our camp

July 3, 1880 (July 3rd) – Work on placer claim in forenoon – In the afternoon we ride over to the Springs to bathe, catch some fish and stay until the 4th

July 4, 1880 (July 4th Sunday) – fished, ate trout, venison, and bear steaks. Had some real milk and butter – Had a pleasant time and rode back to camp in the evening

July 5, 1880 (July 5th) – Commenced locating a 160 acre placer claim – Two gentlemen from Hahns peak visit us to stay all night – Shippy returned bringing mail nearly a month old

July 6, 1880 (July 6th) – Finished staking the claim. Made a plat of same rain in afternoon

July 7, 1880 (July 7th) – Assay – Work on claim – Hunt and Henry Crawford visit.

July 8 – 9, 1880 (July 8th and 9th) – Work at developing claim

July 10, 1880 (July 10th.) – Complete the work on placer claim necessary to hold for one year

July 11, 1880 (Sunday July 11th) – Gathered up our effects – Move to Steamboat Springs

July 12, 1880 (July 12th) – Built a forge – Sharpened and repaired our tools and shod our horses. Got pack saddles in order – put up a supply of provisions

July 13, 1880 (July 13th) – Started for Browns park – at noon camp Crawford found a lode camp for the night at Marshalls ranch 22 miles down the river Out force consists of Crawford and self, Bradley, Shippy, and Brooks and Farnsworth with Mr. Hunt and man who are prospecting in their own interests – Starke is at Hot Sulphur awaiting his brothers arrival

July 14, 1880 (July 14th) – Move 25 miles – Camp on Fortification creek – prospected the gravel and found small quantities of gold

July 15, 1880 (July 15th) – Moved 30 miles – Camp in Big Gulch – country, sand with thin stratas of gravel showing a very little gold – Water very bad. We had to dig for it. Flies, gnats and musquitoes thick and troublesome

July 16, 1880 (July 16th) – Moved 25 miles over a very hard trail Camp on Snake river – country nearly all sand with patches of limestone – We are at Cross mountain with the Silurian formation in sight

July 17, 1880 (July 17th) – Crawford went a way up the mountain while the rest of us getting breakfast and found some fine cropping of carbonates – Moved to Douglass wells and all hands prospect in the afternoon made two good looking discoveries that we think lead to good mines

July 18, 1880 (July 18 Sunday) – Moved 18 miles to Green river just above Lodore Canon, camp – Country sandy – weather very hot and no water between camps – Musquitoes so thick we can hardly breathe

July 19, 1880 (July 19th) – Conclud we can expedite the work and get over more ground to divide our forces – we divide provision Crawford takes Shippy and Farnsworth and starts for Bullion camp about 65 M. farther westward I take Brooks and Bradley and move back to Douglas wells – Got there at 1 P.M. ate a hasty dinner and all went up into the hills to work – got back to camp late and went to bed very tired

July 20, 1880 (July 20th) – Prospected hard all day found fine float but did not locate any lode or carbonate deposit

July 21, 1880 (July 21st) – Traced up a beautiful flow of float to where it cropped out of the mountain – Staked the claim and named it the Copper King – Prospected in the afternoon

July 22, 1880 (July 22nd) – As we were preparing to move camp one of our horses ran off and it took all day to find it

July 23, 1880 (July 23rd) – Moved to Cross mountain – prospect in the afternoon found and staked two splendid looking claims with ore in place think these must certainly prove rich – Bradley found a fine deposit of ore

July 24, 1880 (Sunday July 24th) – Prospected in the forenoon, found and staked two more claims – Had a heavy thunder storm last night as we lay in the sand, our horses stampeded and we had to go after them in the rain and darkness – Soon found them by the flashed of lightning, caught and repicketed and lay down again in our wet blankets to rest and get what sleep we could – Are about out of grub and no game in the country are entirely out of meat Moved in afternoon to Baggs cow ranch on Bear river – shot a sage hen as we were going into camp which was quite a God send

July 25, 1880 (July 25th) – Moved across the country to Yampa peak – Prospect in the afternoon – found nothing   move camp 3 miles to get grass for the horses Killed a fawn today

July 26, 1880 (July 26th) – Moved 30 miles back to Fortification creek – caught a mess of fish

July 27, 1880 (July 27) – Prospect up the creek for placer diggings. Caught some more fish – Rain hard in evening

July 28, 1880 (July 28) – Ride 25 miles   camp at Marshalls ranch rain some during the day. Raining hard tonight but we have a cabin to sleep in

July 29, 1880 (July 29) – Ride 22 miles to Steamboat Springs – arrived in time to take a bath and change clothes – Bradley killed a deer

July 30, 1880 (July 30) – Build a coal pit – Get it fired – Set up furnace, catch a mess of trout – Crush and prepare samples of ore

July 31, 1880 (July 31st) – Work at assaying – Crawford, Hunt and party arrive except Shippy who was paid off at Douglas wells on the return from Utah – Write some letters

Aug 1, 1880 (Sunday Aug 1st) – Rested, wrote letters and fished

Aug 2, 1880 (Aug 2nd) – Worked at assaying – Crawford and

Brooks go west to Ladds Creek to prospect for placers and lodes – Bradley goes east to prospect – Brings in part of a deer

Aug 3, 1880 (Aug 3rd) – Finished assaying – sharpened the tools – Bradley goes prospecting – Crawford and Brooks return having followed the creek up into the Indian reservation

Aug 4, 1880 (Aug 4th) – Crawford goes with Bradley and Garbarino to show them a lode that Crawford and I found four years ago to have them do some digging on while we are gone to Georgetown and to point out a filed for them to prospect in after they get sufficient samples of ore for assay – Brooks get up the teams while I put up some grub and things to use on our way out after a load of supplies – Start for Georgetown

Aug 8, 1880 (Aug 8th) – Having concluded that, as Crawford and I want to go to boulder we can save time to go from Hot Sulphur on stage and cars, and on our return, load here   we leave Brooks with teams to let them rest and recruit – Start for Georgetown on stage As most of the heavy articles needed will have to be freighted in during our absence by the merchants here, had rather pay than haul ourselves

Aug 19 – 20, 1880 (Aug 19 & 20) – Have returned to Hot Sulphur – Met our man Bradley who left the work we had assigned to him – and our employ – He says that he was induced to take this step after reading a letter that Starke had written about us – That Starke had told him that he was going to stop payments of money due us and to break up the company – That Starke was going to buy up a herd of ponies to take back to Missouri and wanted him (Bradley) to help him drive them back – This intelligence is hard to believe although we have always found Bradley to be truthful. We think if it is true that Starke must certainly be crazy – Have always treated him like a brother – load our wagon

Aug 21, 1880 (Aug 21st) – Having come 25 miles today and had time to reflect I write a hasty letter to Tygard (approx.) in regard to Starkes course as far as we have heard

Aug 25, 1880 (Aug 25th) – Reach Steamboat Springs in forenoon

Capt. F. J. Tygard
In 1880 Tygard was serving as the
President of the Bates County National Bank

Bates County National Bank dollar bill, issued 1871
Signed by President Perry A. Burgess and Vice President F. J. Tygard

– See Starke and call him in a room – Mr. Crawford "goes for him" and demands to know why he had wrote back to the company such a string of lies stating what we had heard he had written – Starke denies most of the charges – Admits that he wrote a letter, that he thought as two of our men had left it would be impossible for us to fulfill our part of the contract this season, that he had so written, thought he had done his duty. I had a talk with him afterward in a friendly way He seemed to feel badly – said he had been missinformed in regard to our intentions (approx.) – He declines to eat dinner and leave in company of Shippy who had got with him and is here – Put in afternoon and evening writing letters, write a long letter to Tygard

Aug 26, 1880 (Aug 26th) – Crawford, Brooks, Garbarino and myself start on a prospecting expedition south – take three weeks supplies with us

- - - - - - - - - - - - - -

State of Colorado

(SS)

County of Routt

Personally appeared before the undersigned County and Probate Judge of Routt County, Colorado P. A. Burgess and Jas H. Crawford, who being by me duly sworn, stat that the foregoing record and account of each days travel and work of the expedition of which they are the managers and have charge is true and correct to the best of their knowledge and belief

Sworn before me this
2nd day of October A.D. 1880
Henry A Crawford
County Judge   (SEAL)
Routt County, Colo.

Boulder House Hotel, corner of Eleventh and Pearl streets
Building purchased by Lewis Cheney in 1881
Courtesy of Carnegie Branch Library for Local History,
Boulder Historical Society Collection

Modern day corner of Eleventh and Pearl streets
Buckingham Block, originally called Cheney Block
Built by Charles Cheney in 1906

CHAPTER 11
Colorado Banking – Investing in the New State

B oulder in the latter half of the nineteenth century was a bustling frontier town made up of emigrants from the Midwest and the East Coast and several western European countries. Most were merchants, laborers, and farmers; many were sick and had come to the region hoping that the climate and the outdoor way of life would improve their health.

The Boulder region was originally Kiowa and Comanche territory, but Cheyenne and Arapaho had moved in by the late 1700s, as had their primary enemy, the Ute. Throughout the eighteenth century, the territory was claimed alternately by both Spain and France. Beginning with the first years of the nineteenth century, early explorers such as James Purcell and Zebulon Pike wandered into what was known then as Louisiana Territory. Although they found gold and discovered—but could not climb due to weather conditions—the thirty-first highest peak in the state of Colorado, Louisiana Territory continued to be well known for its desert-like geography. This long-standing misperception allowed the Native Americans there to live virtually undisturbed until the late 1850s.

In late fall of 1858, Missouri farmer Thomas Aikins and Nebraska City mayor and grocer Alfred Brookfield led their prospecting expedition to Boulder Creek, where they constructed eleven primitive cabins. On January 16, 1859, gold was discovered in a small creek bed that the men appropriately named Gold Run. Knowing now that the white men would settle in their hunting ground, the Arapaho were not pleased with this turn of events. Conflict was inevitable, and in 1860, a band of 400 or so Arapaho conducted their final antelope hunt in the area. Five hundred animals fell to the hunters' arrows.

Before 1861 was over, a treaty forced the Arapaho from 90 percent of their hunting ground. White pioneers had taken over the Boulder valley, and relations between the two cultures were at times cordial, at other times tense. Arapaho Chief Left Hand had built strong friendships with some of the settlers, but resentment and distrust still festered on both sides.

Despite the discovery of gold, the small Boulder Creek settlement did not flourish. Mining was backbreaking work, and most men had no idea what they were in for when they signed on as prospectors. Many returned home, disheartened and exhausted. Others left mining but remained in the Boulder valley. They built farms and raised crops and cattle, knowing they had guaranteed buyers in the miners. Still others opened saloons, general stores, barbershops, banks, hotels, and restaurants. Boardinghouses were an easy way for anyone, especially the relatively few adventurous single women who had made the trip west, to make money.

Those who remained in the valley had one thing in common, as historian Amos Bixby—himself a luckless miner in Boulder—said:

> One good effect of the severe trial has been to eliminate the lazy
> and the easily discouraged men, and to leave only those of clear
> grit and sufficient intelligence to see ultimate success.[1]

On February 10, 1859, Aikins called a meeting and formed the Boulder City Town Company for the purpose of establishing and organizing a town on Boulder Creek. More than sixty men signed the association's Articles of Organization. Eighteen parcels of land 50 feet wide and 140 feet deep were granted to each member. Leftover lots were sold for $1,000 each, an exorbitant price that prohibited most settlers from living in Boulder City.

Even in its infancy, Boulder enacted building codes and strict regulations. For instance, all cabins had to be built in a span of sixty days, and all had to face north or south. Streets were to measure eighty feet wide, while alleys were twenty feet. This would not be a town haphazardly thrown together, as so many mining towns were.

Despite thoughtful planning and because of the hefty price of lots, interest in developing Boulder City quickly gave way to interest in gold once there was a break in the snows of the foothills. Even those with shares in the Boulder City Town Company headed back up into the mountains and the area around Gold Run. When it became obvious that many of the influx planned to settle there, miners met and set up a government, calling themselves Mountain District Number One, Gold Hill, Nebraska (Territory). A constitution was adopted, boundaries were established, officers elected, and mining regulations put into place. It was the first mining district in what would become the state of Colorado.

By the end of July 1859, Boulder City—now nearly a ghost town—established its own mining district, and a small amount of gold was found. Still, it was nothing in comparison to what miners were finding at Gold Run. Apparently unalarmed by the lack of people or businesses in Boulder City, Samuel Breath and William Davidson built a double log cabin from which they sold mining equipment and groceries. Their business thrived, and soon the town had a reputation for providing the business-savvy entrepreneur with the opportunity to succeed. Before the end of the year, Boulder was home to a thriving business that provided hay to miners' horses and mules, a mail delivery and passenger service, a grist mill, a saloon, and several farms.

And yet the town remained impoverished in general, owing primarily to lack of sewage and drainage systems. The miners at Gold Hill needed only so much in terms of supplies, and Boulder's muddy terrain was a challenge for anyone going anywhere, especially along Pearl Street, the main road through town. The town's few hundred residents were limited in what they could do. They needed an act of God to jumpstart their determined but struggling community.

In October 1860, a forest fire advanced so rapidly up the canyon that Gold Hill residents had time to save only themselves. The settlement was destroyed, and most of its inhabitants left. Some returned to the East, but most headed to Boulder City and brought their individual business and agricultural expertise with them. The town developed, even as Gold Hill was rebuilt on lower ground with better access to water. The Hill would remain a virtual camp until the mid-1870s and the identification of tellurium, a valuable ore the miners had been overlooking for years.

Boulderites finished construction of the first school building in the territory in October 1860. When school was not in session, the building, largely the product of donated materials and labor, was used for church services and town meetings as well as dances and court trials. The Boulder Post Office was also established in 1860, and A. J. Macky—the same Macky who would cofound the Steamboat Springs Town Company in 1884—built the first frame house on the corner of Fourteenth and Pearl streets.

Considered one of Boulder's first permanent settlers, Macky had invested unwisely in several mining claims and operations before settling in Boulder as a carpenter and butcher. In 1861, he was named postmaster, a position he held for six years. During that time, he also served Boulder as county treasurer, justice of the peace, and school secretary and treasurer. He held various positions in public office throughout the 1870s, and earned a reputation as a man of integrity and fairness as he invested in real estate and lending. Macky remained one of early Boulder's leading developers when he built the first brick business block, located along Pearl Street. He also built the first brick home in Boulder, at 1201 Pine Street. Over time he amassed a respectable amount of wealth and used it generously to fund organizations and projects he deemed worthy to enhance the prosperity of his town.

Throughout the decade, however, mining camps surrounding Boulder developed more quickly than the town itself. The city that would—in one century—become a haven for the hippie counterculture of the 1960s and eventually be listed among the Top Ten Best Cities for the Next Decade by Kiplinger's *Personal Finance Magazine*[2] found itself at a virtual standstill until the 1870s.

Boulder was incorporated on November 4, 1871, and its population increased from just a few hundred residents in the 1860s to 3,060, according to the 1880 national census. The turning point in Boulder's development came in 1870 when the town's business community announced its determination to be connected to the rest of the region by railroad. Finances kept them from their goal for a few years, but in April 1873, the Colorado Central came through Boulder. Several months later, the Denver and Boulder Valley Line began providing service to the town as well.

The 1870s saw an evolving Boulder City, and one of the greatest achievements of the decade was the founding of what today is known as the University of Colorado-Boulder. The territorial legislature had approved Boulder as a site for a university in October 1861, but for various reasons, the school did not open until 1877. Colorado Territory appropriated $15,000 to the creation of the university in 1874, but it came with the condition that Boulder also raise $15,000. A. J. Macky and two other town businessmen led the fund-raising campaign, to which 104 families contributed.

The university benefited from Colorado's admittance to the Union on August 1, 1876. At that time, the school became a land-grant institution and was given seventy-two more lots of land. Added to the twenty-plus acres already allotted to the campus, that grant ensured the possibility of future expansion.

Old Main, the first university building, opened on September 5, 1877, with two teachers and forty-four students, each of whom paid a $10 matriculation fee—and nothing else. In addition to classrooms, Old Main housed the school's first president, Joseph Sewall, and his family, as well as the maintenance man and his wife. Soon, the four-story building included a library, made possible by a $2,000 donation from local banker Charles Buckingham.

Boulder truly was a town built on the generosity of its most prominent citizens. Another such resident was James P. Maxwell. Twenty-four-year-old Maxwell moved to Boulder in 1863 after investing in the mining industry in Central City and Lump Gulch. Along with Captain Clinton Tyler, he built a steam sawmill along Boulder Creek. Maxwell was a key figure in building a toll road up through Boulder Canyon, and he surveyed the town's first municipal water system. He was eventually elected deputy U.S. Mine and Land Surveyor, a position that allowed him to make extensive surveys of the

James P. Maxwell - Boulder Pioneer

burgeoning Boulder region. Throughout the 1870s, Maxwell served in the territorial legislature, and represented the state of Colorado in the U.S. Senate. Maxwell was elected both treasurer and mayor of Boulder County, and he had the honor of becoming the first state engineer of Colorado.

Maxwell enjoyed the distinction of being the stepson of Martha Maxwell, a self-taught taxidermist who single-handedly revolutionized museum display methods. Twenty-two-year-old Martha and her forty-two-year-old husband James had moved to Boulder from Baraboo, Wisconsin. Martha shot her own animals, which she then stuffed and collected. Her collections were exhibited at county fairs and, in 1876, at the famous Philadelphia Exposition. The 4-foot, 11-inch huntress was a lifelong vegetarian whose name today is synonymous with natural history.

Maxwell, like Macky, was generous with his money, and the University of Colorado was one of the recipients of his philanthropy. Boulder's Maxwell Street and Maxwell Lake are named after this active and visionary businessman.

Boulder in the 1870s was much like any other frontier town, and its main thoroughfare—Pearl Street—had a life of its own. Largely commercial, the unpaved road was lined with brick buildings housing various businesses: confectioners, fire insurance offices, drug stores and the like. A popular watering hole—L. Garbarino—sat on the 1300 block (in the twenty-first century, it is a franchise called Old Chicago). Horse-drawn freight wagons and carriages carried people and packages to their destinations, avoiding the numerous ruts as deftly as possible. In the summer, dust swirled constantly owing to the high and frequent winds. Because of its location in the eastern foothills of the Rockies, Boulder falls victim to severe downslope winds. At times gusting up to 100 miles per hour, these winds can turn violent within a matter of seconds and could destroy a cabin just as quickly. Because of these incredibly strong winds, many early cabins and homes were built with outside wall supports. In 1871, a tree-planting program was initiated as a way both to beautify the city and to provide a natural and necessary wind break.

Pearl Street was also home to the prestigious Brainard Hotel. Built in 1874, the hotel boasted a roster of elite guests, including Ulysses S. Grant, Phineas T. Barnum of the Barnum & Bailey Circus, and even the diminutive Tom Thumb and his wife. The city's first hotel, Boulder House, sat on the northeast corner of Eleventh and Pearl Streets. Originally the double log home built by Samuel Breath and William Davidson in 1860, the property was bought by the Squire and Tourtellot families and added onto so that it served as a combination store, hotel/boarding house, and residence. Lewis Cheney acquired the building in 1881.

This progressive and bustling atmosphere attracted many visionary men, including Lewis Cheney and Perry Burgess. No doubt the two entrepreneurs set their sights on Boulder after traveling through on their way between Missouri and Steamboat Springs during their summer excursions between 1874 and 1876. At first only Lewis would make the move to Colorado, but he was followed by Perry less than a year later.

In March 1877, while Perry remained in Missouri managing the Bates County National Bank, Lewis arrived in Boulder accompanied by his friend and partner I. M. Smith. On May 10, they founded the First National Bank of Boulder, located at the corner of Twelfth and Pearl Streets. Lewis owned the property and was acting president of the bank, with I. M. Smith as cashier. Lewis's son-in-law, W. H. Allison, was a director of the bank and would eventually become its president following the death of A. J. Macky in 1906. A well-respected resident of Boulder, Allison served briefly as mayor. Longtime friend and partner James Maxwell was a stockholder in the First National Bank, and A. J. Macky, who seemingly had a stake in every major financial endeavor in town, was another director. The entire banking partnership was extensive and included dozens of men besides these more well-known figures.

Lewis returned to Missouri in June of 1877 to collect his family and household goods. The family required an entire freight car to haul their belongings, which included an extensive art collection and a dining room set adorned with gold leaf.

Less than one year later, Perry replaced I. M. Smith as vice president and cashier of the First National Bank. A January 18, 1878, *Boulder County News* article announced the change in management:

> A Change has occurred in the management of the First National Bank of this town, Mr. I. M. Smith Cashier, resigning, and Mr. P. A. Burgess taking his place. For several months past the directors of the Farmers' and Merchants' Bank, of Paris, Texas, have endeavored to secure the services of Mr. Smith, who was one of their number before coming to Boulder. At last their arguments prevailed, and he resigned his position of Cashier of the First National, to take the position of President of the Farmers' and Merchants'.

Mr. Burgess, a nephew of Lewis Cheney, and former Vice-President and a heavy stockholder of the Bates County National Bank of Butler, Mo., desiring from considerations of health to locate in Colorado, purchased a part of the stock of the First National held by Mr. Smith, Mr. Cheney taking the rest, has come to stay with us permanently, having also purchased the residence property of Mr. Cheney, the latter relieving Mr. Smith of his elegant home, just thoroughly put in order for the summer adornment.

Upon the reassignment of Mr. Smith the Directors held a meeting and elected Mr. Burgess Cashier and W. H. Thompson Ass't Cashier, and are now ready for business, the new arrangement taking effect last Tuesday morning. The selection and promotion of Mr. Thompson to this responsible position will give universal satisfaction to the patrons of the Bank.

Mr. Burgess brings strength and experience to the institution, having been raised in the business by Messrs. Cheney and Smith. The patrons of the bank and the public generally will extend cordial greeting to Mr. Burgess, and will find him a very pleasant gentleman to do business with.

Cheney Family Home - N.E. corner of Broadway and High streets

Lewis quickly became one of the largest real estate holders in the city, "having business blocks upon many of the most prominent corners."[3] The Cheney family home was located on Block 3, on the northeast corner of Broadway (Twelfth) and High Streets. Today the upscale High Street Loft—with the restored and renovated Pomeroy-Cheney House—occupies the same location. The original Cheney family home was razed many years ago. The Pomeroy-Cheney House is a small bungalow on the Cheney property, and in 2010 was one of the ten oldest homes in Boulder. Originally built in 1872 by real estate developer James Pomeroy, the house was sold to Boulder attorney Sylvester Downer in 1884. He lived in it for just a short while before selling to the Cheney family.

Lewis also purchased all of Block 173 of a prestigious residential district in 1877; that neighborhood was formally established as Mapleton Hill in 1882. There, Perry built his home diagonally across the corner from where Lewis's mansion stood at Twelfth and High. Perry's home, located on what is today Broadway, was situated between modern-day Mapleton and Maxwell (named after J. P. Maxwell) Streets. The list of other residents in Mapleton Hill read like a Who's Who roster and included A. J. Macky, J. P. Maxwell, and Colonel Ivers Philips. Perry bought Block 173 from his uncle in 1878.

The other major bank in town, the National State Bank, was owned by brothers Charles G. and W. A. Buckingham. Also located on Pearl Street and about one block from the First National Bank of Boulder, its doors opened for business on April 20, 1874. Although local newspapers reported Lewis as the wealthiest man in Boulder, Buckingham was constantly on his heels. A sort of rivalry existed between the Cheney and Buckingham families on both a private and a public basis.

In 1899, construction of a brick building that replaced the original Boulder House on the corner of Eleventh and Pearl Streets was completed. The front of the building at 1111 Pearl Street included an iron placard designating that corner as "Cheney Block," in honor of Lewis's influence on the city of Boulder. In 1919 it was sold to the

Buckingham family and renamed "Buckingham Block." Little evidence remains today of Lewis Cheney's profound impact on Boulder. Yet in his day, he was one of its favorite citizens, known for his generosity, professional integrity, and dedication to helping Boulder realize its potential.

Macky Hose, a Bank's Best Friend

A frontier bank was only as good as its ability to protect the money it housed. To that end, quality mattered in two distinct areas: safes and fire protection. Never one to let a money-making opportunity pass him by, A. J. Macky opened his own hose company in January 1877. The A. J. Macky Hose Company was the second of two such companies in Boulder, the other being the Boulder Hose and Phoenix Hook and Ladder. Rather than construct its own building, Macky's company moved in with Boulder Hose. The existing quarters were extended, and a formal dedication ceremony took place in December 1877.

In October 1882, fire broke out in Lewis Cheney's building, the Boulder House. A *Boulder County Herald* article dated October 25 reported the incident. Notice how the primary concern was not the building that was actually on fire, but Cheney's bank, which was one block away.

> Another fire has called the department out. A stove to heat soldering irons was standing on the tin roof of Mr. Cheney's new building, corner of 11th and Pearl streets, and by its heat set fire to the boards underneath. When the alarm was given the report that Cheney's block was on fire and the hose carts started for the bank building. This is why Boulder Hose went by the fire. The company, however, returned in time to put a stream on the fire, when the hose burst, an attachment was made to the Macky Hose and the fire put out. The damage was nominal.

Macky Hose Company, on Pearl Street - First National Bank on right
Courtesy of Carnegie Branch Library for Local History, Boulder Historical Society Collection

First National Bank of Boulder, 1883 - Lewis Cheney stands left in doorway
Courtesy of Carnegie Branch Library for Local History, Boulder Historical Society Collection

First National Bank of Boulder - Names on photo are in order from left to right
Courtesy of Carnegie Branch Library for Local History, Boulder Historical Society Collection

Lewis Cheney, circa 1880

High-Profile Socializing

Lewis and his second wife, Sarah Ann Milner, enjoyed an active social life as they raised their many children—Antoinette, Ida, Oliver, Charles Homer, and eventually, Lynette—in the roomy brick home in Mapleton Hill. As a high-profile business-man, Lewis kept busy with his colleagues even outside the office. Although known primarily as a banker, he also had interests in the mining industry, serving as treasurer and director of the Boulder Mining & Concrete Company.

Lewis's name frequently appeared in the local newspa-pers for reasons both professional and personal. The following *Boulder Banner* account of a June 1877 baseball game between the city's prominent men is comical for its complete lack of political correctness.

Base Ball Fever

And in this place, the prominent citizens of town engaged in a match, one side being composed of lean men, and the other fat ones. Imagine such men as J. C. Howe, Col. Ellet, Weisenborn, Major Salsbury, Capt. Graham, B. C. Sawyer, L. Cheney, Lafe Miller and A. W. Bush, should play a game against Tom Graham, Capt. Paddock, Cashier Smith, Walter Buckingham, Marine Smith, A. R. Brown, O. E. Henry, C. M. Farrar and Newt Hockaday, and you have about what was had in this town last week. Even old men can go crazy here.

Cashier Smith is Lewis's partner I. M. Smith; Colonel Ellet, a stockholder in the First National Bank of Boulder, also served as Boulder's mayor for several terms. These men were often professional competitors who necessarily depended upon one another and socialized together. For Boulder's citizenry, they were an endless source of entertainment and curiosity.

As active as Lewis Cheney was in Boulder's development and banking system, his name has largely fallen to the ages. Perry Burgess, who moved to Boulder in 1878, was also a force in the banking business and yet, like that of his uncle, his name rarely appears in connection with early Boulder settlement. Perry was a stockholder, vice president, and cashier (1878–1881) in the First National Bank of Boulder, and he and his family enjoyed a vibrant social life in connection with Lewis.

Although his residency in Boulder lasted three brief years, Perry made a name for himself throughout the city and established lifelong partnerships with some of the earliest pioneers and most prominent citizens.

The Burgess and Cheney families continued to summer in Steamboat Springs during their Boulder years, a tradition maintained by Lewis's son, Charles, throughout his lifetime. In January 1881, Perry and his family relocated to Rich Hill, Missouri, where he

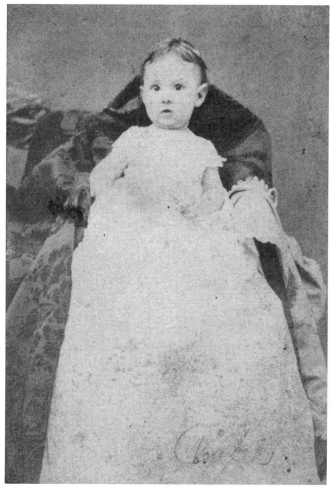

Charles Cheney, circa 1876
'Cousin Charlie' transcribed the 1866 - 1868 Burgess diaries

Quote by Charles Cheney as recalled by a third grade Central school classmate in the *Boulder Daily Camera*, 1953

"The only sure way to make money was in the banking or cattle business... They pay a sure dividend every year... cattle run on the range, cost nothing for feed, and when you loan the other fellows money left on deposit you get good interest, and that also costs you nothing."

founded the Rich Hill Bank. Lewis expanded his Colorado banking interests by opening the First National Bank of Gunnison in May 1882 with James McClure and other longtime partners. That was soon followed by the opening of the People's Bank of Salida, where he again served as president.

Perry remained in Missouri until 1882, at which time he and his family made a final move to Steamboat Springs. There, with the assistance of his friend and neighbor Harvey Woolery, he built a home and began to enjoy the beauty of northwestern Colorado. Although Perry was the only one of the business partners to relocate permanently to Steamboat Springs, he, along with A. E. Lea, Lewis Cheney, A. J. Macky, J. P. Maxwell, and others formed the Steamboat Springs Town Company in 1884 with $160,000 in capital.

The efforts of this primitive chamber of commerce marked the beginning of the Yampa Valley region as a promising place in which to work and live, and Perry was determined to be part of it. In fact, Boulder and Steamboat Springs share a historical connection in that many of the same men who were prominent in the settlement of one were also distinguished leaders, if not citizens, of the other. James Crawford, for example, founded Steamboat Springs but wintered in Boulder, where the climate wasn't so severe. Boulderites Perry and Lewis summered in Steamboat Springs, where Perry was a key figure as the town was established and development flourished. Other men—A. J. Macky and J. P. Maxwell among them—intuitively recognized both areas for what they were and wisely invested in each.

Despite the fact that Colorado was largely a vast wilderness even as it claimed statehood, there is no denying that some of its most important twenty-first-century cities were linked not by roads, but by a handful of visionaries who saw what could be and made the imagined a reality.

Being one of those visionaries, as Lewis Cheney was, had its costs. His early life as a Mormon had been one of persecution and near-constant fugitive status. Perhaps those early years allowed him to hone his survival skills and encouraged him to look for opportunity under even the most remote circumstances. His early career as a freighter on the Mormon Trail and later during the gold rush era was physically challenging, and his later real estate and banking endeavors no doubt added to the stress of losing his wife and being left with four children.

He kept in touch with his beloved nephew Perry all his life as the two men frequently traveled between Steamboat Springs and Boulder. Theirs were full lives, with deep bonds and varied interests. But everything—even something as seemingly mundane as a day trip to visit a loved one—in the nineteenth century was much harder and required more effort than we can imagine now. Life lived at a determined pace was rich, yes, but also exhausting.

And yet it seemed that neither man was willing to slow down. And because of their unyielding dedication to progress, Boulder and Steamboat Springs remain two of the most breathtaking, vibrant cities in the state of Colorado.

First National Bank of Boulder building, corner of Pearl and Broadway
Today, the building is in the heart of the Pearl Street walking district

Burgess Family Ranch - Steamboat Springs, Colorado 1884
Courtesy of Tread of Pioneers Museum, Steamboat Springs, Colorado

CHAPTER 12
Hahns Peak - Perry's Return to Mining

Although technically "discovered" many years earlier, Hahns Peak was officially named on August 27, 1865, when Joseph Hahn led a gold mining expedition there with two friends—William Doyle and Captain George Way. Doyle recorded the event on a scrap of paper on which he wrote, "This is named Hahns Peak by his friend and comrade, William A. Doyle, August 27, 1865."[1]

Hahn had actually been to the mountain peak in 1862 on another prospecting expedition, but bad weather forced his group to conduct just a cursory survey of the creeks and gulches before heading back toward Georgetown, their starting point.

Hahn eventually died on a third expedition in 1867 when unforgiving winter weather conditions and lack of food once again impeded his mission. Refusing to turn back, he paid the ultimate price for his choice.

In the early 1870s, Hahns Peak was the only settlement in Routt County other than Steamboat Springs. During that time, several mining—gold, silver, coal—companies opened and found great success. Hahns Peak was the county seat of Routt County from 1879 until 1912, at which time boundary lines changed and Steamboat Springs was made the new county seat.

One of those mines was co-owned by Perry Burgess, A. J. Macky, F. A. Hinman, and Edward Cody. It was one of the most successful gold-mining ventures in the area. Steamboat Springs historian and promoter C. C. Graham wrote about the company in his February 25, 1888, *Montezuma Millrun* newspaper article:

> Some of the richest gulches are not worked, for want of sufficient water. The Cody Macky & Co. procure water from a ditch seventeen miles long extending from the west branch of the upper Elk river. This company has been prosperous from its inception and was organized in 1886. Miles of water pipes have been laid; expensive booms constructed and many valuable improvements

have been added, entailing a great outlay of labor and money. Outside of all expenses, the company has been able to declare a grand dividend, with encouraging and increasing prospects.

Perry's 1885 Steamboat Springs diary provides an exact date of the agreement—the day he and Macky bought into the company— November 16, 1885, which is slightly different from Graham's account.

> Macky and myself bought each an undivided one-fourth interest in Cody and Hinman's mining interest at Hahn's Peak for which we each paid $20,000.00.

Perry had other mining interests as well. Around the same time he bought into the Cody, Macky & Co. mine, Perry discovered the Republican Mine with Steamboat resident W. H. Dever. That mine, located on Copper Ridge, was relocated twelve years later and bought out by the Copper Ridge Mining & Milling Company.

Though largely considered a man's industry, mining in those early days was an activity that appealed to women as well. Those of means could buy a mine, hire labor, and reap the rewards of someone else's hard day's work. Perry Burgess's wife, Annie, partnered with A. J. Macky's wife, Adelaide, and signed a mine claim on June 28, 1892. Encompassing one hundred acres in Hahns Peak, the mine was known as Woman's Placer. Annie's aunt, Mary Sampson, also got involved in the business. It was a unique mine in ownership alone: One of the wealthiest women in Boulder joined one of the earliest settlers of Steamboat Springs and opened a mine. It wasn't the usual life found in the daily diary and journal entries of women pioneers.

What is Placer Mining?

Gold miners found their treasure in the form of flakes, nuggets, and dust. In order to extract it, the gold had to be separated from the rock it was found in. Water erosion was helpful to this process because it wore down the rock, which allowed the gold to flow into the water until it reached areas where it would slow down, such as river bends. Prospectors would then pan for gold in these areas. They would scoop dirt from the bottom of the stream or river or creek and swirl it in the pan. As water was poured from the pan, only gold was left behind. This use of water to excavate minerals—in this case, gold—is known as placer mining.

Panning wasn't the only method used. For larger-scale mining, prospectors used a sluice box, with barriers along the bottom to trap the gold. Rockers—equipment shaped like cradles—were used to sift sand and water through screens, again leaving the gold behind.

But to do either of these—panning or sluicing—the gold first had to be excavated. And to do that, miners used picks or dynamite to open pits. From there the gravel was shoveled into a trough and then "washed" with water blasted from hydraulic nozzles at a force of 5,000 pounds. While hydraulic mining was remarkably effective, it ravaged the environment permanently. Gravel and sediment traveled naturally downstream to nearby canyons and farmlands, often burying forever whatever lay beneath it, be it fertile fields or once clear-running streams and rivers.

Like thousands of other nineteenth-century settlers, Perry clearly had an interest in seeking his fortune in gold. And, without a doubt, Hahns Peak was the place to do that in northwest Colorado. But something happened, something that made Perry lose interest in his investment and sell his share of the Cody, Macky & Co. mine to Macky on September 24, 1889. That same year, he organized his final bank in Steamboat Springs with F. E. Milner.

Gold mining never made Perry a rich man, but he was a well-respected assayer—*the* official assayer for the town of Steamboat Springs—whose skills prospectors would travel dozens of miles to hire. His name was often published in the *Steamboat Pilot* in relation to gold and silver assaying, and numerous 1887 diary entries attest to his interest and popularity:

Andrew J. Macky, circa 1880

The White Pinecone, Gunnison, Colorado, June 25, 1886
Mr. A. J. Macky Brought to Boulder last week 397 ounces of gold dust valued at
$5,000. Which he had taken out of the placer mine at Hahn's Peak.

July 8 – Made assays and moved a pile of lumber – wrote letters

July 12 – worked at assaying most of the day Helped work on the house went home am very tired tonight

July 17 – worked at assaying rained 3 showers Pd Coulter $10.00 cash on a/c

July 19 – worked at assaying – a cold raw windy day – Storm Peak was clad in new snow this morning

July 20 – worked at assaying and cupel making Couldn't put the foot bridge back across the river today. A big frost this morning Emma and Lulie Prichet visited me at the shop this afternoon.

And yet he sold his interests in the industry and got out. It may well be that Perry's inherent respect for and appreciation of natural beauty and resources were in direct conflict with the hydraulic mining prevalent in that era. His July 14, 1897, *Pilot* recollection article reflects his love of the natural world while providing a vivid description of the Hahns Peak area.

Some Early History
Interesting Region Between Elk River and Hahn's Peak.

At the crossing of Elk river, as we journey toward Hahn's Peak, we pass the first ranch that was settled upon in Elk river valley. S. B. Reid was the first white man to fence, clear and break land, build a habitation and plant and cultivate a crop in this valley. No surveys had yet been made and the settler then had only to select a nice fertile piece of land, with wood, water, pasturage, game, fish and other conveniences near at hand, and, like the badger, go to digging.

At that time the land was open and free for all as air and sunshine, as the Creator intended it should be. It was no uncommon thing for the settler to go out in the morning and see, within easy gun shot of his cabin door, a band of lordly elk or a herd of beautiful deer or antelope or an occasional bruin wending his way toward some cool, shady mountain marsh to spend the hot hours of the day. Flocks of sage hens, dusky grouse and willow grouse would come about his door yard, and the streams were teeming with trout, among which were many old residenters of the salmon variety, lusty, plump fellows eager to snap the bait, and when hooked would make the line fairly hiss as it cut the air, and a strong rod bend and tremble. In those dear early days the spring mornings would be filled with bird songs mingled with the notes of geese, cranes and ducks. This was before the greedy, murderous, vandal pot hunter had invaded our little paradise. This class of bipeds kept away for fear of coming in contact with the frisky Ute, who had a reputation for wanting "heap scalp," or, to be more plain, of coveting other people's hair and the skin upon with it grew. Taxes were light, accidents, lawsuits and sickness were almost unknown.

Passing the old Reid ranch the road leads up a long gulet, bringng us to the summit of the Willow creek divide. Here we halt to drink in the grand scene that lies before us, which is made up of green valleys with beautiful trout streams like silver threads coursing through them, gently sloping, pine clad mountains interspersed with grassy, cool looking parks, rugged hills of lava, the deep rocky gorge through which the waters of many mountain streams that empty into and make Willow creek escapes into Elk river. You can look across and down upon Way's gulch and String ridge, where the first mining operations were conducted. Hahn's Peak rises almost in front of you, a little to the left, while you can see the serrated vertabrae of the North American Continent piercing the blue air a little to the right and looking only a short distance from you. On this sublime height, where, except when disturbed by the elements, eternal solitude reigns, and in an almost inaccessible spot, a fine deposit of mica is known to exist which is pronounced by experts to be nearly as good as the best grade known.

The Hahn's Peak district used to be divided into two distinct settlements or camps. The town that was started on Way's gulch, near the base of String ridge, was known as Bugtown, so called by the boys on account of the bosses and managers of the company having a residence there as well as being the site of the company's office. These men were called the "big-bugs" by the boys, hence the name Bugtown.

A few cabins were built over the divide on the Deep creek side as winter quarters for the miners and prospectors, many of whom had located claims. These cabins were occupied by the laboring class and was named Poverty and the rich placer territory adjacent thereto was known and is now called by the name of Poverty Bar and Poverty Flats. Many thousands of dollars worth of the yellow metal have been washed from the sand and gravel in front of the old row of buildings that once fringed the border of the beautiful pine forest and sheltered the workers. Among the buildings was a boarding house, a saloon, a store of general merchandise, a shop, and later on some county offices.

At the time of the Ute Indian outbreak, in 1878, Routt county's seat of government was at Hayden. The place was depopulated that autumn and the county records moved by one Frank M. Jones to Hahn's Peak, where they still remain.

It is time to select a place to camp and we move on down the hill, cross Willow creek, drive on to and through the future great city, thence out a mile on the old Snake river road and camp on Deep creek, a short distance above its confluence with Willow creek, and will tell in our next what we find out that is worth relating.

Whatever the reason, Perry gradually lost interest in gold mining, but his life in Hahns Peak was anything but empty. In 1887, he managed a general store owned by F. E. Milner and F. A. Metcalf. According to the October 20, 1887, edition of the *Steamboat Pilot*,

> The store at Hahns Peak has by far the largest and best selected stock of any in the county. Mr. Burgess is the courteous manager.

Milner and Metcalf also co-owned the Bank of Hahns Peak, which opened its doors for business on January 1, 1898. That same year, the partners moved their Hahns Peak store to Steamboat Springs, a sure sign that the town was growing. Milner retained an interest in Hahns Peak where his silver mine, the Tom Thumb, was one of the more prosperous and reputable. Milner and his crew were responsible for breaking ground to build a road from Hahns Peak to nearby Columbine, another popular mining community and a stopover for those traveling by buckboard, on foot, or on horseback. The Hahns Peak-Columbine Wagon Road made travel possible in a wilderness that the railroad had ignored.

Milner had another tie to Perry: He was the cousin of Oliver Cheney, Lewis's son. Oliver, or "Ollie," had mining interests in Boulder as well as a financial investment in Milner's Hahns Peak store. Like his father, Lewis, Ollie was an outdoorsman, and took every opportunity to spend time in the area. He found Hahns Peak so appealing that he left Boulder and honeymooned there in 1896. A few years later, Ollie became a resident of Routt County and spent the remainder of his life ranching in the area.

Perry's diary reveals that much of the first half of 1884 was spent expanding his family home and traveling back and forth between Steamboat Springs and Hahns Peak. Although all of Perry's entries are brief, the astute reader can pull small details from his diary and recognize that his life was full and active. His pastimes included snowshoeing, boating, and enjoying dinner company.

> January 24 – Clear and cold-Worked at cabin today – Have it nine logs high – Have a pretty fair view of the comet – It is South of West tonight.

> January 31 – Finished the log work of the cabin and began to cut a doorway-Warm and pleasant

> February 6 – Warm. Snow a little. Out in one casing in window and saw the remaining window. Have concluded to build another small room for a larder or store room.

Oliver Irwin (Ollie) Cheney, circa 1877

Boulder Daily Camera, **1894**
Ollie Cheney is of Age

It amounts to considerable to a young man to come into possession of his majority. He can vote and be free from parental strings. But when he has had property left to him and becomes its sole owner by virtue of inheritance, this 21st anniversary is a great event. Ollie Cheney, son of the lamented Lewis Cheney, the Boulder banker, has recently become of age. The Camera office building and the building occupied by Undertaker Trezise and other pieces of productive Boulder property are now his in fee simple title. He is a young man of excellent presence, good looking, wealthy and -unmarried.

Ollie Cheney with his horse Tony, circa 1890 - Routt County pioneer

February 9 – Finished sawing the door, put in casing, and began digging out sawing more logs. Have concluded to build the house higher. Annie and I went up to the Springs in the evening – Day clear and cold.

March 2 Sunday – Annie, Bruce, John, and I went down in the grove. Shot a porcupine. After dinner we all snow shoed and had lots of fun and some hard falls coasting. Day bright and beautiful. All hands thoroughly tired tonight.

March 23 – Sunday: Quite pleasant. Snow shoed and rode in the river. Elmer called today.

March 24 – Pleasant – Worked at the porch and the cabin. Bruce and I took a little boat ride. Got another mail.

March 25 – Snow in morning, but cleared off and is quite pleasant – Worked at the cabin. Louis Garbarino and Mr. Adair stopped for dinner today.

March 31 – Cold and raw this forenoon but moderated by 3 P.M. and snow hard until bedtime, looks like would continue a week. Humpty about the same. Old Puss has been sick a long time. I shot her today to end her suffering. Annie, Lissie and I snow shoed up to Lissie's ranch today. Snow is crusted and settled very hard. Met Mr. Dever and two other men coming in. Called at Missrs Crawford and Woolery's. Began using hay off the stable, snow all night.

April 23 – Cut wood and tinkered around home. The folks were down from the Springs breaking trails. Took a pack load of hay on a horse. Saw a crane today. The river is getting up.

April 24 – I have a lame back so can hardly get around. Killed a wild goose today, took the vegetables up and picked out the bad ones today. The Springs folks broke a trail down to Mr. Woolery's stacks. Got another mail.

April 25 – Gloomy and stormy. Do nothing but chores.

April 26 – Snow fell about 6 inches last night and snow by spells

Johnny Sampson (L) and Bruce Burgess (R), son of Perry A. Burgess
Courtesy of Tread of Pioneers Museum, Steamboat Springs, Colorado

BRUCE BURGESS

Perry's son, Bruce Burgess, with bear skins, circa 1884
Courtesy of Tread of Pioneers Museum, Steamboat Springs, CO

Montezuma Mill Run, 1888

The bear revels in the mountain ranges and seldom pays the settlers any complimentary visits except in berry time. He is then fat, and his favors consist of a valuable hide and bear lard which is superior in quality and usefulness to the best of Armour's or Fairbank's. Bruin is not dreaded, but his visits are solicited and he is invariably entertained after the manner of Sharp, Remington and Ballard. He spends the springtime in following bands of elk and embraces all opportunities of hugging elk calves, and loving them to death. Bear skins are a prominent feature to a frontier cabin. They denote valor and prowess, and carry with them enough romance for an evening's entertainment.
C.C. Graham, Steamboat Springs Town Promoter

all today. Daisy is snow blind-I loafed around the house. Can see nearly all the top of the garden fence above the snow now. The river is raising very fast. Annie has a nervous headache tonight.

April 27 – Sunday – Annie is better, we snow shoed down to the river. The water begins to show through the snow in places where the ground is very low in the bottom. Elmer was here this evening.

June 8 Sunday – The boys and I went after the balance of the deer, saw another deer. In afternoon I made a gate for cow yard. Louis Garbarino was here this afternoon. Annie and Lissie went up and got the mail.

June 9 – Finished shingling the kitchen and planted potatoes. Dever was here this afternoon.

June 10 – Worked at assaying in forenoon and at the house in the afternoon. Dever was here this afternoon making a wheelbarrow.

June 11 – Rained part of the day. Spaded and sowed some turnips. Laid floor in porch. Dever worked at wheelbarrow. Louis G. was here to dinner.

July 24 – Worked at making fence in forenoon. Annie and I took the horses and went hunting. Killed a fine deer and did not get home until 9 P.M. A stranger who is in route for Hahn's Peak stays tonight here..

July 25 – Commenced to cut hay. Mr. Dever came down from the mine. Mr. Denison came up and had a very severe attack of palpitations of the heart. Thought he was dying for a little while. He recovered and ate a hearty supper. Mr. Crawford and Logan came by him.

July 26 – Worked at haying. The women folks went up to the Springs. AM very tired tonight. Saw Mr. Milner today. Denison is better and went up to the Springs.

July 27 – Kept the Sabbath by fishing and visiting with lots of company that came.

Throughout Perry's life he associated with a wide array of friends and business partners. He was as comfortable in a board meeting as he was prospecting or spending time working on his cabin. Upon examination of the Burgess Steamboat diaries, it becomes evident by the constant flow of visitors just how well known he was in the area. One Hahns Peak resident whose name appears several times in Perry's 1886–1887 diary is Ed Burnett. The following entries are from 1887.

> July 24 – worked at assaying. There was a horserace here today. Ed Burnett brought more samples

> Aug 20 – worked all day at the house   paid Coulter $5.00 Ed Burnett was in this P.M. brought two samples of rock

> Aug 24 – made some bone dust for cupels visited with Col. Steel and wrote Macky. Burnett etals

> Nov 14 – Sunday – Done some Notary work for Mr. Murphy wrote to Burnett. Worked at grading in the afternoon. Aunt May was here to spend the day. Day was a pleasant autumn day

> Nov 16 – put boards on North side of stable roof Partly filed the big saw. Visited with Ed Burnett – Bought a shoulder of fresh pork Read from Co. Clerk Certificate of Election as J. P. for this Precinct. Was very cold this A.M. 6(degrees) below 0 but turned warm and thawed some

> Nov 20 – rec'd from the Crawfords assignment of ½ int. in 3 mining claims. Ed Burnett John (Gait?) et als were here today. I bought a sack of potatoes and attended to various maters. Louis G spent the evening with us.

> Nov 27 – a clear cold day – I worked about home in forenoon and attended a L. E meeting in afternoon. Ed Burnett was here also Mr Youngfield

According to Ed himself, he was "the model bachelor of Elk River."[2] Born in 1865, Burnett was one of those prospectors for whom Hahns Peak was a mistress. The *only* mistress. He built his cabin there in 1906. In 1950, author and historian Thelma Stevenson and

Ed Burnett
Courtesy of Denver Public Library

her husband bought that property. When it came time to renovate Burnett's cabin and barn, they learned more about the former owner than they had ever imagined they would.

Stevenson recalls in her 1976 book, *Historic Hahns Peak*:

> That Burnett was a short man could be deduced from the fact that he constructed a low doored, two-small-windowed, 14 by 16 foot cabin. It was of lightning killed, pine logs that had been felled, straight and sound, from standing dead timber. Gable ends were insulated with gunny sacking, log crevices chinked with mud. The huge, round log, roof beams were covered with four layers of rough sawn boards. Each addition covered cracks of the layer below it. They carried great snow weight effectively, usually kept out the rain ...

Clearly, this bachelor prospector had been his own carpenter and veterinarian with first class photography skills. He had cooked for himself, read books and periodicals and worn out iron picks in the placers. Hard work and harsh weather led to backache and kidney trouble which in turn called for pain killing drugs. He doctored himself, carried water from Two-Mule Spring by the roadside.[3]

Ed served as justice of the peace of Clark, another nearby community, in 1896 and was constable of the 13th precinct of Routt County before 1912. His friends remembered him as philosophical and well read, yet he lived his life alone in his small cabin. By the time he died in 1939, he was nearly blind and had suffered for years from excruciating arthritis.

No one knows how Perry and Ed became friends, but it is clear they were just that. Mining was probably the common thread between the two rustic men. Perhaps they also shared a love of the land. Hahns Peak seemed to have that effect on its residents, especially the men whose livelihoods depended upon its natural resources.

All his life, Perry had observed and recorded, appreciated and honored all the virtues and nuances of the land in which he traveled and lived. This July 2, 1897, *Steamboat Pilot* recollection article embodies not only Perry's deep-seated awe for Hahns Peak and the home he created there, but the respect he showed for nature's grace wherever he went.

On Hahn's Peak

The Glorious View that Can be Obtained from There.

Your new camp on Deep creek, near Willow creek, is pleasant. You have an abundance of pure water, dry firewood and green pasturage for your horses right at your camp. Being very much in love with dame nature, you have taken some walks through bits of moss grown, shady woodlands so invitingly near. Being fond of trout you have wandered up Willow creek and its tributaries with rod and line in hand and have brought back to camp a well filled basket or so of elegant and palatable brook trout, and when up near the head of the green, flower-decked valley have noted some mighty pine trees and perhaps have had a glimpse of bruin's tracks in the old game trails that come to the creek from many directions.

Having a desire to view the landscape from the summit of Hahn's Peak you have been looking in that direction and mentally mapping out a course by which you can make the ascent with the least exertion, by following the gentlest slopes that lead to the top. Some morning you may be awakened by the gentle murmur of the rain on your tent roof. As it is not yet light, and the melody is so gentle and soothing, you will turn in your warm nest and take another nap. Upon awaking you find it broad daylight and the rain has temporarily ceased falling, but a dense fog surrounds you and every sound you make is faithfully repeated from the woods and hills about you and you note that the report of a pistol or rifle seems for a time to gain volume as it goes crashing back and forth and finally dies in a sullen roar. The saucy elf—Miss Echo—gives you a fine exhibition of her power of mimicry this foggy morning.

As you had yesterday planned to ascend the Peak today, and being neither sugar or salt, but an active palpitating body of bone and animal tissue, in the vigor of early manhood, you are not appalled by a few harmless rain drops nor the banks of mist that seem to shut you in, leaving but a bit of landscape of dripping willows and freshly washed greensward about your wagon and tent visible.

In your mind's eye you have a pretty correct map of the route to the summit you had decided to take. You eat a hearty camp breakfast and wash it down with that glorious nectar, camp coffee, then, with your light prospecting pick and a lunch, you strike out in the direction you yesterday decided to take. Your feet and legs are encased in rubber boots, while a light gossamer protects your body from the rain and mist as well as the wet bushes with which you will come in contact.

Your pocket compass gives you the course you wish to take, and, as you have a long climb ahead, you avoid as much as possible any descent, keeping continually ascending, and realizing the fact that often "the more haste the less speed," you walk leisurely, pausing from time to time to take breath and examine the rocks you encounter, breaking off fragments with the pole end of your pick to bring them under the focus of your pocket microscope.

After about three hours of this leisurely climbing you note that it is beginning to grow lighter, in another half hour you can see "Old Sol" faintly outlined through the mist above you, another half hour and you emerge into the sunlight, and finally the summit is gained and you stand in the presence of Ominpotence on what seems to be a miniature earth floating on a mighty ocean of clouds. Instinctively you uncover and gaze in awe at the glorious sight. The busy world beneath you is gone, concealed beneath the sea of clouds upon which you see other specks of landscape floating like small islands. These you recognize as the summits of other peaks, which, like the one on which you are standing, push their heads above the vapor into the crisp fresh air and golden sunlight. You look across to where the "Crest of the Continent" seems to look so solemnly down upon the lower world. As you continue to look the sense of speechless awe begins to wear off and the lump in your throat to subside, and as nature tells you that your long climb has emptied your stomach you remember the lunch in your pocket and eat it with a keen relish that shows not the slightest trace of deficiency in your gastronomical powers. After lunch comes the meditative, nerve soothing and not to be dispensed-with pipe and tobacco, and then you spend another hour "cracking rocks." The pocket in which you carry specimens begins to bulge and grows continually heavier, the clouds have "rolled by" and are gone. The hills, valleys and woodlands beneath you are again in clear view and look astonishingly near.

Your return to camp is comparatively easy. All you have to do is to keep putting one foot ahead of the other, specific gravity does the rest.

After the mining boom, the buildings remained, but their inhabitants took off for parts unknown. The entire region was taken over by a homesteading ranch that was active into the 1960s.

People eventually began to trickle into the area, some interested in renovating old historic buildings, others focused on building new, custom homes. The peak itself is the only well-known and frequently climbed peak in the Elkhead Mountain range.[4]

Today Hahns Peak is a quiet residential town lovingly maintained by the Hahns Peak Historical Society. It continues to offer some of the most breathtaking scenery in the American West, and visitors enjoy camping, hiking, mountain biking, horseback riding, and other adventures.

Perry's deep appreciation for Hahns Peak is evident from his writings published in the *Steamboat Pilot*. For years, visitors to the Burgess cabin would be treated to a picnic or a day at Hahns Peak. Perry Burgess—and his Cheney relatives—understood the value of the beauty and grandeur inherent in the area, and it remained a much beloved region for all of them for the rest of their lives.

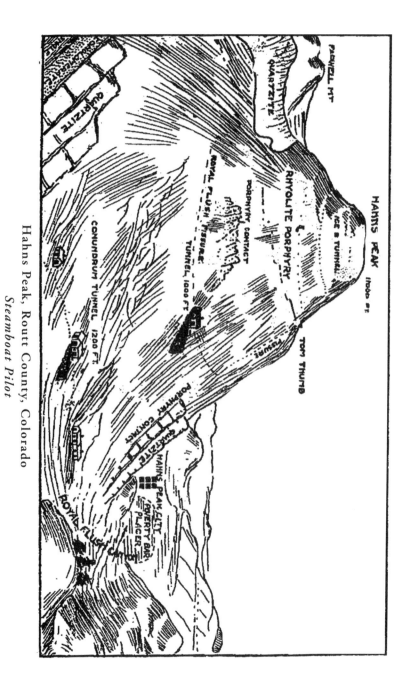

Hahns Peak, Routt County, Colorado
Steamboat Pilot

Burgess Family Ranch, Steamboat Springs, Colorado, circa 1888

(L-R) Bruce (leaning against wall), Helen and Annie Burgess (sitting), J. H. Crawford (on porch), Perry (right of porch, no hat)

Courtesy of Tread of Pioneers Museum, Steamboat Springs, Colorado

CHAPTER 13
Steamboat Springs, Colorado – Home at Last

Perry Burgess and Lewis Cheney were at the height of their professional success by 1883. They owned numerous banks in both Missouri and Colorado, where they were also heavily invested in real estate. Their business interests in Colorado extended to include mining, and both men partnered with James Crawford to help organize the Steamboat Springs Town Company. It was a heady time for uncle and nephew, and the future looked promising.

By this time, it seems Perry and his family were living in a cabin he built in 1881 with the help of friend and next-door neighbor, Harvey Woolery. Before that, they occupied "Little Cabin". Although no known diary belonging to Perry exists for 1881, Crawford's daughter Lulie kept her own diary that year and mentioned Perry's wife, Annie, in an entry:

> Sat., Sept. 24 Crowded again. Seventeen for supper including 8 campers, one of them a Mr. Bigelow. Mrs. Burgess was down from the Little Cabin. She has got a new hat.

"Little Cabin" refers to the cabin built by Sandy Mellen and Charlie Mayo when they were hired by Crawford to protect his homestead claim. The cabin was lived in by the Crawford's upon first settling in the area, while waiting on an Indian trader to move out of "Big Cabin." Once they moved into "Big Cabin," he loaned out "Little Cabin" to others so that they might have a place to live while building their own homes. Perry's own cabin, though hospitable by fall of 1881, was an unending project for him as he worked to expand the main building and add out-buildings over the course of the next several years. Perry's property, like that of the other original settlers in the area, was 160 acres. Unlike some of the others, his cabin was two miles outside of the actual town. Almost adjacent to and bordering his ranch was the Steamboat Springs Cemetery, which remains in use even in the twenty-first century.

Say It With Rocks

Brothers Harvey and Milton Woolery lived across from one another, separated by the Yampa River. At the time, there was no bridge connecting the two river banks, and when the ice broke in the spring, the waters were too deep to wade across.

This was but a mere obstacle for the Woolery brothers, who kept in daily contact by tying notes to rocks and throwing them back and forth to one another. This was how, one morning, Harvey learned the tragic news that his brother's wife had died the night before, as referenced in John Rolfe Burroughs' *Steamboat in the Rockies*:

> Her baby, Clara, was just one year old. Mr. Harvey Woolery went for his wife and Mrs. Burgess. The horses had to swim to take the wagon across (the river) but they forded safely. There was no undertaker, so they took care of the body and made a rude casket from the sideboards of one of the freight wagons. . .[1]

She was originally buried on Dream Island and was later moved to the Steamboat Springs Cemetery, becoming one of the first recorded burials there.

Perry Burgess recorded the event in his 1882 diary as well:

> May 16- Morning bright and pleasant but soon clouded over. Crawford and I started out to hunt. Separated up in Soda Park after a long hard hunt I killed a big bull elk, got home at 4 P.M., Annie met me at the fence with the starting and painful intelligence that Mrs. J. M. Woolery is dead. H. Woolery and Crawford hunted up some horses and took Mrs. W. and Annie down to J.M.'s cabin. Mr. Dever and I are busy making a coffin. Looks like storm tonight. Mail came in at 5 P.M.

> May 17- We finished making the coffin. Ramsden, Smith and Price came. Dug a grave on the island and buried poor Mrs. Woolery a sad pioneer funeral. Only two women and nine men. Annie has taken the motherless baby. Had a thunderstorm tonight.

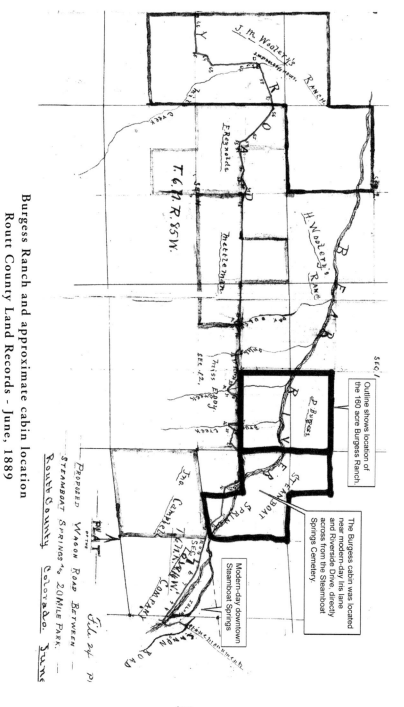

Burgess Ranch and approximate cabin location
Routt County Land Records - June, 1889

Because there were so few settlers in Steamboat Springs in the early 1880s, those who did live there came to depend upon one another for socialization as well as survival. Winters were especially harsh in that mountain climate, and individual cabins became social gathering places in lieu of churches, saloons, and other public buildings. The Burgess cabin was no exception.

Perry's diaries indicate that he and Annie were entertaining and dining with a continuous flow of guests. His 1882 diary mentions many such encounters in April alone:

> April 14 – Clear and cold – in the fore noon I went up Soda Creek after traps and up on the mountains North to look for bear and elk – saw no signs of game – in the afternoon worked at ditching – Annie done a washing Woolery and Paul Wagner came up and took dinner with me.

> April 23 – Warm – Went down the river to fish. Caught none – Henry and Hans. Roger and Murray came and stay all night – Dave came with mail. Roger was here to break trail – raining at 9 P.M.

> April 25 – Day warm and windy. Mail came in badly wet. Dave says it was unavoidable and he reports that he got the mail wet that went out yesterday – Prichard and Dutch Joe came down today in route to the Peak. Read a letter from Crawford.

> April 29 – We made some assays today. Shadbolt took dinner with us today. Weather very pleasant I shot a beautiful white heron today. Mail came in this P.M.

> April 30 – Crawford and Dever went down the R. today – Stafford, Shadbolt, Bruner and Wall were here today – I killed two grouse and one hawk, write some letters.

As years passed, the number and frequency of visitors to his ranch only increased. Perry was very meticulous about recording the names—sometimes just a first name, other times, a last—of people he interacted with on any given day. In addition to names of prominent men such as J. P. Maxwell and A. J. Macky, one name that repeatedly reappears is Elmer Burgess, as seen in these 1898 diary excerpts:

> June 24 – Rain a little in the night last night. Cool and cloudy in the forenoon. Warm and windy in the afternoon. I worked at the fence and ground my ax in the forenoon. Willard, Emma and Gay Burgess and Elmer Burgess family came to visit and spend the afternoon. I paid Delmi 5.00 for work living last fall and winter. Gave a guarantee to the Co. Seat Committee in case the County Seat is moved to Steamboat.

> August 9 – Worked in the shop, made 3 assays for W. W. Adair and 2 for self. Met a new Burgess today, sister of Willard and Elmer. She was here with Gay and Willard. I had a nice visit with Gay. Schaller paid $5.00 rent Aug. 8. Sent a statement to Coleman showing Mrsz. Rent paid March 26/1898 and Schaller paid to August 8/98 and I paid for my trouble to this date. (Side margin-$1.15 Com. Coleman).

> September 20 – Annie is still better. I paid Adair $10.15 for-Freight, bought a bolt of cloth to line a upstairs bedroom, a sack of bran, some tobacco, matches, Stamped envelopes and Postal cards. Winterstern came in with some rock samples for assay. Elmer Burgess came and got Williard's papers. Bruce and Cochran came home from the Peak tonight.

> September 24 – A pleasant day. Mr. Williams passed out of this life, at 9 last night only surviving the amputation 2 hours. Mr. Cochran and I went fishing today. Brought home 35. Milton Woolery's folks were here this afternoon and arranged for Clara to board here again this winter. I got a fish bone lodged in my throat at breakfast. It is sore tonight. Bruce came home from the Peak this evening. Elmer Burgess left his Justice books here tonight.

> November 26 – A wonderful fair day, sky cloudless and very little wind. I send Elmer Burgess $150.00 received for his improvements on Lot 3 Block 3 and sent back $125.00 for Lot 4 in Block 3. Attended to various small matters. Annie sends Mrs. Marginnard $1.00 bal. due her from purchase of a Mackintosh.

Although one would assume Perry was related to any other Burgess in the sparsely populated town of Steamboat Springs, the fact is, he wasn't related to any of them. According to a 1938 issue of the *Steamboat Pilot,*

> Elmer Burgess was an outstanding citizen of pioneer times, industrious, honest and enterprising. Better than all he was a good neighbor. If any one needed help in putting up crops or in other ways they could always depend upon him for cheerful assistance. ... Elmer Burgess is the last of the male members of this important family to cross the divide. They did their full part in the early development of the Steamboat Springs section.

Since Perry had relatives in Utah, Elmer could not possibly be a relative. What's more, Perry enjoyed close relations with his relatives and always used titles like "Aunt" and "Uncle." If any of the Burgesses in his diary were related to him in some capacity, he would have indicated his familiarity with them in such a way. As it was, there were several people in the area with the Burgess surname, none of them related to Perry.

Some of his most frequent visitors were his Cheney relatives. Lewis had been a frequent visitor in the 1880s, and Emma's name was mentioned in Perry's diaries as well. In fact, both Ben and Emma purchased land in Steamboat Springs, though there is no record of their ever having lived there. Regardless, Perry must have encouraged his family to visit this remarkable new wilderness he had "discovered," and his enthusiasm for and love of the area was unmistakable.

It wasn't all work and hosting dinners for Pioneer Perry, however. His 1883 diary reveals a man willing to relax when circumstances allow it:

January 1 – Laid around the house all day.

January 7 – Snow all day. Do not do anything but loaf around the house.

January 14, Sunday – Loaf around the house most all day.

Emma White
Sister of Perry A. Burgess
A frequent visitor to
the Burgess Ranch

Annie Burgess
Wife of Perry A. Burgess

Courtesy of Tread of Pioneers Museum,
Steamboat Springs, CO

March 6 - Day bright and pleasant. I feel lazy today and do not work. Saw a few willow grouse and black bird today.

March 22 – Loafed around the house. Clark came down. Dever came down at night. Wrote Maxwell.

In addition to loafing around the house, Perry clearly found letter-writing to be a source of relaxation. He wrote extensively to friends and family, a habit that allowed him to maintain those close bonds he cherished. Through letters, Perry was able to keep abreast of the events involving his family still living in Utah. As the 1880s progressed, however, those beloved relatives began to die off. William Burgess Sr. died in November of 1880, while Uncle Harrison passed on in February of 1883. Living so far away from this side of his family may have left Perry feeling somewhat isolated at times, despite the fact he was surrounded by his wife, children, and scores of friends. His life, after all, followed a similar pattern to the lives of his Mormon relatives as he settled in the wilderness and made a life for himself as a pioneer.

Perry's Steamboat Springs diaries indicate he enjoyed a healthy balance of physical labor, work as an assayer, recreation, and relaxation. During these early years of the 1880s, he split his time between Steamboat Springs and Rich Hill, Missouri, where he continued to perform the duties of an officer of the bank until 1882, when he and his family permanently relocated to Steamboat Springs. When he wasn't working, he traveled a great deal. Despite the fact that the train had not yet come to Steamboat and that any other mode of transportation was painfully slow compared to modern methods, Perry thought nothing of traveling hundreds of miles and crossing state lines as he visited his businesses and family.

Around the homestead, one of Perry's favorite activities was visiting any one of the many natural springs near his home. An 1882 diary entry indicates his interest ran beyond the occasional bath and therapeutic dip in the hot springs:

April 1 – Haulted the last load of hay down from Spring Creek took a bath in the hot springs just (?) in the balance of the day in digging and ditching around the springs – Have at this writing added four new springs to the group. Day warm and bright it looks a little stormy this evening – am very tired tonight.

Life in early Steamboat Springs moved along at a slow pace. The Steamboat Springs Town Company formed in 1884 to promote the area, and resident and historian Graham—another friend and neighbor of Perry's—wrote newspaper articles touting the town's many virtues in hopes of appealing to homesteader hopefuls far and wide. His March 10, 1888 *Montezuma Millrun* article concluded with a flourish:

> The fertility of the soil, the salubrity of the climate, the plentifulness of coal and timber the purity and wholesomeness of its water, the law abiding and enlightening population render Routt county a desirable place for people to prosper and enjoy the blessings of life and home. It is not subject to extremes of climate or dangers of fatal and destructive convulsion of the elements. It is too undulating for cyclones and too broken for blizzards. For the forgoing account and description there is claimed a truthful and candid purpose and an honest motive, if not terseness and elegance in style and diction. To many intelligent and enterprising residents of the county the writer acknowledges that indispensable aid and encouragement which adds to the importance and interest of the subject and strengthens a forcast of the hope of useful efforts and beneficial results.

Perry's own life was relatively idyllic in those first years on his ranch. Aside from visits from grizzly bears and the occasional cold and temporary bout of snow blindness, his days passed with a calm routine. Life took a turn for the worse, however, in early 1885 when his uncle, Lewis Cheney, became ill and was diagnosed with stomach cancer. Although his diary from that year does not indicate that he knew of his uncle's illness, Perry did make a trip to Boulder that March.

March 21 – Emery and I started for Boulder, nooned at Thayer's.

Stopped for the night with Louis Wilson. We are very tired.

March 22 – Snowed and "stuck" terribly all day. Camped for night in the old Cobberly cabin. Am snow blind.

March 23 – Stuck badly. Made Rock creek, my eyes are very bad-

March 24 – Started from Rock Creek at daylight. Got to Mrs. King's at Troublesome at dark, very tired.

March 25 – Took dinner at Hot Sulphur Springs. Stay all night at Ostrander's. Shoeing was very bad today.

March 26 – Got to Cozen's stay all night.

March 27 – Reached Empire. Stormed hard all day. We came down a long gulch on the East slope that made quite a cutoff. Had a terrible hard days work and are tired out.

March 28 – Walked down to the rail road after breakfast. Took the train for Denver. Thence to Boulder where we arrived at sundown. Found Uncle Lewis very low indeed. He cannot get well. Shook hands with a good many friends.

March 29 – Uncle Lewis is no better. Took dinner at S. C. Brown's. Bought some clothes. Very windy.

March 30 – Slept at Macky's. Took breakfast and dinner there also. Uncle Lewis has been unconscious all day – Seems to be gradually sinking.

March 31 – Uncle Lewis died at 9 o'clock this morning.

April 1 – The post Mortern (?) was made today and preparations for the burial-Stayed at Brown's.

April 2 – Uncle Lewis was buried today. Stay for night at Macky's.

April 3 – Loafed around, wrote to Annie and c.

April 4 – Talked with almost everyone.

April 5 – Sunday. Visited.

The April 3, 1885, edition of the *Boulder News and Banner* published Lewis's obituary. Though at times bordering on the macabre with announcements like, "For some time his life has been hanging by a thread, liable to be severed at any moment," the homage was sincerely flattering to one of the city's most prominent and dedicated citizens:

> The deceased was one of our most representative men, and his loss will be keenly felt by the business man, the wealthy and the poor. Mr. Cheney had the interests of the town at heart, and was always ready to lend assistance to any laudable enterprise that would further advance the interests of the place, as had been shown by the active part he has taken in many of the movements put upon foot with this view. He was one of the largest real estate owners in the city, having business blocks upon many of the most prominent corners besides owning a majority of the stock in the First National Bank, of which he is president, a position held by him since he founded the institution in 1877. That he was a man of considerable means is evident from the fact that in addition to his wealth in this city, he owned stock, until recently, in a bank at Holden, Missouri, and in another at Gunnison, in this State. From the very first outset in life he has been successful in financial matters, which goes to prove that he is a very careful man in his business affairs.

In its entirety, the obituary is long and gives details about Lewis's background and personal life. The one detail that was left out? Lewis Cheney was raised a Mormon. In all likelihood, no one in town—not his closest friends or his business associates—knew this fact.

Boulder's businesses closed for half a day in honor of the passing of Lewis Cheney.

Lewis generously took care of his children and wife in his will, leaving them money, stocks in his various business ventures, and real estate. Between his three youngest children—Oliver, Charles, and Linnie—he equally divided his stock in the Steamboat Springs Town Company. Lewis divided and bequeathed his Pearl Street property to his third daughter, Ida, as well as Oliver, Charles, and Linnie.

If residents of Boulder mourned Lewis Cheney's death, Perry Burgess was devastated by it. In the days immediately following his uncle's burial, Perry took the train to Montrose, Colorado, where he bought into Uncompahgre Valley Bank, an institution owned by McConnell that was originally opened as the Bank of Montrose. The two men knew each other from Gunnison, where McConnell was a shareholder in Lewis's bank.

Montrose seemed to offer Perry little comfort, as indicated in his diary from 1885.

> April 10 – Arrived at Montrose at 4
>
> April 11 – Loaf around all day. This is a very uninviting town and country but will probably come out all O.K.
>
> April 12 – McConnell and I drove out Post and talked over business matters.
>
> April 13 – Loaf around. Awful lonsome. Do not hear from home.
>
> April 25 – Fixed up some business matters today. Very pleasant but the air feels soft like it is going to storm some.
>
> April 26 – Sunday-I am very lonesome and would like to be at home.
>
> May 6 – Hot. Business dull. Mac and I went to see the new machinery that is being put in the flouring mill.
>
> May 7 – Warm and dusty-Very dull today.

Despite his homesickness, Perry seemed, at that point, to want to make a new life for himself in Montrose. He returned home in late May, but by early July was back in Montrose, where he bought six business lots and drew up a contract to build a house.

> July 4 – Went to Denver. Thence to Boulder. Crawford went with me.

July 5 – Sunday-Got the Springs folks together and had a business talk.

July 6 – Visited, went to Denver in the evening. Very hot and dusty.

July 7 – Started for Montrose. Had a hot dusty ride. Got to Montrose at midnight.

July 8 – Read up my accumulated mail and wrote some letters. Business dull-Very hot.

July 9 – Wrote letters. Went out to Mc's ranch for tea-

July 10 – Dull, Hot, Muggy. Bought six business lots.

July 11 – Made a contract for house.

On August 14—one month and three days after signing the contract—Perry agreed to sell his share of the Montrose bank to James McClure. On August 19, he headed home to Steamboat Springs.

Never before had Perry displayed such indecisiveness. Perhaps Lewis Cheney's death at age fifty-five caused Perry to take stock of his own life, where he was compared to where he wanted to be. Whatever his thought process, Perry's diary reveals 1885 to be a major turning point in his life in that he spent more time in recreational activities like hunting and fishing and less time at work. His own health was no longer so robust, as he complained of suffering from cholera in July and then general illness throughout September and October. It may well be that Lewis's death put Perry's own mortality under a magnifying glass, and so he was determined to make more of the time he had with family and friends. His professional life seemed to come to an abrupt standstill.

The year 1885 was a big year in the development of Steamboat Springs for one reason: the birth of the first Northwestern Colorado newspaper, the *Steamboat Pilot*. Founded by Boulder printer James Hoyle, the paper's first issue was published July 31, 1885. But the genesis of the newspaper is as interesting as any news it printed.

James Hoyle—friend of both Perry Burgess and Lewis Cheney— heard rumor of the building of a new town called Steamboat Springs. Knowing it was financially backed by prominent Boulder businessmen like Macky and Maxwell, Hoyle decided to find out more. Macky and Maxwell spoke with Hoyle and encouraged him to make Steamboat Springs home to his yet-to-be published newspaper.

Hoyle purchased a used foot-powered job press from the *Boulder News* while the Steamboat Springs Town Company, eager to have a newspaper to promote the many virtues of the valley, donated the property upon which the first official *Steamboat Pilot* office would sit.

According to Hoyle's widow, Jane, and published in Charles Leckenby's *The Thread of Pioneers*,

> We left Boulder June 20 with three teams, one driven by Maxwell's father, one by Marc Maxwell and the other by Mr. Hoyle.
>
> We went thru the mountains over Berthoud Pass and the Gore Range. We went thru Egeria Park and followed the Yampa River into Steamboat Springs, reaching there with the printing plant on July 1, 1885. . .
>
> There were just five cabins then on the bank of the river, constituting what was the town of Steamboat Springs, our new home. These were the homes of James H. Crawford and family, Harvey Wollery and family, Frank Hull and family, and Emery Milner had a small store. These were all the inhabitants of Steamboat Springs could boast at that time. The Suttle family lived just above town and the Burgess family just below town. . .[2]

Leckenby credits the Hoyles with "carrying enlightenment into the wilderness."[3]

The entrepreneurs set up shop in a temporary location since the donated land had no physical building on it yet, and on July 31, the handful of Steamboat residents read about the death and burial of General Ulysses S. Grant as well as a brief article on the sorry quality of beef cattle presently available for sale.

By fall, the *Pilot's* first permanent office was constructed, an 18' x 24' log building which the Hoyles also called home. James Hoyle, who suffered lead poisoning resulting in tuberculosis, died in this home in December of 1894.

Perry's existing diary entries for 1886 are sporadic and lost to the ages altogether after July. So although the event is not recorded, he and Annie welcomed their first daughter, Helen, into the family, probably during the latter half of the year. Son Bruce was twelve or thirteen years old at the time of his sister's birth. A second daughter, Emma, was born in 1889. Again, there exist no known diary entries to herald the birth or anything else for that year.

The year 1889 was important for Perry from a professional standpoint as well. His Uncle Lewis's death in 1885 seemed to leave Perry floundering. For all of his adult life, Perry had been intimately involved with Lewis both personally and professionally. He depended upon his uncle for guidance and advice, and he owed much of his success to Lewis's dedication and mentoring.

Francis Emery (F. E.) Milner, circa 1890
Nephew of Lewis Cheney

F. E. Milner's famous Cabin Hotel, Steamboat Springs, Colorado

Milk Spring, Steamboat Springs, Colorado

In 1889, Perry helped Francis (F. E.) Milner organize and open the Milner Bank and Trust Company, Northwest Colorado's first bank. Located in Steamboat Springs, it was not Milner's first banking operation, as he had grown up in Boulder among the Cheney family and had, for a short time, run the First National Bank of Boulder. Lewis's youngest sons, Oliver and Charles Cheney, were major investors in the Milner Bank and served on its Board of Directors. Another familiar name was associated with this particular bank. According to an article in the January 2, 1889 *Steamboat Pilot*, A. J. Macky purchased, along with Perry, a bank building. Within months, Milner Bank and Trust opened. Milner's success allowed him to open a second bank on the corner of Lincoln Avenue and Ninth Street. Above the bank and connected by a southeastern-facing staircase were real estate offices. According to John Burroughs's book *Steamboat in the Rockies*, the area surrounding that stairway was the first place the snows would melt each spring, thus making it a favorite after-school haunt for energetic children. That bank still stands today.

Despite the bank's success, Perry could not maintain interest in the endeavor and within a few years, he retired. It was the last bank Perry would ever be associated with. His banking career had finally come to an end.

As for Milner, he opened the popular Cabin Hotel in 1910, which was a famous Steamboat Springs landmark until it burned to the ground in the 1930s. According to a newspaper advertisement, rooms rented for $1.00 to $2.50 per day, a rate reasonable enough to make the hotel a tourist favorite. One curious note: Although the hotel boasted one hundred guest rooms, it provided just one bathroom in the entire building.

Milner became an influential resident of Routt County and the Steamboat Springs area. Nearly every profitable business in the region was connected to him in some way. Among his financial investments were the local telephone company, the stage line, and the brick factory. While most investments were sound, Milner's interests in cattle turned out to be his downfall. After World War I, beef prices plummeted as the global market returned to a normal level of activity and production. Ranchers were left with large herds bought at inflated prices and could no longer get top dollar for the cattle. Milner was left holding mortgages not only on the cattle itself, but on the land on which they grazed. He was forced to close his bank, thus ending his reign as the wealthiest man in Steamboat Springs. In 1900, he sold his home in town and moved to his cattle ranch, located outside the city limits. Today that area is a town called Milner.

Perry's diaries for the years 1887 (partial) through 1894 are not known to exist, and so little can be said of his life during that time period other than what is found in public records. The year 1891 brought more sadness to Perry when his eldest daughter, Helen, died on April 27. She had always been a sickly child and was only about five years old when she was buried across from the Burgess ranch in the Steamboat Springs cemetery. Diary entries from 1895 record Perry visiting his beloved girl's grave, sometimes with young Emma in tow.

> April 19 – Went to look for Bruce's horses did not find them visited and put some flowers on our Little Helen's grave. Saw some geese over the river and heard frogs croaking today for the first this year. Rained again this afternoon.
>
> April 25 – Looks some like a storm is coming. Emma and I went up on the hill where the grave yard is and put some flowers on Little Helen's grave.
>
> May 1 – This is the fourth anniversary of our Little Helen's funeral. I went down to the ranch and hauled a small load of hay home rain hard afternoon and snowed all the forenoon a very disagreeable day.
>
> June 9 Sunday – Went up to the graveyard and put some flowers on the graves of Helen, Hazel, Lissie and Mr. Hoyle. Annie and Emma went to take a walk with Willard's folk after noon. I wrote Cousin Maggie today. Pleasant but rain at night.

Perry's early years as a full-time resident of Steamboat Springs brought both joy and sorrow. They were also years of a sort of shifting within the man himself. Gone was the adventurous spirit, replaced instead by a more introspective attitude that allowed him to walk away from all the businesses he had spent his life developing and maintaining. The Perry Burgess who wrote his diaries from 1895 until the end of his life was not the same man who recorded life's daily activities in years prior. "Work" for him now consisted of writing, homesteading, and assaying. His interests took on a more spiritual nature, and the last years of his life would be spent in a quest for the Truth.

Second generation Milner Bank Building - Corner of 9th and Lincoln

CHAPTER 14
Death of a Pioneer

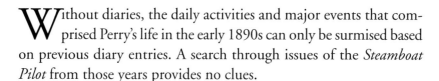

Without diaries, the daily activities and major events that comprised Perry's life in the early 1890s can only be surmised based on previous diary entries. A search through issues of the *Steamboat Pilot* from those years provides no clues.

When his diary entries pick up again in February 1895, it becomes clear that Perry has maintained his letter-writing habit and counts among his correspondents Maggie and Jenny Burgess, his cousins in St. George, Utah; Mrs. Jane Hoyle, widow of the recently deceased founder of the *Steamboat Pilot*; and A. J. Macky, his good friend and business partner, whose correspondence revolves primarily around the Steamboat Springs Town Company.

Specific diary entries from 1895 allow for glimpses into the social activities of Steamboat Springs pioneers:

> March 1 – A beautiful day, clear and bright. The air feels like spring, yet it was 14 below 0 at daylight and zero at 9 P.M. I done some writing today and nursed a sunburn face and eyes that I got yesterday. Tonight there is to be a ball at McWilliam's hall. Bruce is floor manager.

> March 15 – Cold clear and cloudy by spells, mostly clear. There is a big masked ball in town tonight.

> April 29 – Wind blew very hard last night and today we had a dust storm, rain and snow at night. There was a calico ball at Milner's hall. Mary Koll was here to play with us tonight.

> October 11 – Was visiting with Pickett and putting down some accounts. There is to be a ball at Milner's ball hall tonight. Lots of folks in town and Annie had a good day's trade.

As Perry's diary attests, balls were an important form of social activity and communication in an era when technology was nonexistent and people longed for a means to connect and enjoy one another's company. Especially in the relative wilderness of remote towns such as

Steamboat Springs, dance was an easy and acceptable way to socialize with neighbors, potential personal mates, and business associates.

In the October diary entry referenced here, Perry mentions that Annie had a good day's trade. He is referring to his wife's business as a milliner. Her shop and services were often advertised and promoted in the *Steamboat Pilot*:

> Mrs. Burgess invites the ladies of Routt County to call and examine styles of cloaks and skirts, be measured and leave orders for tailor made garments. Prices to suit all classes.[1]

> Mrs. Perry A. Burgess and Mrs. Wren each carry a full line of millinery, notions and children's wear—and a whole lot of other things which a man can't describe which are so dear to the feminine heart.[2]

Perry's 1895 diary reveals something else: He is writing and regularly submits his manuscripts for publication:

> March 3 – Sunday. A cold raw day. Snowed a little by spells all day. I wrote and read. Bruce cleaned his stable. Ada went to stay a month with Mrs. Milner we had roast duck for dinner today that Dr. Kernaghan gave us. I finished my "Anecdotes of the Plains and the Mountains." Snowing very hard at bedtime. Got no mail today. It came in tonight to late to distribute.

> April 1 – Clear most all day, warm and thawed fast. The tra [?] mails that were behind came this afternoon, we have a diluge of papers to read. I sent some main script to the American Field for examination and wrote to Cousin Maggie and Pat Burke and Mr. Standont today.

Perry submitted manuscripts to *Frank Leslie's* and *Harper's* in addition to *American Field*. Although he never says that any of his manuscripts were published, he records days when he writes what he calls "sketches." These may be the *Steamboat Pilot* recollection articles that he published regularly. His diaries from 1896 to the end of his life include mention of these sketches, but the earliest *Pilot* article known to exist today is dated 1897. Even so, it is a reasonable assumption that his diary "sketches" refer to his *Pilot* essays.

Perry, Helen, Annie, and Bruce Burgess with Louis Garbarino (L-R) inside Burgess Cabin, circa 1889
Courtesy of Tread of Pioneers Museum, Steamboat Springs, Colorado

In addition to writing, Perry seemed to be interested in art. Annie and several of her neighbors took painting classes, but Perry's artistic endeavors were limited to doodles and sketches that decorated the pages of his Steamboat Springs diaries.

Perry's diaries also indicate that his health was failing through the second half of the 1890s. It seems that his entire household fall prey to illness quite often in the early months of 1896:

> January 15 – Began rewriting my manuscript today to send to the Ledger. Bruce went to Mr. Turner's to a party last night and slept all day today. My right eye is so I can hardly see out of it today.

> January 20 – As a big storm is so near when us I filled both wood boxes with dry oak wood. Brought in coal, etc. I am afraid I am going to lose my right eye. I fear that a cataract has formed.

> February 5 – Snowed all day. Annie and I both sick with the Grippe. Had the doctor call on Annie. Aunt Mary stayed with us today. Mr. Cody stopped to see us on his way to Denver, wrote to N.Y. Ledger, Farm I. Co. et al.

The Grippe

Perry's February 5 diary entry mentions that he and Annie had "the grippe." Modern doctors recognize it as influenza, a contagious viral disease. But on January 18, 1899, the *Steamboat Pilot* ran an article about the grippe. At the time, Bruce Burgess, Perry's son, was coeditor of the newspaper:

"... It will run the gamut and the sufferer will imagine he has the smallpox, yellow fever, cholera, appendicitis, tape worm, in-growing toenails, hard luck, or a mother-in-law. ... But he'll get over it, and then for the next ten years will lay every pain and ache that afflicts his anatomy to 'that confounded grippe I had in 99. It don't come often but it's a lulu.'"

February 9 Sunday - Was pleasant today, wrote some letters. Kansas Parkinson came home from Montana last night. Emma is quite sick tonight. Annie was not so well today.

February 10 – Pleasant today. Emma had a violent attack of croup this afternoon but seems easier at this 7 P.M. Annie and I are both some better-Sent $10.00 to E. K. & Co. and a Duplicate draft to Hudson Medical Institute.

February 25 – Another clear day, cold in the forenoon but warm in the afternoon, thawed some in the roads and dooryards with a South exposure. Mail came on time. I read and wrote. Annie is taken cold again and is feeling poorly tonight. Quite a number of the neighbors are sick. There is and has been an epidemic of Ear ache, in many cases a gathering which breaks before release hard.

March 4 – A cold blustery day. Annie is so sick that I only leave the house to bring coal and water and go to see the doctor. Aunt Mary is not able to come up today. Grover has only one more year in which to misrepresent and rob this great nation.

Perry A. Burgess, circa 1890

Patent Medicine: Cure or Curse?

Patent medicine was a major industry in America by the mid-nineteenth century. The term "patent medicine" was initially granted to medicines used exclusively by royalty in England. These medicines were exported to America during the seventeenth century, but opportunists quickly began making their own "medicines" at home, using similar yet different—and sometimes deadly—ingredients. Almost none of these medicines or their ingredients were actually patented at all, though some, like Castoria were trademarked. Promoted as near miracle drugs, patent medicines promised to cure everything from venereal disease to cancer.

Unfortunately, these elixirs usually caused more harm than good as many contained generous amounts of alcohol, morphine, cocaine, and opium. Often marketed specifically to children, these drugs sometimes led to the deaths of children whose well-meaning parents confidently administered dose after dose.

With limited medical treatment available, and the rugged conditions of the Colorado frontier, patent medicine was popular as it promised health and vitality. While one will never know, it is possible that Perry and Annie gave patent medicine to their children as well as taking it themselves during times of illness. According to Perry's Steamboat diary his family was often sick, and their daughter Helen died at the age of five.

Perry's March 4, 1896 diary entry reveals more than a wife's illness. It includes one brief but unmistakably disdainful remark concerning President Grover Cleveland, the candidate Perry himself had voted for. Clearly, he disagrees with the president's policies and decisions by this time, which were largely supportive of capitalism. This was the Gilded Age, after all, a time of great industrial expansion and the robber barons who led the way—men like John D. Rockefeller, Andrew Carnegie, and Cornelius Vanderbilt. The rich got wealthier

Helen Burgess, circa 1890
(1886 - 1891)
Courtesy of Tread of Pioneers Museum, Steamboat Springs, CO

while the laboring class worked harder for less pay and under horrific conditions. It was an era of labor strikes and unions; never before had the relationship between politics and money been so obvious. Perry's disillusionment with his country's government must have been severe, for this 1895 diary entry shows his interest in the short-lived Populist Party:

> September 7 – Worked at the ditch in the forenoon and went to the Populist Primary in the afternoon. The weather seems like fall.

It seems that Perry had been undergoing a change of heart, the catalyst for which might have been his uncle Lewis Cheney's death. Though he continued to receive dividend payments from his banks, Perry bowed out of any further day-to-day involvement with them. His attitude toward money and capitalism in general shifted, and he was living a phase of his life dictated by social conscience.

Within three weeks of writing that March 4 diary entry, Perry took on a new job as bookkeeper for the local co-op, a position he would hold until his death.

> March 21 – Last night was warm and windy with some rain and snow. Thawed more today than any day yet. I began work this afternoon on the books of the Co-operative store, went to Lodge for the first time in some months.

Co-ops in the 1890s were much like they are today. Based on the concept of working together and sharing the rewards of the labor, cooperatives are owned and operated by groups of individuals for their own benefit. The roots of the cooperative movement reach back to the late 1790s, and though co-ops in the twenty-first century are no longer considered fringe enterprises but have largely been accepted into mainstream society, that wasn't the case in Perry's day. At that time, co-ops were seen largely as socialist organizations, consisting of people who were frustrated by a perceived inequity inherent in capitalism

Perry clearly fell into this category of consumer and citizen by the late 1890s. His entire life had revolved around the pursuit of money, be it the gold rush or the founding of multiple banks. As a disciple of Lewis's, Perry became an astute businessman who benefited from a capitalistic society. But by the end of the century, it appears he had basically withdrawn from that realm.

Perry wasn't the only Burgess to work in a co-op. His son, Bruce, joined him in the Steamboat Springs co-op for a short period, and his uncle William Burgess Jr. operated his own local co-op in Utah. Perry and William frequently corresponded, so they might have influenced each other in the decision to become an active co-op member.

Uncle William Burgess Jr. (light suit) and family, Utah

Although it would be a stretch to label Perry Burgess a dyed-in-the-wool socialist, there is no denying his shift in attitude. A November 1896 diary entry indicates Perry's involvement with the Ruskin Society:

> November 17 – Worked at Co-op books, wrote Ruskin Co-op Assn. Elmer brought part of a load of coal this P.M. Work at books until 10 P.M.

The Ruskin Cooperative Association was an experimental coop-eration-over-competition colony that existed in Dickson County, Tennessee, from 1894 to 1899. The colony was inspired by the Eng-lish social critic John Ruskin and founded by the American Julius Wayland, who wrote and published a weekly socialist newspaper called *The Coming Nation*. Within fifteen months of its first issue, the paper boasted 60,000 subscribers, making it the country's most popular socialist publication. Profits from the paper financed the development of Wayland's utopian colony, which outsiders monitored and watched with great curiosity. Interestingly, Rich Hill, Missouri, where Perry maintained many connections as a former bank president, became one of the paper's publishing locations in the early 1900s.

Perry's diary shows that Perry and his Aunt Mary enjoyed paid subscriptions to *The Coming Nation*.

> April 2 [1895] – Clear and warm. I hauled hay today and helped Annie wash. Mail is due tonight but at 8 P.M. has not come. Roads are almost impassable. Mary [?] gave me the money to renew her subscriptions to Coming Nation and Light of Truth. Mail came after 9 P.M.

> September 12 [1895] – Wrote out an order Edson Keith [?] for Annie went down to the ranch to see where the new road has cut through the S.E. Core. Sold Kirmaghan and Baur's note the Bk. Paid Willard $25.00 a/c paid Mrs. Bartz a note of Annie's she bought of Stees. Sold the old harness to DeLongi. [Side margin-Sent to Coming Nation for our renewal and books and c.]

> December 14 [1896] – A very cold day, am not well and only read and do a little writing. Help Mr. Leighton with his Treas. a/c. A cold raw day. Send $0.50 to Coming Nation and gave Mr. Parkinson $1.00 to send for the Light of Truth. Read a letter from Mr. Crosby.

The other title mentioned—*The Light of Truth*—was a book published in 1896 that was concerned with spiritualism. Consid-ered by some to be a religion, by others a philosophy, spiritualism is a belief system based on the concept that humans are dual beings, possessing both a physical and a spiritual self. Although the physical ends with death, the spiritual—soul or spirit—continues in another form. Spiritualists allege that communication between the dead and the living is possible via a medium or psychic.

Spiritualism in America took hold in the late 1840s and was particularly appealing as a religion to social reformers who were frustrated with traditional churches for their lack of interest in fighting slavery and promoting women's suffrage. The movement's numbers swelled directly following the Civil War, primarily because those who had lost loved ones in the violence wished to contact them.

By the end of the nineteenth century, the movement's reputation became tarnished as fraudulent mediums were exposed. Even so, believers continued to read any of the numerous newspapers and periodicals pertaining to spiritualism. Perry's diary reveals his interest in the movement, though there is never any mention of séances or meetings with like-minded friends or acquaintances.

It is interesting to consider how far to the left of conservative capitalism Perry had moved by the end of his life. Perhaps his memories of persecution as a Mormon influenced his decision to keep his spiritualist and socialist tendencies and beliefs private. He had, after all, established himself as a reputable businessman, even if he no longer participated actively in those businesses with which he was associated. He had a family to consider as well. If he did indeed have spiritualist leanings, he knew to keep them under wraps. And while there is no way to know exactly *why* he read *The Light of Truth*, he most definitely purchased it.

It could be that Perry was interested in contacting the spirit of his dearly loved daughter Helen, or perhaps even that of his Uncle Lewis. Death may have been a prominent topic in his mind in 1896 because his surviving daughter, Emma, was ill:

> July 4 – A hot dusty day. The people are celebrating on a big
> scale. I do not take any part, but work at the Co-op books in

forenoon and lie about in the shade and read in the afternoon. Went this afternoon for a short walk with little Emma who is now and has for 2 or 3 weeks afflicted with a nervous trouble like St. Vites's Dance, but she is weak and soon worried. At this 10 P.M. a big ball is in progress in the hall next to our rooms.

Although spelled wrong, the disease Perry refers to in his diary was St. Vitus' dance, a disorder characterized by involuntary jerky movements of the face, arms, and/or legs. Associated with rheumatic fever, it was caused by specific strains of streptococci. The jerking and twitching of St. Vitus' Dance disappeared during sleep, but there was no known treatment for the disease, which usually ran its course within several months. Perry's daughter's condition alternately improved and worsened over the course of July until it got so bad he brought in a doctor. By the end of the month, she was well enough to visit the Crawfords at their home.

Perry kept himself busy with hunting and fishing, often with the Crawfords and the Maxwells, old friends and frequent visitors. Fishing in the springs was particularly rewarding. According to Perry's 1898 diary, he caught a total of 125 fish between September 16 and September 25. Subsequent entries reveal that he continually gave away "a mess of fish."

One of his favorite annual activities was to hike to the peak of Mt. Werner, a climb of about 10,564 feet. Travel remained an integral facet of Perry's life, and he frequently visited his family in Adrian, Missouri. Other family members—those still faithful to and active in the LDS Church in Utah—he kept in touch with through regular letters.

The relatives on his mother's side—the Cheneys—were largely uninvolved in the Mormon Church. Perry's Uncle Levi was a force to be reckoned with as he dedicated himself to the RLDS Church and denounced the LDS Church in nearly any public forum that would welcome him. The *Lena Star* newspaper published announcements of Levi's activities:

July 23, 1883: The debate between C.H. Albright and Dr.

Cheney was held last Saturday evening. Three judges were chosen who gave their unanimous descision in favor of C.H. Albright's arguments. If this debate rules the United States, Mormonism will be stopped.

August 10, 1883: Dr. Cheney gave the band boys a lecture on Mormonism last Friday night. The Dr. is the only Mormon we have in Kent and it appears as though he had received a revelation to work in the Mormon cause. We have three churches here now, but there is still room for a new one, if there are any member to build it. "Work while it is called to-day, for the night cometh when no man can work."

EDITOR LENA STAR.- Will you please give me space in your valuable paper to answer your Kent correspondent in your issue of April 18th 1884.

Just so, Mr. C. H. Albright, I did read from the book of mormon, to prove that the practice of all evils and abominations is not mormonism; that is just what we do claim.

But you claimed that polygamy, with all others sins, is mormonism; if as you say, that I read from the book of mormon and proved by the book, that the people at Salt Lake do not follow the teachings of that book; that is just what I did intend to try to show, that polygamy, with all other sins, is not mormonism; and as you say, I proved they do not live after the teachings of the book, they can not be living mormonism; and as C.H. admits that we did make and establish that fact, he thereby admits that all those evils condemned in the book, therefore are not mormonism what he says to the contrary nevertheless.

We thank Mr. Albright for turning around and deciding himself at last in our favor, as two of the judges did in a short time after.

Respectfully yours,
Levi Cheney
Kent, Ill, April 21st 1884

The year 1897 was pivotal in Perry's life. That was the year he began publishing his recollection articles in the *Steamboat Pilot*. His debut article was published on July 7, the last day he wrote in his diary for over a year. Exactly one week later, this advertisement appeared in the *Pilot*:

> For Sale Cheap. 160 acres of patented land, 160 acres timber culture, all fenced, covered by individual water ditches; cuts about 90 tons of hay; thirty acres in grain. Good improvements, residence, stables, sheds, etc. Wagons, carriages and all modern farm machinery; household furniture; thirty odd head of cattle, chickens, hogs, horses, etc. A bargain. Apply to P.A. Burgess, Steamboat Springs.

Perry did sell his ranch and move into town to Oak Street, where he apparently gave up farming—and the writing of his diary—to focus on writing professionally full-time. He also served during his last years as a justice of the peace and the superintendent of the Steamboat Springs Town Company. Perry kept his job as an assayer and added realtor to his résumé in 1898. On February 14, 1900, a *Steamboat Pilot* advertisement announced that Perry had formed a business with Jerry McWilliams, and the partners advertised their services as Burgess & McWilliams, Real Estate, Loan, Rental & Collection Agency.

> Jerry N. McWilliams and Perry A. Burgess have formed a co-partnership, under the firm name of Burgess and McWilliams, to buy and sell on commission, ranches, mining property, houses and lots, ranch products and live stock in quantities, make collections on all accessible points, negotiate loans and promote feasible business enterprises. They will make rental business a specialty. All business entrusted to their care will have prompt, careful, personal attention. Charges reasonable. We respectfully solicit your business.

Age and its accompanying wisdom may have made Perry question his values and beliefs, but it did nothing to slow him down.

Perry's last diary entry was recorded on May 13, 1900. On May 7, he wrote:

> Monday May 7-Since Mar 31st I have been sick, could not work.
> I today pay Killian & J. $10.00 a/c store bill McWilliams paid
> his rent to Coleman to 1st $12.00 less his Com. or his part of it.

He must have been quite seriously ill, for he wrote not at all
between March 31 and May 7. On May 30, this news brief appeared
in the *Steamboat Pilot*:

> The brave old pioneer, Perry A. Burgess, has been making a
> heroic struggle against disease for the past two months. During
> the past week he has been very low and his present condition
> shows little improvement.

On June 6, Perry died, sitting in his chair. He was eight days shy
of his fifty-seventh birthday. He was buried in the Steamboat Springs
Cemetery on the hill overlooking his original 160-acre ranch, next to
his daughter Helen and just feet from C. C. Graham and his child
Charles. His *Steamboat Pilot* obituary read:

> Today, at 1:15 o'clock, the soul of Perry A. Burgess left the pain
> racked body and passed to its reward. While death has long been
> expected it came suddenly while he was sitting in a chair. Mr.
> Burgess was one of Steamboat Springs' pioneers and during his
> long residence here none were ever found to say otherwise than
> that he was a just and honest man. He had to an unwonted
> degree the milk of human kindness, thoughtful, considerate,
> kind and obliging, a good neighbor and a firm friend. His death
> is a shock to the whole community, and the stricken family
> have the sympathy of all. The funeral will be at 1:30 o'clock
> tomorrow afternoon.

Perry—Mormon, pioneer, entrepreneur, prospector, adventurer,
family man—was gone. It was the end of a life, but in a much broader
sense, Perry's death marked the end of a *way* of life. In December
1908, the railroad finally built track through Steamboat Springs.
Residents and investors had been depending upon the development
of the railroad to make Steamboat Springs a major hub of activity
for decades, but it was men like James Crawford, A. J. Macky, and

F. E. Milner whose dogged determination and perseverance made it happen. The debut of the Denver Northwestern & Pacific Railroad in Steamboat was celebrated by hundreds of residents and a brass band, and yet the Perry Burgess who loved the land almost as if it were one of his children would surely have mourned. The railroad crossed over the springs for which the town was named and forever silenced the music of its waters.

While the train connected the Steamboat Springs wilderness with the rest of Colorado and eventually, the whole country, the advent of the motorized automobile just a few years after Perry's death ushered in a culture in which people could come and go on a regular basis without giving much thought to distance and time. As the world became larger, social networking became easier, and soon the car was an icon of technological innovation and progress. How would Perry have fared in this new society?

History has left records of some of those relatives of Perry's. His daughter Emma died of unknown causes on March 13, 1903, in Boulder. A March 6, 1918, *Steamboat Pilot* obituary announced his son Bruce's death:

Bruce B. Burgess

> Word was received Monday that Bruce B. Burgess, a former Routt County resident and pioneer, had passed away following an operation at a Cheyenne hospital. The funeral was held at Boulder, Colo. On March 1, the remains being laid away in the Boulder cemetery. Deceased was the father of Miss Frankie Burgess, who makes her home in Steamboat with her mother Mrs. Frank McClelland, and it was by the daughter that word of Mr. Burgess' death was received. In addition to this daughter he is survived by his mother, Mrs. A. Justis of Stockton Ill. Mrs. Mary L. Sampson, who died in Routt county February 21, was a grand aunt of Mr. Burgess.

Bruce had married Mary Shaw less than one year after his father's death, but the couple divorced in 1912.

Annie Burgess remarried. Her second husband was a longtime Stephenson County, Illinois, friend with the last name of Justus. Annie died in 1926 and was buried next to her son Bruce in Columbia Cemetery in Boulder, Colorado.

The Burgess legacy lives on in Steamboat Springs even today. Burgess Creek—a vacation area boasting townhomes, lodges, and condominiums and located just a mile from Perry's beloved Mt. Werner—is named after him and includes Burgess Creek Road. A chairlift at the Steamboat Ski Resort is named Burgess Creek, and a twenty-first century program called Steamboat Unbridled aimed at developing the businesses at the base of the ski resort included the building of Burgess Creek Plaza.

Perry Burgess was just one man—a man with a yearning for adventure and fortune whose simple Mormon roots led him to the American West, where the call of the wild enticed him to follow path after path of discovery and development. He had a key role in pioneering the Colorado wilderness, from the banks of Boulder to the gold rush at Hahns Peak and eventually amid the vast, breathtaking beauty of Steamboat Springs.

He was a man whose dedication and vision had a major impact on the expansion of the western wilderness, and yet he delighted most in the simple things—the sight of an early spring robin, a day's pleasant weather, the reading of a loved one's letter. He earned himself a small fortune in a society he eventually would come to question, and after a lifetime of doggedly trekking across the country, he found his greatest joy in the placid art of writing.

Perry Abraham Burgess was a simple yet perplexing American trailblazer. One must wonder how many more Perry Burgesses figured in this nation's rich and rewarding history. May his story never be forgotten.

1893

THE "BURGESS" GUN
12-GAUGE REPEATING SHOTGUN.
LATEST—QUICKEST—SIMPLEST—SAFEST.
ADDRESS,
DOUBLE HITS IN 1-8 SECOND.   THE BURGESS GUN CO.,
THREE HITS IN ONE SECOND.
SIX HITS IN LESS THAN THREE SECONDS.   BUFFALO, N. Y.

The Burgess Gun Company, Buffalo, N.Y. Owned by Andrew Burgess, the first cousin of Perry's father Abram. One of the most prolific gun designers of his time, Burgess designed a unique 12 gauge folding pump shotgun. Andrew married Eudora Tiffany, a granddaughter of the founder of Tiffany Jewelers. A true renaissance man like his cousin Perry, Andrew was also known for his long-term partnership with Mathew Brady of Washington, D.C. the father of photojournalism. Together, they photographed some of Washington's most prominent citizens. Burgess later took ownership of the D.C. studio following Brady's departure.

You will find other interesting Burgess relatives of Perry on the following pages.

Biographical Notes

The following people figure prominently within the Burgess diaries or served as business partners in one or more of the Burgess-Cheney enterprises.

William W. Adair – Native of Tennessee, and brother of Samuel Adair. Active in the merchandising business until 1901. Eventually became a rancher with more than 400 acres. Frequently noted in the Burgess Steamboat Springs diary.

William Allison – Husband of Nettie Cheney, the daughter of Lewis and Sarah Milner Cheney. Came to Boulder with Lewis Cheney in the 1870s. Lived on Block 173, near the N.W. corner of Mapleton and Broadway. He became president of the First National Bank after the death of A. J. Macky. President Taft once accepted an invitation by Allison to an Ohio alumni event held in Boulder. Served on the Colorado Chautauqua board of directors. Died tragically from injuries sustained when his Ford Model T ran off a small cliff and "turtled" on top of him.

Abram Burgess – Born 1820 in New York, the son of William and Violate Burgess and father of Perry Burgess. Died on the trail during the Mormon Exodus.

Annie Mapes Burgess – Wife of Perry Burgess, mother of Bruce, Helen and Emma Burgess. Born February 8, 1848, in Ohio, Annie probably spent a majority of her youth in Jo Daviess County, Illinois. Died in 1926, and was buried with her son Bruce and daughter Emma in the Columbia (Pioneer) Cemetery, Boulder, Colorado, near the Cheney family plot.

Bruce Burgess – Only son of Perry Burgess and Annie Mapes, born September 9, 1876, in Bates County, Missouri. During the early years of Steamboat Springs, Bruce was one of few children living in the area. Business partner of Charles H. Leckenby of the *Steamboat Pilot* newspaper near the turn of the century. Moved away from Steamboat

Springs following the death of his father Perry. Died February 26, 1918, and is buried in the Columbia (Pioneer) Cemetery, Boulder, Colorado.

Elmer Burgess – Although mentioned frequently in the Burgess Steamboat diaries, there is no family relationship to Perry A. Burgess. A pioneer resident of Routt county who later died in Perma, Montana, on April 23, 1938. Had two sons and two daughters, Fay Burgess, Harry Burgess, Ruby Burgess and Mrs. William H. Hitchens.

Emma Burgess – Perry and Annie Burgess's third child and second daughter. Born March 9, 1889, in Steamboat Springs Colorado. The namesake of Perry's mother and half sister, Emma Samantha. Mentioned frequently throughout the later years of the Burgess diary, often in regard to health. Died in 1902. Buried in the Boulder Columbia (Pioneer) Cemetery next to her mother Annie and brother Bruce.

Harrison Burgess – Uncle of Perry Burgess. Leader in the Mormon Church and citizen of Utah. Although not involved in the Mountain Meadows Massacre, his descendants would later come to ranch on the property for decades.

Helen Burgess – First daughter of Perry and Annie Burgess. She was born in 1886 and died at the age of five on April 27, 1891. Helen is buried with her father Perry in the Steamboat Springs Cemetery.

Margaret Burgess – Referred to as "Cousin Maggie" in the Burgess Steamboat diaries. A favorite relative of Perry's and sister to "Cousin Jennie Burgess."

Melancthon Wheeler Burgess – Uncle of Perry Burgess. Mormon Pioneer, resident of Utah. Owned one of the first homes in St. George, Utah.

Jennie Caroline Burgess – Cousin of Perry Burgess, sister of "Cousin

Maggie" mentioned frequently in the Burgess Steamboat diaries. Born July 19, 1880, in St. George, Utah. A favorite relative of Perry, and well known throughout the Burgess family. Performed extensive research on William Burgess Sr., and his many descendants that was later part of a project to compile the information for the Library of Congress. Married Samuel Wallace Miles July 11, 1900, and died January 13, 1972, in Parowan, Iron County, Utah.

Semantha Cheney Burgess – Born December 1, 1823, the daughter of Ephraim and Harriet Law Cheney. Married Abram Burgess and later became the mother of diarist Perry Burgess. Following the death of Abram, she married Dr. Ben White. She died sometime after 1900.

Willard H. Burgess – Although mentioned frequently in the Burgess Steamboat diaries, there is no family relationship with Perry Burgess. A pioneer resident of Routt county.

William Burgess Sr. – Grandfather of Perry A. Burgess. A Deacon of the early Mormon Church, and was closely associated with Joseph Smith, Brigham Young, and other leaders of the Church. Was a supervisor during the building of the Kirtland and Nauvoo Mormon temples. Served as a Captain of some of the first wagons to cross from Nauvoo, Illinois, into the Salt Lake Valley.

William Burgess Jr. – Uncle of Perry Burgess. Only one state apart, William and Perry remained in contact throughout their lives. William and Joseph Smith Jr. attended the 'School of the Prophets' together. A colonel in the Utah Militia. Missioned to the Indians at the request of Mormon leadership at Fort Lemhi, the first white settlement in what would later be the state of Idaho.

Charles Cheney – Son of Lewis and Sarah Milner Cheney, and known often as "Cousin Charlie" in the Burgess diary. Born in Holden, Missouri, in 1873. Came to Boulder, Colorado, as a young boy and was greatly involved in the Cheney family enterprises including mining, banking, and real estate. Became president of the First National Bank of Colorado in 1919 and served until the bank failed during the Great Depression. Served as treasurer of Colorado University. Married Louisa "LuLu" Chase, daughter of famed photographer Dana B. (D. B.) Chase of Colorado. Lulu was known for her work on the Board of the Parks Department and support of the Boulder Day School.

Emma Cheney – Daughter of Lewis and Margaret Blair Cheney, and first cousin of Perry A. Burgess. Married Henry Conner in 1875 and was an early socialite of Holden, Missouri.

Dr. Levi Cheney – Uncle of Perry A. Burgess. Longtime resident of Jo Daviess and Stephenson County, Illinois, during Perry's boyhood years. Levi Cheney and Dr. Ben White were both doctors of Indian and patent medicine. Married Amelia Mercy Clark; had daughters Hattie and Samantha. Samantha Cheney (Thompson) is the great grandmother of co-author Travis Thompson and one of multiple children named in honor of Perry Burgess's mother. Levi was associated with Joseph Smith III, the son of the Mormon Prophet, and received multiple visits from Joseph in 1887. Later Dr. Cheney would move to Independence Missouri, and take residence on Short Street. near the temple lot area. Following his death, his daughters would remain on Short Street. and become neighbors of Joseph and his family.

Ida Cheney – Daughter of Lewis Cheney and Margaret Blair Cheney. Educated at Hellmoth College in Canada. Married Seth Bradley, banker from Denver and Kansas City. Held property in Steamboat Springs. Like her father, suffered and died from stomach cancer and was buried in the Cheney family plot in Holden, Missouri.

Lewis Cheney – Uncle and lifelong business partner of Perry A. Burgess. California 49er and Bozeman Trail pioneer who owned multiple banks throughout Missouri and Colorado.

Oliver Cheney – Son of Lewis and Sarah Milner Cheney, and a first cousin of Perry A. Burgess. Born November 23, 1870, in Holden, Missouri. Resident of early Boulder, and later owned a large ranch near the head of Morrison Creek in Steamboat Springs. Received valuable plots of Boulder and Steamboat Springs real estate from the estate of his father. Owned the Camera building, Trestez Funeral Home, and other Boulder real estate holdings. Unlike brother Charles, Ollie held few positions within the family banking businesses. Was involved with F. E. Milner in mining at Hahns Peak. Stockholder of the Yampa Valley Bank at Hayden, Colorado, and served as both vice president and president of the Milner Bank and Trust Company until the time of the bank's failure.

Sarah Milner Cheney – Second wife of Lewis Cheney. Matriarch of the Cheney family. Died 1900 in Cleveland, Ohio, while visiting friends with her daughter. She is buried in the Cheney family plot at the Boulder Cemetery.

Sarah, widow of Lewis Cheney, was a "lady of large means."

Boulder Camera, September 13, 1890

Henry C. Conner – Son-in-law of Lewis Cheney. Resident of Holden, Missouri, and later, Kansas.

Edward Cody – Mining partner of Perry Burgess and Andrew Macky at Hahns Peak, Routt County, Colorado.

John G. Cope – Banking partner of Lewis Cheney and Perry Burgess. Executor of the Lewis Cheney estate along with William H. Thompson and a trustee for Lewis's sons, Oliver and Charles.

John moved from Ohio to Holden, Johnson County, Missouri, in 1869, a true era of success for the community. Entered into the grain and milling business with Henry C. Conner, Lewis Cheney's son-in-law.

Disposed of his partnership with Henry Conner in 1872 and purchased several shares in the First National Bank of Holden. Newly organized by Lewis Cheney and I. M. Smith, the bank experienced significant growth while the town of Holden expanded. John was elected cashier of the bank, a position he held until the departure of Lewis for Boulder to establish the new First National Bank. At the request of Lewis Cheney, was called to Boulder and became an officer of the First National.

Also a partner in The Boulder Land and Improvement Company, which designed and platted the Mapleton Hill area of Boulder. Other members of the company include Boulder pioneer Andrew J. Macky and James P. Maxwell, all partners in the early Cheney enterprises.

Became president of the First National Bank of Boulder following the death of Lewis Cheney in 1885. Unexpectedly, John himself passed away in 1886, at which time A. J. Macky was elected president of the bank. The Cope children remained in Boulder and were often noted in the *Camera* society pages for their lavish children's parties.

Henry A. Crawford – Pioneer of Routt County and brother of Steamboat Springs founder James H. Crawford.

James H. Crawford – James and wife Margarent Crawford are the founders of Steamboat Springs. Had children John, Logan, and Lulie. Built one of the first two cabins at Steamboat Springs and spent his life promoting the area. Friend and business partner of Perry Burgess and Lewis Cheney. The diaries of Lulie Crawford and Perry Burgess are some of the only records of early Steamboat Springs.

Delancy – Childhood friend of Perry Burgess from Jo Daviess County, Illinois. His death is noted in the Burgess Steamboat diaries.

W. H. Dever – Pioneer prospector and assayer of Steamboat Springs, Colorado.

John Ellet – Served as a Union Colonel in the Civil War. Commander of the ram boats Lancaster and later the Switzerland. Together with his uncles and their fleet of ram boats, they attacked the city of Memphis and forced the Confederate surrender. Relocated to Colorado after the war and became an early mayor of Boulder, serving multiple terms. Served as a stockholder and director of the First National Bank of Boulder.

George F. Fonda – Arrived in Boulder in 1874 and played a major role in the town's development. Joined Macky Hose Team in 1875 and was the first foreman. Elected vice president of the First National Bank of Boulder after the turn of the century, long after the deaths of Lewis Cheney and Perry A. Burgess, who never partnered with Fonda. A. J. Macky and Fonda held major interests in the Boulder Milling and Elevator Company, which probably led to later associations in the First National. George and his brother Gilles were well known and active in early Boulder fire control, serving in the Macky and Boulder Hose Companies.

Perry Burgess and Lewis Cheney were Mormons driven from Nauvoo at a young age, and ironically the Fonda family had a connection to the city of Nauvoo as described in the

Portrait and Biographical Record of Denver and Vicinity, Colorado - 1898

> "The parents of our subject are Henry D. and Catherine (Farrell) Fonda, who were natives of the Mohawk Valley, N. Y., and of Pennsylvania, respectively. The father was a civil engineer, and for years in the early days of the New York Central & Hudson River Railroad he was employed in that capacity by the company. Later he removed to Illinois, and settled on a farm in Hancock County, near the town of Augusta. He was county surveyor there for five terms and helped drive the Mormons out of Hancock County when they became obnoxious to the citizens."

Louis Garbarino – Pioneer of Routt County and close friend of Perry A. Burgess as evident by multiple entries in the Burgess Steamboat diaries. Well known throughout the early Steamboat Springs community.

Charles "C. C." Graham – An early settler on Elk River who later moved to Steamboat Springs, where he lived for many years. A local civic leader. Participated in the Populist Party with Burgess. Elected state senator serving in the Ninth and Tenth general assemblies. Sold real estate in early Steamboat and was a public notary. Later moved to California where he resided for more than 15 years until his death. After his death, his body was returned to Steamboat Springs, and buried on the hill in the Steamboat Springs Cemetery.

H. E. Hawes – Judge and prominent citizen of Holden, Johnson County, Missouri. Stockholder in the Bank of Holden and business partner of Perry Burgess and Lewis Cheney. Involved in the real estate and insurance business, of which many of Perry's family were long-time customers. Employed Ben White—stepfather of Burgess—as a livestock broker in the 1870s. "Judge Haws" is included in just one diary entry, when he arrives to visit Perry's mother Semantha in Holden Missouri

James Hoyle – Boulder, Colorado newspaperman. Upon the urging of the Steamboat Springs Town Company, Hoyle relocated to Steamboat Springs in 1885. James, and wife Jane, were close friends of Perry Burgess. Founder of the *Steamboat Pilot* newspaper, first issue published July 31, 1885.

Frank Hull – One of the earliest citizens of Steamboat Springs, Colorado. Took up his land in a pre-emptive claim in March 1884. Sold his land to William W. Adair in 1901.

Alfred E. Lea – Member of the inner circle of Cheney business associates from the beginning when the First National Bank of Boulder was established. A major shareholder in the Steamboat Springs Town

Company until after the turn of the century. The Lea-Cheney relationship may have begun much earlier, as both men were originally from the border counties of Missouri. Alfred Lea has a unique history all his own and is often noted in the Burgess Steamboat diaries.

Alfred's father, Dr. Pleasant Lea, owned property in both Missouri and Boulder, Colorado. Dr. Lea was killed by Kansas soldiers during the Border War. Alfred's brothers fought with Quantrill's Raiders and began training as elite Confederate guerillas. Brother Captain Joseph Lea is attributed with being one of Quantrill's best officers.

Married Hersa Coberly and had one son, Homer Lea, who became a general in the Chinese Army. Homer Lea was instrumental in training the Chinese Imperial Reform Army, using American soldiers as instructors. Lea was also an author of two works on geopolitics: *The Valor of Ignorance* predicted the rise of Japanese militarist aggression and a Japanese empire in the Pacific, while *The Day of the Saxon*, commissioned by British Field Marshal Lord Frederick Roberts, predicted the rise of a greater German Reich based on national supremacy and ethnic purity.

Charles H. Leckenby – Pioneer newspaperman of Northwestern Colorado. Editor of the *Steamboat Pilot* newspaper. Published the book *Thread of Pioneers*, a classic history of Steamboat Springs and Routt County, Colorado. Partnered with Bruce Burgess during his early days with the *Steamboat Pilot*.

Andrew J. Macky – Born in Herkimer County, New York, on November 11, 1834. A carpenter by trade, he came to Boulder in 1859 via an ox team. Organized the First National Bank of Boulder with Lewis Cheney and I. M Smith in 1877. Early stockholder, then director and vice president. Following the death of John G. Cope in 1886, was elected president until his own death June 11, 1907. Macky had no blood heirs and left his estate to Colorado University. As a Steamboat Springs Town Company shareholder, Macky and Burgess remained in constant contact by mail and frequent board meetings.

Following Macky's death, his private compartment was opened at the First National Bank and was found to contain large quantities of paper money, stocks, bond, and numerous bottles filled with gold nuggets. His estate donated over $300,000 for the building the Macky Auditorium, which continues to stand prominently on the Colorado University-Boulder campus today.

Mapes family – Parents of Annie Mapes Burgess and frequent visitors to the Burgess Steamboat Springs cabin. Longtime residents of Jo Daviess County, Illinois, where Perry Burgess spent much of his childhood.

James P. Maxwell – Entered into the lumber business on South Boulder Creek in 1863 along with brother-in-law Captain Clinton Tyler. Later elected to the first session of the Colorado State Senate in 1876 and served until 1880. Maxwell took an interest in securing the appropriations for the state university in Boulder. Elected mayor of Boulder in 1878. Had extensive ranching interests in Colorado. Served as president of the Steamboat Springs Town Company and a frequent visitor to the Burgess Steamboat cabin.

James McClure – Longtime partner in multiple Burgess and Cheney enterprises. Married Martha J. Warford of Montrose, and afterward became interested as a stockholder in six banks from Missouri to Colorado. Served as mayor of Montrose, Colorado, for multiple terms. Represented Montrose and Delta counties in the eleventh state legislature in 1897.

Sam Morrison – Husband of Perry Burgess's half-sister, 'Addie.' Sam and Addie lived in Missouri near Perry's mother in Holden.

Jerry N. McWilliams – A prominent and respected early citizen of Steamboat Springs Colorado. Sold Steamboat Springs real estate with Perry Burgess during his last years. Cattleman and avid investor in Routt County.

Frederick A. Metcalf – Arrived from New York in 1888 and became a early resident of Routt County. Metcalf was a cashier of the Milner and Company Bank for many years, eventually that partnership dissolved. Invested in Steamboat Springs real estate.

Francis Emery Milner – Born near Marion, Indiana, on April 10, 1861. Came to Colorado as a young boy with his parents and settled in Boulder. Son of William I. Milner and nephew of Sarah Milner Cheney. As an impressionable young man, F. E. Milner was exposed to the Burgess and Cheney family enterprises. Arrived 1880 in Steamboat Springs and became closely associated with the advancement of Northwestern Colorado. Homesteaded land near the mouth of Walton Creek. Erected a small store and hotel, two of the earliest structures in Steamboat Springs. In 1889, established Milner and Company Bank with Perry Burgess as cashier, the first bank in Northwest Colorado. The bank eventually became the Milner Bank and Trust, which failed in 1918. Owned a large ranch which later became the town of Milner, Colorado. Major shareholder in the Steamboat Springs Town Company.

Johnny O'Connor – Hahns Peak prospector and partner of Perry Burgess.

J. P. Orr – Attorney from Holden, Missouri. Stockholder and Director in the Bank of Holden. Longtime friend of Perry Burgess and frequently mentioned as "Orr" in the Burgess Steamboat diaries. Elected Holden City Attorney in 1872, 1875, and 1879.

Colonel Ivers Philips – Early stockholder and officer of the First National Bank of Boulder, Colorado. Long-time director of the bank, served with Perry and Lewis during their early years in Boulder. A prominent man of Boulder and a great curiosity to the local press. Lived in a massive, four story home, built in 1882 at the SW corner of 11th and Pine streets in the Mapleton Hill district. Donated a large art collection to Colorado University, which later hung in the classroom of Dr. J. Raymond Brackett, C.U.'s first dean.

Pulsipher Family – In-laws of the Burgess family.

S. B. Reid – Early settler of the Elk River Valley.

> "S. B. Reid was the first white man to fence, clear and break land, build a habitation and plant and cultivate a crop in this valley. No surveys had yet been made and the settler then had only to select a nice fertile piece of land, with wood, water, pasturage, game, fish and other conveniences near at hand, and like the badger go to digging."

> - Perry Burgess, 1896 "Some Early History"

Merrick A. Rogers – Native of Jo Daviess County, Illinois. First cousin of Lucien Rogers, who accompanied Burgess on the 1866 Bozeman Trail cattle drive. The Rogers family owned shares in the Bank of Holden and were lifelong friends and associates of the Burgess and Cheney families. Practiced law in Denver and served as a judge. Later served with James P. Maxwell on the Colorado General Assembly. Perry frequently wrote to or received letters from the Rogers family in his Steamboat diaries. The suicide of Judge Rogers is a well-known incident in Steamboat Springs history.

> Suicide of Judge Rogers

> One of Steamboat's Esteemed Citizens takes the Giant Powder Route.

> ...He had taken a stick of giant powder that he had purchased of Hugus & County a short time before, went down back of the hotel, where he and his wife were boarding, to near the river, took about one-third of the stick attached the fuse and cap, and it is supposed that he lighted the fuse with his cigar, put the cigar back in his mouth, laid down on his back on the giant powder, crossed his legs and calmly waited for the moment to arrive when his soul would be sent to eternity...

> *The Steamboat Pilot* Nov. 27, 1901

O. A. Rogers – Native of Jo Daviess County, Illinois. Stockholder in the Bank of Holden. Brother of Colorado Senator Merrick Rogers and cousin of Lucien Rogers, who joined Burgess on the Bozeman Trail. Burgess was known to call on O. A. Rogers during his visits to Holden, Missouri.

Geo Roush – Mentioned briefly in the Burgess Bozeman Trail diary. This is probably the Geo. Roush who is found in Lena, Illinois, and a member of the local gun club. Geo. Roush is often noted in the *Lena Star* when competing at local sharpshooting events with the White and other families.

Johnny Sampson – Son of Mary Sampson and first cousin of Annie Mapes Burgess. Neighbor of the Burgess family in Routt County. Married Ora L. Adams on May 9, 1900.

Mary Sampson – Aunt of Annie Mapes Burgess. Originally from Jo Daviess County, Illinois, Mary and son John were attracted to Routt County in the 1880s, probably at Perry's urging. Mary and family were neighbors of the Burgess family and are frequently found in the Burgess Steamboat diaries as "Aunt Mary."

Abram Shippy – Present with Burgess and Crawford during their 1880 exploration trip into the Yampa Valley and Steamboat Springs. Found as "Abram Shippy" in Crawford's diary and "A. Shippy" in Burgess's diaries.

Israel M. Smith – Early partner of Perry Burgess and Lewis Cheney. Stockholder and bank officer in the Bank of Holden, Bates County National Bank, and the First National Bank of Boulder. Later was an officer at the Bank of Kansas City. Smith was robbed and killed in 1881 at a Kansas City train station when he was thrown over a cliff by his assailants.

James Harvey Stees – A resident of Lena, Illinois. Married Abigail (Abbie) Sampson on December 3, 1879, and later moved to Routt County where they were neighbors of the Burgess family. Annie Mapes Burgess's mother was also a Sampson from Lena, Illinois. Stees and wife had four children: William, Rueben, Henderson and Lily.

Ingram Starkey – Banking and prospecting partner of Perry Burgess and Lewis Cheney in both Missouri and Colorado. As per the 1870 U.S. Federal census for Holden, Missouri, Ingram was born about 1830. Served in the Civil War and reached the rank of Captain by the end of the conflict. Later became a prominent lumberman from Holden, Missouri. Served as a City Councilman in 1882 with H.C. Conner, son-in-law of Lewis Cheney. Listed in the 1872 Charter of the Bank of Holden as holding only three shares of common stock, with a total value of $300.00.

Horace Suttle – Built and operated the first lumber mill in Steamboat Springs. He resided there briefly before moving on to California. As per the book *San Diego and Imperial Counties, California.* "... his political allegiance is given to the Socialist party."

William H. Thompson – Resident of Boulder and officer of the First National Bank of Boulder. With John G. Cope, was appointed Executor of the Lewis Cheney estate in 1884.

Flavious J. Tygard – Known as Captain F. J. Tygard, a friend and business associate of Perry Burgess and Lewis Cheney. Lived at 113 Pine Street in Butler, Missouri. Served as cashier, vice president and later president of the Bates County Bank following the departure of Burgess and Cheney to Colorado. Led the efforts to bring electric lighting to Butler, now known as the 'Electric City.' Frequently mentioned in the Burgess Steamboat diaries and was a partner in the 1880 prospecting trip into the Yampa Valley with Crawford and Burgess. The Bates County Bank failed in 1906, and Tygard was charged with fraud and sentenced to serve in the federal penitentiary.

William Tygard – Brother of F. J. Tygard. Brokered livestock until July, 1881, when he became a stockholder in the Bank of Rich Hill during Perry Burgess's presidency. Married Minnie Gill and later became president of the bank following Perry's departure to Steamboat Springs. The Bank of Rich Hill failed in 1906, same year as the Bates County Bank. The Tygards were prominent citizens of Bates County, Missouri.

William E. Walton – An early pioneer of Steamboat Springs. Entered the Yampa Valley in 1875 with Perry Burgess following the directions of James H. Crawford. His 160 acre grant included what is today Lincoln Avenue and a large portions of the downtown area of Steamboat Springs. A new marriage to Cora Allen in 1879, the demands of his Missouri banking, and other interests likely drew Walton away from Colorado. He finally returned, decades later on vacation, long after the death of his partners Perry Burgess and Lewis Cheney.

Adalade F. White – Daughter of Ben and Semantha Cheney White. Half-sister of Perry Burgess, and commonly referred to as 'Addie' in the Burgess Steamboat diaries. Born in Jo Daviess County, married Samuel J. Morrison, a favored recipient of Perry's many letters. Lived in Bates and Johnson County, Missouri, and was a frequent visitor to Steamboat Springs. Perry would often write his mother Semantha, his sister Addie, and brother-in-law Sam on the same day.

Dr. Benjamin Franklin White – Known as Ben, he was the second husband of Semantha Cheney Burgess, and the stepfather of Perry Burgess. A doctor and California 49er, White lived in Jo Daviess County, Illinois, and later, Bates and Johnson counties in Missouri. Traveled to Steamboat Springs where he owned property for a short period of time in the 1890s.

Emma Semantha White – Daughter of Ben and Semantha Cheney White, and half-sister of Perry Burgess. Born in Jo Daviess County but moved with her family to Missouri as a young child. Owned property briefly in Steamboat Springs near the Burgess Ranch. Frequently visited Yampa Valley but doesn't seem to have ever been a resident.

Pony Whitmore – Beloved pioneer prospector, outdoorsman of Routt County. With W. H. Dever, located the Gilpen mine at the head of the Elk River.

Harvey Woolery – Early rancher of Routt County. Steamboat Springs neighbor of Perry Burgess. Perry and Harvey lived on the north side of the Yampa River, while Harvey's brother Milton lived on the South. Born in Cooper County, Missouri, very close to the areas that held Cheney, Burgess, and Walton banking interests. Acquired 160 acres in Steamboat through pre-emption laws. Eventually owned over 400 acres of Routt County property. Married Sarah Murphy on Nov. 2, 1871.

Milton Woolery – Brother of Harvey, early settler of Routt County. Lived on the opposite side of the Yampa River from Harvey and Perry Burgess.

Notes

Chapter 1
Hannah Dustin - Perry's Infamous Ancestor

1. In his 1874 book *Indian Wars of New England* (Boston: B. B. Russell & Co.), Robert B. Caverly states that the group traveled approximately 75 miles at that point. He points out that "Indian computations of that time" put the mileage closer to 250 miles (p. 18). Other sources report miles covered at 100 and 60. There is no way to provide an exact number of miles. Regardless, the journey was long and harsh.

2. John Greenleaf Whittier, *Legends of New England* (Baltimore: Genealogical Publishing Company, 1992), 128.

3. From Chapter 10, *Province Laws*, Massachusetts Archive.

4. The letter can be found at www.hannahdustin.com, where it has been reprinted from an account of Hannah's story written by H.D. Kilgore.

5. C. H. Pope, *The Cheney Genealogy*, (Boston: Charles H. Pope, 1897), 222.

6. Ibid, 223.

7. Ibid, 223-24.

8. Franklin Ellis, *The History of Catturaugus, New York: Illustrations and Biographical Sketches of Some of Its Prominent Men and Pioneers* (Philadelphia: L.H. Everts, 1897), pp. 390-99. Available online at http://www.paintedhills.org/CATTARAUGUS/Freedom1879Bios/Freedom1879Hist.htm, courtesy of Painted Hills Genealogy Society.

9. Ibid.

Chapter 2
Early Mormon Era - Birth of Perry Burgess

1. Unlike common seer stones, the Urim and Thummim were purportedly provided by God for the purpose of translating the golden plates.

2. Excerpted from Chapter I: Early Life, http://penelope.uchicago.edu/Thayer/E/Gazetteer/People/William_Hyde/Journal/1*.html, courtesy of Bill Thayer. The original handwritten diary resides in the Historian's Library, The Church of Jesus Christ of Latter Day Saints.

3. Hales, Kenneth G., "Autobiography of Harrison Burgess" in

Windows, a Mormon Family, (Tucson: Skyline Printing, 1985), available online at http://www.sedgwickresearch.com/burgess/ burgess,h.htm, courtesy of Sedgwick Research.

4. Ibid.

5. "The Temple After Half a Century," The New York Times, p. 15, December 25, 1887. Available online at http://query.nytimes.com/ mem/archive-free/pdf?_r=1&res=9805E7D7163AE033A25756C 2A9649D94669FD7CF.

6. "A Short Sketch of the Life of William Burgess, Jr., the son of William Burgess and Violate Stockwell" available online at http:// contentdm.lib.byu.edu/cdm4/document.php?CISOROOT=/ FH30&CISOPTR=45691&REC=18

7. From *The History of Elam Cheney, My Grandfather.* Privately donated and housed in the Salt Lake City LDS Library.

8. Library of Congress, Manuscript Division, WPA Federal Writers' Project Collection.

9. *History of Zerah Pulsipher*, 1789-1872, written by himself. Available online at http://www.johnpratt.com/gen/7/z_pulsipher.html.

10. Rigdon, Sidney, "Oration: Delivered on The 4th of July, 1838." Printed as a pamphlet and housed in the LDS Church Library. Available online at *SaintsWithoutHalos.com*, http:// saintswithouthalos.com/p/sr_380704.phtml.

11. Jensen, Andrew, *The Historical Record, a Monthly Periodical* (Salt Lake City: self-published, December 1888), p. 673.

12. McBride, James, *The Autobiography of James McBride, 1818-1876*, pp. 12-13. Typescript, L. Tom Perry Special Collections, Harold B. Lee Library, Brigham Young University. Available online at http://www.heartslinked.com/peterson_families/ancestors/james_ mcbride_autobiography_3.htm#massacre.

13. Pulsipher, John, and Donald N. Burgess, *A Mormon Diary as Told by John Pulsipher, 1835-1891*, 2008.

14. Known in many historical documents as P.A. Burgess.

15. Woods, Fred E., "Gathering to Nauvoo: Mormon Immigration 1840-46," in *Nauvoo Journal*, Fall, 1999, p. 50. Available online at http://www.mormonhistoricsitesfoundation.org/publications/ nj_fall1999/NJ11.2_Woods.pdf.

16. Smith, Inez Davis, *The History of the Church* (Independence: Price

Publishing Company, 1966), p. 343.

17. Daniels, William M. *A Correct Account of the Murder of Generals Joseph and Hyrum Smith, at Carthage on the 27th Day of June, 1844,* (Nauvoo, Ill: John Taylor).

Chapter 3
The Mormon Exodus - Perry's First Trail Ride

1. According to the Nauvoo Temple Endowment Name Index of the Church of Jesus Christ of Latter-day Saints.

2. Reprinted in Inez Smith Davis' *The History of the Church*, p. 345.

3. According to Hubert H. Bancroft's *History of Utah: 1540-1866*, as reprinted in Davis' *The History of the Church*, p. 346.

4. According to Frank McLynn's *Wagons West: The Epic Story of America's Overland Trails*, Grove Press, 2002.

5. C. Alden Harper and Gail Holmes, *More History of the Mormon Trail*. Available online at http://omaha.adamhaeder.com/trails/history2.htm.

6. According to LDS.org, *Gathering the Dispersed Nauvoo Saints, 1847-1852*.

7. According to the LDS Web site, http://www.lds.org/churchhistory/library/pioneerdetails/1,15791,4018-1-1849,00.html.

Chapter 4
California Gold Rush - Family Business Begins

1. Cheney, Thomas E. ed., *Lore of Faith and Folly*, (Salt Lake City: University of Utah Press), p. 192.

2. Ibid, p. 187.

3. Ibid, p. 193.

4. Allen, W. W. and R. B. Avery, *California Gold Book, First Nugget*, (San Francisco and Chicago: Donohue & Henneberry), p. 72. Although Marshall's 1857 account of the discovery specifically indicates he was alone at the time he first spied the gold, other accounts include Wimmer on the scene. In addition, Marshall's account places the date between the 18th and 20th of January. Historians now know the date was actually January 24th.

5. Ibid, 73.

6. Bishop, M. Guy, *Henry William Bigler* (Logan: Utah State University Press), 1998, p. 59.

7. Cunningham, Erin, and Annette Randall, "The California Gold Rush," September 23, 2002.
8. California Gold Rush Letters, compiled by Ray W. Justus, October 27, 1998. Available online at http://jodaviess.ilgenweb.net/Goldrush/goldrushtoc.htm.

Chapter 5
Utah War—Perry's Uncles Go to War

1. Also known as Dry Creek, Sulpher Springs, Snow's Springs.
2. Named after a Nephite king in the *Book of Mormon.*
3. *Emery County Pioneer Settlers of the 19th Century: William Burgess, Jr.* Originally found at www.lofthouse.com; now available online at http://tthompsonmedia.com/cheney/histories/WilliamBurgessJr.pdf.
4. McClurg, Gilbert, *The Official Proceedings of the Eleventh National Irrigation Congress* (Ogden, Utah: The Proceedings Publishing Co.), 1904, p. 419.
5. Quoted from the GOP Convention of 1856 in Philadelphia at "Republican Philadelphia," available online at http://www.ushistory.org/gop/convention_1856.htm.
6. Taken from a Springfield, Illinois speech. Douglas had once been a supporter of the Mormons. Printed in Sally Denton's *American Passage, the Tragedy at Mountain Meadows, September 1857* (New York: Alfred A Knopf), 2003, p. 107.
7. Hafen, Leroy R. and Ann W. Hafen, eds., *Mormon Resistance: A Documentary Account of the Utah Expedition, 1857-1858* (Lincoln: University of Nebraska Press, reprint), 2005, p. 199.
8. Ramos, Donna G. "Utah War: U.S. Government Versus Mormon Settlers," available online at http://www.historynet.com/utah-war-us-government-versus-mormon-settlers.htm.
9. From *The Utah Expedition, 1857-1858: Letters of Jesse A. Gove, of Concord, to Mrs. Gove, & Special Correspondence of the N.Y. Herald* (Concord: New Hampshire Historical Society), 1928, p. 58.
10. Hafen, p. 208.
11. Ibid, pp. 208-09.
12. Ibid, pp. 172-73.
13. Ibid, pp. 221-25.

14. Inman, Colonel Henry and Colonel William F. Cody, *The Great Salt Lake Trail* (Topeka: Crane & Company), 1914, pp. 394-95.

15. Moorman, Donald L. and Gene A. Sessions, *Camp Floyd and the Mormons: The Utah War at 49.*

16. Schindler, Hal. "Bullwhacking Was No Snap, Occupied Lowest Rung on the Social Ladder," *Utah History to Go*, October 29, 1995. Available online at http://historytogo.utah.gov/salt_lake_tribune/in_another_time/102995.html.

17. According to a privately published family history titled *Pulsipher Family History Book* by Nora Hall Lund.

18. Hafen, p. 236.

19. Inman, p. 126.

20. According to Lund.

21. According to William P. McKinnon in *Causes of the Utah War.*

22. Inman, p. 157.

Chapter 7
'Bloody Bozeman' Trail - Perry's Montana Diaries & Recollections

1. Also known as Alder Gulch.

2. *Journeys to the Land of Gold*, p. 21.

3. Found online at http://freepages.history.rootsweb.ancestry.com/~familyinformation/fpk/car_2.html.

Chapter 9
Missouri Banking - A Change in Careers

1. According to the *Bates County, MO Sesquicentennial 1841-19*, p. 15.

2. One month and one day after this momentous occasion, Perry opened up the Bank of Rich Hill in Missouri.

3. Reprinted in the Butler, Missouri Chamber of Commerce informational pamphlet, *Welcome to Butler Missouri!*, p. 5.

4. Ibid.

5. Page 192.

Chapter 10
The Founding of Steamboat Springs

1. Page 8.

2. "Routt County, Colorado: Its Livestock and Range," February 1888.

3. July 11, 1911, p. 5. Available online at the Colorado Historic Newspaper Archives.
4. *Montezume Millrun*, No. 36, February 25, 1888.
5. Pages 3-4.

Chapter 11
Colorado Banking—Investing in the New State

1. "History of Boulder County," in *History of Clear Creek and Boulder Valleys, Colorado*, (O.L. Baskin & Co.: Chicago, IL), 1880, p. 389.
2. According to a *Daily Camera* article, May 27, 2010.
3. According to Lewis's obituary, published in the *Boulder News & Banner*, April 3, 1885.

Chapter 12
Hahns Peak - Perry's Return to Mining

1. According to Thelma V. Stevenson in *Historic Hahns Peak*, (Robinson Press: Fort Collins, CO), 1976, p. 2.
2. Ibid, p. 87.
3. Ibid, pp. 89-90.
4. Climbers argue about which mountain range Hahns Peak falls into. Some believe it is part of the Sierra Madre. But according to the book *The History of the Elkhead Mountains*, Hahns Peak is the eastern-most point of that range.

Chapter 13
Steamboat Springs, Colorado - Home At Last

1. Page 23.
2. Pages 65-68.
3. Pages 64-65.
4. According to his booklet, *Steamboat Springs, the First Forty Years* (1972).

Chaper 14
Death of a Pioneer

1. September 29, 1897.
2. December 30, 1894.

Selected Bibliography

The resources that follow were either those most consulted in the development of this book or titles the authors believe will be most beneficial to readers wanting further information. Other sources used and cited can be found in the Notes section.

Books

Allen, W. W. and R. B. Avery. *California Gold Book, First Nugget, Its Discovery and Discoverers and Some of the Results Proceeding Therefrom*. San Francisco & Chicago: Donohue & Henneberry, 1893.

Benson, Maxine. *Martha Maxwell, Rocky Mountain Naturalist*. Lincoln: University of Nebraska Press, 1986.

Bishop, M. Guy. *Henry William Bigler*. Logan: Utah State University Press, 1998.

Brundage, W. Fitzhugh. *A Socialist Utopia in the New South: The Ruskin Colonies in Tennessee and Georgia, 1894-1901*. Chicago: University of Illinois, 1996.

Caverly, Robert B. *Heroism of Hannah Duston, Together with The Indian Wars of new England*. Boston: B. B. Russell & Co., 1874.

Cheney, Thomas E. *The Lore of Faith & Folly*. Salt Lake City: University of Utah Press, 1971.

Crawford, James Logan. *Pritchett Ranch*. 2006.

Davis, Kenneth C. *America's Hidden History: Untold Tales of the First Pilgrims, Fighting Women, and Forgotten Founders Who Shaped a Nation*. New York: HarperCollins, 2008.

Doyle, Susan Badger, ed. *Journeys to the Land of Gold: Emigrant Diaries From the Bozeman Trail, 1863-1866*, 2 Volumes. Helena: Montana Historical Society Press, 2000.

The Duston-Dustin Family Association Genealogists. *The Duston-Dustin Family: Thomas and Elizabeth (Wheeler) Duston and Their Descendants*. Decorah: Anundsen Publishing Company, date unknown.

Early Boulder Series, Number 2 Fire Protection. Sanford Charles Gladden, date unknown.

Daughters of Utah Pioneers, *An Enduring Legacy, Vols. I-XII*. Salt Lake City: Utah Printing Company, 1978.

Davis, Inez Smith. *The Story of the Church*. Independence: Price Publishing Company, 1996.

Fleming, Elvis E. *Captain Joseph C. Lea: From Confederate Guerrilla to New Mexico Patriarch*. Las Cruces: Yucca Tree Press, 2002.

Forbes, Allan, compiler. *Other Indian Events of New England*, Volume II. Boston: State Street Trust Company, 1941.

Fort Phil Kearny Bozeman Trail Association. *Portraits of Fort Phil Kearny*. Banner: The Fort Phil Kearny/Bozeman Trail Association, 1993.

Gardner, Hamilton. *The History of Lehi*. Salt Lake City: The Deseret News, 1913.

Goodell, Jotham. *A Winter with the Mormons*. Salt Lake City: University of Utah, 2001.

Hafen, Leroy R. and Ann W. Hafen, eds. *Mormon Resistance: A Documentary Account of the Utah Expedition, 1857-1858*. Lincoln: University of Nebraska Press, 2005.

The Historical Guide to Routt County. Steamboat Springs: The Tread of Pioneers Museum, 1979.

History of Clear Creek and Boulder Valleys, Colorado. Chicago: O. L Baskin & Co., 1880.

Lambrecht, Mona and the Boulder History Museum. *Boulder 1859-1919*. Charleston: Arcadia Publishing, 2008.

Lea, Homer. *The Valor of Ignorance*. New York: Harper & Brothers, 1942.

Leckenby, Charles H. *The Tread of Pioneers*. Steamboat Springs: The Pilot Press, 1945.

McConnell, William John. *Early History of Idaho*. Caldwell: Idaho State Legislature, 1913.

McClurg, Gilbert. *The Official Proceedings of the Eleventh National Irrigation Congress*. Ogden: The Proceedings Publishing Co., 1904.

Mulder, William and A. Russel Mortensen, *Among the Mormons: Historic Accounts by Contemporary Observers*. New York: Knopf, 1958. Reprint, Lincoln: University of Nebraska Press, 1973. Reprint. Salt Lake City: Western Epics Publishing Co., 1994.

Olsen, Deborah. *Steamboat Springs Legends, A Centennial Collection*. Steamboat Springs: Steamboat Chamber Resort Association, 1999.

Owens, Kenneth N. *Gold Rush Saints: California Mormons and the Great Rush for Riches.* Spokane: The Arthur H. Clarke Company, 2004.

Pettem, Silvia. *Boulder: Evolution of a City.* Niwot: University Press of Colorado, 1994.

——. *Positively Pearl St.: A Chronicle of the Center of Boulder, Colorado, 1859 to Present.* Ward: The Book Lode, LLC, 2007.

Pritchett, Lulita. *The Shining Mountains.* Chicago: Albert Whitman & Co., 1939.

Roach, Delbert E. and Barbara B., eds. *A Heritage of Faith and Courage: William and Violate Burgess and Their Family.* Murray: Family Heritage Publishers, 2006.

Smith, Phyllis. *A Look at Boulder from Settlement to City.* Boulder: Pruitt Publishing Company, 1981.

Smith, Sybil. *Hannah Duston's Sister.* Lincoln: iUniverse, 2005.

Spears, Clarence L. *Boulder, Colorado in 1883.* self-published, 1939.

Stevens, Walter Barlow. *Missouri the Center State: 1821-1915*, Volume 3. Chicago-St. Louis: The S. J. Clarke Publishing Company, 1915.

Stevenson, Thelma V. *Historic Hahns Peak.* Fort Collins: Robinson Press, 1976. Reprint. 1979.

Stone, Wilbur Fiske. *History of Colorado*, Volume II. The S. J. Clarke Publishing Company, Chicago, 1918.

Whittier, John Greenleaf. *Legends of New England.* Baltimore: Clearfield Company, 1992. Reprint.

Periodicals

Aethern, Robert G., ed. "From Illinois to Montana in 1866: The Diary of Perry A. Burgess," *Pacific Northwest Quarterly*, January 1950, Vol. 41, Number 1, pp. 65.

Boulder, Colorado: 150 Years, 1859-2009, Official Guide. Boulder: Boulder Sesquicentennial Celebration Committee, 2009.

Leckenby, Charles H. "The Founding of Steamboat Springs and of Hahns Peak," *The Colorado Magazine*, May 1929, Volume VI, Number 3, pp. 92-98.

Powell, Lee A. *Steamboat Springs The First Forty Years.* 1972.

Web sites

Author names have been indicated where provided.

About The Pilot & Today. Steamboat Today.
http://www.steamboatpilot.com/about/.

Amerson, Annie Dismukes. Jennie Wimmer Tested Gold in Her Soap
Kettle. Gold Rush Gallery Inc.
http://www.goldrushgallery.com/news/wimmer.html.

Bailey, Clay. Ruskin Cooperative Association. The Tennessee
Encyclopedia of History and Culture. http://
tennesseeencyclopedia.net/imagegallery.php?EntryID=R067.

Boulder's Downslope Winds. University Corporation for Atmospheric
Research.http://www.ucar.edu/communications/factsheets/winds.
html.

Perry Burgess Steamboat Diaries. Bud Werner Memorial Library.
http://www.yampavalley.info

The Colorado Gold Rush. Western History Mining.
http://www.westernmininghistory.com/articles/11/page1/.

Doerner, John. Bozeman Trail Forts (1866-1868). Friends of the Little
Bighorn Battlefield. http://www.friendslittlebighorn.com/Frontier-
military-posts.htm.

Gallatin: What's the Mormon War? Daviies County Historical Society.
http://www.daviesscountyhistoricalsociety.com/modules.php?op=
modload&name=News&file=article&sid=127.

Henry W. Bigler "Autobiography." Huntington Library, Art Collections,
and Botanical Gardens. http://www.huntington.org/education/
GoldRush/advent/hm57034tran.html.

History of Bates County. Bates County.
http://www.batescounty.net/bates_county.htm.

A History of Social Dance in America. American Antiquarian Society.
http://www.americanantiquarian.org/Exhibitions/Dance/.

History—Mining Towns. Folsom History Museum.
http://www.folsomhistorymuseum.org/1mining_towns.htm.

Joseph Smith, Prophet: Joseph Smith Funeral. Prophet Joseph Smith.
http://www.prophetjosephsmith.org/joseph_smith_
timeline/1834-1844/joseph_smith_funeral.

Lulita Crawford Pritchett.
   http://www.lulitacrawfordpritchett.com/.

Mather Family Times. Rev. Richard Mather. Free Pages.
   http://freepages.genealogy.rootsweb.ancestry.com/~mather/
   Mather/Richard.shtml.

McKeever, Bill. LDS and RLDS (Community of Christ): Differences &
   Similarites. Mormonism Research Ministry. http://www.mrm.org/rlds.

The Mormon Battalion. Web Books Publishing. http://www.web-books.
   com/Classics/ON/B1/B1120/30MB1120.html.

Mormon Handcart Trek. Pilgrimage Publications.
   http://www.pilgrimagepublications.com/mormon.htm.

Mormon History, Kirtland. Dear Elder.
   http://www.dearelder.com/index/inc_name/Mormon/title2/
   Mormon_History,_Kirtland.

Nauvoo Temple Endowment Name Index.
   http://www.xmission.com/~research/family/familypage.htm.

New Perspectives on the West: William Clarke Quantrill. PBS.
   http://www.pbs.org/weta/thewest/people/i_r/quantrill.htm.

Ramos, Donna G. Utah War: U. S. Government Versus Mormon
   Settlers. HistoryNet. http://www.historynet.com/utah-war-us-
   government-versus-mormon-settlers.htm.

Sam Brannan. Sierra Foothills Magazine.
   http://www.sierrafoothillmagazine.com/brannan.html.

Silver Lake Ditch. The Ditch Project. http://bcn.boulder.co.us/basin/
   ditchproject/?Our_Ditches:Silver_Lake_Ditch.

Steamboat Springs, Colorado. Steamboat Springs Chamber of
   Commerce. http://www.steamboat-chamber.com/info/facts.asp.

Thompson Media. The Genealogy of Dr. Levi Cheney, Mormon Pioneer
   and California 49er, & Amelia Clark. http://tthompsonmedia.
   com/cheney/index.php.

———.The Story of Hannah Dustin/Duston of Haverhill, Massachusetts.
   http://www.hannahdustin.com/index2.html.

Who Was the Ninety-Second Illinois Volunteer Mounted Infantry? 92nd
   Illinois Infantry. http://www.92ndillinoisinfantry.com/Brief%20
   History.htm.

Index

C